POCKET GUIDE TO

baby names

POCKET GUIDE TO

baby names

Clare Gibson

Published by SILVERDALE BOOKS
An imprint of Bookmart Ltd
Registered number 2372865
Trading as Bookmart Ltd
Blaby Road
Wigston
Leicester LE18 4SE

© 2007 D&S Books Ltd

D&S Books Ltd
Kerswell,
Parkham Ash, Bideford
Devon, England
EX39 5PR

e-mail us at:- enquiries@d-sbooks.co.uk

This edition printed 2007

ISBN 13: 9-781-84509-465-2

DS0168. Baby Names

Creative Director: Sarah King
Designer: Debbie Fisher

Material from this book previously appeared in The
handbook of Baby Names
Fonts: Gill Sans, Lucida Handwriting and Myriad Roman

Printed in Thailand

1 3 5 7 9 10 8 6 4 2

contents

introduction

What is a name? Well, a dictionary would define 'name' as a word by which something or someone is known. But if you subtly change the wording of the question and ask yourself what's in a name, you suddenly find yourself leaving the realms of dry lexicality and entering a fluid world, in which a rich myriad of meanings and associations – portraits of historical personages, snatches of music, images of paintings, passages of literature and memories of faces – each tinted by personal experience, constantly shift and merge like the jewel-bright pieces of a kaleidoscope.

Apart from life itself, perhaps the most fundamentally important gift that parents can bestow upon their newborn child is its name, for a name both identifies and defines identity, a requirement that is as significant for the child as for the countless people whom it will encounter during the course of its life. Some indigenous cultures endow names with such power that their members are given two, one for everyday use and a second, secret name that is believed to contain the essence of the individual bearer and must never be divulged to strangers for fear of thus giving them the means to establish absolute control over him or her (a concept that is vividly encapsulated in the German fairytale 'Rumpelstiltskin').

But will a child's name prove a blessing or a curse? Will its name help this brand-new person to enjoy an easy passage as it sets sail on the unpredictable waters of life, or will it throw up rocky obstacles in the form of countless self-esteem-sapping, petty humiliations? Indeed, a name is so inextricably bound up with its bearer's sense of identity, and with how others see him or her, that an ill-considered choice may have life-long repercussions. (One wonders whether the Canadian communications scholar Marshall McLuhan held a long-standing grudge against his parents when he wrote, in his work *Understanding Media*, 'The name of a man is a numbing blow from which he never recovers.')

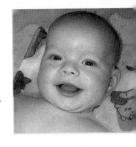

The wrong choice?

Names can, of course, be changed, be it by recourse to a nickname, a second name or even a completely new one, yet the original name will continue to live on in other people's memories. To give an example, a friend of mine (who, if you'll pardon the pun, shall remain nameless) stoically endured being called by her much-loathed first name throughout her school years, but on entering a new phase of her life, which involved moving to a different town and making new acquaintances, had no qualms about discarding it and replacing it with her second name. If that wasn't confusing enough for her childhood friends and family, on her marriage shortly thereafter, she replaced her maiden name with her husband's family name, thus completing her rebranding. Yet while those who knew her in her previous incarnation respect her decision, long-held memories cannot be erased that easily: the name that springs to mind whenever I think of her remains the one by which I originally knew her.

In my friend's case, the despised name was a traditional one with saintly connotations, but, due to notorious namesakes, others are redolent with sinister associations, notably Adolf, thanks to Herr Hitler. It is a sad truth that the actions of certain historical – or contemporary – individuals have besmirched the names of their bearers, but not necessarily forever: Guy, for example, was eschewed in England for many centuries on account of the treasonable activities of Guy Fawkes in 1603, but has now been rehabilitated.

When choosing a name for their baby, apart from avoiding names that have been tainted by infamous namesakes, there are a few other potential pitfalls that parents should be aware of.

Firstly, a sequence of names whose initials would spell out a word for which their child would be mocked, such as P(atrick) I(an) G(regson). Secondly, in an era of increasing globalisation and multiculturalism, a name that may have offensive connotations in other cultures (a prime example of which can be found in Sue Browder's *The New Age Baby Name Book*, in which a certain boy's name is noted as meaning 'witness' in South African, the name in question being Paki, which, to Britons, is an overtly racist word for a person of Pakistani origin). Finally, consider how – if at all – a name could become a nickname (would Natasha become Nasty?) and if a prospective first name will partner a family name sympathetically (would little Robyn Banks grow up to become law-abiding or would Primrose Wood rejoice in her emphatically sylvan name?)

The right choice?

In the end, however, the name that is chosen for a child will be one that sounds pleasing to parental ears, although it will probably, snapshot-like, reflect the conventions, values and fashions that prevailed at the time of the baby's birth, social mores that have generally become increasingly tolerant in the twenty-first century (that is, apart from such countries as France and Brazil, where parents are still required to select a name from a legally approved list).

If a delightful-sounding name also has personal significance for the parents, then a child will be doubly blessed, and will probably be enthralled to learn the origin, or a notable bearer, of his or her name. This book differs from comparable compendiums in that it contains a wealth of notable namesakes that will not only send prospective parents on a nostalgic voyage of rediscovery through long-forgotten aspects of their past, but offers a gallery of interesting figures from history, sports and the arts to illustrate the potential of a name. Although they shouldn't be regarded as role models (and some are more notorious than notable), they will certainly act as illuminating starting points. Also included are characters drawn from fiction and legend, along with venerable figures from numerous mythological traditions and such world religions as Hinduism, Judaism, Christianity and Islam.

The natural world is yet another rich source of names, from the jewel and flower names so beloved in Victorian times, through names that evoke the sterling qualities of various birds and beasts, to sunny- or tempestuous-sounding names inspired by weather phenomena and thence to the celestial realms of the stars. Time and space can provide additional inspiration, such as a name based on the date, day or season when your baby made its world début or the place where it was conceived or born. Other potential naming possibilities include your child's appearance – and within these pages you'll find names that, for instance, echo the dark, golden or auburn hues of a person's crowning glory – as well as their behavioural characteristics, be they gentle or spirited.

Last (but not least, because there is no limit to the human imagination), the key to finding the perfect name for a baby could be an evocative name, perhaps a first name already borne by a family member or cherished friend or, if she has relinquished it, the baby's

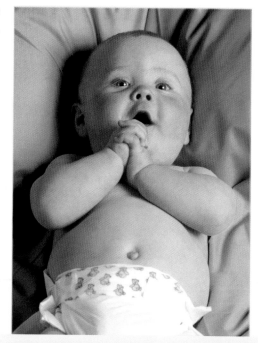

mother's maiden name, another family name that you think sounds attractive or one that celebrates your baby's cultural or national heritage. And don't let the inconvenience of a potential namesake's alternative sex put you off: a Nigel can always be commemorated in a gurgling Nigella which is also the name of a delicate flower.

The meaning of names

Whatever name you settle on, knowing its meaning will add another layer of magic to an already evocative appellation. Due to the fluid nature of language, however, meanings are not always as clear-cut as one would hope, especially when many of the names that are commonplace today originated hundreds, if not thousands, of years ago within the potent brew of a linguistic melting pot. To explain further, some historical background needs to be drawn to the fore.

Most of the languages used in the Western world evolved from Proto-Indo-European, a language that was in use before 3000 BC and that scholars speculate was derived from the tongue used by the Kurgan people of the steppes of southern Russia, nomads who eventually wandered to the Danube and Adriatic regions of Europe and beyond. A prolific progenitor, Proto-Indo-European gave life to the Indo-European family of languages, categorised in vastly simplified form below.

The Indo-European family of languages

1) Indo-Aryan, including Sanskrit, Hindi or Urdu and Romany

2) Iranian, including Persian

3) Armenian

4) Anatolian

5) Greek

6) Albanian

7) Latin (or Italic) and, through Vulgar Latin, the Romance languages, French, Italian, Spanish, Catalan, Portuguese, Rumansch or Rhaeto-Romanic, Romanian and Provençal

8) Celtic, including Celtiberian, Gaulish and Galatian; the Brythonic languages, Cumbrian, Welsh, Cornish and Breton; and the Goidelic languages, Irish Gaelic, Manx and Scots Gaelic

9) Germanic, subdivided as follows:

a) East Germanic, including Gothic

b) West Germanic, which today includes German, English, Frisian, Flemish, Yiddish Dutch and Afrikaans

c) North Germanic, including Danish, Swedish, Norwegian, Faeroese and Icelandic

10) Balto-Slavonic (or Slavic), subdivided as follows:

a) Baltic, including Latvian and Lithuanian

b) Slavonic, including Czech, Slovak, Bulgarian, Macedonian, Serbo-Croat, Slovene, Belorussian, Russian and Ukrainian

To clarify the attributions of many of the names in this book further, we should now home in on the evolution of the West and North German branches of Germanic, as set out below.

The evolution of West Germanic and North Germanic

1) West Germanic evolved into two languages: Low German and High German, which in turn evolved as follows:

a) Low German evolved into three branches, Anglo-Saxon (or Old English) which was spoken from around AD 400, Old Saxon and Low Franconian

i) Anglo-Saxon (or Old English) evolved into Middle English in around AD 1100, which in turn gave way to Modern English in around 1550

ii) Old Saxon evolved into Middle Low German and thence into Plattdeutsch (or Low German)

iii) Low Franconian evolved into Middle Dutch and thence into Dutch and Flemish

b) High German (or Old High German, spoken from around AD 770 to 1050) evolved into Middle High German (1050–1350) and thence into Modern German

2) North Germanic evolved into Old Norse, spoken from around AD 700 to 1350, from which are derived Norwegian, Swedish, Danish, Faeroese and Icelandic

The relevance of the evolution of the Indo-European languages to this book is that many have contributed to the 'British' names that fill these pages through the successive invasions of Britain effected by their speakers. If the British Isles can be said to have an indigenous language, it is Celtic, which somehow survived both the first Roman invasion of Latin-speakers between 55 and 54 BC and the subsequent invasions of West Germanic peoples – the Jutes appropriating Kent and the Isle of Wight, the Saxons parts of the south and the Angles infiltrating the Midlands and North – from around AD 449, whose contribution was Anglo-Saxon (or Old English). Next came the Norsemen, Danish (and Norwegian) Vikings, whose eventual northern English realm, the Danelaw, established in AD 886, became the province of Old Norse. Following the death of Edward the Confessor, the penultimate Anglo-Saxon king, another breed of Norsemen – the Normans, led by William, Duke of Normandy – arrived on English shores in 1066, whereafter Norman French, a dialect of Old French heavily influenced by the Old Norse spoken by the Normans' Norwegian forebears, became the prevalent language. Finally, however, the invasions ceased, and the dominant language of the British Isles gradually assimilated its Anglo-Saxon (or Old English), Old Norse and Norman French components to emerge as Middle English (which replaced French as the language of the law in England in 1362), and then Modern English.

The point of our canter through the evolution of Indo-European languages is to establish that all are to a greater or lesser extent inter-related, so that if a name's meaning is ascribed to the Old English language, it could sometimes equally have been designated as being of Germanic (given when the specific Germanic source is unclear) or Old Norse origin, so similar are many of these tongues' root components. Equally, as a consequence of both the Claudian Roman conquest of Britain in AD 43 and the Norman Conquest of 1066, as well as the influence of Christianity, whose lingua franca was once Latin, many names identified as having an Old English source could equally be deemed to have Latin or Old French roots, while to cloud the picture further, Latin in turn borrowed many words from Greek. Yet amid this minefield of potential misattribution, the spirit of the name's meaning shines through, a far more important consideration than any etymological nitpicking or onomastic navel-gazing (which is also why, in this book, you've been spared the details of a name's original incarnation, for example, Hrodebert being the nominal ancestor of Robert).

Can the names contributed by the different peoples who, over the course of time, made up what is now the native stock of the British Isles be said to have certain characteristics? To an extent they can: Celtic names reflect personal characteristics veiled with an aura of mysticism, while Germanic and Old Norse names (which typically consist of two components, as shown in this book, which could be mixed and matched at will) convey, on the one hand, a yearning for prosperity and, on the other, a relish of savagery and a statement of noble intent.

Two other general categories were also popular among the ancestors who bequeathed us their names. Firstly, in a pious age, those drawn from the Bible, whether Hebrew, Latin or Greek in origin, along with a host of saintly names, remained perennial favourites. The more 'popish' appellations, however, were abhorred by the 17th-century Puritans, who instead preferred rugged Old Testament names – and often the more obscure, the better – or appropriated the names of qualities that

they felt their children should aspire to, such as obedience, prudence and chastity. And, secondly, family names, which in turn usually owe their origin either to the first name, nickname or occupational name of a medieval ancestor – naming practices thus coming full circle – or to a place name. (Be aware, however, that, as with numerous first names, the meanings of some family names have been obscured by the many mistranslations and mispronunciations that were propagated in an age of general illiteracy.) Although usually restricted to the naming of boys, the practice of assigning first-name duties to family names was particularly prevalent during the 19th century, but today a girl is as likely to be called Taylor as a boy. Today, in fact, apart from the danger of causing a child life-long embarrassment, it seems that anything goes.

About this book

Collating all of the names that have ever existed in every culture would certainly have proved a life-long task, which would have been impractical for me, and of no use to you if you are eagerly anticipating the birth of your baby. For this reason, the names that have been included in this book are broadly traditional, but with a liberal sprinkling of imports from non-Western cultures, many of which, in our age of multiculturalism, will not sound as alien to an ear attuned to the English language as you may expect. In addition, to broaden your options even further, most names are accompanied by a generous selection of variants and diminutives: related names, alternative spellings and nicknames, which may not have separate entries (equally, the notable namesakes of similar names may have been telescoped into one entry). Finally, note that if a name is 'unisex', this is indicated after its meaning, but that the name will not usually appear in both the boys' and girls' sections.

In the days before baby-name books became the publishing phenomenon that has resulted in booksellers' shelves groaning with such tomes, my parents had to resort to borrowing a teacher's register in their search for inspiration for my first name (my second was originally my grandmother's). I doubt whether there were more than ten female names to choose from, and sometimes wonder who my young namesake was and what became of her. By contrast, today's parents are spoiled for choice, but choice can bring its own problems. Naming a child is an awesome responsibility, and I hope that you'll find this book a useful guide in your baby-naming quest. Above all, remember that 'A good name is rather to be chosen than great riches' (Proverbs, Chapter 21, verse 9).

Boys'
Names

Aaron

Variants and diminutives: Aaran, Aarao, Aharon, Ahron, Aranne, Arek, Aren, Arend, Ari, Arin, Arn, Arni, Arny, Aron, Aronek, Aronne, Aronos, Arron, Haroun, Harun, Ron, Ronnie, Ronny.
Meaning: 'high mountain', 'mountaineer' or 'exalted' (Hebrew); 'messenger' (Arabic).

Abdul

Variants and diminutives: Ab, Abdal, Abdalla, Abdel, Abdullah, Del.
Meaning: 'servant of Allah [God]' (Arabic).

Abel

Variants and diminutives: Abe, Abelard, Abeles, Abell, Abelot, Abi, Able, Hevel, Nab.
Meaning: 'breath' (Hebrew); 'son' (Assyrian).

Abner

Variants and diminutives: Ab, Abbey, Abby, Avner, Eb, Ebbie, Ebner.
Meaning: 'my father is light' or 'father of light' (Hebrew).

Abraham

Variants and diminutives: Ab, Abe, Abi, Abie, Abrahamo, Abrahan, Abram, Abramo, Abran, Arram, Aubrey, Avram, Avrom, Avrum, Bram, Ham, Ibrahim.
Meaning: 'father of a multitude' (Hebrew)

Absolom

Variants and diminutives: Absalom, Absolon, Axel.
Meaning: 'my father is peace' or 'father of peace' (Hebrew).

Ace

Variants and diminutives: Acelet, Acelin, Acey, Acie, Asce, Asselin, Azzo, Ezzelin.
Meaning: 'unity' or 'a unit' (Latin).

Adair

Meaning: 'ford made by an oak tree' (Scots Gaelic); 'happiness' or 'riches' and 'spear' (Old English) as a variant of Edgar.

Adam

Variants and diminutives: Ad, Adamec, Adamek, Adamik, Adamka, Adamko, Adamnan, Adamo, Adamok, Adams, Adamson, Adan, Adao, Adas, Addie, Addis, Addison, Addos, Addoson, Addy, Ade, Adekin, Adem, Adhamh, Adi, Adinet, Adnon, Adok, Adom, Adomas, Damek, Edie, Edom.
Meaning: 'red' or 'red earth' (Hebrew).

Adar

Variants and diminutives: Addar, Addi, Addie, Adin, Adino, Adir, Adna, Ard, Arda.
Meaning: 'fire', 'exalted' or 'dusky and cloudy' (Hebrew); 'prince' or 'ruler' (Syrian).

Adler

Meaning: 'eagle' (German and Old English).

Adlai

Meaning: 'my ornament' (Hebrew).

Adolphus
Variants and diminutives: Ad, Adolf, Adolfo, Adolph, Adolphe, Adolpho, Aethelwulf, Dolf, Dolly, Dolph, Dolphus.
Meaning: 'noble' and 'wolf' (Germanic).

Adrian
Variants and diminutives: Ade, Adi, Adie, Adorjan, Adriann, Adriano, Adrianus, Adrien, Adrik, Andreian, Andreyan, Andri, Andrian, Andriyan, Arne, Hadrian.
Meaning: 'from Adria' (a city in northern Italy) or 'dark one' (Latin).

Adriel
Variants and diminutives: Adri, Adrial.
Meaning: 'God's majesty' or 'of God's congregation' (Hebrew).

Adwin
Meaning: 'creativity' (Ghanaian).

Aeneas
Variants and diminutives: Angus, Aonghus, Eneas, Enne, Oenghus, Oengus.
Meaning: 'worthy of praise' (Greek).

Ahmed
Variants and diminutives: Ahmad.
Meaning: 'greatly adored' or 'praised the most' (Arabic)

Ahren
Meaning: 'eagle' (Germanic).

Aidan
Variants and diminutives: Adan, Ade, Aden, Adie, Aedan, Aiden, Eden, Haden, Hayden, Haydon, Haydn.
Meaning: 'to help' (Middle English); 'small fiery one' (Irish Gaelic).

Ainsley
Variants and diminutives: Ainie, Ainslee, Ainslie.
Meaning: 'my clearing' or 'my meadow' (Old English); derived from a family name, in turn derived from the Nottinghamshire place name Annesley.

Akash
Meaning: 'sky' (Hindi).

Akil
Variants and diminutives: Ahkeel, Akeel.
Meaning: 'intelligent one' (Arabic).

Akin
Variants and diminutives: Ahkeen, Akeen.
Meaning: 'courageous' (Yoruban).

Akio
Variants and diminutives: Akira.
Meaning: 'bright boy' (Japanese).

Alan
Variants and diminutives: Ailean, Ailin, Al, Alain, Alair, Aland, Alano, Alanus, Alao, Alawn, Alein, Alen, Aleyn, Aleyne, Allain, Allan, Allayne, Allen, Alleyn, Allie, Allwyn, Ally, Allyn, Alun, Alyn.
Meaning: 'rock' (Breton); 'harmony' (Celtic); 'good-looking' or 'cheerful' (Irish Gaelic).

Alaric

Variants and diminutives: Alarick, Alarico, Alarik, Rich, Rick, Ricky, Ulric, Ulrich.
Meaning: 'noble ruler' or 'ruler of all' (Germanic).

Alastair

Variants and diminutives: Al, Alasdair, Alastair, Alastar, Alaster, Alastor, Aleister, Alisdair, Alistair, Alister, Allaster, Allister, Aly.
Meaning: 'defender of men' or 'warrior' (Greek). A Scots Gaelic variant of Alexander.

Alban

Variants and diminutives: Al, Alba, Albany, Albek, Alben, Albie, Albion, Albin, Albinek, Albino, Albins, Alby, Alva, Alvah, Alvan, Alvin, Alwin, Alwyn, Aubin, Auburn, Binek, Elva, Elvin, Elvis.
Meaning: 'from Alba Longa' (a Roman city) or, as Alben and Albin, 'white' (Latin).

Albert

Variants and diminutives: Adalbert, Adel, Adelbert, Adell, Aethelbert, Ailbert, Al, Albe, Albek, Alberik, Alberti, Albertino, Alberto, Albertus, Albie, Albrecht, Ales, Aliberto, Alvertos, Aubert, Bechtel, Berco, Bert, Bertchen, Bertek, Bertel, Berti, Bertie, Bertik, Berto, Berty, Burt, Elbert, Elbie, Elvert, Ethelbert, Hab, Halbert, Imbert, Olbracht, Ulbricht.
Meaning: 'noble' and 'bright' or 'famous' (Germanic).

Aldo

Variants and diminutives: Al, Aldan, Alden, Aldin, Aldis, Aldivin, Aldon, Aldous, Aldos, Aldren, Aldus, Ealder, Eiden, Elder, Eldon, Eldor, Elton.
Meaning: 'old and wise' (Germanic).

Aldred

Variants and diminutives: Al, Dred, Eldred.
Meaning: 'old' and 'counsel' (Old English).

Aldrich

Variants and diminutives: Al, Aldric, Aldridge, Audric, Eldredge, Eldric, Eldridge, Elric, Rich, Richie, Richy.
Meaning: 'old' and 'powerful ruler' (Old English).

Aldwyn

Variants and diminutives: Aldan, Alden, Aidin, Aldwin, Edlwin.
Meaning: 'old' and 'friend' (Old English).

Alec

Variants and diminutives: Al.
Meaning: 'defender of men' or 'warrior'. A diminutive of Alexander.

Aled

Variants and diminutives: Al.
Meaning: 'offspring' or 'noble brow' (Welsh); derived from the river Aled in North Wales.

Alexander

Variants and diminutives: Al, Alasdair, Alastar, Alastair, Alaster, Alec, Aleister, Alejandro, Alejo, Alek, Alekko, Aleks, Aleksander, Aleksandr, Aleksei, Alesaunder, Alessander, Alessandro, Alex, Alexandr, Alexandre, Alexandros, Alexis, Alexius, Ali, Alic, Alick, Alik, Aliks,

Alisander, Alisandre, Alistair, Alister, Alix, Allesandro, Alysanyr, Alysaundre, Axel, Leks, Leksik, Lekso, Lex, Lexi, Sacha, Sande, Sander, Sanders, Sandey, Sandie, Sandor, Sandro, Sandy, Sasha, Saunder, Saunders, Sender, Xander, Zander.
Meaning: 'defender of men' or 'warrior' (Greek).

Alfred

Variants and diminutives: Aelfric, Ailrid, Al Alf, Alfie, Alfredo, Alfric, Alfrick, Alfrid, Alfy, Alured, Auveray, Avere, Avery, Elfrid, Fred, Freddie, Freddy.
Meaning: 'elf' or 'good' and 'counsel' (Old English).

Algar

Variants and diminutives: Aelgar, Alger, Algor, Elgar, Eylgar.
Meaning: 'elf' and 'spear' (Old English).

Algernon

Variants and diminutives: Al, Alger, Algie, Algy.
Meaning: 'moustachioed' or 'whiskered' (French).

Ali

Meaning: 'Allah [God]' (Arabic).

Alim

Variants and diminutives: Aleem, Alem.
Meaning: 'wise' (Arabic).

Alon

Variants and diminutives: Allon.
Meaning: 'oak' (Hebrew).

Aloysius

Meaning: 'famed' and 'warrior' (Germanic). A French Provençal variant of Louis.

Alphonso

Variants and diminutives: Affonso, Afonso, Al, Alf, Alfie, Alfio, Alfo, Alfons, Alfonso, Alfonsus, Alfonzo, Allon, Alon, Alonso, Alonzo, Alphonse, Alphonsine, Alphonso, Alphonsus, Fons, Fonsie, Fonz, Fonzie, Fonzo, Lanzo, Lon, Lonnie, Lonny, Lonzo.
Meaning: 'noble' and 'ready' (Germanic).

Alton

Variants and diminutives: Alten, Altin, Elton.
Meaning: 'of the old town' (Old English).

Alva

Variants and diminutives: Alvah.

Meaning: 'exalted', 'brightness' or 'injustice' (Hebrew).

Alvar

Meaning: 'elf' and 'warrior' or 'army' (Old English).

Alvin

Variants and diminutives: Al, Albin, Aloin, Aluin, Aluino, Alvan, Alvi, Alvino, Alwin, Alwyn, Aylwin, Elvin, Elwyn.
Meaning: 'elf' or 'noble' and 'friend' (Old English).

Alvis
Variants and diminutives: Elvis.
Meaning: 'knowing all' (Norse).

Amal
Meaning: 'pure' (Hindi).

Ambrose
Variants and diminutives:
Ambrogio, Ambroise, Ambrosi,
Ambrosio, Ambrosius, Ambrus,
Emrys.
Meaning: 'divine' or 'immortal'
(Greek).

Amin
Variants and diminutives: Ameen,
Amen, Amitan, Ammon, Amnon,
Amon.
Meaning: 'the truth' (Hebrew and
Arabic); 'faithful' (East Indian).

Amir
Variants and diminutives: Ameer,
Emir.
Meaning: 'prince' or 'ruler' (Arabic).

Amory
Variants and diminutives: Amati,
Amery, Ames, Amias, Amice, Amiot,
Amor, Amyas, Embry, Emory, Imray,
Imrie.
Meaning: 'loving person' (Latin);
'renowned' and 'ruler' (Germanic).

Amos
Meaning: 'weighed down' or 'carried'
(Hebrew).

Anatole
Variants and diminutives: Anatol,
Anatolio, Anatoly, Antal.
Meaning: 'rising sun' (Greek).

Andrew
Variants and diminutives: Aindreas,
Aindrias, Anders, Andersen,
Anderson, Andi, Andie, Andor,
Andras, André, Andreas, Andrei,
Andrej, Andres, Andrey, Andrik,
Andros, Andy, Drew.
Meaning: 'manly' (Greek).

Aneurin
Variants and diminutives: Aneirin,
Nye.
Meaning: 'man of honour' (Latin), a
variant of Honorius; 'pure gold'
(Welsh).

Angel
Variants and diminutives: Angelico,
Angelino, Angell, Angelo, Angelos.
Meaning: 'messenger' (Greek). Also a
girl's name.

Angus
Variants and diminutives: Aeneas,
Aengus, Aonghas, Aonghus.

Meaning: 'single choice' (Scots
Gaelic).

Anselm
Variants and diminutives:
Amselmo, Ancel, Ancell, Ancelm,
Ancelmo, Ansel, Anselino, Ansell,
Anselmo, Ansil, Ansill, Anzelmo,
Enselmo, Selmo, Semo.
Meaning: 'divine' and 'helmet'
(Germanic); 'related to nobility' (Old
French).

Anthony
Variants and diminutives:
Andonios, Andonis, Ant, Antaine,
Antal, Antek, Anti, Antoin, Antoine,
Anton, Antone, Antoni, Antonin,
Antonio, Antonius, Antony, Antos,
Toni, Tonio, Tony.
Meaning: 'flourishing' (Greek);
'without price' (Latin); derived from
the Roman family name Antonius.

Apollo
Meaning: 'to push back' or 'destroy'
(Greek).

Archibald
Variants and diminutives: Arch,
Archaimbaud, Archambault,
Archbold, Archibaldo, Archie, Archy,
Arkady, Arky, Ercanbald, Erkenwald,
Baldie.

Arfon

Meaning: 'facing Anglesea' (Welsh).

Ari

Variants and diminutives: Aaron, Ari, Aristotle, Arri.
Meaning: 'lion' (Hebrew).

Armand

Variants and diminutives: Arek, Arman, Armande, Armando, Armen, Armin, Armine, Armino, Armon, Armond, Armonde, Armondo, Herman, Mandek, Mando, Ormond.
Meaning: 'army' and 'man' (Germanic). A variant of Herman.

Arnold

Variants and diminutives: Arn, Arnald, Arnaldo, Arnaud, Arnauld, Arnaut, Arnd, Arndt, Arnel, Arnell, Arne, Arnet, Arnett, Arney, Arni, Arnie, Arno, Arnoldo, Arnoll, Arnolt, Arnot, Arnott, Arny, Ernald, Ernaldus, Wado.
Meaning: 'eagle' and 'strength' or 'rule' (Germanic).

Arsen

Variants and diminutives: Arcenio, Arsanio, Arsemio, Arsenio, Eresenio.
Meaning: 'virile' (Greek).

Arthur

Variants and diminutives: Acur, Art, Artair, Arth, Arte, Artek, Artey, Artie, Artis, Arto, Artor, Artuir, Artur, Arturo, Artus, Arty, Atur.
Meaning: 'bear-keeper' (Greek); 'bear' (Celtic); 'stone' (Irish Gaelic); 'noble' (Welsh); 'follower of Thor' (Norse); derived from the Roman name Artorius.

Asa

Meaning: 'physician' or 'healer' (Hebrew); 'born in the morning' (Japanese).

Asad

Variants and diminutives: Aleser, Alisid, Asid, Assid.
Meaning: 'lion' (Arabic).

Asher

Variants and diminutives: Aser, Ash, Ashur, Asser.
Meaning: 'happy' (Hebrew); as Ashur, 'martial' (eastern Semitic); 'born during Ashur [a Moslem month]' (Swahili).

Ashley

Variants and diminutives: Ash, Ashleigh, Ashlie.
Meaning: 'ash wood' (Old English). Also a girl's name.

Aslan

Variants and diminutives: Arslan.
Meaning: 'lion' (Turkish).

Aswad

Meaning: 'black' (Arabic).

Athelstan

Variants and diminutives: Stan.
Meaning: 'noble' and 'stone' (Old English).

Athol

Variants and diminutives: Atholl, Athole.
Meaning: 'new Ireland' (Scots Gaelic); derived from a Scottish family name, in turn derived from a Scottish place name.

Auberon

Variants and diminutives: Aubrey, Oberon.
Meaning: 'noble' or 'like a bear' (Germanic).

Aubrey

Variants and diminutives: Alberic, Alberich, Aubary, Aubery, Auberon, Aubri, Aubrie, Aubry.
Meaning: 'elf' and 'strength' or 'ruler' (Germanic). Also a girl's name.

Augustus

Variants and diminutives: Agostin, Agostino, Agosto, Aguistin, Agustin, August, Auguste, Augustin, Augustine, Augustino, Augusto, Austen, Austin, Gus, Gussie, Gustus.
Meaning: 'venerable' or 'great' (Latin); a name assumed by Roman emperors, notably the first, Caius (or Gaius) Julius Caesar Octavianus.

Aulay

Variants and diminutives: Amhlaigh, Olaf, Olave.
Meaning: 'forebear' and 'relics' (Old Norse) as a Scots Gaelic variant of Olaf.

Avery

Meaning: 'elf' and 'ruler' (Old English).

Axel

Variants and diminutives: Aksel.
Meaning: 'oak' (Germanic); 'divine reward' (Scandinavian). Also a variant of Absolom and Alexander.

Aylmer

Variants and diminutives: Ailemar, Athel, Eilemar, Elmer.
Meaning: 'noble' and 'renowned' (Old English).

Azariah

Variants and diminutives: Azaria, Azriel.
Meaning: 'God is my help' (Hebrew). Also a girl's name.

Bailey

Variants and diminutives: Bail, Bailie, Baillie, Baily, Bayley.
Meaning: 'to enclose' or 'bailiff' (Old French).

Baird

Variants and diminutives: Bard.
Meaning: 'poet' or 'singer of poetry' (Welsh and Scots Gaelic).

Bal

Meaning: 'hair' (Sanskrit, Tibetan, English Gypsy).

Balder

Variants and diminutives: Baldewin, Baldur, Baldwin, Ball, Baudier, Baudoin.
Meaning: 'white god' or 'god of lightness' (Old Norse); derived from the name of a benevolent god of Norse mythology, loosely equated with Jesus Christ.

Baldric

Variants and diminutives: Baldarich, Baldri, Baudrey, Baudri.
Meaning: 'bold' and 'ruler' (Germanic).

Baldwin

Variants and diminutives: Baldawin, Baudoin, Bawden, Bealdwine, Boden, Bodkin, Bowden.
Meaning: 'bold' and 'friend' (Germanic).

Balthazar

Variants and diminutives: Baltasar, Balthasar, Belshazzer.
Meaning: 'Bel [a god of Babylon] be the king's protector' (Greek).

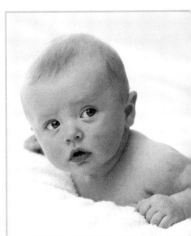

Barak

Meaning: 'flash of light' or 'lightning' (Hebrew).

Bardolf

Variants and diminutives: Bardell, Bardolph.
Meaning: 'bright' and 'wolf' (Germanic).

Barnabas

Variants and diminutives: Bane, Barn, Barna, Barnaba, Barnabe, Barnaby, Barnebas, Barney, Barnie, Barny, Bernabe, Burnaby.
Meaning: 'son of encouragement' (Hebrew).

Baron

Variants and diminutives: Baran, Barron.
Meaning: 'warrior' or 'man' (Latin); 'free man' (Germanic); a British family name derived from the title of nobility.

Barrett

Variants and diminutives: Barret.
Meaning: 'bear' and 'strength' (Germanic); derived from an English family name.

Barry

Variants and diminutives: Bairre, Bari, Barnard, Barnett, Barra, Barre, Barret, Barrfind, Barri, Barrie, Barrie, Barrington, Barris, Barrymore, Bearach, Fionbharr.
Meaning: 'spear' or 'fair-haired boy' (Irish Gaelic); 'barrier' (Old French).

Bartholomew

Variants and diminutives: Bardo, Barholomee, Bart, Bartel, Bartelot, Barth, Batholomaus, Bartholomieu, Bartie, Bartle, Bartlemey, Bartlet, Bartlett, Bartley, Bartold, Bartolo, Bartolome, Bartolomé, Barton, Barty, Bat, Bate, Batkin, Batly, Batty, Bertel, Meo, Mewes, Tholy, Tolly, Tolomieu, Tolomey.
Meaning: 'son of Tolmai [or Talmai]' (Hebrew).

Barton

Meaning: 'barley settlement' (Old English); derived from an English family name.

Baruch

Variants and diminutives: Barush.
Meaning: 'blessed' (Hebrew); 'good-doer' (Greek)

Basil

Variants and diminutives: Bale, Bas, Basie, Basile, Basilie, Basilio, Basilius, Basine, Basle, Baz, Bazek, Bazel, Bazil, Brasil, Breasal, Bresal, Vas, Vasil, Vasile, Vasilek, Vasili, Vasilis, Vasily, Vassily, Vasya, Vasyl, Vazul.
Meaning: 'kingly' or 'royal' (Greek); 'war' (Irish Gaelic).

Bavol

Variants and diminutives: Bevel.
Meaning: 'wind' or 'air' (English Gypsy).

Beau

Meaning: 'handsome' (French).

Beck

Meaning: 'brook' or 'stream' (Old Norse).

Bede

Meaning: 'prayer' (Old English).

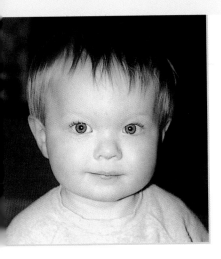

Beldon

Variants and diminutives: Belden, Beldin.
Meaning: 'small, beautiful place' (Old English).

Benedict

Variants and diminutives: Banet, Banko, Ben, Benayt, Bence, Benci, Bendek, Bendik, Benditto, Benedek, Benedetto, Benedick, Benedicto, Benedik, Benedikt, Benedo, Benek, Bendix, Benedetto, Benedicto, Benes, Benet, Benett, Beneyt, Bengt, Beni, Benigno, Benitin, Benito, Beniton, Benke, Bennet, Bennett, Bennie, Benny, Benoist, Benoit, Bento, Bettino, Betto, Boruch, Dick, Dix, Dixie, Venedict, Venedikt, Venka, Venya.
Meaning: 'blessed' (Latin).

Benjamin

Variants and diminutives: Bannerjee, Ben, Benji, Benjie, Benjy, Benmajee, Bennie, Benno, Benny, Berihert, Yemin.
Meaning: 'son of my right hand' or 'favourite son' (Hebrew).

Bentley

Variants and diminutives: Benm, Benny, Bently.
Meaning: 'place where there is bent grass' (Old English); derived from an English family name, in turn derived from a number of English place names.

Berenger

Meaning: 'bear' and 'spear' (Germanic).

Berg

Variants and diminutives: Bergen, Berger, Bergin, Borg, Borje, Bourke, Burke.
Meaning: 'mountain' (German); derived from a German family name, in turn derived from a number of German place names.

Berkeley

Variants and diminutives: Barclay, Barcley, Berk, Berke, Berkley, Berkly.
Meaning: 'birch wood' (Old English); derived from an English family name, in turn derived from an English place name.

Bernard

Variants and diminutives: Banet, Baretta, Barn, Barnard, Barnet, Barnett, Barney, Barnie, Barny, Barr, Barre, Barret, Barrett, Barry, Bear, Benek, Beno, Benno, Bern, Bernat, Barnadin, Bearnard, Bernado, Bernal, Bernardel, Bernardin, Bernardino, Bernardito, Bernardo, Bernardyn, Bernarr, Bernd, Berndt, Bernek, Berend, Berngards, Bernhard, Bernhardi, Bernhardt, Berni, Bernie, Bernis, Berno, Bernt, Berny, Bjarne, Björn, Bjorne, Burnard, Burnie, Burny, Levar, Nardo, Vernados.
Meaning: 'bear' and 'strength' (Germanic).

Bersh

Variants and diminutives: Besh.
Meaning: 'a year' (English Gypsy).

Berthold

Variants and diminutives: Bert, Bertell, Bertie, Bertil, Bertin, Bertol, Bertold, Bertole, Bertolt, Berton, Labert.
Meaning: 'bright' and 'power' (Germanic).

Bertram
Variants and diminutives: Bert, Berteram, Bertie, Bertran, Bertrand, Bertrando, Bertrem, Berty.
Meaning: 'bright' and 'raven' (Germanic).

Berwin
Meaning: 'supportive' and 'friend' (Old English); 'harvest' and 'friend' (Middle English).

Bevan
Variants and diminutives: Bev.
Meaning: 'son of Evan' (Welsh).

Bevis
Variants and diminutives: Beavis, Bev, Bevan, Bevin, Bivian, Bix, Buell.
Meaning: 'beef' or else 'cherished' or 'handsome' and 'son' (Old French); possibly also derived from Beauvais, a French place name.

Bill
Variants and diminutives: Billy, William.
Meaning: 'will' and 'helmet' or 'protection' (Germanic). A diminutive of William.

Björn
Variants and diminutives: Bernard.
Meaning: 'bear' and 'strength' (Germanic). A Scandinavian variant of Bernard.

Blaine
Variants and diminutives: Blain, Blane, Blayne.
Meaning: 'narrow' or 'servant of Saint Blane' (Irish Gaelic). Also a girl's name.

Blair
Variants and diminutives: Blaire.
Meaning: 'flat land' or 'plain' (Scots Gaelic); derived from a Scottish family name, in turn derived from a Scottish place name. Also a girl's name.

Blaise
Variants and diminutives: Balas, Balasz, Ballas, Biagio, Blaisot, Blas, Blase, Blasi, Blasien, Blasius, Blayze, Blaze, Blazek, Braz, Vlas.
Meaning: 'stammering' (Latin); 'taste' (Celtic); 'torch' (Old English). Also a girl's name.

Blake
Variants and diminutives: Blanchard, Blanco.
Meaning: 'pale' or 'black' (Old English).

Blythe
Variants and diminutives: Bligh, Blithe.
Meaning: 'carefree' (Old English).

Boaz
Meaning: 'strong man' or 'swiftness' (Hebrew).

Bob
Variants and diminutives: Bobbie, Bobby, Robert.
Meaning: 'fame' and 'bright' (Germanic). A diminutive of Robert.

Bonamy
Variants and diminutives: Bonaro, Boni, Bunn.
Meaning: 'good' and 'friend' (Old French).

Bonar
Meaning: 'courteous' (Old French).

Bond
Variants and diminutives: Bonde, Bondie, Bondon, Bonds, Bondy.
Meaning: 'to bind' (Old Norse); 'earth-tiller' (Old English).

Boniface
Variants and diminutives: Boneface, Boni, Bonyface, Facio, Fazio.
Meaning: 'destined to receive blessings', 'good-doer' or 'good-looking' (Latin).

Boris
Variants and diminutives: Borislav.
Meaning: 'battle' or 'stranger', (Old Slavonic); 'small' (Tartar).

Boyce
Meaning: 'wood' (Old French); derived from an English family name, in turn

derived from a number of English place names.

Boyd

Variants and diminutives: Bow, Bowen, Bowie.
Meaning: 'yellow' or 'from the Island of Bute' (Scots Gaelic); derived from a Scottish family name.

Braden

Variants and diminutives: Brad, Bradan, Bradin, Bradon, Brady, Bray, Braydan, Brayden, Braydin, Braydon, Braydun, Broadus.
Meaning: 'to broaden' (Old English); derived from an English family name.

Bradford

Variants and diminutives: Brad.
Meaning: 'broad ford' (Old English); derived from an English family name, in turn derived from a number of English place names.

Bradley

Variants and diminutives: Brad, Bradlee, Bradleigh, Bradly, Brady, Lee, Leigh.
Meaning: 'broad' and 'wood' or 'clearing' (Old English); derived from an English family name, in turn derived from a number of English place names.

Bramwell

Variants and diminutives: Bram, Branwell.
Meaning: 'raven' and 'well' (Cornish); 'brambles' and 'stream' (Old English); derived from an English family name, in turn derived from a number of English place names.

Bran

Meaning: 'raven' (Welsh).

Brandon

Variants and diminutives: Bran, Brandan, Branton, Brendan.
Meaning: 'broom' and 'hill' (Old English); derived from an English family name, in turn derived from a number of English place names.

Brant

Variants and diminutives: Brand, Brandi, Brandon, Brandt, Brent.
Meaning: 'fire' or 'firebrand' (Old English).

Brendan

Variants and diminutives: Bran, Brand, Brandan, Brandon, Brannon, Branon, Brant, Breandan, Bren, Brenain, Brend, Brenden, Brendin, Brendon, Brennan, Brenon, Brondan.
Meaning: 'prince' or 'royal' (Irish Gaelic).

Brent

Variants and diminutives: Brendt, Brenten, Brenton.
Meaning: 'high place' (Celtic); 'burned' (Old English); derived from an English family name and a number of English place names.

Brett

Variants and diminutives: Bret, Bretton, Brit, Briton, Britton.
Meaning: 'Breton' or 'Briton' (Latin); 'the ardent one's son' (Celtic).

Brian
Variants and diminutives: Briano, Briant, Brianus, Briar, Brareus, Brien, Brienus, Brion, Brior, Bruinal, Bryan, Bryant, Byron.
Meaning: 'strong', 'hill' or 'elevated' (Irish Gaelic)

Brock
Variants and diminutives: Badger, Braxton.
Meaning: 'badger' or 'brook' (Old English); 'young deer' (Old French).

Broderick
Variants and diminutives: Brod, Broddy.
Meaning: 'renowned' and 'ruler' (Germanic). A variant of Roderick.

Bruce
Variants and diminutives: Brucey, Brucie, Bruis, Brus.
Meaning: uncertain, possibly 'wood' (French); derived from the French family name Brieuse or the Scottish family name de Brus.

Bruno
Variants and diminutives: Brewis, Bronson, Browse, Bruin, Bruns, Labron, Lebron.
Meaning: 'brown' or 'like a bear' (Germanic).

Bryce
Variants and diminutives: Brice, Brick, Brycen, Brychan, Bryson, Bryston.
Meaning: 'son of the powerful ruler' (Germanic); 'dappled' (Welsh). Also a girl's name.

Bryn
Variants and diminutives: Brin, Brinn, Bryne, Brynmor, Brynn, Brynne.
Meaning: 'hill' (Welsh). Also a girl's name.

Brynmor
Meaning: 'large hill' (Welsh).

Bud
Variants and diminutives: Budd, Buddy.
Meaning: 'friend' or 'brother' (English).

Burr
Variants and diminutives: Burbank, Burrell, Burris, Burton.
Meaning: 'youth' (Scandinavian); 'roughly edged' (Middle English).

Burt
Variants and diminutives: Bert, Burty.
Meaning: 'bright' (Old English).

Byron
Variants and diminutives: Biron, Buiron, Byram, Byrom.
Meaning: 'cowshed' or 'cattle-herder' (Old English); 'landed estate' or 'cottage' (Old French).

Cadfael
Meaning: 'battle' and 'metal' (Welsh).

Cadwallader
Variants and diminutives: Cadwaladar, Cadwalader, Cadwaladr, Cadwalladr.
Meaning: 'battle' and 'leader' (Welsh).

Caerwyn
Meaning: 'white castle' (Welsh).

Caesar
Variants and diminutives: Arek, Casar, Cecha, Cesar, César, Cesare, Cesareo, Cesario, Cezar, Cezary, Cezek, Czar, Kaiser, Kesar, Sarito, Seasar, Sezar, Tsar.
Meaning: 'to cut', 'blue-grey', 'dark hair', 'long hair' or 'head of hair' (Latin); a Roman family name and title assumed by Roman emperors (emulated by the German kaisers and Russian tsars).

Cahil
Meaning: 'young' or 'inexperienced' (Turkish).

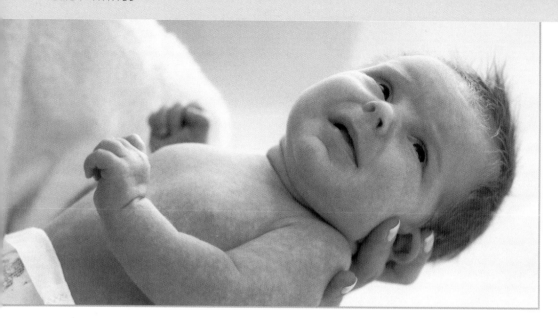

Caius
Variants and diminutives: Cai, Kai, Kay.
Meaning: 'to rejoice' (Latin). A variant of Gaius.

Cal
Variants and diminutives: Calen, Calin, Kail, Kale, Kalen, Kayle.
Meaning: 'thin' (Irish Gaelic).

Caleb
Variants and diminutives: Cal, Cale, Kalb, Kale, Kaleb, Kalev.
Meaning: 'without fear' or 'bold' (Hebrew); 'brave in victory' (Arabic).

Calum
Variants and diminutives: Callum, Colm, Colum, Kallum, Kalum.
Meaning: 'dove-like' (Latin); 'servant of Saint Columba' (Scots Gaelic). A variant of Columbus or a diminutive of Malcolm.

Calvin
Variants and diminutives: Caiv, Cal, Calvino, Kal, Kalvin, Vin, Vinnie, Vinny.
Meaning: 'bald' (Latin).

Cam
Meaning: 'beloved' (English Gypsy).

Cameron
Variants and diminutives: Cam, Camaron, Camron, Kam, Kamaron, Kameron, Kamron.

Meaning: 'crooked nose' (Scots Gaelic); also the name of a Scottish clan.

Camillus
Variants and diminutives: Camille, Camillo.
Meaning: 'messenger' or 'attendant at ritual' (Latin); derived from the Roman family name Camillus.

Camlo
Variants and diminutives: Cam.
Meaning: 'friendly' or 'lovely' (English Gypsy); 'sweet dew' (Vietnamese).

Campbell
Variants and diminutives: Cam, Camp, Campie, Campy.
Meaning: 'beautiful plain' (Latin); 'crooked mouth' (Scots Gaelic); also the name of a Scottish clan.

Caradoc
Variants and diminutives: Caractacus, Caradawg, Caractacos, Caradog, Carthac, Carthach, Carghage, Cerdic.
Meaning: 'dear' or 'friendly' (Welsh).

Carew
Meaning: 'dear' or 'coach' (Latin).

Carl
Variants and diminutives: Carlo, Carlos, Karl.
Meaning: 'man' or 'free man' (Germanic). A variant of Charles.

Carr
Variants and diminutives: Karr, Kerr.
Meaning: 'marshland' (Old Norse); derived from an English family name, in turn derived from a number of place names.

Carter
Meaning: 'cart-maker' or 'cart-driver' (Old English); also an English family name and a girl's name.

Carvel
Variants and diminutives: Carvell.
Meaning: 'song' (Manx); 'from the marsh' (Old French).

Cary
Variants and diminutives: Carey.
Meaning: 'much loved' or 'costly' (Latin); 'castle-dweller' (Welsh); derived from an English family name and a number of British place names.

Casimir
Variants and diminutives: Cachi, Casey, Cashi, Casimer, Casimiro, Cass, Cassie, Cassy, Kasimier, Kasimir, Kazek, Kazik, Kazimir, Kazio, Kazmer.
Meaning: 'peace is proclaimed' (Old Slavic).

Caspar
Variants and diminutives: Cash, Casper, Cass, Cassie, Cassy, Gaspar, Gaspard, Gaspare, Gasparo, Gasper, Gazsi, Jaspar, Jasper, Josper, Kaspar, Kasper.
Meaning: 'jewel' (Greek); 'treasurer-keeper' (Persian); 'imperial' (Germanic). A variant of Jasper.

Cassidy
Variants and diminutives: Caiside, Cass, Cassady, Cassie, Cassy, Kass, Kassady, Kassidy.
Meaning: 'curly' or 'intelligent' (Irish Gaelic); 'trickster' (Welsh). Also a girl's name.

Cassius
Variants and diminutives: Case, Casey, Cash, Casius, Caskey, Cass, Cassie, Cassy, Cazzie, Cazzy, Cez, Chaz, Kas.
Meaning: 'vain' (Latin).

Cathal
Variants and diminutives: Cal.
Meaning: 'strong in battle' (Irish Gaelic).

Cecil
Variants and diminutives: Caecilianus, Caecilius, Cece, Cecile, Cecilio, Cecilius, Ceese, Ces, Cis, Kilan, Seisyllt, Sissy, Sitsyllt.
Meaning: 'blind' (Latin); 'sixth' (Welsh).

Cedric
Variants and diminutives: Cad, Caddaric, Caradoc, Caradog, Ced, Cedrych, Cerdic, Ceredic, Rick, Rickie, Ricky.
Meaning: uncertain; possibly 'welcome sight' (Welsh); 'generous pattern' (Celtic); 'friendly' (Old English); possibly coined by Scottish writer Sir Walter Scott for his character Cedric Rotherwood in the novel Ivanhoe; possibly a misspelling of Cerdic.

Cemal
Variants and diminutives: Kamal.
Meaning: 'handsome' (Arabic).

Chad
Variants and diminutives: Ceadda, Chadd, Chaddie, Chaddy.
Meaning: 'battle' (Welsh); 'martial' (Old English).

Chaim
Variants and diminutives: Chaimek, Chayim, Chayyim, Chayym, Haim, Hayim, Haym, Hayyim, Hy, Hyam, Hyman, Hymie, Khaim, Mannie, Manny.
Meaning: 'life' (Hebrew).

Chand
Variants and diminutives: Chandran.
Meaning: 'the moon' (Sanskrit).

Chandler
Variants and diminutives: Chan, Chane, Chaney, Cheney, Shandler.
Meaning: 'candle-maker' or 'candle-seller' (Old French).

Chang
Meaning: 'free' (Chinese).

Channing
Variants and diminutives: Chan, Chane, Chann, Channe, Channon.
Meaning: 'channel' (Latin); 'wolf cub' (Irish Gaelic). Also a girl's name.

Chanticleer
Meaning: 'to sing clearly' (Old French).

Charles
Variants and diminutives: Alcuin, Carel, Carl, Carleton, Carlie, Carling, Carlino, Carlisle, Carlo, Carlos, Carlson, Carlton, Carlus, Carly, Carlyle, Carol, Carolle, Carolo, Carolos, Carolus, Carroll, Cary, Caryl, Cathal, Cathaoir, Chad, Chaddie, Chaddy, Char, Charlet, Charley, Charlie, Charlot, Charis, Charlton, Charly, Charlys, Chas, Chay, Chaz, Chic, Chick, Chicky, Chico, Chilla, Chip, Cholly, Chuck, Corliss, Curley, Curlie, Curly, Kale, Kalle, Kalman, Karcsi, Karel, Kari, Karl, Karlen, Karlens, Karlik, Karlin, Karlis, Karol, Karole, Karolek, Karolus, Karoly, Siarl, Tearlach, Turlogh.
Meaning: 'man' or 'free man' (Germanic).

Charlton
Variants and diminutives: Carleton, Carlton, Charleton.
Meaning: 'settlement of free men' (Old English); derived from an English family name and a number of English place names.

Chauncey
Variants and diminutives: Chance, Chancey, Chaunce, Chaune.
Meaning: 'to fall' (Latin); 'chance' (Old French); 'chancellor' (Old English).

Chen
Meaning: 'great' (Chinese).

Chester
Variants and diminutives: Caster, Castor, Ches, Cheslav, Chesleigh, Chesley, Chet.
Meaning: 'military camp' or 'Roman site'

(Latin); derived from an English family name and a number of English place names.

Chevalier
Variants and diminutives: Chev, Chevi, Cheviot, Chevy.
Meaning: 'knight' (Old French); derived from the French title of nobility.

Christian
Variants and diminutives: Chrétien, Chris, Chrissie, Chrissy, Christen, Christiaan, Christiano, Christianos, Christie, Christien, Christy, Chrystian, Crispin, Cristao, Cristi, Cristian, Cristianito, Cristiano, Cristino, Crystek, Karston, Kerestel, Keresztyen, Kerstan, Kit, Kito, Kreston, Kris, Krischan, Krispin, Krist, Krista, Krister, Kristian, Kristjan, Kristo, Kristos, Krists, Krys, Krystek, Krystian, Jaan, Zan.
Meaning: 'Christian' (Latin).

Christopher
Variants and diminutives: Chippy, Chris, Chrissie, Chrissy, Christal, Christie, Christof, Christofer, Christoff, Christoffer, Christoforo, Christoforus, Christoph, Christophe, Christophorus, Christoval, Christovano, Christy, Chrystal, Cris, Cristi, Cristo, Cristobal, Cristoforo, Cristovao, Crystal, Gilchrist, Gillecriosd, Kester, Kit, Kris, Kriss, Kristo, Kristof, Kristofel, Kristofer, Kristoffer, Kristofor, Kristopher, Krisus, Stoffel, Tobal, Tobalito, Xit.
Meaning: 'carrier of Christ' (Greek).

Ciaran
Variants and diminutives: Ciaren, Keeran, Kiaran, Kieran, Kiraren, Kyran.
Meaning: 'dark' (Irish Gaelic).

Cid
Variants and diminutives: Cyd, Sid, Syd.
Meaning: 'master' or 'lord' (Arabic).

Clancy
Variants and diminutives: Clance, Clancey.
Meaning: 'offspring' or 'son of the red warrior' (Irish Gaelic); also an Irish family name.

Clarence
Variants and diminutives: Clair, Claire, Clancy, Claral, Clare, Claron, Sinclair.
Meaning: 'of Clare' (Latin); derived from the British title duke of Clarence, in turn derived from French and Irish place names; 'clear', 'bright' or 'famous' (Latin) as the male version of Clare.

Clark
Variants and diminutives: Clarke, Claxton.
Meaning: 'inheritance' (Greek); 'cleric' or 'clerk' (Old English).

Claude
Variants and diminutives: Claud, Claudell, Claudian, Claudianus, Claudio, Claudius, Claus, Glade, Klaus.
Meaning: 'lame' (Latin); derived from a Roman family name.

Clay
Variants and diminutives: Clayland, Clayten, Claytin, Clayton, Cle, Clea, Cletis, Cletus.
Meaning: 'clay' (Old English).

Clement
Variants and diminutives: Clem, Cleme, Clemen, Clemens, Clément, Clemente, Clementius, Clemento, Clemenza, Clemmie, Clemmons, Clemmy, Clemon, Clim, Kal, Kalman, Kaloymous, Kelemen, Klema, Klemens, Klement, Kelmet, Klemo, Klim, Klimek, Kliment, Klimka, Klimt, Klyment, Menz.
Meaning: 'merciful' or 'mild' (Latin).

Clifford
Variants and diminutives: Clif, Cliff, Cliffe, Clifton, Clyfford.
Meaning: 'ford by a cliff' (Old English); derived from an English family name and place name.

Clinton
Variants and diminutives: Clint, Clintin.
Meaning: 'hill settlement' (Old English); derived from an English family name, in turn derived from a place name.

Clive
Variants and diminutives: Cleavant, Cleavon, Cleve, Cleveland, Clevey, Clevie, Clif, Cliff, Cliffe, Clifton.
Meaning: 'cliff' (Old English); derived from an English family name, in turn derived from a place name.

Clyde
Variants and diminutives: Cly, Clydel, Clywd.
Meaning: 'heard from a distance' (Welsh); derived from a family name, itself derived from the name of the Clyde river in Scotland.

Cole
Variants and diminutives: Colby, Cole, Coleman, Colier, Colin, Colis, Collayer, Colley, Collie, Collier, Collis, Collyer, Colman, Colton, Colville, Colvin, Colyer, Comghhall.
Meaning: 'swarthy' (Old English); 'hostage' or 'pledge' (Irish Gaelic); 'coal' (Middle English). Also a diminutive of Nicholas.

Colin
Variants and diminutives: Cailean, Coilin, Colan, Cole, Colino, Collie, Collin, Collins, Colly, Colyn.
Meaning: 'victory of the people' (Greek) as a diminutive of Nicholas; 'youth' or 'puppy' (Scots Gaelic); 'young man' (Irish Gaelic); 'chieftain' (Celtic).

Columba
Variants and diminutives: Callum, Calum, Colin, Colm, Colmicille, Colon, Colum, Columb, Columbus, Culva.
Meaning: 'dove-like' (Latin).

Coman
Meaning: 'noble' (Arabic).

Conal
Variants and diminutives: Congal, Connall, Connell.
Meaning: 'mighty' (Celtic).

Conan
Variants and diminutives: Con, Conant, Conn, Conney, Connie, Connor, Conny, Conor, Kinan, Kynan.

Meaning: 'high' (Celtic); 'wolf' or 'hound' (Irish Gaelic); 'to be able to' (Middle English).

Conor

Variants and diminutives: Con, Conchobar, Conner, Connery, Connor, Connors.
Meaning: 'high desire', 'wilful', 'lover of wolves' or 'lover of hounds' (Irish Gaelic); derived from an Irish family name.

Conrad

Variants and diminutives: Con, Conn, Conni, Connie, Conny, Conrade, Conrado, Conrao, Conroy, Cort, Curt, Koenraad, Konni, Konrad, Kort, Kurt.
Meaning: 'brave' and 'advice' (Germanic).

Constantine

Variants and diminutives: Con, Conney, Connie, Considine, Consta, Constans, Constant, Constantin, Constantinius, Constantino, Costa, Costain, Costane, Costin, Custance, Konstantin.
Meaning: 'constancy' (Latin).

Corbin

Variants and diminutives: Corban, Corben, Corbet, Corbett, Corby, Corbyn, Korbin, Korby, Korbyn.

Meaning: 'raven' (Old French).

Cordell

Variants and diminutives: Cord, Cordas, Cordel, Cordelle, Kord, Kordel, Kordell.
Meaning: 'instrument string' (Greek); 'cord' or 'cord-maker' (Old French).

Corin

Variants and diminutives: Caren, Carin.
Meaning: 'spear' (Sabine).

Cormac

Variants and diminutives: Cormack, Cormick.
Meaning: 'tree trunk' (Greek); 'charioteer' (Irish Gaelic).

Cornelius

Variants and diminutives: Conney, Connie, Cornall, Cornel, Cornell, Corney, Cornie, Corny, Cory, Neil, Neilus, Nelly.
Meaning: 'horn' or 'cornel tree' (Latin); derived from a Roman family name.

Corrigan

Variants and diminutives: Cori, Corigan, Corrie, Corry, Cory, Kori, Korigan, Korrie, Korrigan, Korry, Kory.
Meaning: 'small spear' (Irish Gaelic).

Cory

Variants and diminutives: Corey, Cori, Correy, Corry, Cory, Korey, Kori, Korrey, Korry, Kory.
Meaning: 'helmet' (Greek); 'hollow-dweller' or 'pool-dweller' (Irish and Scots Gaelic). Also a girl's name.

Cosmo

Variants and diminutives: Cosimo, Cosmas.
Meaning: 'order' (Greek).

Craig

Variants and diminutives: Kraig.
Meaning: 'rock' (Scots Gaelic); derived from a Scottish family name.

Crispin

Variants and diminutives: Crepin, Crispian, Crispianus, Crispinian, Crispinianus, Crispino, Crispo, Crispus, Krispin.
Meaning: 'curly' (Latin).

Crosby

Variants and diminutives: Crosbey, Crosbie.
Meaning: 'from the place of the cross' (Old Norse).

Cullen

Variants and diminutives: Cull, Cullan, Culley, Cullie, Cullin, Cully.

Meaning: 'cub' (Celtic); 'holly' (Irish Gaelic); 'from the nook' (Scots Gaelic); 'to select' (Middle English).

Curran

Variants and diminutives: Curr, Currey, Currie, Curry, Kurran, Kurrey, Kurrie, Kurry.
Meaning: 'champion' (Irish Gaelic); 'to churn' (Old English).

Curtis

Variants and diminutives: Cort, Cortie, Corty, Court, Courtenay, Courtland, Courtlandt, Courtney, Courts, Curcio, Curt, Curtell, Kurt, Kurtis.
Meaning: 'courtyard' (Latin); 'courteous' (Old French); 'short stockings' (Middle English); derived from an English family name.

Cuthbert

Variants and diminutives: Cudbert, Cudbright, Cuddie, Cuddy, Cumbert, Cuthbrid, Bert.
Meaning: 'famous' and 'bright' (Old English).

Cyprian

Variants and diminutives: Sy.
Meaning: 'of Cyprus' (Latin).

Cyril

Variants and diminutives: Ciril, Cirill, Cirillo, Cirilo, Ciro, Cy, Cyriack, Cyrill, Cyrille, Cyrillo, Girioel, Kiril, Kyril, Sy, Syriack.
Meaning: 'ruler' or 'lord' (Greek).

Cyrus

Variants and diminutives: Ciro, Cy, Cyrie, Kir, Kiril, Russ, Sy.
Meaning: 'sun', 'throne' or 'shepherd' (Persian).

Dacey

Variants and diminutives: Dace, Daci, Dacie, Dacy, Dasey, Dasi, Dasy, Daycee, Dayci, Daycie, Daycy.
Meaning: 'southerner' (Irish Gaelic). Also a girl's name.

Dalai

Meaning: 'mediator' (Sanskrit).

Dalbert

Variants and diminutives: Bert, Bertie, Berty, Dal.
Meaning: 'valley' and 'bright' (Germanic).

Dale

Variants and diminutives: Dael, Dail, Daile, Dal, Daley, Dali, Dalibor, Dallan, Dallas, Dallin, Dalt, Dalton, Dalva, Daly, Dayle, Delles, Dillon, Dolan.
Meaning: 'valley' (Old English). Also a girl's name.

Damian

Variants and diminutives: Dag, Dagan, Dagget, Dailey, Daily, Daly, Daman, Dame, Damiano, Damien, Damion, Damek, Damjan, Damlan, Damlano, Damon, Damyan, Darmon, Day, Dayman, Daymon, Daymond, Dayton, Demian, Dal, Delbert, Dema, Demyan.
Meaning: 'to tame', 'gentle' or 'fate' (Greek); 'demon' (Latin); 'bright day' (Old English).

Dane

Variants and diminutives: Dain, Daine, Dana, Daniel, Dayne, Dean.
Meaning: 'Dane' (Old Norse).

Daniel

Variants and diminutives: Dacso, Dainial, Dan, Dana, Dane, Daneal, Daneil, Danek, Dani, Daniela, Daniele, Daniels, Danil, Danila, Danilka, Danilo, Danko, Dano, Dannet, Dannie,

Dannson, Danny, Danson, Danukas, Danya, Danylets, Danylo, Deiniol, Denils, Dennel, Domhnall, Donal, Donois, Dusan, Kamiela, Nelo, Taneli.
Meaning: 'judgement of God' (Hebrew).

Dante

Variants and diminutives: Duran, Durant, Durante, Durrant, Duryea.
Meaning: 'steadfast' (Latin); 'to endure' (Italian). A diminutive of Durante, an Italian version of Durand.

Darby

Variants and diminutives: Dar, Darb, Darbey, Darbie, Derby, Derland, Dero, Deron, Diarmaid, Dorset, Dorsey, Dorsie, Dove, Dover, Dovey.
Meaning: 'deer park' or 'settlement by the water' (Old English); derived from an English family name and place name;

'free' (Irish Gaelic). Also a girl's name.

Darius

Variants and diminutives: Daare, Dar, Dare, Dareios, Daren, Daria, Darian, Darien, Darin, Dario, Darn, Darnel, Daron, Daroosh, Darrel, Darren, Darrin, Darrius, Daryl, Derry, Dorian.
Meaning: 'rich' (Greek).

Darrell

Variants and diminutives: Dar, Dare, Darel, Darell, Darlin, Darol, Darold, Darrel, Darrill, Darrol, Darroll, Darry, Darryl, Daryl, Daryle, Derel, Derial, Derland, Derral, Derrell, Derrill, Derry, Derryl, Deryl, Dorrel.
Meaning: 'dear' (Old English); 'of Airelle' (French); derived from an English family name, in turn derived from a French place name. Also a girl's name.

Darren

Variants and diminutives: Dar, Daran, Dare, Daren, Darien, Darin, Dario, Darn, Darnell, Daron, Darran, Darrin, Darring, Darron, Darun, Daryn.
Meaning: uncertain; possibly 'rich' (Greek) as a variant of Darius; possibly 'great small one' (Irish Gaelic) when derived from an Irish family name.

Darwin

Variants and diminutives: Dar, Derwin, Derwyn, Durwin.
Meaning: 'sea' or 'dear' and 'friend' (Old English).

David

Variants and diminutives: Dab, Dabbey, Dabby, Dabko, Dabney, Daffy, Dafyd, Dafydd, Dahi, Dai, Daibhead, Daibhi, Daibhidh, Daith, Daithi, Daithin, Dakin, Dako, Dathi, Daud, Daue, Dav, Dave, Daveed, Davey, Davi, Davidas, Davidde, Davide, Davidek, Davidyne, Davie, Davin, Daviot, Davis, Davit, Davito, Davy, Davyd, Daw, Dawe, Dawes, Dawid, Dawood, Dawoodji, Dawson, Dawud, Deakin, Deio, Devi, Devlin, Dew, Dewer, Dewey, Dewi, Dodya, Dowid, Dov, Dow, Dowe, Kavika, McTavish, Tab, Tafydd, Taffy, Tavi.
Meaning: 'beloved' or 'friend' (Hebrew).

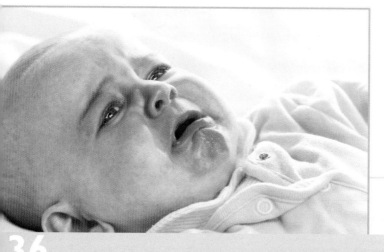

Dean

Variants and diminutives: Deane,
Dee, Dene, Dennit, Deno, Denton,
Dino.
Meaning: 'one in charge of ten' or
'dean' (Latin); 'valley' (Old English);
derived from an English family name.

Decimus

Meaning: 'tenth' (Latin).

Declan

Variants and diminutives: Deaglan.
Meaning: uncertain; possibly 'good'
(Irish Gaelic).

Dee

Meaning: a diminutive of any name
beginning with 'D-'. Also a girl's name.

Delano

Variants and diminutives: Del,
Delan, Delane, Delaine, Delainey,
Delaney, Delann, Lane, Laine.
Meaning: 'dark' or 'healthy' (Irish
Gaelic); 'of the night' (French).

Delmar

Variants and diminutives: Del,
Delmer, Delmor, Delmore.
Meaning: 'of the sea' (Latin).

Delroy

Variants and diminutives: Del, Roy.

Meaning: 'of the king' (Old French)

Demetrius

Variants and diminutives: Deems,
Demeter, Demetre, Demetri, Demetrio,
Demitri, Demetrios, Demitrios,
Demitrius, Demitry, Demmy, Dima,
Dimitr, Dimitre, Dimitri, Dimitrios,
Dimitry, Dimos, Dmitri, Dmitrik, Dmitry,
Dometer, Domotor, Dymmek, Dymitry,
Dyzek, Mimis, Mitros, Mitsos, Takis.
Meaning: 'of Demeter' (Greek),
Demeter being the Greek earth
goddess.

Denholm

Variants and diminutives: Den,
Dennie, Denny.
Meaning: 'valley' and 'island' (Old
English); derived from an English
family name, in turn derived from an
English place name.

Dennis

Variants and diminutives: Deenys,
Den, Denes, Denis, Denison, Denit,
Denka, Denman, Dennes, Dennet,
Denney, Dennie, Dennison, Dennit,
Denny, Denote, Denya, Denys,
Denzel, Denzell, Denzil, Deon, Diniz,
Dinny, Dion, Dione, Dionigi, Dionis,
Dionisio, Dionysios, Dionysius,
Dionysos, Dionysus, Diot,
Donnchadh, Donnet, Donoghm,

Dwight, Enis, Ennis, Enzo, Nicho,
Tennis.
Meaning: 'deity of the Nysa' (Greek),
Nysa being the birthplace of
Dionysus, the Greek god of wine,
fecundity, vegetation and revelry,
from whose name Dennis is derived.

Denton

Variants and diminutives: Dennie,
Denny.
Meaning: 'valley' and 'settlement'
(Old English); derived from an
English family name, in turn derived
from a number of English place
names.

Denver

Variants and diminutives: Den,
Dennie, Denny.
Meaning: 'Danes' crossing' (Old
English); 'little forested valley' (Middle
English); 'green' (French); derived
from an English family name, in turn
derived from an English place name.

Denzil

Variants and diminutives: Dennie,
Denny, Denzel, Denzell.
Meaning: uncertain; possibly
'fortress' (Celtic); 'high' (Cornish);
derived from a Cornish family name,
in turn derived from the Cornish
place name Denzell.

Derek

Variants and diminutives: Darick, Darik, Darrek, Darrick, Darrik, Dederick, Dek, Dekker, Del, Der, Derec, Dereck, Deric, Derick, Derk, Derrec, Derreck, Derrek, Derric, Derrick, Derrik, Derry, Deryck, Deryk, Diederick, Dirck, Dirk, Durk, Dyryke, Rick, Ricky, Terry, Theoderic, Thierry, Tedrick.
Meaning: 'people' and 'ruler' (Germanic). A variant of Theodoric.

Dermot

Variants and diminutives: Darby, Der, Derby, Dermott, Diarmad, Diarmaid, Diarmait, Diarmid, Diarmit, Diarmuid, Diiarmuit, Kermit.
Meaning: 'lacking in envy' (Irish Gaelic).

Deror

Variants and diminutives: Derori, Dror.
Meaning: 'free' or 'a swallow' (Hebrew).

Derry

Variants and diminutives: Dare, Darrey, Darrie, Dary.
Meaning: 'red-headed' (Irish Gaelic); 'oak trees' (Welsh). Also a diminutive of names beginning with 'Der-'.

Desiderio

Variants and diminutives: Desi, Desideratus, Desiderius, Desito, Diderot, Didi, Didier, Didon, Didot, Dizier.
Meaning: 'desiring' (Latin).

Desmond

Variants and diminutives: Demon, Des, Desi, Dezi.
Meaning: 'of the world' (Latin); 'from south Munster' (Irish Gaelic), Munster (Deas-Mhumhan in Irish Gaelic) being an Irish province; derived from an Irish family name.

Deval

Variants and diminutives: Dev, Deven, Devmani, Devraj.
Meaning: 'divine' (Sanskrit).

Devin

Variants and diminutives: Deavon, Dev, Devan, Deven, Devlin, Devon, Devron, Devy, Devyn.
Meaning: 'poet' (Irish Gaelic). Also a girl's name.

Dexter

Variants and diminutives: Decca, Deck, Dek, Dex.
Meaning: 'right-sided' or 'right-handed' (Latin).

Dhani

Variants and diminutives: Dan, Dannie, Danny, Dhan, Dhanni, Dhannie, Dhanny.
Meaning: 'rich' (Hindi).

Dick
Variants and diminutives: Dickie,
Dickon, Dicky.
Meaning: 'ruler' and 'hard'
(Germanic). A diminutive of Richard.

Diego
Meaning: 'supplanter' (Hebrew). A
Spanish variant of James, in turn a
variant of Jacob.

Dietrich
Variants and diminutives: Dedrick,
Dedrik, Detrik, Dierck, Dierk, Dieter,
Dieterich, Dietz, Dirk, Dtrik, Dytrych.
Meaning: 'powerful' and 'rich' or
'ruler of the people' (Germanic).

Digby
Meaning: 'to dig a ditch' (Old
French); 'farm by a ditch' (Old
English); derived from an English
family name, in turn derived from an
English place name.

Diggory
Variants and diminutives: Digory.
Meaning: uncertain; possibly 'gone
astray' (French).

Dominic
Variants and diminutives: Chuma,
Chumin, Chuminga, Deco, Dom,
Domek, Domenic, Domenick,
Domenico, Domenikos, Domenyk,
Domi, Domicio, Domingo, Domingos,
Dominick, Dominik, Dominique,
Dominy, Domo, Domokos, Domonkos,
Don, Donek, Dumin, Menico, Mingo,
Nick, Nickie, Nicky, Niki.
Meaning: 'of the lord' (Latin).

Donald
Variants and diminutives: Bogdan,
Bohdan, Domhnal, Domhnall, Don,
Donahue, Donal, Donaldo, Donalt,
Donn, Donne, Donner, Donnie,
Donny, Donahue, Donovan, Donya,
MacDonald, Tauno.
Meaning: 'global might' (Scots
Gaelic); also a Scottish clan name.

Donato
Variants and diminutives: Dodek,
Don, Donary, Donat, Donatello,
Donati, Donato, Donatus, Donny.
Meaning: 'gift' (Latin).

Donnel
Variants and diminutives: Donn,
Donnell, Donnelly, Donny, Doon, Dun.
Meaning: 'hill' or 'hillfort' (Irish Gaelic).

Donovan
Variants and diminutives: Don,
Donnie, Donny, Donovon, Dunavan,
Van.
Meaning: 'dark' (Irish Gaelic); 'dark
warrior' (Celtic); derived from an Irish
surname.

Doran
Variants and diminutives: Darren,
Dore, Dorey, Dorian, Dorie, Doron,
Dorran, Dory.
Meaning: 'gift' (Greek); 'exiled' or
'estranged' (Irish Gaelic).

Dorian
Variants and diminutives: Dor,
Dorrie, Dory.
Meaning: 'of the sea' or 'of Doris'
(Greek), Doris being a Greek region
north of the Gulf of Corinth. Also a
girl's name.

Dougal

Variants and diminutives: Doug, Dougie, Doyle, Dug, Dugald, Duggy, Dughall, Dubhghall.
Meaning: 'dark stranger' (Irish Gaelic).

Douglas

Variants and diminutives: Doug, Dougal, Dougie, Douglass, Dougy, Dugald, Duggie.
Meaning: 'dark water' (Scots Gaelic); derived from a Scottish family name, in turn derived from a Scottish place name.

Dov

Variants and diminutives: Dovev.
Meaning: 'bear' (Hebrew).

Doyle

Variants and diminutives: Dougal.
Meaning: 'assembly' (Irish Gaelic); 'dark stranger' (Irish Gaelic) as a variant of Dougal.

Drake

Meaning: 'snake' or 'dragon' (Greek).

Drogo

Variants and diminutives: Drew, Drewe, Drews, Dru, Druce, Drue, Drugo.
Meaning: 'to carry' (Germanic).

Duane

Variants and diminutives: Duwayne, Dwain, Dwain, Dwane, Dwayne.
Meaning: 'dark and little' (Irish Gaelic).

Dudley

Variants and diminutives: Dud, Dudd, Dudly
Meaning: 'Duddha's clearing' (Old English); derived from an English family name, in turn derived from an English place name.

Duff

Meaning: 'dark' (Scottish and Irish Gaelic); derived from a Scottish family name; 'dough' (northern English).

Duke

Variants and diminutives: Dukey, Dukie, Duky.
Meaning: 'leader' (Latin) as a derivation of the title of nobility; 'servant of [Saint] Maedoc' (Irish Gaelic) as a variant of Marmaduke.

Duncan

Variants and diminutives: Dun, Dunc, Dune, Dunkie, Dunn, Donncha, Donnchadh.
Meaning: 'brown warrior' (Irish and Scots Gaelic) or 'princely battle' (Scots Gaelic).

Dunstan

Variants and diminutives: Donestan, Dunn, Dunne, Dunst, Dustie, Dustin, Dusty.
Meaning: 'grey-brown', 'dark stone' or 'stony hill' (Old English).

Durand

Variants and diminutives: Dante, Duran, Durant, Durante, Durrant, Duryea.
Meaning: 'steadfast' (Latin); 'to endure' (Italian).

Dustin

Variants and diminutives: Dust, Dustie, Dusty.
Meaning: uncertain; possibly 'Thor's stone' (Old Norse); possibly 'a warrior' (Germanic); derived from an English family name.

Dwight

Variants and diminutives: Dewitt, DeWitt, Diot, Doyt, Wit, Wittie, Witty.
Meaning: uncertain; possibly 'white' (Old English and Old Dutch); possibly 'deity of the Nysa' (Greek), Nysa being the birthplace of Dionysus, the Greek god of wine, fecundity, vegetation and revelry, from which the name may be derived via a family name in turn derived from the name Diot, a variant of Dionysus.

Dylan

Variants and diminutives: Dill, Dillan, Dillie, Dillon, Dilly.
Meaning: 'son of the wave' or 'influence' (Welsh).

Eamon

Variants and diminutives: Eamonn, Edmund.
Meaning: 'happiness' or 'riches' and 'protector' (Old English) as the Irish Gaelic variant of Edmund.

Earl

Variants and diminutives: Earland, Earle, Earlie, Early, Erie, Erl, Erle, Errol, Erroll, Eryl, Jarl, Rollo.

Meaning: 'chieftain' (Old English); derived from the title of nobility.

Ebenezer

Variants and diminutives: Ben, Benezer, Eb, Eban, Ebanezer, Eben, Ebeneezer, Ebenezar, Even.
Meaning: 'help-giving stone' (Hebrew).

Edan

Variants and diminutives: Ed, Eddie, Eddy, Eden.
Meaning: 'fire' (Celtic).

Edgar

Variants and diminutives: Adair, Eadgar, Ed, Eddie, Eddy, Edek, Edgard, Edgardo, Edgars, Edko, Edus, Garek, Ned, Neddie, Neddy, Ted, Teddie, Teddy.
Meaning: 'happiness' or 'riches' and 'spear' (Old English).

Edmund

Variants and diminutives:
Eadmond, Eamon, Eamonn, Ed, Eddie, Eddy, Edmon, Edmond, Edmondo, Edmundo, Edmunds, Esmond, Mundek, Mundo, Ned, Neddie, Neddy, Odi, Odon, Ted, Teddie, Teddy.
Meaning: 'happiness' or 'riches' and 'protector' (Old English).

Edom

Variants and diminutives: Adam, Idumea.
Meaning: 'red' or 'red earth' (Hebrew). A variant of Adam.

Edric

Variants and diminutives: Ed, Eddie, Eddy, Edred, Edrich, Edrick, Ric, Rick, Rickie, Ricky.
Meaning: 'happiness' or 'riches' and 'powerful' or 'ruler' (Old English).

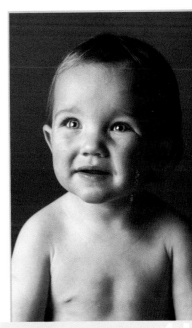

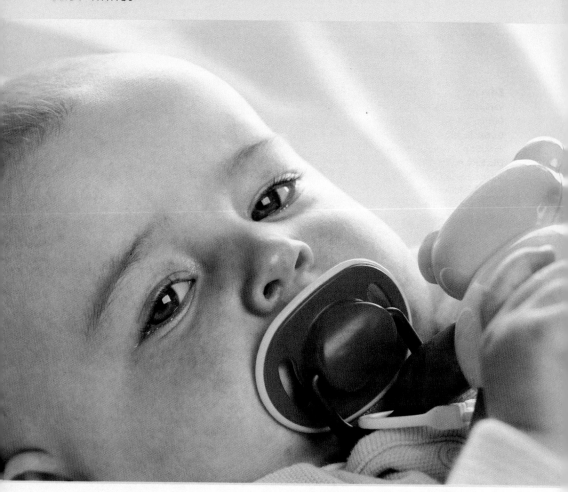

Edward

Variants and diminutives: Duardo, Duarte, Eadbard, Eadbhard, Eamon, Ed, Edd, Eddard, Eddie, Eddy, Ede, Edek, Edgard, Edik, Edison, Edko, Edo, Edoardo, Edouard, Edouardo, Edrardo, Edson, Eduard, Eduardo, Eduardus, Eduarelo, Eudardo, Edus, Edvard, Edwardo, Edwardus, Edzio, Eideard, Emile, Eward, Guayo, Ned, Nedd, Neddie, Neddy, Ted, Tedd, Teddie, Teddy.

Meaning: 'happiness' or 'riches' and 'guardian' (Old English).

Edwin

Variants and diminutives: Eaduin, Ed, Eddie, Eddy, Edred, Eduin, Eduino, Eduinus, Edwinn, Edwy, Edwyn, Ned, Neddie, Neddy, Ted, Teddie, Teddy.

Meaning: 'happiness' or 'riches' and 'friend' (Old English).

Egan

Variants and diminutives: Aeduca, Aodhagan, Egon.

Meaning: 'small fire' (Irish Gaelic).

Egbert

Variants and diminutives: Bert, Bertie, Berty.

Meaning: 'shining' or 'famous' and 'sword' or 'blade' (Old English).

Elan

Variants and diminutives: Ela, Elah, Elai, Elon.

Meaning: 'tree' (Hebrew); 'spirited' (Latin); 'friendly' (Native American).

Eldon

Variants and diminutives: Edlen, Edlon, Elden, Elder, Eldor, Elton.

Meaning: 'Ella's mound' (Old English); derived from an English family name, in turn derived from a place name; 'old and wise' (Germanic) as a variant of Aldo.

Eldred

Variants and diminutives: Aldred.

Meaning: 'old' and 'counsel' (Old English).

Eleazar

Variants and diminutives: El, Elazar, Elazaro, Elie, Eliezer, Ely, Lazar, Lazarus.

Meaning: 'God is my help' (Hebrew).

Eli

Variants and diminutives: El, Eloy, Ely, Ilie.

Meaning: 'elevated' or 'Jehovah' (Hebrew).

Elijah

Variants and diminutives: El, Eli, Elia, Elias, Elie, Eligio, Elihu, Elija, Elio, Eliot, Eliott, Elis, Elisio, Elison, Eliyahu, Elliot, Elliott, Ellis, Ellison, Elly, Elsen, Elson, Ely, Elyas, Elye, Elyot, Elys, Ilie, Ilija, Ilya.

Meaning: 'Jehovah is God' (Hebrew).

Elisha

Variants and diminutives: Elias, Eliot, Elis, Elissee, Eliseo, Elison, Elizur, Elkan, Elkanah, Ellas, Elliot, Elliott, Ellis, Ellison, Elly, Elrad, Elrod, Elsden, Elsen, Elson, Elstone, Ely, Hrod.

Meaning: 'God is my salvation' (Hebrew).

Elliot

Variants and diminutives: Elias, Eliot, Elliott, Ellis.

Meaning: 'Jehovah is God' (Hebrew) as a variant of Elias (Elijah); 'noble' and 'battle' (Old English); derived from an English family name.

Ellis

Variants and diminutives: Eelia, Eelusha, Elek, Eli, Elia, Elias, Eliasz, Elie, Elihu, Elis, Elisee, Eliseo, Elison, Ellas, Ellison, Elly, Elsden, Elsen, Elson, Elston, Ely, Elya, Ilias, Ilya.

Meaning: 'Jehovah is God' (Hebrew) as a variant of Elias (Elijah); derived from an English family name; 'benevolent' (Welsh).

Elmer

Variants and diminutives: Ailemar, Athel, Aylmar, Aylmer, Aymer, Edmar, Edmer, Eilemar, Elma, Elman, Elmo, Elmore.
Meaning: 'noble' and 'renowned' (Old English). A variant of Aylmer.

Elroy

Meaning: 'the king' (Old Spanish). A variant of Leroy.

Elton

Variants and diminutives: Elden, Elsdon, Elston.
Meaning: 'Ella's settlement', 'old' or 'noble' and 'town' (Old English); derived from an English family name, in turn derived from a place name.

Elvis

Variants and diminutives: Alby, Alvis.
Meaning: 'knowing all' (Old Norse) as a variant of Alvis; 'white' (Latin) as a variant of Alby (Alben and Albin, see Alban).

Elwin

Variants and diminutives: Al, Albin, Aloin, Aluin, Aluino, Alvan, Alvi, Alvin, Alvino, Alwin, Alwyn, Aylwin, El, Elva, Elvert, Elvin, Elwin, Elwyn.
Meaning: 'fair' and 'brow' (Welsh); 'old' and 'friend' (Old English); 'elf' or 'noble' and 'friend' (Old English) as a variant of Alvin.

Emery

Variants and diminutives: Almericus, Almery, Amalric, Amalrich, Amerigo, Amory, Emerick, Emericus, Emerson, Emil, Emilio, Emlin, Emlyn, Emmerich, Emmerlich, Emmery, Emmory, Emory, Imray, Imre, Imrich, Imrus.
Meaning: 'diligent' and 'ruler' (Germanic); 'powerful' and 'noble' (Old English).

Emile

Variants and diminutives: Amal, Emielo, Emil, Emilek, Emilio, Emilian, Emiliano, Emilio, Emils, Hemilio, Imelio, Melo, Milko, Milo, Miyo.
Meaning: 'eager', 'flatter' or 'rival' (Latin); derived from the Roman family name Aemilius.

Emlyn

Meaning: uncertain; possibly 'rival' (Latin) when derived from the Roman family name Aemilianus; possibly derived from the name of a Welsh town, Newcastle Emlyn. Also a girl's name.

Emmanuel

Variants and diminutives: Emanuel, Emanuele, Imanuel, Immanuel, Mani, Manny, Mannye, Mano, Manoel, Manuel.
Meaning: 'God is with us' (Hebrew).

Emmet

Variants and diminutives: Emmett, Emmit, Emmitt.
Meaning: 'truth' (Hebrew); 'ant' (Old English).

Emrys

Meaning: 'divine' or 'immortal' (Greek) as a Welsh variant of Ambrose.

Engelbert

Variants and diminutives: Bert, Bertie, Berty, Englebert, Ingelbert, Inglebert.
Meaning: 'angel' and 'bright' (Germanic).

Enoch

Meaning: 'dedicated', 'sacred to God', 'educated' or 'teacher' (Hebrew).

Enos

Variants and diminutives: Enosh.
Meaning: 'man' (Hebrew).

Ephraim

Variants and diminutives: Efim, Efraim, Efrain, Efrasha, Efrat, Efrayim, Efrem, Efren, Efron, Ephrayim, Ephrem, Ephrim, Rema.
Meaning: 'fruitful' (Hebrew).

Erasmus

Variants and diminutives: Elmo, Erasme, Erasmo, Eraste, Erastus, Ras, Rastus.
Meaning: 'beloved' or 'desired' (Greek).

Eric

Variants and diminutives: Erek, Erich, Erick, Erico, Erik, Eriks, Ric, Rick, Ricki, Rickie, Ricky.
Meaning: 'eternal', 'honourable' or 'island' and 'ruler' (Old Norse).

Ernest

Variants and diminutives: Earnan, Earnest, Ern, Erneis, Erneste, Ernestino, Ernesto, Ernestus, Ernie, Ernis, Erno, Ernst, Erny, Neto.
Meaning: 'earnest' (Old English).

Eros

Meaning: 'erotic love' (Greek).

Errol

Variants and diminutives: Earl, Erroll, Eryl, Harold, Rollo, Rolly.
Meaning: uncertain; possibly 'chieftain' (Old English) as a variant of Earl; possibly derived from a Scottish family name, in turn derived from a Scottish place name; possibly 'watcher' (Welsh) when the spelling Eryl is used.

Esau

Meaning: 'hairy' (Hebrew).

Esmond

Variants and diminutives: Esmund.
Meaning: 'grace' and 'defence' (Old English).

Ethan

Variants and diminutives: Etan, Ethe.
Meaning: 'constancy' or 'strength' (Hebrew).

Ethelbert

Variants and diminutives: Adalbert, Adelbert, Elbert, Elbie.
Meaning: 'noble' and 'bright' (Old English).

Ethelred

Variants and diminutives: Aethelraed, Aillred, Alret, Edred.
Meaning: 'noble' and 'counsel' (Old English).

Eugene

Variants and diminutives: Egen, Eoghan, Eugen, Eugène, Eugenio, Eugenios, Eugenius, Evgeni, Evgenios, Ewan, Ewen, Geka, Gencho, Gene, Genek, Genie, Genio, Genya, Jano, Jenci, Jeno, Jensi, Owain, Owen, Yevgeniy, Yevgeny, Zenda, Zheka, Zhenka.

Meaning: 'well-born' (Greek).

Eustace

Variants and diminutives: Eustache, Eustachius, Eustasius, Eustathius, Estatius, Eustazio, Eustis, Stace, Stacey, Stacy.
Meaning: 'fruitful', 'good' or 'ear of corn' (Greek).

Evan

Variants and diminutives: Ev, Evin, Ewan, Owen, Eoin.

Meaning: 'God has favoured', 'God is gracious' or 'God is merciful' (Hebrew) as a variant of Ieuan, in turn a Welsh variant of John; 'young warrior' or 'young archer' (Old Welsh).

Evander

Meaning: 'good man' (Greek).

Evelyn

Variants and diminutives: Evel, Evelio, Evelle.
Meaning: 'hazelnut' (Germanic); 'bird' (Latin). Also a girl's name.

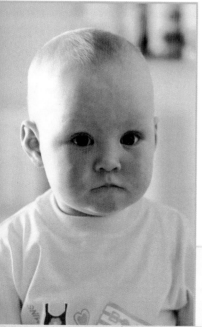

Everard

Variants and diminutives: Averitt, Devereux, Eberhard, Eberhart, Eberle, Ebert, Everart, Everet, Everett, Everette, Everhard, Everley, Evert, Eward, Ewart.
Meaning: 'boar' and 'tough' (Old English).

Ewan

Variants and diminutives: Eaven, Eoghan, Eugene, Ev, Evan, Evander, Evans, Evin, Evo, Ewen, Euan, Owain, Owen.
Meaning: 'youth' (Scots Gaelic); 'well-born' (Greek) as a variant of Eugene; 'God has favoured', 'God is gracious' or 'God is merciful' (Hebrew) as a variant of Ieuan, in turn a Welsh variant of John.

Ewart

Variants and diminutives: Euel, Ewell.
Meaning: 'settlement by the river' (Old English); derived from an English family name, in turn derived from a place name; 'ewer' (Old French).

Ezekiel

Variants and diminutives: Ezechial, Ezell, Eziechiele, Haskel, Haskell, Hehezkel, Yehezekel, Zeke.
Meaning: 'God give strength' (Hebrew).

Ezra

Variants and diminutives: Azariah, Azrikam, Azur, Esdras, Esra, Ezar, Ezer, Ezera, Ezri, Ezzard, Ezzret.
Meaning: 'help' (Hebrew).

Fabian

Variants and diminutives: Fabe, Fabek, Faber, Fabert, Fabi, Fabiano, Fabianus, Fabien, Fabio, Fabius, Fabiyan, Fabyan.
Meaning: uncertain; possibly 'bean' or 'skilful' (Latin); derived from the Roman family name Fabius.

Faisal

Variants and diminutives: Faisel, Faisil, Faisl, Faizal, Fasil, Faysal, Faysul, Fayzal, Fayzel.
Meaning: 'a fair judge' (Arabic).

Farid

Meaning: 'unique' (Arabic).

Farouk

Variants and diminutives: Farook, Farooq, Faruq.
Meaning: 'detector of lies' (Arabic).

Farquhar
Variants and diminutives: Fearchar.
Meaning: 'dear' or 'amiable' and 'man' (Scots Gaelic).

Farrell
Variants and diminutives: Farell, Farr, Farrall, Farril, Ferrel, Ferrell.
Meaning: 'superior' or 'valiant' (Irish Gaelic).

Felix
Variants and diminutives: Bodog, Fee, Fela, Felex, Felic, Felice, Felicio, Felike, Feliks, Felis, Felixiano, Felizano, Feliziano, Felizio, Phelim.
Meaning: 'happy' or 'fortunate' (Latin).

Ferdinand
Variants and diminutives: Fardie, Fardy, Faron, Farran, Farren, Fearn, Ferando, Ferd, Ferde, Ferdenando, Ferdi, Ferdie, Ferdinando, Ferdino, Ferdy, Fern, Fernand, Fernandas, Fernandeo, Fernando, Fernandus, Ferni, Ferrand, Ferrando, Ferrant, Ferrante, Ferren, Ferrentus, Hernán, Hernándo, Nando, Nano.
Meaning: 'spirited' (Latin); 'journey' or 'peace' and 'prepare' or 'venture' (Germanic).

Fergal
Variants and diminutives: Fearghal.
Meaning: 'brave' (Irish Gaelic).

Fergus
Variants and diminutives: Fearghas, Feargus, Fergie, Ferguson, Fergy.
Meaning: 'strong and brave' or 'supreme choice' (Irish and Scots Gaelic).

Fidel
Variants and diminutives: Fedele, Fidelio.
Meaning: 'trust' or 'faithful' (Latin).

Finbar
Variants and diminutives: Fin, Finbarr, Finn, Fionnbharr.
Meaning: 'fair-haired' (Irish Gaelic).

Finlay
Variants and diminutives: Fin, Findlay, Findley, Findlaech, Finley, Finn, Fionnlagh.
Meaning: 'fair-haired' and 'warrior' or 'hero' (Scots Gaelic).

Finn
Variants and diminutives: Eifion, Finan, Finian, Finnegan, Finnian, Fion, Fionn.

Meaning: 'fair' (Irish Gaelic); also a citizen of Finland.

Fisk
Variants and diminutives: Fish, Fiske.
Meaning: 'fish' or 'to fish' (Germanic).

Fitz
Variants and diminutives: Fitzgerald, Fitzpatrick, Fitzroy.
Meaning: 'son' (Old English).

Flavius
Variants and diminutives: Flavian, Flavio.
Meaning: 'yellow' (Latin).

Fletcher
Variants and diminutives: Fletch.
Meaning: 'arrow-maker' (Old English); derived from an English family name.

Florian
Variants and diminutives: Ferenc, Fiorello, Florence, Florentino, Florents, Florentz, Florenz, Florus, Flory.

Meaning: 'flowering' or 'blossoming' (Latin). A male version of Florence.

Floyd

Variants and diminutives: Lloyd.
Meaning: 'grey' (Welsh) as a variant of Lloyd.

Flynn

Variants and diminutives: Flin, Flinn, Flyn.
Meaning: 'son of the red-headed man' (Irish Gaelic).

Forbes

Meaning: 'fodder' (Greek); 'field-owner' or 'prosperous' (Irish Gaelic).

Ford

Meaning: 'river crossing' (Old English).

Fortunatus

Variants and diminutives: Fortunato, Fortune, Fortunio.
Meaning: 'luck' (Latin). A male version of Fortuna.

Foster

Variants and diminutives: Forest, Forester, Forrest, Forrester, Forster, Foss.
Meaning: 'forester' (Old English), when derived from an English family name; 'foster child' (Old English).

Francis

Variants and diminutives: Chicho, Chico, Chilo, Chito, Cisco, Currito, Curro, Farruco, Fenenc, Fra, Fran, Franc, Franca, Francesco, Franchot, Francie, Francisco, Franciscus, Franciskus, Franck, Franco, François, Farnio, Frank, Frankie, Franky, Frannie, Frans, Frants, Franus, Franz, Franzen, Franzi, Frasco, Frascuelo, Frenz, Firso, Paco, Pacorro, Palani, Panchito, Pancho, Paquito, Proinnsias, Quico.
Meaning: 'French' (Latin).

Frank

Variants and diminutives: Cisco, Fenenc, Ferenc, Feri, Fran, Franc, Franca, Franck, Franco, Franek, Franio, Franki, Frankie, Franky, Frannie, Frans, Frants, Franus, Franz, Franzl, Frenz, Paco.
Meaning: 'free' (Latin); derived from the name of the Franks, a Germanic tribe whose western kingdom is now France, while their eastern kingdom is Germany. Also a diminutive of Francis and Franklin.

Franklin

Variants and diminutives: Francklyn, Frank, Franki, Frankie, Franklyn.
Meaning: 'free man' (Middle English); derived from an English family name.

Fraser

Variants and diminutives: Frase, Frasier, Fraze, Frazer, Frazier.
Meaning: uncertain; possibly 'curly' (Old English); possibly 'charcoal-burner' or 'strawberry' (Old French); possibly derived from a Scottish family name, in turn derived from the French place name La Fraselière.

Frederick

Variants and diminutives: Bedrich, Eric, Erich, Erick, Erik, Federico, Federigo, Federoquito, Fred, Freddie, Freddy, Fredek, Frédéric, Frederic, Frederich, Frederico, Frederigo, Frederik, Fredi, Fredric, Fredrick, Fredrik, Freed, Freeman, Frides, Fridrich, Friedel, Friedrich, Frits, Fritz, Fritzchen, Fritzi, Lico, Ric, Rich, Rick, Rickey, Rickie, Ricky, Rico, Riki.
Meaning: 'peace' and 'ruler' (Germanic).

Fulbert

Variants and diminutives: Bert, Berty, Filbert, Filberte, Filibert, Fulbright, Phil, Philbert, Philibert.
Meaning: 'very' and 'bright' (Germanic).

Gabriel

Variants and diminutives: Gab, Gabby, Gabe, Gabi, Gabian, Gabie, Gabiel, Gabirel, Gabko, Gabo, Gabor, Gabrial, Gabriele, Gabrielli, Gabriello, Gabris, Gaby, Gabys, Gavril, Gay, Riel.
Meaning: 'man of God' or 'my strength is God' (Hebrew).

Gaius

Variants and diminutives: Caius, Kay.
Meaning: 'to rejoice' (Latin).

Galahad

Variants and diminutives: Gwalchafed.
Meaning: 'battle hawk' or 'falcon of summer' (Welsh).

Gale

Variants and diminutives: Gael, Gail, Gaile, Gallard, Gay, Gayle.
Meaning: 'gallant' (Old French); 'lively' (Old English); 'stranger' (Irish Gaelic). Also a male version of Gail.

Galen

Variants and diminutives: Gaelan, Gail, Gailen, Gale, Galeno, Gay, Gayle, Gaylen.
Meaning: 'calm' (Greek).

Galvin

Variants and diminutives: Gal, Galvan, Galven.
Meaning: 'sparrow' or 'brilliant white' (Irish Gaelic).

Gamaliel

Variants and diminutives: Gamliel.
Meaning: 'God's recompense' (Hebrew).

Gandalf

Meaning: 'the elf of the wand' in the

49

fictional language of the Men of the North in Middle Earth; coined by British writer J R R Tolkien for a leading character – a wizard – in his epic fantasies *The Hobbit* and *The Lord of the Rings*.

Gareth

Variants and diminutives: Gary, Garry, Garth.
Meaning: 'gentle' (Welsh).

Garfield

Variants and diminutives: Gar, Field.
Meaning: 'triangle' and 'field', 'promontory' or 'spears' and 'field' (Old English); derived from an English family name, in turn derived from a place name.

Garrick

Variants and diminutives: Garek, Garick, Garik, Garreck, Garrek, Garrik, Garry, Gary, Gerek, Gerick, Gerreck, Gerrek, Gerrick, Gerrik, Rick, Rickie, Ricky, Rik, Rikky.
Meaning: 'spear' and 'ruler' (Old English).

Garth

Variants and diminutives: Gareth, Garret, Garton, Garvie, Garvin, Garry, Gary.

Meaning: 'enclosure' (Old Norse); 'garden' (Old English); derived from an English family name, in turn derived from a place name. Also a variant of Gareth.

Gary

Variants and diminutives: Gareth, Gareym Garfield, Gari, Garret, Garrett, Garri, Garry, Garth, Gerold.
Meaning: dependent on the meaning of the name of which it is a diminutive, for example: 'gentle' (Welsh) as a diminutive of Gareth; also derived from a British family name.

Gavin

Variants and diminutives: Gauen, Gauvain, Gauvin, Gav, Gavan, Gaven, Gavino, Gavvy, Gawain, Gawaine, Gawen, Gawin, Gwalchmai, Gwalchmei, Walwain, Walwyn.
Meaning: 'falcon of May' or 'hawk of the plain' (Welsh); 'district' (Germanic).

Gaylord

Variants and diminutives: Gae, Gail, Gaile, Gallard, Gay, Gayelord, Gayle, Gayler, Gaylor.
Meaning: 'merry' (Old French); derived from an English family name. Recently rendered unfashionable by its homosexual connotations.

Geoffrey

Variants and diminutives: Geof, Geoff, Giotto, Gisfrid, Godfrey, Godofredo, Gottfried, Gotz, Govert, Jef, Jeff, Jefferies, Jefferson, Jeffery, Jeffie, Jeffrey, Jeffries, Jeffry, Jeffy.
Meaning: uncertain; possibly 'God', 'good', 'district', 'traveller' or 'pledge' and 'peace' (Germanic) as a variant of Godfrey.

George

Variants and diminutives: Deòrsa, Dod, Durko, Egor, Geo, Geordie, Georg, Georges, Georgi, Georgie, Georgio, Georgios, Georgius, Georgiy, Georgy, Giorgis, Giorgos, Gogos, Goran, Gyorgy, Gyuri, Gyurka, Igor, Jarge, Jeorg, Jerzy, Jiri, Jörgen, Jorgen, Jorge, Jorgen, Jorje, Jorn, Jur, Juraz, Jurek, Jurg, Jürgen, Jurgen, Jurgi, Jurgis, Juri, Jurik, Jurko, Juro, McGeorge, Seoirse, Seòras, Sior, Siors, Siorys, Xorge, Yegor, Yorick, York, Yura, Yurchik, Yuri, Yurik, Yurko, Yusha, Zhorka.
Meaning: 'farmer' (Greek).

Geraint

Variants and diminutives: Gerontius.
Meaning: 'old man' (Greek); a Welsh variant of the Latin name Gerontius.

Gerald

Variants and diminutives: Erhard, Garald, Garet, Garett, Garey, Garo, Garold, Garolds, Garret, Garrett, Garritt, Garry, Gary, Geaóid, Gearóid, Ged, Gerallt, Ger, Gerado, Geralde, Geraldo, Gerardo, Geraud, Gerek, Gerold, Gerret, Gerrie, Gerrit, Gerritt, Gerry, Gerwald, Cherardo, Giraldo, Girald, Girard, Giraud, Girauld, Girault, Giraut, Herrardo, Jarett, Jarrett, Jed, Jerald, Jeraldo, Jerrald, Jerral, Jerre, Jerrel, Jerrel, Jerrie, Jerrold, Jerry.
Meaning: 'spear' and 'rule' (Germanic).

Gerard

Variants and diminutives: Erhard, Garald, Garey, Garo, Garold, Garolds, Garrard, Garret, Garrett, Garry, Gary, Gearard, Ged, Gellart, Gellert, Ger, Gerado, Geraud, Gerek, Gerhard, Gerharde, Gerhart, Gerrard, Gerret, Gerrie, Gerrit, Gerry, Gerwald, Gherardo, Giralt, Girard, Giraud, Girauld, Girault, Giraut, Herrado, Jarett, Jarrett, Jed, Jerald, Jeraldo, Jerrald, Jerral, Jerrard, Jerre, Jerrel, Jerrell, Jerrie, Jerrold, Jerry.
Meaning: 'spear' and 'hard' (Germanic).

Gervaise

Variants and diminutives: Gervais, Gervase, Gervasius, Gervis, Jarvis.
Meaning: uncertain; possibly 'spear' (Germanic) and 'servant' (Celtic).

Gerwin

Variants and diminutives: Gerwyn.
Meaning: 'fair' and 'love' (Welsh).

Gibor

Meaning: 'strong' (Hebrew).

Gibson

Variants and diminutives: Gib, Gibb, Gibbie, Gibby.
Meaning: 'son of Gilbert' (Old English), Gilbert meaning 'pledge' or

'hostage' and 'bright' (Germanic), 'servant', 'servant of Saint Bridget' or 'servant of Saint Gilbert' (Scots Gaelic); derived from a British family name.

Gideon

Variants and diminutives: Gedeon, Gid, Gideone, Hedeon.
Meaning: uncertain; possibly 'hewer', 'powerful warrior', 'maimed' or 'stump' (Hebrew).

Gilbert

Variants and diminutives: Bert, Bertie, Berty, Burt, Burtie, Birty, Gib, Gibb, Gibbie, Gibbon, Gibby, Gibson, Gil, Gilberto, Gilbride, Gilburt, Gilibeirt, Gill, Gilleabart, Gilli, Gillie, Giselbert, Guilbert, Wilbert, Wilbur, Wilburt, Will.
Meaning: 'pledge' or 'hostage' and 'bright' (Germanic); 'servant', 'servant of Saint Bridget' or 'servant of Saint Gilbert' (Scots Gaelic).

Giles

Variants and diminutives: Egide, Egidio, Egidius, Gide, Gidie, Gil, Gile, Gilean, Gileon, Gill, Gilles, Gillette, Gillian, Gyles.
Meaning: 'kid' or 'goatskin' (Greek); derived from the Roman name Aegidius; 'servant' (Scots Gaelic).

Gillespie

Variants and diminutives: Gill.
Meaning: 'bishop's servant' (Scots Gaelic); derived from a Scottish family name.

Gilroy

Variants and diminutives: Gill, Gilly, Roy.
Meaning: 'servant of the red-headed man' or 'servant of the king' (Scots Gaelic).

Glen

Variants and diminutives: Glenard, Glenn, Glennard, Glennon, Glyn, Glynn.
Meaning: 'valley' (Scots Gaelic); derived from a Scottish family name, in turn derived from a geographical feature. As Glenn, also a girl's name.

Glyndwr

Variants and diminutives: Glendower.
Meaning: 'valley' and 'water' (Welsh).

Godfrey

Variants and diminutives: Goraidh.
Meaning: 'God', 'good', 'district', 'traveller' or 'pledge' and 'peace' (Germanic).

Godwin

Variants and diminutives: Godewyn, Godwyn, Goodwin, Win, Winny, Wyn.
Meaning: 'God' or 'good' and 'friend' (Old English).

Gordon

Variants and diminutives: Goran, Gordan, Gorden, Gordey, Gordie, Gordy, Gore, Gorham, Gorrell, Gorton.
Meaning: uncertain; possibly 'large' and 'fort' or 'marsh' and 'wooded dell' (Scots Gaelic); derived from a Scottish family name, in turn derived from a Scottish or Norman place name.

Grady

Variants and diminutives: Gradey.
Meaning: 'step' (Latin); 'bright one' or 'exalted one' (Irish Gaelic).

Graham

Variants and diminutives: Graeham, Graeme, Graemer, Graenem, Graenum, Grahame, Gram, Gramm.
Meaning: 'Granta's', 'gravelly', 'grey' or 'grant' and 'homestead' (Old English); derived from Grantham, an English town; also a Scottish family name.

Grant

Variants and diminutives: Grantland, Grantley.
Meaning: 'large', 'tall' or 'to bestow' (French); derived from a Scottish family name.

Granville

Variants and diminutives: Grenville.
Meaning: 'large' and 'town' (French); derived from an English family name, in turn derived from a Norman place name.

Gray

Variants and diminutives: Graydon, Grey, Greyson.
Meaning: 'grey' or 'bailiff' (Old English).

Gregory

Variants and diminutives: Gero, Greg, Gregg, Greggory, Gregoire, Gregor, Gregorio, Gregorios, Gregorius, Gregors, Gregos, Gregour, Gregus, Greig, Greis, Gries, Grigoi, Grigor, Grigorios, Grigory, Griogair, Grischa.
Meaning: 'watchful' (Greek).

Griffith

Variants and diminutives: Griff, Griffin, Gruffudd, Gruffydd, Gryphon.
Meaning: uncertain; possibly 'strong warrior' or 'lord' (Welsh) as a variant of Gruffydd; also a British family name.

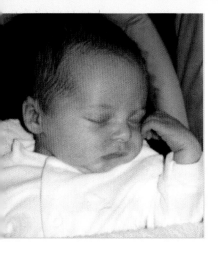

Gustave

Variants and diminutives: Gus, Gussie, Gustaf, Gustaff, Gustav, Gustavo, Gustavs, Gustavus, Gusti, Gustik, Gusty, Gustus, Kosti, Tabo, Tavo.
Meaning: 'staff' and 'of the gods' or 'of the Goths' (Swedish).

Guy

Variants and diminutives: Gui, Guido, Guyon, Gye, Vitus, Viti, Wido, Wyatt.
Meaning: 'wood', 'wide', 'warrior' or 'guide' (Germanic).

Gwyn

Variants and diminutives: Gwynne, Wyn, Wynne.
Meaning: 'fair' (Welsh). A male version of Gwen.

Gwynfor

Meaning: 'fair' and 'lord' or 'place' (Welsh).

Gyan

Meaning: 'erudite' (Sanskrit).

Habib

Meaning: 'lover' or 'beloved' (Arabic).

Hadar

Meaning: 'glory' (Hebrew).

Hadrian

Variants and diminutives: Ade, Adi, Adie, Adorjan, Adriann, Adriano, Adrianus, Adrien, Adrik, Andreian, Andreyan, Andri, Andrian, Andriyan, Arne, Hadrian.
Meaning: 'from Adria' (a city in northern Italy) or 'dark one' (Latin) as a variant of Adrian.

Hadyn

Variants and diminutives: Aidan, Hayden, Haydon.
Meaning: uncertain; possibly 'to

help' (Middle English) or 'small fiery one' (Irish Gaelic) as a variant of Aidan; possibly 'hay' and 'hill' (Old English) when derived from an English family name, in turn derived from a number of English place names.

Haidar

Meaning: 'lion' (Arabic).

Hakan

Meaning: 'fiery' (Native American).

Hakeem

Variants and diminutives: Hakim.
Meaning: 'wise' (Arabic).

Hakon

Variants and diminutives: Haakon, Hacon, Hak, Hako.
Meaning: 'useful' or 'exalted race' (Old Norse).

Hale

Variants and diminutives: Hal, Haley, Halford, Halley, Hallie, Halsey, Halsy, Hollis, Holly.
Meaning: 'safe', 'healthy' or 'whole' (Old English).

Halil
Variants and diminutives: Hallil.
Meaning: 'flute' (Hebrew); 'close friend' (Turkish).

Hallam
Variants and diminutives: Halam, Hallum.
Meaning: 'nook', 'stone' or 'far-off valley' (Old English); derived from an English family name, in turn derived from an English place name.

Ham
Variants and diminutives: Abraham.
Meaning: 'hot' or 'swarthy' (Hebrew); 'home' or 'village' (Old English); also a name for cured pork.

Hamal
Meaning: 'lamb' (Arabic).

Hamilton
Variants and diminutives: Hamel, Hamil, Hamill, Tony.
Meaning: 'home' and 'lover' or 'place' (Old English); derived from a Scottish family name, in turn derived from a number of British place names.

Hamish
Variants and diminutives: Seamus, Shamus, Shemais.
Meaning: 'supplanter' (Hebrew) as an anglicised Scots Gaelic version of James (Jacob).

Hamlet
Variants and diminutives: Amleth, Amlothi, Haimes, Ham, Hamelin, Hames, Hamil, Hamilton, Hamlin, Hamlyn, Hammond, Hamnet, Hamo, Hamon, Hamond, Hampden, Hampton, Haymund, Haymo, Tony.
Meaning: 'home' (Germanic); 'small village' (Old English).

Hamza
Meaning: 'powerful' or 'strong' (Arabic).

Hannibal
Variants and diminutives: Annibal, Annibale, Hanniball, Honeyball.
Meaning: 'grace' (Punic) and 'Baal' [the chief god of the Phoenicians and Cananites] or 'lord' (Semitic).

Hans
Variants and diminutives: Hanan, Handley, Hanes, Hanley, Hanns, Hansel, Hansen, Hanson, Haynes, Heinz, Henlee, Honus, Johannes.
Meaning: 'God has favoured', 'God is gracious' or 'God is merciful' (Hebrew) as a northern European version of John.

Hanuman
Meaning: 'leader of the monkeys' (Hindi).

Hardy
Variants and diminutives: Eberhard, Hardee, Harden, Hardey, Hardie, Hardin, Harding.
Meaning: 'bold' or 'tough' (Germanic); derived from an English family name.

Harley
Variants and diminutives: Harl, Harlan.
Meaning: 'archer' or 'deer hunter' (Teutonic); 'flax' and 'field' (Middle Low German); 'hare' and 'clearing' (Old English); derived from an English family name, in turn derived from a number of English place names.

Harold
Variants and diminutives: Arailt, Araldo, Aralt, Arold, Aroldo, Arrigo, Enric, Eral, Errol, Garald, Garold, Gerahd, Giraldo, Hal, Haldon, Hale, Halford, Harailt, Harald, Haraldr, Haralds, Haroldas, Haroldo, Hardoldus, Harivlad, Hariwald, Harlow, Haroldus, Harolt, Harry, Heral, Hereweald, Heronim, Hieronim, Hiraldo, Jindra, Kharald, Parry, Rigo.
Meaning: 'army' and 'ruler' or 'power' (Old English).

Harper

Meaning: 'sickle' (Latin); 'harp-player' (Old English). Also a girl's name.

Harrison

Variants and diminutives: Harris, Harrisen.
Meaning: 'son of Harry' or 'son of', 'home' and 'ruler' as a variant of Henry.

Harte

Variants and diminutives: Hart, Hartley, Hartman, Hartwell, Hartwig, Heartley, Hersch, Herschel, Hersh, Hershel, Hertz, Hertzl, Heschel, Heshel, Hirsch, Hirsh.
Meaning: 'hart' or 'stag' (Old English); a diminutive of Hartley, 'hart' and 'clearing' (Old English), derived from an English family name, in turn derived from a number of English place names.

Harvey

Variants and diminutives: Ervé, Harv, Harve, Harveson, Harvie, Hervé, Hervey, Hervi.
Meaning: 'battle' and 'worthy' (Breton); derived from an English family name.

Hassan

Meaning: 'nice' or 'handsome' (Arabic).

Heath

Meaning: 'heath' or 'place where wild plants grow' (Old English); derived from an English family name, in turn derived from a number of English place names.

Hector

Variants and diminutives: Eachann, Eachdonn, Ector, Ettore, Heck, Heckie, Hecky.
Meaning: 'holding firm' (Greek).

Hedley

Variants and diminutives: Headley, Hedly.
Meaning: 'heather' or 'male sheep' and 'clearing' (Old English); derived from an English family name, in turn derived from a number of English place names.

Helios

Variants and diminutives: Heller, Heli.
Meaning: 'sun' (Greek).

Helmut

Variants and diminutives: Hellmut, Helm, Helmuth.
Meaning: 'spirited' and 'brave' (Teutonic); 'helmet' (Germanic).

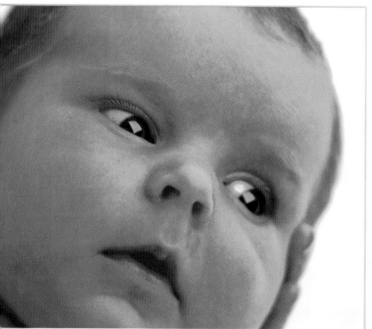

Henry

Variants and diminutives: Anraoi, Anrique, Arrigo, Bambis, Eanraig, Enri, Enric, Enrico, Enrikos, Enrique, Enriquillo, Enzio, Erizio, Erizo, Guccio, Hagan, Haimirich, Hal, Halkin, Hank, Hanraoi, Haralpos, Harris, Harrison, Harry, Hawkin, Hedric, Hecrich, Hedrick, Heimadall, Heiman, Heindrick, Heine, Heinemann, Heinie, Heinrich, Heinrick, Heinrik, Heinz, Hen, Hendri, Hendric, Hendrick, Hendrik, Heneli, Heniek, Henier, Henke, Henning, Henny, Henri, Henric, Henrico, Henricus, Henrik, Henrim, Henriot, Henrique, Henryk, Henty, Heriot, Herriot, Herry, Hersz, Hinrich, Honok, Inriques, Jindra, Jindrich, Khambis, Kharlambos, Kiko, Lambos, Quico, Quinto, Quique, Rico, Rik, Riki, Rogberto.
Meaning: 'home' and 'ruler' (Germanic).

Herbert

Variants and diminutives: Bert, Bertie, Berty, Eberto, Harbert, Heber, Hebert, Herb, Herbertus, Herbie, Herby, Heriberto.
Meaning: 'army' and 'bright' (Germanic).

Hercules

Variants and diminutives: Hacon, Heracles, Herakles, Herc, Hercule, Herk, Herkie, Herky.
Meaning: 'glory of Hera' (Greek), Hera being the wife of Zeus and goddess of marriage in Greek mythology.

Hereward

Meaning: 'army' and 'protection' (Old English).

Herman

Variants and diminutives: Armand, Armando, Armant, Armin, Armino, Ermanno, Ermin, Harman, Harmen, Harmon, Herenan, Herm, Hermann, Hermanze, Hermie, Herminio, Hermon, Hermy.
Meaning: 'army' and 'man' (Germanic).

Hermes

Variants and diminutives: Hermus.
Meaning: 'support' or 'stone' (Greek).

Hesketh

Variants and diminutives: Hezeki, Hezekiah.
Meaning: 'God's strength' (Hebrew) as a variant of Hezekiah.

Hippolytus

Variants and diminutives: Hippolyte, Ipppolitus, Ypolit, Ypolitus.
Meaning: 'horse' and 'release' (Greek).

Hiram

Variants and diminutives: Ahiram.
Meaning: 'brother' and 'elevated' (Hebrew).

Hiroshi

Meaning: 'generous' (Japanese).

Ho

Meaning: 'good' (Chinese).

Holden

Variants and diminutives: Holbrook.
Meaning: 'hollow' and 'valley' or 'watcher' (Old English); derived from an English family name, in turn derived from a number of English place names.

Homer

Variants and diminutives: Homero, Omero.
Meaning: uncertain; possibly 'hostage' (Greek); 'helmet-maker' (Old French); 'pool in a hollow' (Old

English) when derived from an English family name, in turn derived from a number of English place names.

Horace

Variants and diminutives: Horacio, Horatio, Horatius, Horry, Orazio.
Meaning: uncertain; possibly 'time' or 'hour' (Latin); derived from the Roman family name Horatius.

Howard

Variants and diminutives: Haoa, Hogg, Howey, Howie, Ward.
Meaning: uncertain; possibly 'heart' and 'protector' or 'bold' (Germanic); possibly 'hogwarden' or 'swineherd', 'eweherd' or 'fence-keeper' (Old English); derived from the family name of the ducal house of Norfolk.

Howi

Meaning: 'dove' (Native American).

Hubert

Variants and diminutives: Berdy, Bert, Bertie, Berto, Berty, Bart, Bartie, Barty, Hobard, Hobart, Hub, Hubbard, Hubbell, Hube, Huber, Huberd, Hubertek, Huberto, Hubi, Hubie, Huet, Huey, Hugh, Hughie, Hugi, Hugibert, Hutchin, Huw, Uberto.
Meaning: 'spirit', 'heart' or 'mind' and 'bright' (Germanic).

Hugh

Variants and diminutives: Aodh, Hew, Hewe, Huet, Huey, Hughie, Hugi, Hugin, Hugo, Hugolino, Hugon, Hugues, Huguito, Huw, Shug, Shuggie, Shuggy, Ugo, Ugolino, Ugone, Uisdean.

Meaning: 'spirit', 'heart' or 'mind' (Germanic); 'inspiration' or 'flame' (Celtic).

Humbert

Variants and diminutives: Bert, Bertie, Berty, Hum, Humbaldo, Humberto, Hunfredo, Hunfrido, Umberto.
Meaning: 'home', 'warrior' or 'giant' and 'bright' (Germanic).

Humphrey

Variants and diminutives: Amhlaoibh, Dumpty, Hum, Humfrey, Humfrid, Humfried, Hump, Humph, Humphry, Humpty, Humpo, Hundredo, Hunfredo, Hunfrey, Onfre, Onfroi, Onofre, Onofredo, Umphrey.
Meaning: 'home', 'warrior', 'giant' or 'strength' and 'peace' (Germanic).

Hunter

Variants and diminutives: Hunt, Huntington, Huntley, Lee, Leigh.
Meaning: 'to grasp' (Old Norse); 'hunter' (Middle English). Also a girl's name.

Hussain

Variants and diminutives: Hosein, Hossein, Husain, Hussein.
Meaning: 'good' or 'handsome' (Arabic).

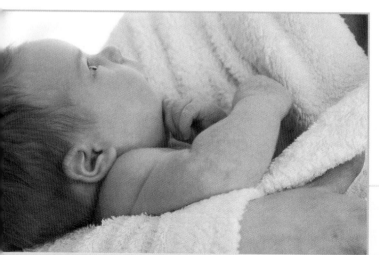

Hyman

Variants and diminutives: Chaim, Hy, Hyam, Hymie.
Meaning: 'life' (Hebrew).

Hywel

Variants and diminutives: Hoel, Hough, Houghton, Howe, Howel, Howell, Howey, Howland, Hulett, Hywell, Powell.
Meaning: 'conspicuous' or 'eminent' (Welsh); 'swine' and 'hill' (Old English).

Iago

Variants and diminutives: James.
Meaning: 'supplanter' (Hebrew) as a Spanish and Welsh version of James (Jacob).

Ian

Variants and diminutives: Ean, Iain, Ieuan, Iwan.
Meaning: 'God has favoured', 'God is gracious' or 'God is merciful' (Hebrew) as a Scottish version of John.

Idris

Meaning: 'lord' and 'ardent' (Welsh).

Idwal

Meaning: 'master' and 'wall' (Welsh).

Ignatius

Variants and diminutives: Egnacio, Eneco, Hignacio, Iggie, Iggy, Ignace, Ignacio, Ignacius, Ignasio, Ignatio, Ignatius, Ignatz, Ignaz, Ignazio, Ignocio, Inigo, Inigue, Nacho, Nacio, Nas, Ygnasio, Ygnocio.
Meaning: uncertain; possibly 'fiery' (Latin); derived from a Roman family name.

Igor

Variants and diminutives: Inge, Ingmar, Ingvar.
Meaning: 'Ing's warrior' (Old Norse), Ing being a Norse fertility god, as a Slavic variant of Ingvar; 'farmer' (Greek) as a variant of George.

Ingram

Variants and diminutives: Ingamar, Ingemar, Inglis, Ingmar, Ingo, Ingra, Ingrim.
Meaning: 'Ing's raven' (Germanic), Ing being a Norse fertility god; derived from an English family name.

Inigo

Variants and diminutives: Eneco, Ignatius, Inigue.

Meaning: uncertain; possibly 'fiery' (Latin) as a variant of Ignatius.

Iorwerth

Variants and diminutives: Iolo, Yorath.
Meaning: 'lord' and 'value' (Welsh).

Ira

Meaning: 'stallion' (Aramaic); 'watchful' (Hebrew).

Irvin

Variants and diminutives: Earvin, Eireambon, Erv, Erve, Ervin, Erwin, Irv, Irvine, Irving, Irwin, Irwyn.
Meaning: uncertain; possibly 'handsome' (Irish Gaelic); possibly 'white river' (Welsh); possibly 'sea' or 'boar' and 'friend' (Old English); possibly 'green water' (Scots Gaelic); derived from a Scottish family name, in turn derived from a number of British place names.

Isaac

Variants and diminutives: Aizik, Eisig, Ike, Ikey, Ikie, Isaacus, Isaak, Isac, Isacco, Isak, Itzhak, Itzik, Izaak, Izak, Izik, Yitzhak, Yithak, Yitzchak, Zack, Zak.
Meaning: 'laughter' (Hebrew).

Isaiah

Variants and diminutives: Esaias, Ikaia, Is, Isa, Isaias, Issa, Yeshaya, Yeshayahu.
Meaning: 'God is salvation' or 'God is generous' (Hebrew).

Ishmael

Variants and diminutives: Esmael, Isamel, Ishmael, Ismael, Ismail, Ismeal, Ismeil, Ysmael.

Meaning: 'God hears' or 'outcast' (Hebrew).

Isidore

Variants and diminutives: Dore, Dory, Isador, Isadore, Isidor, Isidoro, Isidro, Izzy.
Meaning: 'gift of Isis' (Greek), Isis being the supreme goddess of Egyptian mythology whose cult was subsequently adopted by the Greeks and Romans.

Israel

Variants and diminutives: Irving, Issy, Izzy, Srully.
Meaning: 'struggle with God' or 'God prevail' (Hebrew).

Ithel

Meaning: 'munificent lord' (Welsh).

Ivan

Variants and diminutives: Evo, Evon, Ivo, Vanya, Yvan,

Yvon.

Meaning: 'God has favoured', 'God is gracious' or 'God is merciful' (Hebrew) as a Slavic version of John.

Ivo

Variants and diminutives: Ives, Ivon, Ivor, Yves.
Meaning: 'yew' or 'small archer' (Germanic).

Ivor

Variants and diminutives: Ifor, Iomhar, Ivair, Ivar, Ivarr, Ive, Iver, Ivon, Yvon, Yvor.
Meaning: uncertain; possibly 'bow made of yew' and 'warrior' (Old Norse); possibly, as Ifor, 'lord' or 'archer' (Welsh).

Jabez

Meaning: 'born in pain' or 'born in sorrow' (Hebrew).

Jack

Variants and diminutives: Jackey, Jackie, Jackson, Jacky, Jake, Jakson, Jan, Jankin, Jock, John.
Meaning: 'God has favoured', 'God is gracious' or 'God is merciful' (Hebrew) as a diminutive of John.

Jacob

Variants and diminutives: Akevy, Akiba, Akiva, Akkoobjee, Akkub, Cob, Cobb, Cobbie, Cobby, Como, Coppo, Cub, Diego, Gemmes, Giacobbe, Giacobo, Giacomo, Giacopo, Hamish, Iago, Iakabos, Iakov, Iakovos, Ikov, Jaap, Jacinto, Jaco, Jacobo, Jacobos, Jacobs, Jacobson, Jacobus, Jacoby, Jacopo, Jacomus, Jacque, Jacques, Jacquet, Jago, Jaime, Jakab, Jake, Jakie, Jakiv, Jakob,

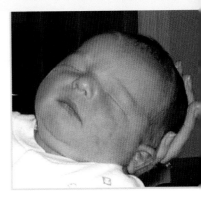

Jakon, Jakov, Jakub, Jakubek, Jalu, James, Jamie, Jaques, Jaquot, Jasha, Jascha, Jaschenka, Jasha, Jayme, Jeb, Jecis, Jekebs, Jeks, Jem, Jemmy, Jeska, Jockel, Jokubas, Kivi, Kobi, Kub, Kuba, Kubaa, Kubes, Kubik, Kubo, Kubus, Lapo, Santiago, Seumuis, Yaagov, Yaakov, Yago, Yakov, Yanka, Yashko, Yuki.
Meaning: 'supplanter' (Hebrew).

Jahan
Meaning: 'the world' (Sanskrit).

Jake
Variants and diminutives: Jack, Jacob, Jakey, Jakie.
Meaning: 'supplanter' (Hebrew) as a diminutive of Jacob; 'God has favoured', 'God is gracious' or 'God is merciful' (Hebrew) as a variant of Jack (John).

Jamal
Variants and diminutives: Cemal, Gamal, Jahmal, Jamaal, Jamael, Jamahl, Jamall, Jameel, Jamel, Jamiel, Jamil, Jamile.
Meaning: 'handsome' (Arabic).

James
Variants and diminutives: Chago, Chango, Chanti, Dago, Diago, Diego, Giacomo, Giamo, Hamish, Jaco, Jacob, Jacobus, Jacomus, Jacques, Jaime, Jaimie, Jaimito, Jam, Jamesy, Jamey, Jamie, Jas, Jay, Jayme, Jaymie, Jem, Jim, Jimbo, Jimmie, Jimmy, Santiago, Séamas, Seamus, Seumas, Seumus, Shamus, Shay, Sheumais, Tiago, Zebedee.
Meaning: 'supplanter' (Hebrew) as a variant of Jacob.

Janus
Variants and diminutives: Januarius, Jarek.
Meaning: 'archway' (Latin).

Japheth
Variants and diminutives: Japhet, Yafet, Yaphet.
Meaning: 'enlargement' or 'handsome' (Hebrew).

Jared
Variants and diminutives: Gerard, Jareth, Jarod, Jarred, Jarret, Jarrod, Jed, Jerrod.
Meaning: 'rose' or 'heir' (Hebrew); 'spear' and 'hard' (Germanic) as a variant of Gerard.

Jaron
Variants and diminutives: Yartron.
Meaning: 'to sing' or 'to call out' (Hebrew).

Jarvis
Variants and diminutives: Gary, Gervais, Gervaise, Gervase, Gervise, Jary, Jarry, Jerve, Jervis.
Meaning: uncertain; possibly 'spear' (Germanic) and 'servant' (Celtic) as a variant of Gervaise.

Jason
Variants and diminutives: Jace, Jaeson, Jaison, Jase, Jasen, Jay, Jayce, Jaycen, Jaysen, Jayson, Joshua.
Meaning: uncertain; possibly 'to heal' (Greek); possibly 'God saves' (Hebrew) as a variant of Joshua.

Jasper
Variants and diminutives: Cash, Casper, Cass, Cassie, Cassy, Gaspar, Gaspard, Gaspare, Gasparo, Gasper, Gazsi, Jaspar, Jasper, Josper, Kaspar, Kasper.
Meaning: 'jewel' (Greek); 'treasurer-keeper' (Persian); 'imperial' (Germanic).

Jay

Variants and diminutives: Jaye, Jey, Jeye.

Meaning: 'supplanter' (Hebrew) as a diminutive of James (Jacob); 'victory' (Sanskrit). Also a diminutive of any other name beginning with 'J' and a girl's name.

Jed

Variants and diminutives: Jedd.
Meaning: 'hand' (Arabic).

Jedidiah

Variants and diminutives: Didi, Jed, Jedadiah, Jedd, Jeddy, Jedediah, Jediah, Yehiel.
Meaning: 'loved by the Lord' (Hebrew).

Jeffrey

Variants and diminutives: Fred, Fredo, Frici, Friedl, Geof, Geoff, Geoffrey, Geoffroi, Geoffroy, Geofredo, Geofri, Giotto, Gisfrid, Godfrey, Godofredo, Godfrids, Godofredo, Godoired, Gofredo, Gotfrid, Gotfryd, Gottfrid, Gottfried, Gotz, Govert, Jef, Jeff, Jefferey, Jefferies, Jefferson, Jeffery, Jeffie, Jeffrey, Jeffries, Jeffry, Jeffy, Jeoffroi, Sheary, Sheron, Sieffre.
Meaning: uncertain; possibly 'God', 'district', 'traveller' or 'pledge' and 'peace' (Germanic) as a variant of Godfrey.

Jem

Variants and diminutives: James, Jemmie, Jemmy, Jeremy, Jeremiah.
Meaning: 'supplanter' (Hebrew) as a diminutive of James (Jacob); 'appointed by God' or 'exalted by God' (Hebrew) as a diminutive of Jeremy (Jeremiah).

Jephthah

Variants and diminutives: Jephtah, Yiftach, Yiftah.
Meaning: 'to open' (Hebrew).

Jeremiah

Variants and diminutives: Diarmaid, Geremia, Gerome, Gerrie, Gerry, Jem, Jere, Jereme, Jeremia, Jeremias, Jeremija, Jeremy, Jerre, Jerrie, Jerrome, Jerry, Yirmeehayu.
Meaning: 'appointed by God' or 'exalted by God' (Hebrew).

Jeremy

Variants and diminutives: Ember, Geremia, Gerome, Gerrie, Gerry, Jem, Jemmie, Jemmy, Jemy, Jer, Jereme, Jeremiah, Jeremie, Jeremija, Jerr, Jerre, Jerrie, Jerrome, Jerry, Katone, Nemet, Yeremey, Yerik, Yirmeeyahu.
Meaning: 'appointed by God' or 'exalted by God' (Hebrew) as an English version of Jeremiah.

Jermaine

Variants and diminutives: Germain, Germane, Germayne, Jamaine, Jermain, Jermaine, Jermane, Jermayn, Jermayne, Jerr, Jerrie, Jerry.
Meaning: 'brother' (Latin) or 'German' (French).

Jerome

Variants and diminutives: Gerome, Geronima, Gerrie, Gerry, Hieremas, Hieronymus, Jere, Jereme, Jérôme, Jeromo, Jeronim, Jerram, Jerre, Jerrie, Jerrome, Jerry.
Meaning: 'holy' and 'name' (Greek) as a French variant of Hieronymus (Hyeronimos).

Jerry

Meaning: 'spear' and 'rule' (Germanic) as a diminutive of Gerald; 'spear' and 'hard' (Germanic) as a diminutive of Gerard; 'appointed by God' or 'exalted by God' (Hebrew) as a diminutive of Jeremy; 'holy' and 'name' (Greek) as a diminutive of Jerome.

Jesse

Variants and diminutives: Jess, Jessie, Jessy.
Meaning: 'gift' or 'God exists' (Hebrew).

Jesus

Variants and diminutives: Hesus, Jesous, Jesu, Jesuso, Jezus, Joshua.
Meaning: 'God saves' (Hebrew) as a variant of Joshua.

Jethro

Variants and diminutives: Jeth, Jett.
Meaning: 'excellence' or 'abundance' (Hebrew).

Jim

Variants and diminutives: James, Jimbo, Jimi, Jimmie, Jimmy.
Meaning: 'supplanter' (Hebrew) as a diminutive of James (Jacob).

Joab

Meaning: 'God the father' or 'praise the Lord' (Hebrew).

Joachim

Variants and diminutives: Akim, Giachimo, Jehoiachin, Jehoiakim, Joa, Jochim, Joaquin, Yehoiakim.
Meaning: 'God exalts', 'God establishes' or 'God judges' (Hebrew).

Job

Meaning: 'persecuted' (Hebrew).

Jock

Variants and diminutives: Jack, Jocko, John.
Meaning: 'God has favoured', 'God is gracious' or 'God is merciful' (Hebrew) as a Scottish diminutive of John.

Joe

Variants and diminutives: Joey, Jojo.
Meaning: 'God will increase' (Hebrew) as a diminutive of Joseph.

Joel

Variants and diminutives: Yoel.
Meaning: 'Jehovah is God' or 'God is willing' (Hebrew).

John

Variants and diminutives: Ansis, Eoin, Evan, Ewan, Gehan, Gennaro, Geno, Gian, Gianetto, Gianni, Giannini, Giannis, Giannos, Gioannes, Giovanni, Haines, Hanan, Hannes, Hannu, Hans, Hansel, Hansl, Hanus, Hasse, Hazze, Honza, Hovhannes, Iain, Ian, Iancu, Ianos, Iban, Ieuan, Ifan, Ignac, Ioan, Ioann, Ioannes, Ioannis, Ion, Ionel, Ivan, Ivanchik, Ivano, Ivas, Iwan, Jack, Jackie, Jackman, Jakon, Jan, Janco, Jancsi, Janek, Janes, Jani, Janika, Jankiel, Janko, Janne, Jano, Janos, Jas, Jasio, Jean, Jeanno, Jeannot, Jehan, Jenda, Jenkin, Jenner, Jennings, Jens, Joanico, Joannes, Joao, Joba, Jochanan, Jock, Jocko, Jofan, Johan, Johanan, Johann, Johannes, Johnie, Johnnie, Johnny, Jon, Jonam, Jonas, Jone, Jonelis, Jonni, Jonnie, Jonny, Jonukas, Jonutis, Jovan, Juan, Juanch, Juancho, Juanito, Juhana, Juho, Jukka, Jussi, Ohannes, Owen, St John, Sean, Seann, Seonaidh, Shane, Shaughn, Shaun, Shawn, Sion, Sionym, Vanek, Vanka, Vanko, Vanya, Vanni, Yan, Yana, Yancy, Yank, Yanka, Yankee, Yanni, Yannis, Yochanan, Yohanan, Yves, Zan, Zane, Zebedee.
Meaning: 'God has favoured', 'God is gracious' or 'God is merciful' (Hebrew).

Jolyon

Variants and diminutives: Jolly, Joly, Julian.
Meaning: uncertain; possibly 'fair-skinned' (Latin) as a variant of Julian.

Jonah

Variants and diminutives: Giona, Guisepe, Iona, Jonas, Yona, Yonah, Yunus.
Meaning: 'dove' (Hebrew).

Jonathan
Variants and diminutives: Johnathan, Johnathon, Jon, Jonathon, Jonnie, Jonny, Jonty, Yonatan.
Meaning: 'God's gift' (Hebrew).

Jordan
Variants and diminutives: Giordano, Ira, Jared, Jarrod, Jerad, Jordain, Jordane, Jordann, Jordie, Jordy, Jordyn, Jorey, Jori, Jorie, Jorrie, Jorry, Jory, Jourdain, Judd, Yarden.
Meaning: 'to flow down' (Hebrew); derived from the Middle Eastern river Jordan. Also a girl's name.

Joseph
Variants and diminutives: Beppe, Beppi, Beppo, Che, Cheche, Chepe, Chepito, Guiseppe, Jazeps, Iosep, Ioseph, Iosif, Jaska, Jo, Jobo, Joce, Jodi, Jodie, Jody, Joe, Joey, Joie, Jojo, Joosef, Jooseppi, Jos, Josce, José, Josecoto, Josef, Joseito, Joselito, Josep, Josephe, Josephus, Joses, Josip, Joska, Josko, Joszef, Joza, Joze, Jozef, Jozhe, Jozhef, Jozio, Jozka, Jozsef, Jozsi, Jupp, Juzef, Juziu, Osip, Osya, Pepa, Pepe, Pepik, Pepillo, Pepin, Pepito, Peppi, Peppo, Pino, Pipo, Seosamh, Seosap, Seosaph, Sepp, Yazid, Yeska, Yesya, Yosayf, Yosef, Yosel, Yoseph, Yosi, Yosif, Yossel, Yossele, Yousef, Yusef, Yusif, Yussuf, Yusuf, Yusup, Yuzef, Zeusef.
Meaning: 'God will increase' (Hebrew).

Joshua
Variants and diminutives: Giosia, Hosea, Hoshayah, Iosua, Jason, Jesous, Jesus, Joaquim, Joaquin, Jos, Josh, Joss, Josua, Josue, Jozsua, Mosha, Yehoshua, Yeshua.
Meaning: 'God saves' (Hebrew).

Josiah
Variants and diminutives: Josh, Josias, Josie, Josy.
Meaning: 'God heals' or 'God supports' (Hebrew).

Jotham
Meaning: 'God is perfect' (Hebrew).

Judd
Variants and diminutives: Jordan, Judah.
Meaning: 'to flow down' (Hebrew), derived from the Middle Eastern river Jordan, as a diminutive of Jordan; 'praise' (Hebrew) as a diminutive of Judah.

Jude
Variants and diminutives: Jud, Juda, Judah, Judas, Judd, Judson, Yehuda, Yehudah, Yehudi.
Meaning: 'praise' (Hebrew) as a diminutive of Judah. Also a girl's name as a diminutive of Judith.

Jules
Variants and diminutives: Julian, Julius.
Meaning: uncertain; possibly 'fair-skinned' (Latin) as a French variant of Julian. Also a girl's name as a diminutive of Julia, Julie and Juliana.

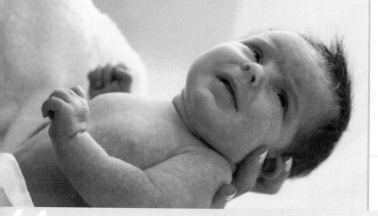

Julian

Variants and diminutives: Giuliano, Giulio, Guliano, Halian, Iola, Iolo, Jellon, Jolin, Jolian, Jollanus, Jolyon, Jule, Jules, Julianus, Julien, Julio, Julius, Julot, Julyan.
Meaning: uncertain; possibly 'fair-skinned' (Latin); derived from the Roman family name Julianus.

Junior

Variants and diminutives: Junius.
Meaning: 'younger' (Latin); derived from the US practice of adding 'Junior' (Jr) to a boy's name when he shares it with his father.

Justin

Variants and diminutives: Giustino, Giusto, Inek, Iustin, Jusa, Just, Justas, Justek, Justen, Justinian, Justinas, Justino, Justins, Justinus, Justis, Justo, Justs, Justukas, Justus, Justyn, Jut, Jute, Tuto, Ustin, Yestin, Yusts, Yustyn.

Meaning: 'just' (Latin); derived from the Roman family name Justinus.

Kahil

Variants and diminutives: Kahlil, Kalil.
Meaning: 'beloved' (Arabic).

Kai

Variants and diminutives: Cai, Caius, Kay.
Meaning: 'rejoice' (Latin) as a Welsh variant of Caius (Gaius); 'sea' (Hawaiian).

Kalil

Variants and diminutives: Kahil, Kahlil, Kailil, Kal, Kallie, Kalton, Khaleel, Khalil.
Meaning: 'good friend' (Arabic); 'beautiful' (Greek); 'wealth' or 'crown' (Hebrew).

Kalman

Variants and diminutives: Kal.
Meaning: 'man' or 'free man' (Germanic) as a variant of Charles; 'merciful' or 'mild' (Latin) as a variant of Clement.

Kamil

Variants and diminutives: Kameel.
Meaning: 'perfection' (Arabic).

Kane

Variants and diminutives: Cathair, Kain, Kaine, Kayne.
Meaning: uncertain; possibly 'warrior' (Irish Gaelic); possibly 'lovely' (Welsh); possibly 'battlefield' (Old French) when derived from Caen, a French town; possibly 'tribute', 'battler' or 'dark' (Celtic); 'golden' (Japanese); 'man' (Hawaiian).

Kaniel

Variants and diminutives: Kan, Kani, Kanny.
Meaning: 'reed' or 'stalk' (Hebrew); 'spear' (Arabic).

Karim

Variants and diminutives: Kareem, Kario.
Meaning: 'noble' or 'generous' (Arabic).

Karl

Variants and diminutives: Carl, Carlo, Carlos, Charles.
Meaning: 'man' or 'free man' (Germanic) as a German variant of Charles.

Kavi

Meaning: 'poetic' (Sanskrit).

Keane

Variants and diminutives: Kane, Kani, Kayne, Kean, Keen, Keenan, Keene, Kene, Kian, Kienan.
Meaning: 'warrior's son' (Irish Gaelic); 'clever' or 'sharp' (Old English).

Kedem

Meaning: 'eastern' or 'ancient' (Hebrew).

Keefe

Variants and diminutives: Keeffe, Keever, Kief, Kiefer, Kif.
Meaning: 'euphoria' (Arabic); 'the handsome one's grandson' (Irish Gaelic) when derived from an Irish family name.

Keir

Variants and diminutives: Kerr.
Meaning: 'dark-skinned' or 'spear' (Irish Gaelic); 'marshland containing brushwood' (Old Norse); derived from a Scottish family name, in turn a variant of Kerr.

Keith

Meaning: 'battlefield' (Irish Gaelic); 'wood' (Scots Gaelic); derived from a Scottish family name.

Kelsey

Variants and diminutives: Kelcey, Kelci, Kelcie, Kelley, Kellog, Kellow, Kelo, Kelsi, Kelsie, Kelson, Kelsy, Kelton.
Meaning: 'warrior' (Irish Gaelic); 'ship's keel' (Old English). Also a girl's name.

Kelvin

Variants and diminutives: Kelvan, Kelven, Kelwin.
Meaning: uncertain; possibly 'ship's keel' and 'friend' (Old English); possibly 'narrow stream' (Scots Gaelic) when derived from a British family name, itself derived from the name of a Scottish river.

Kendal

Variants and diminutives: Ken, Kendahl, Kendale, Kendall, Kendel, Kendell, Kendyl, Kenn, Kennie, Kenny, Kyndal.
Meaning: 'ruler' and 'valley' (Old English); 'valley of the Kent river' (Old English) when derived from an English family name, in turn derived from a Cumbrian place name; 'spring' and 'valley' (Old English) when derived from an English family name, in turn derived from Kendale, a place in Humberside. Also a girl's name.

Kenelm

Variants and diminutives: Ken, Kennie, Kenny.
Meaning: 'brave' and 'helmet' (Old English).

Kennedy

Variants and diminutives: Cinneidid, Kemp, Ken, Kenman, Kenn, Kennard, Kennie, Kenny.
Meaning: 'head' and 'ugly' (Irish Gaelic) when derived from an Irish family name; 'ruler' (Old English). Also a girl's name.

Kenneth

Variants and diminutives: Cainnech, Caioneach, Canice, Cennydd, Cenydd, Cinaed, Cynnedd, Ken, Kene, Kenney, Kennie, Kenny, Kenya, Kesha.
Meaning: 'born of fire' or 'handsome' (Scottish and Irish Gaelic); 'royal oath' (Old English).

Kenrick

Variants and diminutives: Cynric, Ken, Kendig, Kendric, Kendrick, Kendrik, Kendrix, Kenerick, Kenn, Kennie, Kenny, Kenric, Kenrik, Kenward, Kerrick, Kerrik, Ric, Rick, Rickie, Ricky.
Meaning: 'hero' and 'chief' (Welsh); 'royal' and 'ruler' (Old English).

Kent

Variants and diminutives: Ken, Kenton, Kenyon.
Meaning: 'white' or 'border' (Celtic); derived from an English family name, in turn derived from the name of the English county of Kent.

Kentigern

Variants and diminutives: Ceanntigher, Kent.
Meaning: 'chief lord' or 'not condemned' (Celtic).

Kenton

Variants and diminutives: Ken, Kent, Kenyon.

Meaning: uncertain; possibly 'royal manor' (Old English).

Kenward

Variants and diminutives: Cenweard, Ken, Kennie, Kenny.
Meaning: 'brave' and 'protector' (Old English).

Kermit

Variants and diminutives: Dermott, Diarmad, Diarmaid, Diarmait, Diarmid, Diarmit, Diarmuid, Diiarmuit, Ker, Kerm, Kermie, Kermode, Kermy, Kerr.
Meaning: 'church' (Dutch); 'lacking in envy' (Irish Gaelic) as a variant of Diarmaid (Dermot).

Kerr

Variants and diminutives: Keir.
Meaning: 'dark-skinned' or 'spear' (Irish Gaelic); 'marshland containing brushwood' (Old Norse); derived from a British family name, itself derived from a British place name.

Kevin

Variants and diminutives: Caoimhinn, Caomhghin, Coemgen, Kev, Kevan, Keven, Kevvie, Kevvy.
Meaning: 'handsome' or 'loved' and 'at birth' (Irish Gaelic).

Kiefer

Variants and diminutives: Kief.
Meaning: uncertain; possibly 'pine tree' or 'jaw' (German).

Kieran

Variants and diminutives: Cianon, Ciaran, Kearn, Kearne, Keeran, Keiran, Keiren, Keiron, Kern, Kerne, Kiaran, Kieren, Kieron.
Meaning: 'dark' (Irish Gaelic).

Killian

Variants and diminutives: Cilian, Cillian, Cillin, Kilian, Killie, Killy, Kilmer.
Meaning: 'church' or 'little warrior' (Irish Gaelic).

Kimball

Variants and diminutives:
Cymbeline, Kim, Kimbell, Kimble,
Kimmie, Kimmy.
Meaning: uncertain; possibly 'empty
vessel' (Greek); possibly 'kin' or 'royal'
and 'bold' (Old English); possibly
'chief' and 'war' (Welsh); derived from
a British family name.

King

Variants and diminutives: Kingsley.
Meaning: 'king' (Germanic); derived
from an English family name.

Kingsley

Variants and diminutives: King,
Kingsleigh, Kingsly, Kingston,
Kinnaird, Kinsey, Kinsley.
Meaning: 'king's clearing' or 'king's
wood' (Old English); derived from an
English family name, in turn derived
from a number of English place names.

Kipp

Variants and diminutives: Kip,
Kipper, Kippie, Kippy.
Meaning: 'pointed hill' (Old English).

Kiral

Meaning: 'king' (Turkish).

Kiran

Meaning: 'ray of light' (Sanskrit).

Kirk

Variants and diminutives: Kerby,
Kerk, Kirby, Kirklan, Kirkland, Kirklen,
Kirklin, Kirtland, Kirtley, Kirtly, Kyrk,
Kyrksen.
Meaning: 'church' (Old Norse);
derived from a British family name.

Kit

Variants and diminutives: Kitt.
Meaning: 'carrier of Christ' (Greek) as
a diminutive of Christopher. Also a
girl's name.

Knut

Variants and diminutives: Canute,
Canutus, Knud, Knute, Note, Nute,
Nutkin, Nutt.
Meaning: 'knot' (Old Norse); 'type' or
'race' (Old Danish).

Koji

Meaning: 'child' (Japanese).

Kumar

Meaning: 'son' (Sanskrit).

Kurt

Variants and diminutives: Curt,
Curtis, Kurtis.
Meaning: 'brave' and 'advice'
(Germanic) as a diminutive of Konrad
(Conrad).

Kyle

Variants and diminutives: Kiel, Kile,
Kiley, Ky, Kylie.
Meaning: 'crowned with laurel'
(Hebrew); 'narrow' or 'narrow strait'
(Scots Gaelic); derived from a
Scottish family name, in turn derived
from a Scottish place name. Also a
girl's name.

Laban

Meaning: 'white' (Hebrew).

Lachlan

Variants and diminutives: Lachann,
Lachie, Lachlann.
Meaning: 'from the land of the
lakes [Norway]' or 'martial' (Scots
Gaelic); derived from a Scottish
family name.

Lal

Meaning: 'beloved' (Hindi).

Lambert

Variants and diminutives: Bert,
Bertie, Berty, Lamberto, Lammie,
Landbert.
Meaning: 'land' and 'bright'
(Germanic).

Lamont

Variants and diminutives: Lammond, Lamond, LaMont, Lamonte, Lemont, Monty.
Meaning: 'the mountain' (Old French); 'lawgiver' (Scots Gaelic).

Lance

Variants and diminutives: Lancelot, Lancing, Lansing, Launce, Launcelot.
Meaning: 'lance' (Latin); 'spear' (Old French); 'land' (Germanic). Both the origin and diminutive of Lancelot.

Lancelot

Variants and diminutives: Lance, Lancing, Lansing, Launce, Launcelot.
Meaning: 'lance' (Latin); 'spear' (Old French); 'land' (Germanic).

Lang

Variants and diminutives: Laing, Langdon, Langer, Langford, Langhorne, Langley, Langly, Langsdon, Langston, Langtry, Lanny, Largo, Longfellow.
Meaning: 'long' (Old English).

Larry

Variants and diminutives: Labhrainn, Lary, Laurence, Laurie, Lawrence, Lawrie, Lorrie, Lorry.
Meaning: 'from Laurentum' (Latin), Laurentum being the Roman name of an Italian town, as a diminutive of Laurence.

Lars

Variants and diminutives: Larse, Laurans, Laurence, Lawrence, Lorens.

Meaning: 'from Laurentum' (Latin), Laurentum being the Roman name of an Italian town, as a Scandinavian version of Laurence.

Laurence

Variants and diminutives: Brencis, Chencho, Inek, Labhrainn, Labhras, Labhruinn, Labrencis, Labrentsis, Lanty, Larikin, Larka, Larkin, Larns, Larrance, Larrence, Larry, Larya, Lars, Larse, Larson, Lary, Laudalino, Laurans, Laurel, Lauren, Laurencho, Laurencio, Laurens, Laurent, Lauri, Laurie, Lauriston, Lauritz, Lauro, Lavr, Lavrik, Lavro, Lawrance, Lawrence, Lawrey, Lawrie, Lawry, Lencho, Lenci, Lochlainn, Lon, Lonnie, Lonny, Loran, Lorant, Lorcan, Loren, Lorence, Lorenco, Lorens, Lorentz, Lorenz, Lorenzo, Loretto, Lorin, Loring, Lorn, Lorne, Lornic, Lorrie, Lorry, Lourenco, Lowrence, Rance, Raulas, Raulo, Renzo.
Meaning: 'from Laurentum' (Latin), Laurentum being the Roman name of an Italian town.

Lazarus

Variants and diminutives: Eleazar, Lazar, Lazare, Lazaro, Lazer, Lazlo, Lesser.
Meaning: 'God is my help' (Hebrew) as a Greek variant of Eleazar.

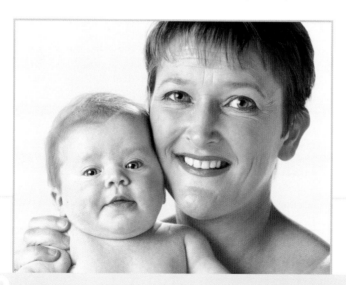

Leander

Variants and diminutives: Ander, Andor, Lea, Leandre, Leandro, Leanther, Lee, Leo, Leon, Maclean.
Meaning: 'lion' and 'man' (Greek).

Leben

Meaning: 'life' (Yiddish and German).

Lee

Variants and diminutives: Leigh.
Meaning: 'meadow', 'clearing' or 'wood' (Old English); derived from an English family name, in turn derived from a number of English place names. Also a girl's name.

Leif

Variants and diminutives: Lief.
Meaning: 'beloved' (Old Norse).

Leighton

Variants and diminutives: Latton, Lay, Layton, Leigh.
Meaning: 'herb garden' (Old English).

Lemuel

Variants and diminutives: Lem, Lemmie, Lemmy.
Meaning: 'dedicated to God' (Hebrew).

Len

Variants and diminutives: Lendal, Lendall, Lendon, Lennie, Lennon, Lennnox, Lenvil, Lenny, Lenwood Leonard.
Meaning: 'tenant house' (Old English); 'flute' (Hopi); 'lion' and 'hard' (Germanic) as a diminutive of Leonard; 'elms' and 'water' (Scots Gaelic) as a diminutive of Lennox.

Lennox

Variants and diminutives: Len, Lenn, Lenox.
Meaning: 'elms' and 'water' (Scots Gaelic); derived from a Scottish family name, in turn derived from a Scottish place name.

Leo

Variants and diminutives: Label, Leander, Leao, Lee, Leib, Leibel, Len, Leni, Lenn, Lennie, Leodis, Leofric, Léon, Leon, Leonard, Leonardo, Leonas, Leondaus, Leone, Leonid, Leonida, Leonidas, Leonis, Leopold, Leos, Leosko, Lev, Leva, Levka, Levko, Levnek, Levya, Lio, Lion, Lionel, Lionello, Liutas, Llewellyn, Llywellyn, Loeb, Loew, Loewy, Lon, Lonnie, Lowe, Lyon, Lyonel, Lyons, Lyron.
Meaning: 'lion' (Latin).

Leofric

Variants and diminutives: Leo.
Meaning: 'dear' and 'ruler' (Old English).

Leonard

Variants and diminutives: Laya, Lee, Len, Lenard, Lennard, Lenn, Lennard, Lennart, Lenne, Lennie, Lenny, Leo, Leon, Leonala, Leonardo, Leonards, Leonek, Leonerd, Leongard, Leonhard, Leonhards, Leonid, Leons, Lewenhart, Lienard, Linek, Lionardo, Lon, Lonnard, Lonnie, Lonny, Nardek, Nenne.
Meaning: 'lion' and 'hard' (Germanic).

Leopold

Variants and diminutives: Leo, Leopoldo, Leupold, Poldi, Poldie, Poldo.
Meaning: 'people' and 'bold' (Germanic).

Leor

Meaning: 'light' (Hebrew).

Leron

Variants and diminutives: Lerond, Lerone, Lerin, Lerrin, Liron, Lirone.
Meaning: 'my song' (Hebrew); 'the circle' (Old French).

Leroy
Variants and diminutives: Elroy, Lee, Lee Roy, Leroi, Roy.
Meaning: 'the king' (Old French); derived from a French family name.

Leslie
Variants and diminutives: Lee, Les, Lesley, Lesly.
Meaning: 'garden' and 'pool' or 'hollies' (Scots Gaelic); derived from a Scottish family name, in turn derived from a number of Scottish place names. Also a girl's name (generally Lesley).

Lester
Variants and diminutives: Leicester, Les, Letcher, Leycester.
Meaning: 'Roman clearing' (Old English); derived from an English family name, in turn derived from the English town of Leicester.

Levi
Variants and diminutives: Lavey, Lavi, Lavy, Leavitt, Lev, Levic, Lever, Levey, Levy, Lewi.
Meaning: 'attached' or 'pledged' (Hebrew).

Lewis
Variants and diminutives: Laoiseach, Lew, Llewellyn, Lothar, Lothair, Louis, Ludovicus, Lughaidh, Lutwidge, Ludwig.
Meaning: 'famed' and 'warrior' (Germanic) as a variant of Ludwig.

Lex
Variants and diminutives: Alexander, Laxton, Lexton.
Meaning: 'word' (Greek). 'defender of men' or 'warrior' (Greek) as a diminutive of Alexander.

Liam
Variants and diminutives: Uilliam, William.
Meaning: 'will' and 'helmet' or 'protection' (Germanic) as a diminutive of Uilliam, in turn an Irish Gaelic variant of William.

Liang
Meaning: 'excellent' (Chinese).

Lincoln
Variants and diminutives: Linc, Link.
Meaning: 'Roman colony by the pool' (Old English); derived from an English family name, in turn derived from the English town of Lincoln.

Linfred
Variants and diminutives: Lin, Linnie, Linny, Fred, Freddie, Freddy.
Meaning: 'gentle' and 'peace' (Germanic).

Linus
Variants and diminutives: Linos.
Meaning: uncertain; possibly 'flax' (Latin).

Lionel
Variants and diminutives: Len, Lennie, Lenny, Leo, Léon, Leon, Leonel, Lionell, Lonnell, Lonnell.
Meaning: 'little lion' (Latin) as a variant of Leon (Leo).

Llewellyn
Variants and diminutives: Fluellen, Leoline, Lew, Lewlin, Lleelo, Llew, Llewelyn, Llywellwyn, Llywelyn, Lyn.
Meaning: 'leader' or 'lion' and 'resemblance' (Welsh).

Lloyd
Variants and diminutives: Floyd, Llwyd, Loy, Loyd.
Meaning: 'grey' (Welsh).

Logan
Variants and diminutives: Login.
Meaning: 'little hollow' (Scots Gaelic); derived from a Scottish family name, in turn derived from a Scottish place name; 'record' (Old English).

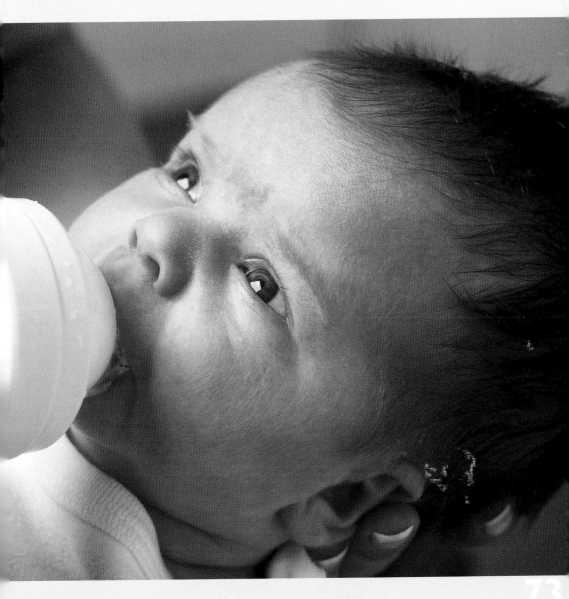

Lorcan
Variants and diminutives: Laurence.
Meaning: 'silent' or 'fierce' (Irish Gaelic); 'from Laurentum' (Latin), Laurentum being the Roman name of an Italian town, as an Irish variant of Laurence.

Lorne
Variants and diminutives: Lorn.
Meaning: uncertain; derived from a Scottish place name; possibly 'from Laurentum' (Latin), Laurentum being the Roman name of an Italian town, as a diminutive of Laurence; possibly 'forlorn' (Old English) as a male version of Lorna.

Louis
Variants and diminutives: Aloys, Aloysius, Chlodovech, Clovis, Elois, Hluodowig, Lew, Lewellen, Lewes, Lewi, Lewie, Lewis, Llewelyn, Llwellyn, Loeis, Lon, Lothar, Lothair, Lou, Louie, Lowes, Lude, Ludeg, Ludek, Ludirk, Ludis, Ludko, Ludovic, Ludovici, Ludovicus, Ludvig, Ludvik, Ludwig, Ludwik, Lui, Luigi, Luis, Lutek, Lutwidge.
Meaning: 'famed' and 'warrior' (Germanic) as a variant of Ludwig.

Lovell
Variants and diminutives: Lovel, Lowell, Loyal, Loyte.

Meaning: 'wolf cub' (Old French); derived from a British family name.

Lucas
Variants and diminutives: Luc, Lucais, Lucan, Luka, Lukas, Luke.
Meaning: 'from Lucania' (Greek), Lucania being a southern Italian region, as a variant of Luke.

Lucian
Variants and diminutives: Luc, Luciano, Lucien, Lucio.
Meaning: uncertain; derived from the Roman family name Lucianus.

Lucius
Variants and diminutives: Lu, Luc, Lucais, Luce, Lucian, Luciano, Lucien, Lucio, Lusio.
Meaning: 'light' (Latin).

Ludovic
Variants and diminutives: Lewis, Lodowick, Louis, Ludo, Ludovick, Ludovico, Ludovicus, Ludwig, Vic.
Meaning: 'famed' and 'warrior' (Germanic) as a diminutive of Ludovicus (Ludwig).

Ludwig
Variants and diminutives: Chlodevech, Clovis, Hluodowig, Lewis, Lothar, Lothair, Louis, Ludeg, Ludek, Ludirk, Ludis, Ludko, Ludvic, Ludovic, Ludovici, Ludovicus, Ludvig, Ludwik, Lutek.
Meaning: 'famed' and 'warrior' (Germanic).

Luke
Variants and diminutives: Loukas, Lucan, Lucas, Luce, Luchok, Luck, Lucky, Luka, Lukacs, Lukas, Lukash, Lukasha, Lukass, Lukasz, Lukyan.
Meaning: 'from Lucania' (Greek), Lucania being a southern Italian region.

Luther
Variants and diminutives: Lotario, Lothaire, Lothar, Lothario, Lother, Lothur, Lutero.
Meaning: 'famous' and 'people' or 'army' (Germanic); derived from the family name of the protestant German religious reformer Martin Luther.

Lyle
Variants and diminutives: Lille, Lisle, Ly, Lyall, Lyell.
Meaning: 'the island' (Old French); derived from a British family name, in turn derived from English and French place names.

Lyndon
Variants and diminutives: Lin, Lindon,

Lindy, Lyn, Lynn.
Meaning: 'lime tree' and 'hill' (Old English); derived from an English family name, in turn derived from an English place name.

Lysander

Variants and diminutives: Sandie, Sandy.
Meaning: 'freer of men' (Greek).

Lyulf

Variants and diminutives: Ligulf, Liul, Lyolf, Lyulph.
Meaning: 'flame' and 'wolf' (Old English).

Mac

Variants and diminutives: Macaulay, Mack.
Meaning: 'son of' (Scots Gaelic). Also a diminutive of any name beginning with 'Mac-', such as Macaulay.

Macauley

Variants and diminutives: Mac, Macalay, MacAulay, Macaulay, MacAuley, MacAuliffe, Macauliffe, Mack, McAulay, McAuley, McAuliffe,

Maccauley, Macawlay.
Meaning: 'son of Olaf' (Irish and Scots Gaelic); derived from a British family name.

Mackenzie

Variants and diminutives: Mac, Mack, MacKensie, Mackensie, MacKenzie, McKensie, McKenzie, Kensie, Kenzie.
Meaning: 'son of Comely [the handsome one]' (Scots Gaelic); derived from a Scottish family name. Also a girl's name.

Maddison

Variants and diminutives: Maddi, Maddie, Maddy, Madison.
Meaning: 'son of Maud', 'son of Matthew' or 'son of Magdalene' (Old English); derived from an English family name. Also a girl's name.

Madoc

Variants and diminutives: Maddoc, Madoch, Maedoc, Marmaduke.
Meaning: 'lucky' or 'generous' (Welsh).

Magnus

Variants and diminutives: Manas, Manus.
Meaning: 'great' (Latin).

Maitland

Variants and diminutives: Mait, Maitie, Maity, Mate, Matey.
Meaning: uncertain; possibly 'inhospitable' (Old French); derived from a British family name, in turn derived from the French place name Mautalant.

Majid

Variants and diminutives: Magid, Maj, Majdi, Majeed.
Meaning: 'glorious' (Arabic).

Malachy

Variants and diminutives: Mal, Malachai, Malachi, Malachias.
Meaning: 'my messenger' (Hebrew).

Malcolm

Variants and diminutives: Callum, Calum, Colm, Colum, Columba, Kallum, Kalum, Mal, Malcom, Maolcolm.
Meaning: 'servant of Saint Columba' (Scots Gaelic).

Malik

Variants and diminutives: Mal, Mali.
Meaning: 'master' (Arabic).

Malise

Variants and diminutives: Mal, Mali.

Meaning: 'servant of Jesus' (Scots Gaelic).

Mallory

Variants and diminutives: Lory, Mal, Mallorey, Mallori, Mallorie, Malori, Malorie, Malory.
Meaning: 'unlucky' (Latin); derived from a British family name. Also a girl's name.

Manasseh

Variants and diminutives: Manasses.
Meaning: 'to forget' (Hebrew).

Manchu

Meaning: 'pure' (Chinese).
Notable namesakes: the Chinese region of Manchuria, homeland of the Manchu people and of the Manchu dynasty that once ruled China.

Manfred

Variants and diminutives: Fred, Freddie, Freddy, Manifred, Mannie, Manny, Mannye.
Meaning: 'man' and 'peace' (Germanic).

Manley

Variants and diminutives: Manly.
Meaning: 'manly' (Middle English); derived from an English family name.

Mansa

Meaning: 'king' (African).

Mansel

Variants and diminutives: Mansell.
Meaning: 'from Le Mans', 'from Maine' or 'dweller in a manse' (Old French); derived from an English family name, in turn derived from a number of French place names.

Mansur

Meaning: 'divinely helped' (Arabic).

Manuel

Variants and diminutives: Eman, Emanuel, Emanuele, Emek, Emmanuel, Emmanuil, Immanuel, Maco, Mango, Mannie, Manny, Mano, Manoel, Manolo, Manue, Manuelito, Manuil, Manuyil, Mel, Minel, Nelo.
Meaning: 'God is with us' (Hebrew) as a Spanish diminutive of Emmanuel.

Marcel

Variants and diminutives: Marc, Marceau, Marcelino, Marcellino, Marcello, Marcellus, Marcelo, Marcelo, Marci, Marco, Marcus.
Meaning: uncertain; possibly 'martial' (Latin) through association with Mars, the god of war in Roman mythology, as a French diminutive of Marcellus (Marcus).

Marcellus

Variants and diminutives: Marc, Marcel, Marcelino, Marcellin, Marcellino, Marcello, Marcelo, Marco, Marcus.
Meaning: uncertain; possibly 'martial' (Latin) through association with Mars, the god of war in Roman mythology, as a Latin variant of Marcus.

Marco

Variants and diminutives: Marc, Marceau, Marcos, Marcus, Mark, Markos.
Meaning: uncertain; possibly 'martial' (Latin) through association with Mars, the god of war in Roman mythology, as an Italian variant of Marcus.

Marcus

Variants and diminutives: Marc, Marcel, Marcellin, Marcellus, Marco,

Marcos, Mark, Markos, Markus.
Meaning: uncertain; possibly
'martial' (Latin) through association
with Mars, the god of war in Roman
mythology; derived from the Roman
family name Marcius.

Mario

Variants and diminutives: Marcus,
Mark, Mari, Marilo, Marion, Marius.
Meaning: uncertain; possibly
'martial' (Latin) through association
with Mars, the god of war in Roman
mythology, as an Italian version of
Marius; possibly 'longed-for child' or
'rebellion' (Hebrew) as a male Italian
and Spanish version of Maria (Miriam
via Mary).

Marius

Variants and diminutives: Marcus,
Mari, Mario, Marion, Mark.
Meaning: uncertain; possibly
'martial' (Latin) through association
with Mars, the god of war in Roman
mythology; derived from a Roman
family name.

Mark

Variants and diminutives: Marc,
Marceau, Marcel, Marcelino,
Marcellin, Marcellino, Marcello,
Marcellus, Marcelo, March, Marci,
Marcilka, Marco, Marcos, Marcus,

Marcy, Marek, Mari, Marilo, Marinos,
Mario, Marion, Marius, Marka, Marko,
Markos, Markus, Markusha, Marques,
Marquis, Mars, Marsh, Marshe, Martin,
Marts.
Meaning: uncertain; possibly
'martial' (Latin) through association
with Mars, the god of war in Roman
mythology. A variant of Marcus.

Marlon

Variants and diminutives: Mar,
Mario, Marle, Marlen, Marlin, Marlis,
Marlo, Marlow, Marlowe, Marne,
Marnin, Merlin.
Meaning: uncertain; possibly 'pond'
and 'remnant' (Old English) as a
variant of Marlow; possibly 'sea' and
'hill' or 'fort' (Welsh) as a variant of
Merlin.

Marlow

Variants and diminutives: Marlon,
Marlowe.
Meaning: 'pond' and 'remnant' (Old
English); derived from an English
family name, in turn derived from an
English place name.

Marmaduke

Variants and diminutives: Duke,
Dukie, Madoc.
Meaning: 'servant of [Saint] Madoc'
(Irish Gaelic).

Marnin

Meaning: 'rejoicer' or 'singer'
(Hebrew).

Marquis

Variants and diminutives: Mark,
Marq, Marques, Marquess, Marquette.
Meaning: 'count of the march
[border]' (Old French) when derived
from a European rank of nobility; 'son
of Mark' (Latin) when derived from
Marques, a Spanish family name.

Marshall

Variants and diminutives: Marsh,
Marshal, Marshe, Marshel, Marshell.
Meaning: 'servant of the horse'
(Germanic).

Martin

Variants and diminutives: Maarten,
Mairtin, Marci, Marcilki, Marcin, Mart,
Martainn, Martan, Martel, Marten,
Martey, Marti, Martie, Martijn,
Martinas, Martine, Martinet,
Martinho, Martiniano, Martinka,
Martino, Martinos, Martins, Martlet,
Marto, Marton, Martoni, Marty,
Martyn, Mertil, Mertin, Tino, Tynek.
Meaning: uncertain; possibly
'martial' (Latin) through association
with Mars, the god of war in Roman
mythology; derived from the Roman
family name Martinus.

Marvin

Variants and diminutives: Marv, Marve, Marven, Marvine, Marvyn, Marwin, Mervin, Mervyn, Merwin, Merwyn, Myrwyn.
Meaning: 'famous' or 'sea' and 'friend' (Old English).

Mason

Meaning: 'mason' or 'stone-worker' (Old French).

Masud

Meaning: 'lucky' (Arabic).

Matthew

Variants and diminutives: Macey, Mack, Maitiu, Mat, Mata, Mate, Matei, Matek, Mateo, Mateus, Matfei, Matfey, Matha, Mathe, Matheiu, Mathern, Mathew, Mathia, Mathias, Mathieu, Mati, Matia, Matiah, Matias, Matok, Matomon, Matt, Mattaeus, Mattathias, Matteo, Matteus, Matthaios, Matthaus, Mattheo, Matthia, Matthias, Matthieu, Matti, Mattie, Mattieu, Mattmias, Matty, Matus, Matvey, Matyas, Matyi, Matyo, Mayo, Motka, Motya, Teo.
Meaning: 'gift of God' (Hebrew).

Matthias

Variants and diminutives: Macey, Mack, Mat, Mata, Mateo, Mateus, Matheiu, Mathern, Mathew, Mathia, Mathias, Mathieu, Mati, Matia, Matiah, Matias, Matok, Matomon, Matt, Mattaeus, Mattathias, Matteo, Matteus, Matthaios, Matthaus, Matthia, Matthias, Matthieu, Matti, Mattie, Mattieu, Mattmias, Matty, Matus, Matyas, Mayo.
Meaning: 'gift of God' (Hebrew) as a Greek variant of Matthew.

Maurice

Variants and diminutives: Maolmuire, Maryse, Maur, Maurey, Mauricio, Maurie, Mauris, Maurise, Maurits, Mauritius, Maurizio, Mauro, Maury, Merrick, Meuric, Meuriz, Meyrick, Mo, Morets, Morey, Morie, Moris, Moritz, Moriz, Morrey, Morrice, Morrie, Morris, Morriss, Morry, Morys, Morus, Moss, Muirgheas.
Meaning: 'Moorish' or 'African' (Latin).

Max

Variants and diminutives: Mac, Mack, Maks, Maxey, Maxie, Maxim, Maxime, Maximilian, Maximilianus, Maximilien, Maximino, Maxwell, Maxy.
Meaning: generally 'great' (Latin) as a diminutive of both boys' and girls' names beginning with 'Max-', but 'the spring' or 'the well' and 'of Magnus' (Scots Gaelic) as a dimunitive of Maxwell.

Maximilian

Variants and diminutives: Mac, Mack, Makimus, Maks, Maksim, Maksimka, Maksym, Maksymilian, Makszi, Massimiliano, Massimo, Max, Maxey, Maxi, Maxie, Maxim, Maximalian, Maxime, Maximilianus, Maximiliao, Maximilien, Maximillian, Maximino, Maximo, Maximus, Maxwell, Maxy, Miksa, Sima.
Meaning: 'greatest' (Latin).

Maxwell

Variants and diminutives: Mac, Mack, Maks, Max, Maxey, Maxie, Maxim, Maxime, Maximilian, Maxy.
Meaning: 'the spring' or 'the well' and 'of Magnus' (Scots Gaelic); derived from a Scottish family name, in turn derived from a Scottish place name.

Maynard

Variants and diminutives: May, Mayne, Menard.
Meaning: 'strength' and 'hard' (Germanic); derived from an English family name.

Mehmet

Variants and diminutives: Mahomet, Mohamma, Mohammed, Muhammad, Muhammed.
Meaning: 'deserving praise' or 'deserving glory' (Arabic) as a variant of Mohammed.

Meical

Variants and diminutives: Meic, Michael.
Meaning: 'who is like God?' (Hebrew) as a Welsh variant of Michael.

Melchior

Variants and diminutives: Melchi, Melchie, Melchisadek, Melchizedek, Melchs, Melchy.
Meaning: uncertain; possibly 'king' or 'king of the city' (Hebrew).

Melville

Variants and diminutives: Mel, Melbourne, Melburn, Meldon, Melford, Mell, Melton, Melwood, Melvin, Melvyn.
Meaning: uncertain; possibly 'Amalo's settlement' (Germanic); possibly 'bad' and 'town' (Old French); derived from a Scottish family name, in turn derived from a Scottish place name.

Melvin

Variants and diminutives: Malvin, Mel, Mell, Melville, Melvyn, Vinny, Vynnie.
Meaning: uncertain; possibly 'council' and 'friend' (Old English); possibly 'Amalo's settlement' (Germanic) or 'bad' and 'town' (Old French) as a variant of Melville.

Menachem

Variants and diminutives: Manasseh, Mann, Mannes, Menasseh, Menahem, Mendel, Mendeley.
Meaning: 'comforter' (Hebrew).

Mercury

Variants and diminutives: Mercurius.
Meaning: 'messenger of Jupiter' (Latin); derived from the name of the messenger of the gods and god of trade in Roman mythology.

Merlin

Variants and diminutives: Marlin, Marlon, Merle, Merlo, Merlon, Merlyn, Myrddin.
Meaning: 'sea' and 'hill' or 'fort' (Welsh); possibly derived from the Welsh town Carmarthen. Also a girl's name (generally Merlyn).

Merrick

Variants and diminutives: Maurice, Merick, Merik, Meril, Merle, Merrik, Merrill, Meryl, Meuric, Meyrick, Myril, Myrl.
Meaning: 'Moorish' or 'African' (Latin) as a Welsh variant of Maurice.

Merton

Variants and diminutives: Mert, Mertie, Merty.

Meaning: 'lake' and 'place' (Old English); derived from an English family name, in turn derived from a number of English place names.

Mervyn

Variants and diminutives: Marvin, Marvyn, Merfyn, Merv, Merven, Mervin.

Meaning: 'famous' or 'sea' and 'friend' (Old English) as a variant of Marvin.

Micah

Variants and diminutives: Mica, Micha, Michael, Misha, Mishka, Miska.

Meaning: 'who is like God?' (Hebrew) as a variant of Michael.

Michael

Variants and diminutives: Dumichel, Machas, Maguel, Makis, Meic, Meical, Mica, Micah, Micha, Michail, Michak, Michal, Michalek, Michau, Micheal, Micheil, Michel, Michelangelo, Michele, Michiel, Micho, Michon, Mick, Mickel, Mickey, Micki, Mickie, Micky, Mietek, Miguel, Migui, Mihail, Mihailo, Mihal, Mihalje, Mihaly, Mihangel, Mihas, Mihel, Mihkel, Mika, Mikael, Mikas, Mike, Mikel, Mikelis, Mikey, Mikhail, Mikhalis, Mikhalka, Mikhos, Miki, Mikk, Mikkel, Mikko, Miks, Mikus, Miles, Milkins, Min, Minka, Mique, Misa, Mischa, Misha, Mishca, Misi, Miska, Misko, Miso, Mitch, Mitchel, Mitchell, Mitchele, Mitchill, Mitchiel, Myall, Mychal, Myles.

Meaning: 'who is like God?' (Hebrew).

Mick

Variants and diminutives: Michael, Mickey, Micky.

Meaning: 'who is like God?' (Hebrew) as a diminutive of Michael.

Miles

Variants and diminutives: Michael, Mihel, Milan, Mills, Milo, Myles.

Meaning: uncertain; possibly 'soldier' (Latin); possibly 'grace' (Old Slavic) or 'merciful' (Germanic) as a variant of Milo; possibly 'gentle' or 'of Michael' (Old English); possibly 'beloved servant of Mary' (Irish Gaelic).

Milo

Variants and diminutives: Miles, Myles.

Meaning: 'grace' (Old Slavic); 'merciful' (Germanic).

Milton

Variants and diminutives: Millard, Miller, Mills, Milt, Miltie, Milty, Mull, Muller.

Meaning: 'middle' or 'mill' and 'settlement' or 'farm' (Old English); derived from an English family name, in turn derived from a number of English place names.

Mitchell

Variants and diminutives: Michael, Mitch, Mitchel.

Meaning: 'who is like God?' (Hebrew) as a variant of Michael; 'big' (Old English); derived from a British family name.

Mohammed

Variants and diminutives: Ahmad, Ahmed, Amad, Amed, Hamdrem, Hamdun, Hamid, Hammad, Hammed, Humayd, Mahmud, Mahmoud, Mahomet, Mehemet, Mehmet, Mohamad, Mohamet, Mohammad, Muhammad, Muhammed.

Meaning: 'deserving praise' or 'deserving glory' (Arabic).

Mohan

Variants and diminutives: Mohandas.

Meaning: 'delightful' (Sanskrit),

Monroe

Variants and diminutives: Monro, Munro, Munroe.

Meaning: 'mouth of the Roe', the Roe being a river in Ireland (Irish Gaelic); derived from a British family name.

Montague

Variants and diminutives: Mante, Montacute, Montagu, Monte, Monty.
Meaning: 'hill' and 'pointed' (Old French); derived from a French and British family name, in turn derived from a French place name.

Montgomery

Variants and diminutives: Monte, Montgomerie, Monty.
Meaning: 'hill' and of 'the powerful man' (Old French); derived from a British family name, in turn derived from two French place names.

Monty

Variants and diminutives: Monte, Montague, Montgomery.
Meaning: 'hill' and 'pointed' (Old French) as a diminutive of Montague; 'hill' and 'of the powerful man' (Old French) as a diminutive of Montgomery.

Mordecai

Variants and diminutives: Marduk, Mord, Mordechai, Mordkhe, Mordy, Mort, Mortie, Morty.
Meaning: 'follower of Marduk' (Hebrew), Marduk being the supreme god of Babylonian mythology.

Mordred

Variants and diminutives: Modred, Modris.
Meaning: uncertain; possibly 'to bite' (Latin); possibly 'host' or 'own' and 'course' (Welsh).

Morley

Variants and diminutives: Morle, Morlie, Morley.
Meaning: 'moor' or 'fen' and 'clearing' (Old English); derived from an English family name, in turn derived from a number of English place names.

Morris

Variants and diminutives: Maurey, Maurie, Maury, Mo, Moor, Moreton, Morey, Morgan, Morie, Morrey, Morrie, Morrissey, Morrison, Morry, Morse, Mort, Mortimer, Morton, Morty, Myrton.
Meaning: 'Moorish' or 'African' (Latin) as a variant of Maurice.

Mortimer

Variants and diminutives: Mort, Mortie, Morty.
Meaning: 'dead' and 'sea' (Old French); derived from an English family name, in turn derived from a French place name.

Morton

Variants and diminutives: Mort, Mortie, Morty.
Meaning: 'moor' or 'fen' and 'settlement' or 'farm' (Old English); derived from an English family name, in turn derived from a number of English place names.

Moses

Variants and diminutives: Moe, Moise, Moisei, Moises, Moisey, Moishe, Moisis, Moke, Mose, Moshe, Mosheh, Moss, Mosya, Mosze, Moszek, Moy, Moyes, Moys, Moyse, Moze, Mozes.
Meaning: uncertain; possibly 'son' (Egyptian); possibly 'drawn out' or 'saved [from the water]' (Hebrew).

Mostyn
Variants and diminutives: Moss, Mostie, Mosty.
Meaning: 'field of the fortress' (Welsh); 'moss' and 'settlement' (Old English); derived from a British family name, in turn derived from a Welsh place name.

Mungo
Variants and diminutives: Kentigern.
Meaning: uncertain; possibly 'beloved' or 'friendly' (Scots Gaelic).

Muraco
Meaning: 'white moon' (Native American).

Murdoch
Variants and diminutives: Muireadhach, Murdo, Murdock, Murtagh, Murtaug, Murtaugh.
Meaning: 'mariner' (Scottish and Irish Gaelic).

Murphy
Variants and diminutives: Meriadoc, Morty, Murph, Murphey, Murphie.
Meaning: 'descendent of the sea warrior' (Irish and Scots Gaelic); derived from a British family name. Also a girl's name.

Murray
Variants and diminutives: Moray, Muirioch, Murrey, Murry.
Meaning: 'seaboard' and 'settlement' (Scots Gaelic); derived from a British family name, in turn derived from the Scottish area and former county of Moray.

Myron
Variants and diminutives: Miron, My, Ron, Ronnie, Ronny.
Meaning: 'myrrh' (Aramaic and Arabic). A male version of Myrna.

Nabil
Variants and diminutives: Nadiv, Nagid.
Meaning: 'noble' (Arabic).

Nagid
Meaning: 'noble', 'wealthy' or 'ruler' (Hebrew).

Nahum
Meaning: 'comforting' (Hebrew).

Namid
Meaning: 'star dancer' (Native American).

Namir
Meaning: 'leopard' (Arabic).

Napier
Variants and diminutives: Nape, Napper, Neper.
Meaning: 'naperer [a keeper of table linen]' (Old French); derived from an English family name.

Napoleon
Variants and diminutives: Leon, Nap, Nappie, Nappy.
Meaning: 'new town' (Greek); derived from Neapolis, the ancient Greek name of the Italian town of Naples (Napoli).

Narcissus
Variants and diminutives: Cissus, Narcie, Narcisse, Narcy.
Meaning: 'numbness' (Greek); derived from the name of the self-absorbed youth of Greek mythology who pined away to become the narcissus flower.

Naren
Meaning: 'manly' (Sanskrit).

Naresh
Meaning: 'lord' or 'king' (Sanskrit).

Nasser
Variants and diminutives: Nassor.
Meaning: 'victorious' (Arabic).

Nathan
Variants and diminutives: Nata, Natan, Nat, Nate, Nathon, Natt, Natty.
Meaning: 'gift' (Hebrew).

Nathaniel
Variants and diminutives: Nat, Nata, Natan, Natanael, Natale, Nataniel, Nataniele, Nate, Nathan, Nathanael, Nathon, Natt, Natty, Neal, Niel, Noel, Nowell.
Meaning: 'gift of God' (Hebrew).

Ned
Variants and diminutives: Edmund, Edward, Neddie, Neddy, Ted, Teddie, Teddy.
Meaning: 'happiness' or 'riches' and 'guardian' (Old English) as a diminutive of Edward; 'happiness' or 'riches' and 'friend' (Old English) as a diminutive of Edmund. Also a diminutive of other names beginning with 'Ed-'.

Neil
Variants and diminutives: Neal, Neale, Neall, Nealson, Neaton, Neely, Neill, Neils, Neilson, Neilus, Nellie, Nels, Nelsi, Nelson, Nial, Niall, Niel, Niels, Nigel, Nil, Niles, Nilo, Nils, Nilson, Nilya, Niul, Nyles.
Meaning: 'champion', 'cloud' or 'vehement' (Irish Gaelic).

Nelson
Variants and diminutives: Nealson, Neaton, Neil, Nels, Nelsen, Nils, Nilsen, Nilson.
Meaning: 'son of Nell' or 'son of Neil' (Old English); derived from an English family name.

Nestor
Variants and diminutives: Nest, Nesty, Tory.
Meaning: 'journey' or 'safe return' (Greek).

Neville
Variants and diminutives: Nev, Nevil, Nevile, Nevill, Newton.
Meaning: 'new' and 'place' or 'town' (Old French); derived from an English family name, in turn derived from a number of French place names.

Nevin
Variants and diminutives: Nefen, Nev, Nevan, Neven, Nevins, Niven.
Meaning: 'little saint' or 'worshipper of the saint' (Irish Gaelic); 'nephew' (Germanic).

Newton
Variants and diminutives: Neville, Newgate, Newland, Newman, Newt, Niland.
Meaning: 'new' and 'place' or 'settlement' (Old English); derived from an English family name, in turn derived from a number of English place names.

Nicholas
Variants and diminutives: Claus, Col, Cola, Colas, Cole, Colet, Colin, Collet, Collett, Colley, Collis, Colly, Kalya. Klaas, Klaus, Kola, Kolya, Micu, Miki, Miklos, Mikolai, Milek, Nic, Nicanor, Niccolo, Nichol, Nick, Nickie, Nickolas, Nickolaus, Nicky, Nico, Nicodemus, Nicol, Nicola, Nicolaas, Nicolai, Nicolaio, Nicolas, Nicolau, Nicolaus, Nicole, Nicoll, Nicolo, Nicy, Niel, Nik, Nike, Niki, Nikita, Nikki, Nikkie, Nikky, Niklas, Niklavs, Niklos, Nikola, Nikolai, Nikolais, Nikolaos, Nikolas, Nikolaus, Nikolos, Nikos, Nikula, Nikulas, Nilo, Nils.
Meaning: 'victory of the people' (Greek).

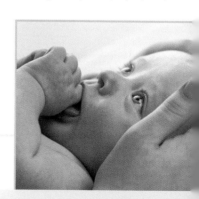

Nicodemus
Variants and diminutives: Demus, Nico, Nicholas.
Meaning: 'victory of the people' (Greek).

Nigel
Variants and diminutives: Neil, Nidge, Nig, Nige, Niguel, Nye.
Meaning: 'champion', 'cloud' or 'vehement' (Irish Gaelic) as a Latinised form of Neil.

Ninian
Variants and diminutives: Nennus, Ninidh.
Meaning: uncertain; derived from the name of a Christian saint.

Noah
Variants and diminutives: Noach, Noak, Noe, Noel, Noi, Noy.
Meaning: 'comfort', 'respite' or 'long-lived' (Hebrew).

Noam
Meaning: 'pleasant' or 'my delight' (Hebrew). A male version of Naomi.

Noël
Variants and diminutives: Natal, Natale, Noel, Nowell.
Meaning: 'birthday' (Latin); 'Christ's birthday' or 'Christmas' (French).

Nolan
Variants and diminutives: Noland.
Meaning: 'son of the noble one' (Irish Gaelic); derived from an Irish family name.

Norbert
Variants and diminutives: Bert, Bertie, Berty, Norrie, Norry.
Meaning: 'north' and 'bright' or 'famous' (Germanic).

Norman
Variants and diminutives: Norm, Normand, Normann, Normie, Norrie, Norris, Norry, Tormod.
Meaning: 'north' and 'man' [Norseman or Viking] (Germanic).

Norris
Variants and diminutives: Norice, Noris, Norman, Norreys, Norrie, Norriss, Norry.
Meaning: 'northerner' or 'nurse' (Old French).

Norton
Variants and diminutives: Nort, Nortie, Norty.
Meaning: 'northern' and 'place' or 'settlement' (Old English); derived from an English family name, in turn derived from a number of English place names.

Noy
Meaning: 'bejewelled by nature' (Hebrew). A male version of Noya.

Nuncio
Variants and diminutives: Nunzio.
Meaning: 'messenger' (Latin).

Nye
Variants and diminutives: Aneirin, Aneurin, Ny, Nyle.
Meaning: 'man of honour' (Latin) or 'pure gold' (Welsh) as a diminutive of Aneurin.

Odo
Variants and diminutives: Aodh, Audo, Oates, Oddie, Oddo, Oddy, Odey, Odinal, Ody, Otes, Othes. Otho, Otis, Ottes, Otto.
Meaning: 'riches' (Germanic).

Ogden
Variants and diminutives: Oak, Oakden, Oakes, Oakie, Oakleigh, Oakley, Oaks, Ogdan, Ogdon.
Meaning: 'oak' and 'valley' (Old English); derived from an English family name, in turn derived from a number of English place names.

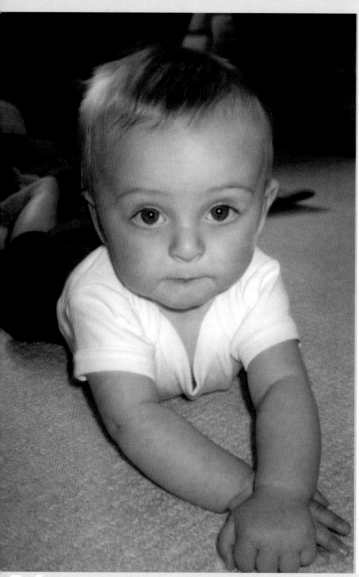

Olaf

Variants and diminutives: Amhlaigh, Anleifr, Aulay, Olafur, Olav, Olave, Olay, Ole, Olen, Olif, Olin, Oliver.
Meaning: 'forebear' and 'relics' (Old Norse).

Oliver

Variants and diminutives: Alvar, Noll, Nollie, Nolly, Oli, Olivero, Olivier, Oliviero, Olley, Olli, Ollie, Olly, Olvan.
Meaning: uncertain; possibly 'olive' (Old French); possibly 'elf' and 'army' (Germanic); possibly 'forebear' and 'relics' (Old Norse) as a variant of Olave (Olaf); derived from a French and English family name.

Omar

Variants and diminutives: Oner, Omri.
Meaning: 'eloquent' (Hebrew); 'long-lived', 'first son', 'follower of the Prophet' or 'highest' (Arabic).

Oran

Variants and diminutives: Odhran, Oren, Orin, Orren.
Meaning: 'sallow' or 'greenish' (Irish Gaelic).

Orde

Variants and diminutives: Ordell.
Meaning: 'order' (Latin).

Orestes
Variants and diminutives: Orest, Oreste, Orin.
Meaning: 'mountain' (Greek).

Orlando
Variants and diminutives: Arland, Arlando, Land, Lando, Lannie, Lanny, Ordando, Orlan, Orland, Orleans, Orley, Orlin, Orio, Orval, Orville, Roland.
Meaning: 'fame' and 'land' (Germanic) as an Italian variant of Roland.

Ormerod
Variants and diminutives: Ormie, Ormy, Rod, Roddie, Roddy.
Meaning: 'Orm's clearing' (Old Norse and Old English); derived from an English family name, in turn derived from an English place name.

Ormonde
Variants and diminutives: Orma, Orman, Ormand, Ormond.
Meaning: 'snake' (Old Norse); 'elm' (French); 'from east Munster' (Irish Gaelic), Munster being an Irish province, when derived from an Irish family name.

Orson
Variants and diminutives: Sonnie, Sonny, Urson.
Meaning: 'bear cub' (Old French).

Ortho
Variants and diminutives: Orth, Othie, Orthy.
Meaning: 'straight' (Greek).

Orville
Variants and diminutives: Orval.
Meaning: uncertain; possibly 'gold' and 'town' (Old French); coined by the English writer Fanny Burney for her character Lord Orville, the hero of the novel *Evelina*.

Osbert
Variants and diminutives: Osgood, Osborne, Osric, Ossie, Ossy, Oz, Ozzie, Ozzy.
Meaning: 'god' and 'bright' (Old English).

Osborne
Variants and diminutives: Osborn, Osbourn, Osbourne, Osburn, Oz, Ozzie, Ozzy.
Meaning: 'god' and 'bear' or 'man' (Old English); derived from an English family name.

Oscar
Variants and diminutives: Oke, Oskar, Ossie, Ossy, Ozzie, Ozzy.

Meaning: 'god' and 'spear' (Old English); 'deer' or 'dear' and 'friend' or 'love' (Irish Gaelic).

Osmond
Variants and diminutives: Esmand, Esme, Osman, Osmand, Osmanek, Osmant, Osmen, Osmon, Osmont, Osmund, Osmundo, Oswin, Oz, Ozzi, Ozzie, Ozzy.
Meaning: 'god' and 'protector' (Old English and Old Norse); derived from an English family name.

Ossian
Variants and diminutives: Oisin, Ossin.
Meaning: 'little deer' or 'fawn' (Irish Gaelic).

Oswald
Variants and diminutives: Ossie, Osvald, Oswal, Oswaldo, Oswall, Oswold, Oz, Ozzie, Ozzy, Waldo, Waldy.
Meaning: 'god' and 'ruler', 'power' or 'wood' (Old English and Old Norse).

Oswin
Variants and diminutives: Oz, Ozzie, Ozzy.
Meaning: 'god' and 'friend' (Old English).

Otis
Variants and diminutives: Otes, Otto.
Meaning: 'riches' (Germanic) as a variant of Otto (Odo); derived from an English family name.

Otto
Variants and diminutives: Audr, Odo, Odon, Onek, Osman, Otek, Otello, Otfried, Othello, Othman, Othmar, Otho, Othon, Otik, Otilio, Otis, Otman, Oto, Oton, Ottmar, Ottomar, Otton, Ottone, Tilo, Tonek.
Meaning: 'riches' (Germanic) as a variant of Odo.

Owen
Variants and diminutives: Bowen, Bowie, Eoghan, Eugene, Euan, Evan, Ewan, Ewen, Owain, Owayne, Ovin, Uwen, Ywain.
Meaning: 'well-born' (Greek) as a Welsh variant of Eugene.

Pablo
Variants and diminutives: Paolo, Paul.
Meaning: 'small' (Latin) as a Spanish variant of Paul.

Paco
Variants and diminutives: Francis, Frank.
Meaning: 'bald eagle' (Native American); 'French' (Latin) as a Spanish version of Francis; 'free' (Latin) as a Spanish version of Frank.

Paddy
Variants and diminutives: Patrick.
Meaning: 'noble' or 'patrician' (Latin) as a diminutive of Patrick (and of Patricia).

Palmer
Meaning: 'palm' or 'hand' (Latin); 'pilgrim' (Old French); derived from an English family name.

Pan
Meaning: 'all' (Greek).

Pancho
Variants and diminutives: Panchito.
Meaning: 'French' (Latin) as a Spanish diminutive of Francisco (Francis).

Paolo
Variants and diminutives: Pablo, Paul.
Meaning: 'small' (Latin) as an Italian variant of Paul.

Paris
Variants and diminutives: Parris.
Meaning: uncertain; possibly 'marshes of the Parisii' (Latin), the Parisii being a Gaulish Celtic tribe; possibly 'pouch' (Greek) when derived from the name of the Trojan prince.

Parish
Variants and diminutives: Parrie, Parrish, Parry.
Meaning: 'neighbour' (Greek); derived from an English family name.

Parker
Variants and diminutives: Park, Parke.
Meaning: 'park-keeper' (Old French); derived from an English family name.

Parnell
Variants and diminutives: Parnall, Parnel, Parrnell, Pernel, Pernell.
Meaning: uncertain; possibly 'rock' (Greek) as a diminutive of Petronella, in turn derived from the Roman family name Petronius; derived from an English family name. Also a girl's name.

Parry
Variants and diminutives: Harry.
Meaning: 'son of Harry' (Welsh); derived from a Welsh family name.

Pascal
Variants and diminutives: Pace, Paco,

Pascalo, Paschal, Pasco, Pascoe, Pascual, Pascualo, Pashell, Pasqual, Pasquel, Pasqul, Pesach.
Meaning: 'to pass over' (Hebrew); 'of Easter' (Old French).

Pascoe
Variants and diminutives: Pascal, Pasco.
Meaning: 'to pass over' (Hebrew) or 'of Easter' (Old French) as a variant of Pascal.

Patrick
Variants and diminutives: Pad, Paddie, Paddy, Padhra, Padhraic, Padi, Padraic, Padraig, Padriac, Padrig, Padruig, Paidin, Pat, Patek, Paton, Patraic, Patric, Patrice, Patricio,

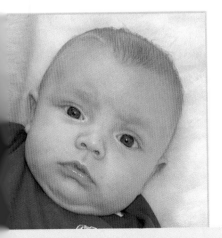

Patricius, Patrizio, Patrizius, Patsy, Patten, Patti, Pattie, Pattison, Patty, Paxton, Payton, Peter, Peyton, Ticho.
Meaning: 'noble' or 'patrician' (Latin).

Paul
Variants and diminutives: Oalo, Pablo, Pail, Pal, Paley, Pali, Palika, Pall, Paolo, Pasha, Pashka, Paulie, Paulin, Paulino, Paulinus, Paulis, Paullus, Paulo, Paulos, Paulot, Pauls, Paulus, Pauly, Pavel, Pavils, Pavlik, Pavlo, Pawel, Pawl, Pawley, Pewlin, Pol, Poul, Powel, Powle.
Meaning: 'small' (Latin).

Paxton
Variants and diminutives: Pax, Paxon.
Meaning: a composite name comprising 'peace' (Latin) and 'place' or 'settlement' (Old English); derived from an English family name.

Pedro
Variants and diminutives: Peter.
Meaning: 'rock' (Greek) as an Italian, Portuguese and Spanish variant of Peter.

Pelham
Variants and diminutives: Pel, Pellie, Pelly, Plum.

Meaning: 'Peola's' or 'hide' and 'place' (Old English); derived from an English family name, in turn derived from an English place name.

Pepin
Variants and diminutives: Pep, Pepi, Peppie, Peppy, Pipi, Pippi.
Meaning: 'petitioner' or 'perseverant' (Germanic).

Percival
Variants and diminutives: Parsifal, Parzival, Perce, Perceval, Perciful, Percival, Percy, Peredur.
Meaning: uncertain; possibly 'pierce' and 'valley' (Old French); coined by the French poet Chrétien de Troyes for a knight of Arthurian legend in his romance *Perceval, ou le conte du Graal* (*Percival, or the Story of the Grail*).

Percy
Variants and diminutives: Perce, Perceval, Percival, Perseus.
Meaning: uncertain; derived from the Roman first name Percius as a British family name, in turn derived from a number of French place names; possibly 'pierce' and 'valley' (Old French) as a diminutive of Percival.

Peregrine

Variants and diminutives: Perry.
Meaning: 'pilgrim', 'foreigner' or 'traveller' (Latin).

Perry

Variants and diminutives: Peregrine, Peter.
Meaning: 'pear tree' (Old English) when derived from a British family name; 'pilgrim', 'foreigner' or 'traveller' (Latin) as a diminutive of Peregrine; 'rock' (Greek) as a diminutive of Peter.

Peter

Variants and diminutives: Farris, Ferris, Padraig, Panos, Parlett, Parnell, Parren, Parry, Peadair, Peadar, Peader, Pearce, Peder, Pedrin, Pedro, Peet, Peeter, Peirce, Pequin, Per, Perequin, Perico, Perka, Perkin, Pernell, Pero, Perren, Perry, Petar, Pete, Peterus, Petey, Petie, Petinka, Petko, Petr, Petras, Petrelis, Petro, Petronio, Petros, Petru, Petrukas, Petruno, Petrus, Petrusha, Petter, Petur, Peyo, Pictrus, Pier, Pierce, Piero, Pierre, Pierrot, Piers, Piet, Pieter, Pietr, Pietrek, Pietro, Piotr, Piotrek, Piti, Petits, Pettis, Pettus, Piran, Pyatr, Pyotr, Rock, Rockey, Rockie, Rocky, Takis.
Meaning: 'rock' (Greek).

Peyton

Variants and diminutives: Pate, Payton.
Meaning: 'Paega's' and 'place' or settlement' (Old English); derived from an English family name, in turn derived from a number of English place names.

Phelan

Variants and diminutives: Phel, Phele.
Meaning: 'wolf' (Irish Gaelic).

Philander

Variants and diminutives: Phil.
Meaning: 'lover' and 'men' (Greek).

Philbert

Variants and diminutives: Bert, Berty, Filbert, Filberte, Filibert, Fulbert, Fulbright, Phil, Philbert, Philibert.
Meaning: 'very' and 'bright' (Germanic) as a variant of Filibert (Fulbert).

Philemon

Variants and diminutives: Phil, Philo.
Meaning: 'kiss' (Greek).

Philip

Variants and diminutives: Feeleep, Felip, Felipe, Felipino, Felippe, Fil, Filip, Filipek, Filipo, Filipp, Filippo, Filips, Filya, Fischel, Fulop, Hippolytos, Lipp, Lippo, Pepe, Phelps, Phil, Philipot, Philipp, Philippe, Philippus, Phill, Phillip, Phillipos, Phillipp, Phip, Pilib, Pip, Pippo.
Meaning: 'horse-lover' (Greek).

Phineas

Variants and diminutives: Phinehas, Phinhas, Pinchas, Pinchos, Pincus, Pini, Pink, Pinkus, Pinky.
Meaning: uncertain; possibly 'black' (Egyptian); possibly 'oracle' (Hebrew).

Pierce

Variants and diminutives: Pearce, Peter, Piers, Pierse.
Meaning: 'rock' (Greek) as a variant of Peter.

Pierre

Variants and diminutives: Peter, Piers.
Meaning: 'rock' (Greek) as a French variant of Peter.

Pierro

Variants and diminutives: Piero, Pierrot, Pirro.
Meaning: 'flame-haired' (Greek); 'little Peter' (Old French).

Piers

Variants and diminutives: Pearce, Peers, Peter, Piaras, Pierce, Pierre, Pierse.
Meaning: 'rock' (Greek) as a variant of Peter.

Pip

Variants and diminutives: Philip.
Meaning: 'horse-lover' (Greek) as a diminutive of Philip.

Piran

Variants and diminutives: Perran, Peter.
Meaning: uncertain; possibly 'rock' (Greek) as a variant of Peter.

Pius

Variants and diminutives: Pitkin.
Meaning: 'pious' or 'dutiful' (Latin).

Placido

Variants and diminutives: Placedo, Placid, Placijo, Plasido, Plasio.
Meaning: 'peaceful' (Latin).

Porter

Variants and diminutives: Port.
Meaning: 'door-keeper' or 'gate-keeper' (Latin); 'to carry' (Old French); derived from an English family name.

Pravin

Meaning: 'skilful' or 'able' (Hindi).

Prem

Meaning: 'endearing' or 'affectionate' (Sanskrit).

Prentice

Variants and diminutives: Prent, Prentis, Prentise, Prentiss.
Meaning: 'apprentice' (Old French); derived from an English family name.

Preston

Variants and diminutives: Prescott.
Meaning: 'priest's' and 'place' or 'farm' (Old English); derived from an English family name, in turn derived from a number of English place names.

Price

Meaning: 'son of Rhys' (Old Welsh); derived from a Welsh family name.

Prior

Variants and diminutives: Pry, Pryor.
Meaning: 'before' (Latin); 'prior [the deputy head of a monastery]' (Old French and Old English); derived from an English family name.

Prince

Meaning: 'first', 'leader' or 'chief' (Latin); derived from a British family name, in turn derived from a title of nobility.

Prosper

Variants and diminutives: Prospero.
Meaning: 'successful' (Latin).

Putnam

Meaning: 'Putta's homestead' (Old

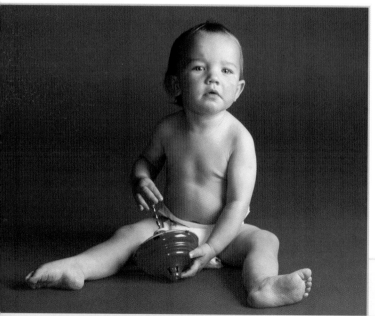

English); derived from an English family name, in turn derived from a number of English place names.

Quentin
Variants and diminutives: Quent, Quentin, Quenton, Quincy, Quinn, Quint, Quintin, Quintus, Quito.
Meaning: 'fifth' (Latin) as a variant of the Roman family name Quintus.

Quillan
Variants and diminutives: Quill, Quillie, Quilly.
Meaning: 'cub' (Irish Gaelic).

Quincy
Variants and diminutives: Quentin, Quincey, Quintus.
Meaning: 'fifth' (Latin) as a variant of the Roman family name Quintus; derived from a French family name, in turn derived from a number of French place names.

Quinlin
Variants and diminutives: Quinley, Quinn.
Meaning: 'strong' (Irish Gaelic).

Quinn
Variants and diminutives: Quin, Quine, Quinney.
Meaning: 'son of' and 'counsel' (Irish Gaelic); derived from an Irish family name.

Quirinal
Variants and diminutives: Quirino, Quirinus.
Meaning: 'of Romulus' (Latin), Romulus being a son of Mars and Rhea Silvia and a founder of Rome, who was deified as Quirinus after his death.

Rab
Variants and diminutives: Rabbie, Rabby, Robert.
Meaning: 'fame' and 'bright' (Germanic) as a Scottish diminutive of Robert.

Rabi
Meaning: 'breeze' (Arabic). A male version of Rabia.

Radburn
Variants and diminutives: Burnie, Burny, Rad, Radborn, Radborne, Radbourne, Radburne, Radd, Raddie, Raddy, Radley.
Meaning: 'reed' or 'red' and 'stream' (Old English); derived from an English family name, in turn derived from a number of English place names.

Radcliff
Variants and diminutives: Cliff, Cliffe, Clyffe, Racliff, Racliffe, Rad, Radcliffe, Radclyffe, Radd, Raddie, Raddy, Redcliff, Redcliffe.
Meaning: 'red' and 'cliff' (Old English); derived from an English family name, in turn derived from a number of English place names.

Radomil
Variants and diminutives: Rad, Rado.
Meaning: 'peace-loving' (Slavic).

Rafe
Variants and diminutives: Rafer, Ralf, Ralph.
Meaning: 'advice' or 'might' and 'wolf' (Germanic) as a variant of Ralph.

Rafferty
Variants and diminutives: Rafe, Rafer, Raff, Raffer.
Meaning: uncertain; possibly

'descendant of' and 'prosperity', 'wielder' or 'floodtide' (Irish Gaelic); derived from an Irish family name.

Rahim

Variants and diminutives: Rahman.
Meaning: 'compassionate' (Arabic).

Rahman

Variants and diminutives: Rahim, Rahmet.
Meaning: 'compassionate' or 'merciful' (Arabic).

Raja

Variants and diminutives: Raj.
Meaning: 'king' (Sanskrit); 'anticipated' or 'hoped for' (Arabic). Also a male version of Rani.

Raleigh

Variants and diminutives: Lee, Leigh, Rally, Rawleigh, Rawley.
Meaning: 'red', 'roe deer' or 'rye' and 'clearing' (Old English); derived from an English family name, in turn derived from a number of English place names.

Ralph

Variants and diminutives: Raaf, Rafe, Raff, Raffy, Ralf, Ralston, Randolph, Ranulf, Raol, Raoul, Raoulin, Rauf, Rauffe, Raul, Raulio, Rawley, Relman, Rolf, Rolph, Rulo.
Meaning: 'advice' or 'might' and 'wolf' (Germanic).

Rama

Variants and diminutives: Ramah.
Meaning: 'black', 'dark' or 'pleasing' (Sanskrit); 'exalted' (Hebrew). Also a girl's name.

Ramón

Variants and diminutives: Raymond.
Meaning: 'advice' or 'might' and 'protector' (Germanic) as a Spanish version of Raymond.

Ramsay

Variants and diminutives: Ram, Ramsey, Ramsy.
Meaning: 'wild garlic', 'ram' or 'raven' and 'island' (Old English); derived from a

British family name, in turn derived from a number of English place names.

Randall

Variants and diminutives: Rand, Randal, Randel, Randell, Randi, Randie, Randl, Randle, Randolph, Randy, Rankin, Ranulf.
Meaning: 'shield' or 'raven' and 'wolf' (Old English).

Randolph

Variants and diminutives: Dolf, Rand, Randal, Randall, Randel, Randell, Randi, Randie, Randl, Randle, Randolf, Randulf, Randulfus, Randy, Rankin, Ranulf, Raoul.
Meaning: 'shield' or 'raven' and 'wolf' (Germanic) as a variant of Randall.

Ransom

Variants and diminutives: Rance, Rand, Ransome, Ranson.
Meaning: 'son of Rand' (Old English), Rand meaning 'shield' or 'raven' and 'wolf' (Old English and Old German) as a diminutive of Randall or Randolph; derived from an English family name.

Ranulf

Variants and diminutives: Ralph, Ranulph.
Meaning: 'advice' or 'might' and 'wolf' (Germanic) as a variant of Ralph.

Raoul

Variants and diminutives: Ralph, Raolin, Raul.
Meaning: 'advice' or 'might' and 'wolf' (Germanic) as a French variant of Ralph.

Raphael

Variants and diminutives: Felio, Raf, Rafael, Rafaelle, Rafaello, Rafaelo, Rafe, Rafeal, Rafel, Raffael, Raffaello, Rafi, Rafito, Raphel, Refael, Refi, Rephael.
Meaning: 'healed by God' (Hebrew).

Rashid

Variants and diminutives: Rasheed.
Meaning: 'follower of the correct path' (Sanskrit and Arabic); 'righteous' (Swahili).

Ravi

Meaning: 'conferring' (Hindi).

Raviv

Meaning: 'dew' or 'rain' (Hebrew).

Ray

Variants and diminutives: Raymond, Rayner, Reigh, Reo, Rey, Rio, Riordan, Roy.
Meaning: 'king' (Old French); 'roe deer', 'stream' or 'rye' (Old English); 'advice' or 'might' and 'protector' (Germanic) as a diminutive of Raymond; 'advice' or 'might' and 'army' (Germanic) as a diminutive of Rayner.

Raymond

Variants and diminutives: Monchi, Mondo, Mundo, Raimon, Raimond, Raimondo, Raimund, Raimundo, Rajmund, Ramon, Ramond, Ramone, Ramundo, Ray, Raymon, Raymondo, Raymund, Raymundo, Raynard, Rayner, Reamonn, Redmond, Reimond.
Meaning: 'advice' or 'might' and 'protector' (Germanic).

Rayner

Variants and diminutives: Ragnar, Ragnor, Rain, Raine, Rainer, Raines, Rainier, Rains, Ranier, Ray, Raynor, Reiner.
Meaning: 'advice' or 'might' and 'army' (Germanic).

Redford

Variants and diminutives: Ford, Red, Redd.
Meaning: 'red' or 'reedy' and 'ford' (Old English); derived from an English family name, in turn derived from an English place name.

Reeve

Variants and diminutives: Reave, Reeves.
Meaning: 'bailiff', 'overseer' or 'chief magistrate' (Old English); derived from an English family name.

Reginald

Variants and diminutives: Naldo, Raghnall, Ranald, Reg, Reggie, Reggy, Reginauld, Regnauld, Regnault, Reinald, Reinaldo, Reinaldos, Reinhold, Reinold, Reinwald, Renaldo, Renato, Renaud, Renault, René, Rex, Reynaldo, Reynaldos, Reynold, Reynolds, Rinaldo, Rinold, Ronald.
Meaning: 'advice' or 'might' and 'power' (Germanic) as a variant of Reynold.

Remus

Variants and diminutives: Remer, Rémi, Remy.
Meaning: 'oar' (Latin).

René

Variants and diminutives: Renato, Renatus, Reni.
Meaning: 'reborn' (French).

Reuben

Variants and diminutives: Reuven, Revie, Ribbans, Rouvin, Rube, Ruben, Rubens, Rubin, Ruby, Ruvane, Ruvim.
Meaning: 'behold, a son' (Hebrew).

Rex

Variants and diminutives: Ray,

Rayner, Regino, Regis, Rexer, Rexford, Rey, Reynaud, Reyner, Roy.

Meaning: 'king' (Latin) and, as such, a male version of Regina; 'advice' or 'might' and 'power' (Germanic) as a diminutive of Reginald (Reynold).

Reynard

Variants and diminutives: Rainardo, Ray, Raynard, Regnard, Reinhard, Reinhart, Renard, Renart, Renaud, Renke, Rey, Reynaud, Raynauld, Reyner.

Meaning: 'advice' or 'might' and 'hard' (Germanic).

Reynold

Variants and diminutives: Ranald, Reginald, Reinald, Reinaldo, Reinaldos, Reinhold, Reinwald, Renaldo, Renaud, Renault, Rene, Reynaldos, Reynolds, Rinaldo, Rinold, Ronald.

Meaning: 'advice' or 'might' and 'power' (Germanic).

Rhett

Variants and diminutives: Rhet, Rhys.

Meaning: 'advice' (Germanic) when derived from a Dutch family name; 'the ardent one' (Old Welsh) as a variant of Rhys.

Rhys

Variants and diminutives: Price, Race, Rase, Ray, Reece, Rees, Reese, Rey, Rhett, Rhyence, Rice, Royce.

Meaning: 'the ardent one' (Old Welsh).

Richard

Variants and diminutives: Aric, Arick, Arri, Dic, Diccon, Dick, Dickie, Dickon, Dicky, Dix, Dixey, Dixie, Dixy, Dizzy, Hicks, Hickson, Hudd, Hudde, Hudi, Hudson, Juku, Rab, Reku, Ric, Ricard, Ricardo, Riccardo, Ricciardo, Ricoo, Rice, Rich, Richardo, Richardon, Richards, Richart, Richerd, Richi, Richie, Richy, Rici, Ricci, Ricco, Rick, Rickard, Rickert, Rickey, Ricki, Rickie, Ricky, Rico, Riczi, Rico, Rihardos, Rihards, Riik, Rik, Rikard, Riki, Riks, Riocard, Riqui, Risa, Risardas, Ritch, Ritchie, Ritchy, Rocco, Rolli, Rostik, Rostislav, Rostya, Rye, Rysio, Slava, Slavik, Slavka.

Meaning: 'ruler' and 'hard' (Germanic).

Rider

Variants and diminutives: Rid, Riddle, Ridgeley, Ridley, Ryder, Ryerson.

Meaning: 'rider', 'knight' or 'cavalryman' (Old English).

Ridley

Variants and diminutives: Rid, Riddle, Rigeley.

Meaning: 'wood-cleared' or 'reedy' and 'clearing' (Old English); derived from an English family name, in turn derived from a number of English place names.

Riley

Variants and diminutives: Reilly, Reyly, Ryley.

Meaning: 'descendant of the valiant one' (Irish Gaelic); 'rye' and 'clearing' (Old English); derived from a British family name.

Riordan

Variants and diminutives: Rearden, Riorden.

Meaning: 'descendent of the royal bard' (Irish Gaelic); derived from an Irish family name.

Ripley

Variants and diminutives: Lee, Leigh, Rip, Ripp.

Meaning: 'strip-like' and 'wood' or 'clearing' (Old English); derived from an English family name, in turn derived from a number of English place names.

River

Variants and diminutives: Rivers, Riverton, Rivington.

Meaning: 'river bank' (Latin). Also a girl's name.

Roald

Variants and diminutives: Roderick.

Meaning: 'renowned' and 'ruler' (Germanic) as a Norwegian variant of Roderick.

Robert

Variants and diminutives: Bert, Bertie, Berto, Berty, Bob, Bobbi, Bobbie, Bobby, Bobek, Dob, Dobb, Dobbs, Dobs, Dobson, Hab, Hob, Hobs, Hobson, Hodge, Hodges, Hopkins, Hopson, Hutchins, Nob, Nobbie, Nobby, Rab, Rabbie, Rabby, Raibeart, Ralf, Riobard, Rip, Rob, Roban, Robard, Robart, Robb, Robben, Robbi, Robbie, Robby, Rober, Robers, Roberto, Roberts, Robertson, Robers, Robi, Robin, Robinet, Robinson, Robson, Robyn, Roibeard, Rolf, Rori, Rosertas, Roy, Rubert, Ruberto, Rudbert, Rupert, Ruperto, Ruprecht, Tito.
Meaning: 'fame' and 'bright' (Germanic).

Robin

Variants and diminutives: Hob, Rob, Robbie, Robby, Robert, Robinet, Robinson, Robyn.
Meaning: 'fame' and 'bright' (Germanic) as a diminutive of Robert. Also a girl's name.

Rocco

Variants and diminutives: Rocky.
Meaning: 'rock' (Italian).

Rocky

Variants and diminutives: Rocco.
Meaning: 'rocky' (English). Also an anglicised version of Rocco.

Roderick

Variants and diminutives: Broderick, Drigo, Eric, Erick, Gigo, Rhodric, Rhydderch, Rick, Rickie, Ricky, Roald, Rod, Rodd, Roddie, Roddy, Roden, Roderic, Roderich, Roderigo, Rodi, Rodito, Rodrego, Rodrich, Rodrick, Rodrigo, Rodrique, Rori, Roric, Rory, Ruaraidh, Rurich, Rurik, Ruy.
Meaning: 'renowned' and 'ruler' (Germanic).

Rodney

Variants and diminutives: Rod, Rodd, Roddie, Roddy.
Meaning: 'Hroda's' or 'reed' and 'island' (Old English); derived from an English family name, in turn derived from a number of English place names.

Rodrigo

Variants and diminutives: Drigo, Rod, Roddie, Roddy, Roderick, Roderigo, Rodito, Rodrego.
Meaning: 'renowned' and 'ruler' (Germanic) as a Spanish variant of Roderick.

Rogan

Meaning: 'red-haired' (Irish and Scots Gaelic).

Roger

Variants and diminutives: Dodge, Gerek, Hodge, Rod, Rodge, Rodger, Rodgers, Rog, Roge, Rogelio, Rogerio, Rogerios, Rogers, Rogier, Roj, Rozer, Rudiger, Rüdiger, Rugero, Ruggerio, Ruggero, Rutger, Ruttger.
Meaning: 'fame' and 'spear' (Germanic).

Rohan

Variants and diminutives: Rowan.
Meaning: 'sandalwood' (Hindi); 'mountain ash' (Old Norse) or 'red' (Irish Gaelic) as a variant of Rowan.

Roland

Variants and diminutives: Lando, Lorand, Lorant, Olo, Orland, Orlando, Orlo, Rolando, Roldan, Rolek, Rolla, Rollan, Rolland, Rollen, Rollin, Rollins, Rollo, Rollon, Rolly, Rolon, Roly, Rowe, Rowland, Rudland, Ruland.
Meaning: 'fame' and 'land' (Germanic).

Rolf

Variants and diminutives: Ralf, Rolfe, Rollo, Rolph, Rolphe, Roul, Roulf, Rudolf, Rudolph.
Meaning: 'fame' and 'wolf' (Germanic) as a German and Scandinavian variant of Rudolf (Rudolph).

Rollo

Variants and diminutives: Rolf, Rolly, Rolon, Roul, Rudolf, Rudolph.
Meaning: 'fame' and 'wolf' (Germanic) as a variant of Rolf (Rudolph).

Romain

Variants and diminutives: Roman, Romano, Romeo, Romulus.
Meaning: 'of Rome' (French).

Roman

Variants and diminutives: Mancho, Romain, Romano, Romao, Romarico.
Meaning: 'of Rome' (Latin). A male version of Roma.

Romeo

Variants and diminutives: Romain, Romallus, Roman, Romanus, Romao, Rommie, Romney, Romolo, Romulus.
Meaning: 'of Rome' (French). A male version of Roma.

Romulus

Variants and diminutives: Quirinus, Romain, Romeo, Romolo, Romulo, Rómulo.
Meaning: uncertain; possibly 'strength' (Latin); derived from the name of the co-founder of Rome in Roman mythology.

Ronald

Variants and diminutives: Naldo, Raghnall, Rainald, Ranald, Ranaldo, Raynaldo, Reginald, Reinaldo, Renaldo, Rey, Reynaldo, Reynold, Rinhaldo, Roald, Ron, Ronel, Ronello, Roni, Ronnie, Ronny, Roone.
Meaning: 'advice' or 'might' and 'power' (Germanic) as a Scottish variant of Reynold.

Ronan

Variants and diminutives: Rónán.
Meaning: 'little seal' (Irish Gaelic).

Rory

Variants and diminutives: Roderick, Ruadidhri, Ruairi, Ruari, Ruaridh, Rurik.
Meaning: 'red' (Scottish and Irish Gaelic) as an anglicised form of Ruaridh (Scots Gaelic) and Ruairi (Irish Gaelic).

Ross

Variants and diminutives:
Roosevelt, Roscoe, Rosey, Rosie, Rosano, Rosse, Rossie, Rossy, Roswald, Royce.
Meaning: 'cape' or 'promontory' (Scots Gaelic); 'wood' (Scottish and Irish Gaelic); 'moor' (Cornish and Welsh); 'horse' or 'fame' (Germanic) or 'rose' (Latin) as a male version of Rose.

Rowan

Variants and diminutives: Rohan, Rooney, Rowen, Rowney.
Meaning: 'mountain ash' (Old Norse); 'red' (Irish Gaelic). Also a girl's name.

Roy

Variants and diminutives: Deroy, Elroy, Leroy, Loe, Ray, Rey, Roi, Royal, Royce, Roye, Royle, Royston.
Meaning: 'red' (Scots Gaelic); 'king' (Old French).

Rudolph

Variants and diminutives: Dodek, Dolf, Dolfe, Dolfi, Dolph, Ralph, Raoul, Raul, Rezso, Rodolfo, Rodolph, Rodolphe, Rodolpho, Rodulfo, Rolf, Rolfe, Rollo, Rolo, Rolph, Roul, Ruda, Rude, Rudek, Rudi, Rudie, Rudolf, Rudolfo, Rudolfs, Rudy, Rufo, Rutz.

Meaning: 'fame' and 'wolf' (Germanic).

Rudyard

Variants and diminutives: Rudd, Ruddie, Ruddy, Rudel, Rudi, Rudy, Rutledge, Rutter.
Meaning: 'red' and 'pole' (Germanic).

Rufus

Variants and diminutives: Rufe, Rush, Rushkin, Russ, Rusty.
Meaning: 'red' (Latin).

Rupert

Variants and diminutives: Robert, Rubert, Ruberto, Rudbert, Rupe, Ruperto, Ruprecht.
Meaning: 'fame' and 'bright' (Germanic) as a German variant of Robert.

Russell

Variants and diminutives: Rosario, Rus, Russ, Russel, Rustie, Rustin, Rusty.
Meaning: 'red-haired' or 'red-faced' (Old French).

Ryan

Variants and diminutives: Rian, Ryen, Ryon.
Meaning: uncertain; possibly 'little king' or 'descendant of a worshipper of Riaghan' (Irish Gaelic), Riaghan referring to a water deity; derived from an Irish family name.

Sacha

Variants and diminutives: Alexander, Sasha.
Meaning: 'defender of men' or 'warrior' (Greek) as a Russian diminutive of Alexander. Also a girl's name (generally Sasha).

Sacheverell

Variants and diminutives: Sach, Sacheverall.
Meaning: 'kid's' and 'leap' (Old French); derived from an English family name, in turn derived from the French place name Sault-Chevreuil.

Sakima

Meaning: 'king' (Native American).

Salim

Variants and diminutives: Saleem.
Meaning: 'peace' or 'safe' (Arabic).

Salvador

Variants and diminutives: Sal, Sallie, Sally, Salvator, Salvatore, Sauveur.
Meaning: 'saviour' (Latin).

Samir
Variants and diminutives: Zamir.
Meaning: 'entertainment' (Arabic).

Samson
Variants and diminutives: Sam, Sami,
Samm, Sammie, Sammy, Sampson, Sams,
Samy, Sansao, Sansom, Sanson, Sansone,
Sansum, Shem, Simson.
Meaning: 'sun' (Hebrew).

Samuel
Variants and diminutives: Sahm, Sam,
Samaru, Sami, Samko, Samm, Sammel,
Sammie, Sammy, Samo, Samouel, Samu,
Samuele, Samuelis, Samuil, Samvel,
Samy, Sawyl, Schmuel, Sem, Shem,
Shemuel, Somhairle, Uel, Zamiel.
Meaning: 'asked of God', 'heard by God'
or 'name of God' (Hebrew).

Sandy
Variants and diminutives: Alexander,
Sandee, Sandi, Sandie.
Meaning: 'defender of men' or 'warrior'
(Greek) as a diminutive of Alexander
(and, as a girl's name, also of Alexandra).

Santiago
Variants and diminutives: Antiago,
Chago, Chano, Sandiago, Sandiego,
Saniago, Tago, Vego.
Meaning: 'Saint James' (Spanish), James
(Jacob) meaning 'supplanter' (Hebrew).

Santo
Variants and diminutives: Santos.
Meaning: 'holy' (Latin); 'saint'
(Portuguese and Spanish). A male
version of Santa.

Saul
Variants and diminutives: Paul, Saulo,
Shaul, Sol, Sollie, Solly, Zollie, Zolly.
Meaning: 'prayed for' or 'asked for'
(Hebrew).

Saxon
Variants and diminutives: Sasanach,
Sass, Sasunn, Sax, Saxe.
Meaning: 'of the sea', 'of the dagger' or
'of the short sword' (Germanic); derived
from the name of the western Germanic
tribe. Also a girl's name.

Scott
Variants and diminutives: Scot, Scoti,
Scotti, Scottie, Scotty.
Meaning: 'a Scot', 'Scots' or 'Scottish'
(English).

Seamus
Variants and diminutives: Hamish,
Séamas, Seumas, Seumus, Seusmas,
Shamus, Shay, Shaymus.
Meaning: 'supplanter' (Hebrew) as an
Irish Gaelic variant of James (Jacob).

Sean
Variants and diminutives: Eoin, Séan,
Shane, Shanen, Shannon, Shanon,
Shaughn, Shaun, Shawn, Shoon.
Meaning: 'God has favoured', 'God is
gracious' or 'God is merciful' (Hebrew) as
an Irish Gaelic variant of John.

Sebastian
Variants and diminutives: Basti,
Bastian, Bastiano, Bastiao, Bastien,
Bastion, Seb, Sebastiao, Sebastiano,
Sebastien, Sebo, Steb.
Meaning: 'venerable' or 'from Sebastia'
(Greek), Sebastia being a city in the
ancient kingdom of Pontus, in Asia
Minor.

Segel
Meaning: 'treasure' (Hebrew).

Selwyn
Variants and diminutives: Selwin, Silas, Silvanus, Silvester, Win, Winnie, Winny, Wyn, Wynn.
Meaning: uncertain; possibly 'sylvan' or 'of the woods' (Latin) as an Old English variant of Silvanus; possibly 'wild' or 'savage' (Old French); possibly 'hall' or 'house' and 'friend' (Old English); possibly 'ardour' and 'fair' (Old Welsh); derived from a British family name.

Sepp
Variants and diminutives: Joseph.
Meaning: 'God will increase' (Hebrew) as a German diminutive of Joseph.

Septimus
Variants and diminutives: Sep.
Meaning: 'seventh' (Latin). A male version of Septima.

Serge
Variants and diminutives: Cergio, Checho, Checo, Serg, Sergai, Sergei, Sergeo, Sergey, Sergeyka, Sergi, Sergie, Sergio, Sergiu, Sergius, Sergiusz, Sergo, Sergunya, Serhiy, Serhiyko, Serjio, Serzh, Sewek, Syarhey, Zergio.
Meaning: uncertain; possibly 'silk' (Greek).

Seth
Meaning: uncertain; possibly 'to appoint', 'to settle' or 'compensation' (Hebrew).

Sextus
Meaning: 'sixth' (Latin).

Seymour
Variants and diminutives: Seymor, Seymore.
Meaning: 'Saint-Maur' (Old French); derived from an English family name, in turn derived from a number of French place names named for Saint Maur (or Maurus), Maur meaning 'Moorish' or 'African' (Latin) as a diminutive of Maurice.

Shane
Variants and diminutives: Sean, Shaine, Shanen, Shannon, Shanon, Shaughn, Shaun, Shawn, Shayn, Shayne, Shoon.
Meaning: 'God has favoured', 'God is gracious' or 'God is merciful' (Hebrew) as an anglicised version of Sean, in turn an Irish Gaelic variant of John.

Sharif
Meaning: 'honest' or 'noble' (Arabic).

Shaun
Variants and diminutives: Sean, Shane, Shaughn, Shawn, Shonn, Shoon.
Meaning: 'God has favoured', 'God is gracious' or 'God is merciful' (Hebrew) as an anglicised version of Sean, in turn an Irish Gaelic variant of John.

Shaw
Meaning: 'small wood', 'thicket' or 'copse' (Old English); derived from an English family name, in turn derived from a number of English place names.

Sheldon

Variants and diminutives: Shel, Shelden, Shelley, Shelly, Shelton.
Meaning: 'steep' and 'valley' or 'flat-topped' and 'hill' (Old English); derived from an English family name, in turn derived from a number of English place names.

Shem

Variants and diminutives: Shammai, Shemuel.
Meaning: 'fame' or 'name' (Hebrew and Yiddish).

Sheridan

Variants and diminutives: Sheridon.
Meaning: uncertain; possibly 'descendant of Siridean', 'eternal' and 'treasure', 'peaceful' or 'wild' (Irish Gaelic);

derived from an Irish family name. Also a girl's name.

Sherman

Variants and diminutives: Sharman, Shearman, Sher, Shermann.
Meaning: 'shears' and 'man' (Old English); derived from an English family name.

Shing

Meaning: 'victorious' (Chinese).

Shiva

Variants and diminutives: Siv, Siva.
Meaning: 'the auspicious [one]' (Sanskrit); derived from the name of the god of destruction and personal destiny, one of the three leading gods in Hindu mythology.

Sholto

Variants and diminutives: Sioltaich
Meaning: 'sower' (Scots Gaelic).

Sidney

Variants and diminutives: Cid, Cyd, Cydney, Si, Sid, Sidon, Sidonio, Syd, Sydney, Sydny.
Meaning: 'wide' and 'island' or 'well-irrigated land' or 'south of the water' (Old English) when derived from an English family name, in turn derived from a number of English place names; 'Saint-Denis' (Old French), when derived from the name of the French town, in turn named for Saint Denys, Denys (Dennis) meaning 'deity of the Nysa' (Greek). Also a girl's name as a diminutive of Sidony.

Siegfried

Variants and diminutives: Fredo, Friedl, Seifert, Seifried, Siffre, Sig, Sigefriedo, Sigfrid, Sigfrido, Sigfried, Sigfroi, Siggi, Siggy, Sigifredo, Siguefredo, Sigurd, Sigvard, Singefrid, Siurt, Szigfrid, Zigfrid, Zigfrids, Zygfryd, Zygi.
Meaning: 'victory' and 'peace' (Germanic).

Sigmund

Variants and diminutives: Siegmond, Siegmund, Sig, Siggi, Siggy, Sigismondo, Sigismund, Sigsmond.
Meaning: 'victory' and 'protection' (Germanic).

Sigurd
Variants and diminutives: Siegfried.
Meaning: 'victory' and 'guardian'
(Old Norse).

Silas
Variants and diminutives: Selwyn,
Silo, Silus, Silvanus, Silvester.
Meaning: 'sylvan' or 'of the woods'
(Latin) as a Greek variant of Silvanus;
'to borrow' (Aramaic); 'snub-nosed'
(Latin).

Silvanus
Variants and diminutives: Selwyn,
Silas, Silvain, Silvan, Silvano, Silvanus,
Silvester, Silvio, Sly, Sy, Sylvan,
Sylvanus, Sylveanus, Sylvester.
Meaning: 'sylvan' or 'of the woods'
(Latin).

Silvester
Variants and diminutives: Selwyn,
Silas, Silvain, Silvan, Silvano, Silvanus,
Silvestio, Silvestre, Silvestro, Silvio, Sly,
Sy, Sylvan, Sylvanus, Sylveanus,
Sylvester, Sylvestre, Vesta, Vester.
Meaning: 'sylvan' or 'of the woods'
(Latin) as a variant of Silvanus.

Simeon
Variants and diminutives: Imon,
Shimeon, Shimone, Si, Sim, Simen,
Simion, Simmy, Simon.

Meaning: 'God has heard', 'listening'
or 'little hyena' (Hebrew).

Simon
Variants and diminutives: Cimon,
Imon, Samein, Semon, Shimon,
Shimone, Si, Silas, Sim, Simao, Simen,
Simeon, Simi, Simie, Simion, Simkin,
Simmie, Simmy, Simone, Simp,
Simpson, Sims, Sy, Symon, Ximenes,
Ximenez.
Meaning: 'God has heard', 'listening'
or 'little hyena' (Hebrew) as a variant
of Simeon; 'snub-nosed' (Greek).

Sinclair
Variants and diminutives: Clarence,
Sinclaire, Sinclar.
Meaning: 'Saint-Clair' (Old English),
Clair (Clare) meaning 'clear', 'bright' or
'famous' (Latin); derived from a
Scottish family name, in turn derived
from a French place name named for
a Norman martyr.

Skelly
Variants and diminutives: Skelley,
Skellie.
Meaning: 'story-teller' (Irish Gaelic).

Solomon
Variants and diminutives:
Lasimonne, Salaman, Salamen,
Salamon, Salamun, Salaun, Salman,

Salmen, Salmon, Salo, Saloman,
Salome, Salomo, Salomon,
Salomonas, Salomone, Selim,
Selman, Shelomo, Shelomoh,
Shlomo, Sol, Solaman, Sollie, Solly,
Solmon, Solom Soloman, Suleiman,
Zalman, Zalmon, Zelmen, Zelmo,
Zollie, Zolly.
Meaning: 'peace' (Hebrew).

Spencer
Variants and diminutives: Spence,
Spens, Spense, Spenser.
Meaning: 'butler', 'house steward' or
'controller of the spence [larder or
buttery]' (Old French); derived from
an English family name.

Spike
Meaning: 'sharp point', 'ear' or 'tuft'
(Latin).

Spiro
Meaning: 'I breathe', 'I exist' or 'I am
inspired' (Latin).

Stafford
Variants and diminutives: Ford,
Staff, Stanford.
Meaning: 'landing place' or 'staithe',
'stony' or 'steers' and 'ford' '(Old
English); derived from an English
family name, in turn derived from a
number of English place names.

Stanford
Variants and diminutives: Ford, Stafford, Stan, Stamford, Standford.
Meaning: 'stony' and 'ford' (Old English); derived from an English family name, in turn derived from a number of English place names.

Stanislas
Variants and diminutives: Estanislao, Estanislau, Lao, Slava, Slavik, Slavka, Stan, Stana, Stando, Stane, Stanislao, Stanislau, Stanislaus, Stanislav, Stanislaw, Stanislus, Stanni, Stanny, Stano, Stas, Stashko, Stasiek, Stasio, Staska, Tano, Tanix, Tilo.
Meaning: 'camp' and 'glory' (Old Slavic).

Stanley
Variants and diminutives: Stan, Stanfield, Stanleigh, Stanly, Stanton.
Meaning: 'stony' and 'clearing' or 'field' (Old English); derived from an English family name, in turn derived from a number of English place names.

Stephen
Variants and diminutives: Astevan, Este, Esteban, Esteben, Estefan, Estefon, Estes, Estevan, Estevao, Estiban, Estien, Estienne, Estiennes, Estifa, Estovan, Estvan, Etienne, Etiennes, Istevan, Isti, Istvan, Stamos, Stavros, Steenie, Stef, Stefan, Stefano, Stefanos, Stefans, Steffan, Steffel, Steffen, Stefos, Stepan, Stenya, Stepan, Stepanya, Steph, Stephan, Stéphane, Stephanos, Stephanus, Stepka, Stevan, Steve, Steven, Stevie, Stevy, Stiofan, Tapani, Teb, Teppo, Tiennot.
Meaning: 'crown' (Greek).

Stirling
Variants and diminutives: Sterling.
Meaning: uncertain; possibly 'dwelling of Melyn' (Old Welsh); possibly 'little star' (Middle English); derived from a Scottish family name, in turn derived from the name of a Scottish town.

Stuart
Variants and diminutives: Steuart, Stew, Steward, Stewart, Stu.
Meaning: 'steward' or 'seneshal' (Old English); derived from a Scottish family name.

Sullivan
Variants and diminutives: Sullavan, Sullevan, Sullie, Sully.
Meaning: 'descendant of' and 'the black person' or 'the hawk-eyed person' (Irish Gaelic); derived from an Irish family name.

Sven
Variants and diminutives: Svarne, Svend, Swen.
Meaning: 'boy' (Old Norse).

Swithin
Variants and diminutives: Swithun.
Meaning: 'strong' (Old English).

Tabbai
Variants and diminutives: Tab, Tabb, Tabbie, Tabby, Tavi.
Meaning: 'good' (Aramaic).

Tabib
Meaning: 'doctor' (Turkish).

Tabor
Variants and diminutives: Tab, Tabb, Tabbie, Tabby, Tabor.
Meaning: 'drum' (Persian).

Taffy
Variants and diminutives: Daffy, Dafyd, Daffyd, David, Taafe, Tab, Tafydd, Taffy, Tavi.
Meaning: 'beloved' or 'friend' (Hebrew) as a Welsh diminutive of David.

Tahir

Variants and diminutives: Taher.
Meaning: 'pure' (Arabic).

Taj

Variants and diminutives: Tahj.
Meaning: 'crown' (Urdu and Arabic). A
male version of Taja.

Tal

Variants and diminutives: Talor.
Meaning: 'dew' (Hebrew). Also a girl's
name.

Talbot

Variants and diminutives: Tal, Talbert,
Tallie, Tally.
Meaning: uncertain; possibly 'dale' or
'valley' and 'command' or 'offer'
(Germanic); possibly 'cut' and 'bundle' or
'faggot' (Old French); derived from an
English family name, in turn derived
from a number of English place names.

Talib

Meaning: 'seeker' (Arabic).

Taliesin

Meaning: 'shining' or 'radiant' and
'brow' (Welsh).

Talman

Variants and diminutives: Tal, Tallie,
Tally, Talmon.
Meaning: 'to oppress' or 'to injure'
(Aramaic).

Talor

Variants and diminutives: Tal.
Meaning: 'morning dew' (Hebrew). Also
a girl's name.

Tam

Variants and diminutives: Tammie,
Tammy, Thomas.
Meaning: 'twin' (Aramaic) as a Scottish
diminutive of Thomas; 'eighth child'
(Vietnamese).

Tamir

Variants and diminutives: Timur.
Meaning: 'date palm' or 'palm tree'
(Hebrew) as a male version of Tamar.

Tancred

Meaning: 'think' and 'advice' (Germanic).

Tanner

Variants and diminutives: Tan, Tann,
Tanney, Tannie, Tanny.
Meaning: 'tanner [a tanner of hides or
skins]' (Old English); derived from an
English family name.

Tariq

Variants and diminutives: Tareek,
Tarick, Tarik.
Meaning: 'knocker at the door' (Arabic).

Taro

Meaning: 'first son' or 'big boy'
(Japanese).

Tarquin

Variants and diminutives: Quin, Tarq.
Meaning: uncertain; possibly 'of
Tarquinni' (Latin), Tarquinni being an
ancient Etruscan town; derived from the
Roman family name Tarquinius.

Tate

Variants and diminutives: Tait, Taite,
Tatum, Tayte.
Meaning: uncertain; possibly 'windy' or
'garrulous' (Native American); possibly
'cheerful' (Old Norse), 'dear', 'happy', 'dice',
'hilltop', 'tress of hair', 'father' or 'teat' (Old
English) when derived from an English
family name.

Tavi

Variants and diminutives: David, Tabbai, Tov, Tovi, Tuvia.
Meaning: 'good' (Aramaic); 'beloved' or 'friend' (Hebrew) as an Israeli diminutive of David.

Tavish

Variants and diminutives: Tammas, Tav, Tavis, Tevis, Thomas.
Meaning: 'twin' (Aramaic) as a Scottish variant of Thomas.

Tayib

Meaning: 'delicate' or 'good' (Arabic).

Taylor

Variants and diminutives: Tailer, Tailor, Tayler, Taylour.
Meaning: 'tailor' or 'cutter' (Old French); derived from an English family name. Also a girl's name.

Teague

Variants and diminutives: Tadhg, Taig, Taogh, Teagan, Tegan, Teige, Teigue, Thady.
Meaning: 'poet' or 'philosopher' (Irish Gaelic); 'lovely' (Welsh) as a male version of Tegan.

Ted

Variants and diminutives: Edmund, Edward, Tedd, Teddie, Teddy,

Theobald, Theodore, Theodoric.
Meaning: 'happiness' or 'riches' and 'guardian' (Old English) as a diminutive of Edward; 'happiness' or 'riches' and 'protector' (Old English) as a diminutive of Edmund; 'God's gift' (Greek) as a diminutive of Theodore. Also a diminutive of other names beginning with 'Ed-' or 'Theo-'.

Teman

Variants and diminutives: Temani.
Meaning: 'right side' or 'south' (Hebrew).

Terence

Variants and diminutives: Tel, Telly, Terencio, Terrance, Terrel, Terrence, Terris, Terry, Terryal, Toirdhealbhach, Torn, Torrance, Torrence, Torrey, Tory, Turlough.
Meaning: uncertain; possibly 'to wear out' or 'to polish' (Latin) when derived from the Roman family name Terentius; 'initiator of an idea' (Irish Gaelic).

Terry

Variants and diminutives: Tel, Telly, Terence, Terrel, Terris, Terryal, Theodoric, Torry, Tory.
Meaning: 'people' and 'ruler' (Germanic) as a diminutive of Theodoric; possibly 'to wear out' or

'to polish' (Latin) or 'initiator of an idea' (Irish Gaelic) as a diminutive of Terence. Also a girl's name as a diminutive of Theresa.

Tertius

Variants and diminutives: Tert, Tertie, Terty.
Meaning: 'third' (Latin). A male version of Tertia.

Tex

Variants and diminutives: Texan.
Meaning: 'Texan' (English), referring to the US state of Texas.

Thaddeus

Variants and diminutives: Faddei, Fadey, Jude, Tad, Tadd, Taddeo, Taddeus, Taddeusz, Taddy, Tade, Tadeas, Tadek, Tadeo, Tades, Tadey, Tadzio, Thad, Thadd, Thaddaeus, Thaddaus, Thaddeo, Thaddy, Thadee, Thadeus, Thady, Theodore.
Meaning: 'valiant' (Hebrew); 'God's gift' (Greek) as a variant of Theodore.

Thane

Variants and diminutives: Thain, Thaine, Thayne.
Meaning: 'thane' or 'tenant by military service', 'chieftain of a Scottish clan' or 'monarch's baron' (Old English); derived from a British

family name, in turn derived from various ranks of lesser nobility.

Theo

Variants and diminutives: Theobald, Theodore, Theodoric, Theophilus.
Meaning: 'God' (Greek); 'God's gift' (Greek) as a diminutive of Theodore; 'people' and 'bold' (Germanic) as a diminutive of Theobald; 'people' and 'ruler' (Germanic) as a diminutive of Theodoric; 'God-loving' (Greek) as a diminutive of Theophilus. Also a male version of Thea.

Theobald

Variants and diminutives: Tebald, Ted, Tedd, Teddie, Teddy, Thebault, Theo, Theodore, Theophilus, Thibaud, Thibault, Thibaut, Tibald, Tibbald, Tibold, Tiebout, Toiboid, Tybalt.
Meaning: 'people' and 'bold' (Germanic).

Theodore

Variants and diminutives: Bohdan, Dorek, Fedar, Fedinka, Fedir, Fedor, Fedya, Feodor, Feodore, Fyoder, Tad, Tadd, Taddeo, Taddeus, Taddeusz, Tadeo, Ted, Tedd, Teddie, Teddy, Tedik, Telly, Teodomiro, Teodor, Teodorek, Teodoro, Teodus, Teos, Tewdor, Tewdwr, Thad, Thaddaus, Thadeus, Thaddeus, Thaddy, Thady, Theo, Theobald, Theodor,

Theodoric, Theodoro, Theodosiuus, Theophilus, Tivadar, Tod, Todd, Todor, Todos, Tolek, Tudor.
Meaning: 'God's gift' (Greek).

Theodoric

Variants and diminutives: Derek, Derk, Derrick, Deryck, Deryk, Dieter, Dietrich, Dirk, Ric, Rick, Rickie, Ricky, Ted, Tedd, Teddie, Teddy, Teodorico, Terrie, Terry, Theo, Theobald, Theodore, Theophilus, Thierry.
Meaning: 'people' and 'ruler' (Germanic).

Theophilus

Variants and diminutives: Theo, Theobald, Theodore, Theodoric, Théophile, Theophillus.
Meaning: 'God-loving' (Greek).

Theron

Variants and diminutives: Tharon.
Meaning: 'hunter' or 'wild beast' (Greek).

Thomas

Variants and diminutives: Chumo, Foma, Fomka, Formo, Masaccio, Maso, Massey, Slawek, Tam, Tamas, Tameas, Tamlane, Tammany, Tammen, Tammie, Tammy, Tamsen, Tamson, Tavis, Tavish, Tevis, Tevish, Thom, Thoma, Thompson, Thurmas, Tip, Tom, Tomas, Tomás, Tomaso, Tomasso, Tomcio, Tome, Tomek,

Tomelis, Tomi, Tomie, Tomislaw, Tomm, Tommie, Tommy, Tomos, Toomas, Tuomas, Tuomo.
Meaning: 'twin' (Aramaic).

Thor

Variants and diminutives: Thurston, Tor, Torquil.
Meaning: 'the thunderer' (Old Norse); derived from the name from the god of thunder in Norse mythology.

Thorley

Variants and diminutives: Thornton.
Meaning: 'thorn' and 'wood' or 'clearing' (Old English); derived from an English family name, in turn derived from a number of English place names.

Thornton

Variants and diminutives: Thorley, Thorn, Thorndike, Thorne, Thornie, Thorny.
Meaning: 'thorn' and 'place' or 'settlement' (Old English); derived from an English family name, in turn derived from a number of English place names.

Thorpe

Variants and diminutives: Thorp.
Meaning: 'farm' or 'village' (Old Norse and Old English); derived from an English family name, in turn derived from a number of English place names.

Thurston

Variants and diminutives: Stan, Thor, Thurstan, Thursting, Torquil.
Meaning: 'Thor's', Thor referring to the thunder god of Norse mythology, and 'stone' or 'farm' (Old English); derived from an English family name, in turn derived from an English place name.

Tiernan

Variants and diminutives: Tiarnan, Tierney.
Meaning: 'son of the lord' (Irish Gaelic); derived from an Irish family name.

Tiger

Variants and diminutives: Tige, Tigger.
Meaning: 'tiger' (Greek); derived from the common name of the *Panthera tigris* genus of striped big cat.

Tilden

Variants and diminutives: Tilford, Tilton.
Meaning: 'convenient' and 'valley' (Old English); derived from an English family name, in turn derived from an English place name.

Timothy

Variants and diminutives: Tim, Tima, Timka, Timkin, Timmie, Timmy, Timo, Timofei, Timofey, Timok, Timon, Timot, Timotei, Timoteo, Timoteus, Timothe, Timothee, Timotheos, Timotheus, Tiomoid, Tisha, Tishka, Tymek, Tymon.
Meaning: 'in honour of God' (Greek).

Tirion

Variants and diminutives: Tyrion.
Meaning: 'gentle' and 'kind' (Welsh).

Titus

Variants and diminutives: Titan, Tite, Titek, Tito, Titos, Toto, Totos, Tytus.
Meaning: uncertain; possibly 'giant', 'day' or 'sun' (Greek); derived from a Roman name.

Tivon

Variants and diminutives: Tibon, Tiv, Tivvie, Tivvy.
Meaning: 'nature-lover' (Hebrew). A male version of Tivona.

Tobias

Variants and diminutives: Tavi, Tivon, Tobe, Tobey, Tobiah, Tobie, Tobin, Tobit, Toby, Tobye, Tobyn.
Meaning: 'God is good' (Hebrew).

Toby

Variants and diminutives: Tobe, Tobey, Tobiah, Tobias, Tobie, Tobin, Tobit, Tobye, Tobyn.
Meaning: 'God is good' (Hebrew) as a diminutive of Tobias.

Todd

Variants and diminutives: Reynard, Tad, Tod, Toddie, Toddy.
Meaning: 'fox' (Middle English); derived from an English family name.

Tom

Variants and diminutives: Thomas, Tomas, Tomás, Tomlin, Tommie, Tommy.
Meaning: 'twin' (Aramaic) as a diminutive of Thomas.

Tony

Variants and diminutives: Antony, Toni, Tonio.
Meaning: 'flourishing' (Greek) or 'without price' (Latin) as a diminutive of Anthony.

Torquil

Variants and diminutives: Thor, Thurston, Torcal, Torcul.
Meaning: 'Thor [the Norse god of thunder]' and 'cauldron' (Old Norse).

Townsend

Variants and diminutives: Town, Townend, Townie, Townshend.
Meaning: 'town' and 'end' (Old English); derived from an English family name.

Trahern

Variants and diminutives: Traherne, Tray.
Meaning: 'excellent' and 'iron' (Welsh).

Travis

Variants and diminutives: Traver, Travers, Travus.
Meaning: 'tollgate', 'tollbridge' or 'crossing' (Old French); derived from an English family name.

Tremaine

Variants and diminutives: Tremain, Tremayne, Trey.
Meaning: 'farm' or 'place' and 'of the stone' (Cornish); derived from a Cornish family name, in turn derived from a Cornish place name.

Trevor

Variants and diminutives: Tref, Trefor, Trev, Trevar, Trever.
Meaning: 'village' and 'big' (Welsh); derived from a Welsh family name, in turn derived from two Welsh place names.

Trey

Variants and diminutives: Tremaine.
Meaning: 'third' (Middle English); 'farm' or 'place' and 'of the stone' (Cornish) as a diminutive of Tremaine.

Tristan

Variants and diminutives: Drest, Driscoll, Durst, Drystan, Tris, Trist, Tristram, Tristrem, Trys, Tryst, Trystan, Trystram.
Meaning: 'noise' or 'tumult' (Celtic) or 'sad' (Old French) as a French, German and Welsh variant of Tristram.

Tristram

Variants and diminutives: Drest, Driscoll, Drust, Drystan, Tris, Trist, Tristan, Tristrem, Tryst, Tryst, Trystan, Trystram.
Meaning: 'noise' or 'tumult' (Celtic) or 'sad' (Old French) as an English variant of Tristan.

Troy

Variants and diminutives: Troilus.
Meaning: 'Troyes' (Old French) when derived from an English and French family name, in turn derived from a French place name; 'son of the footsoldier' (Irish Gaelic). Also a girl's name.

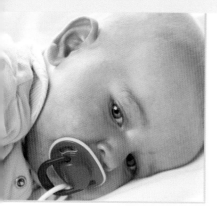

Tudor

Variants and diminutives: Tewdwr, Theodore, Theodoric, Tudur, Tudyr.
Meaning: 'people' and 'ruler' (Germanic) as a Welsh variant of Theodoric; 'God's gift' (Greek) as a Welsh variant of Theodore; derived from a Welsh family name.

Tyler

Variants and diminutives: Tiler, Ty, Tye.
Meaning: 'tiler' or 'tile-maker' (Old English); derived from an English family name.

Tyrone

Variants and diminutives: Ty, Tye, Tyron.
Meaning: 'Eoghan's [or Euen, Eugene,

Ewan or Owen's] country' (Irish Gaelic); derived from the name of a county in Northern Ireland.

Tyson

Variants and diminutives: Tie, Ty, Tye, Tysen, Tysone.
Meaning: 'firebrand' (Old French); derived from an English family name. Also a girl's name.

Udell

Variants and diminutives: Del, Dell, Udale, Udall.
Meaning: 'yew' and 'valley' (Old English); derived from an English family name, in turn derived from an English place name.

Ulim

Variants and diminutives: Ulem.
Meaning: 'wise' or 'learned' (Arabic). A male version of Ulima.

Ulric

Variants and diminutives: Alaric, Ric, Rich, Richie, Richy, Rick, Ricki, Rickie, Ricky, Ulf, Ulfa, Ull, Ulrich, Ulrick, Ulu, Wolfrid, Wolfrich, Wulfric, Wulfrich.
Meaning: 'wolf' and 'ruler' (Germanic).

Ultimus

Variants and diminutives: Ult, Ulti, Ultimo, Ulty.
Meaning: 'furthest' or 'last ' (Latin). A male version of Ultima.

Ulysses

Variants and diminutives: Odysseus, Uileos, Ulick, Ulises, Uluxe.
Meaning: uncertain; possibly 'hater' (Greek) as a Latin version of Odysseus.

Umberto

Variants and diminutives: Bert, Berto, Humbert, Humberto, Umber.
Meaning: 'shade' (Latin); 'earth shadow' (Italian); 'home', 'warrior' or 'giant' and 'bright' (Germanic) as an Italian diminutive of Humberto (Humbert).

Upton

Meaning: 'upper' and 'farm' or 'place' (Old English); derived from an English family name, in turn derived from a number of English place names.

Uranus

Variants and diminutives: Ouranos.
Meaning: 'heaven' (Greek); derived from the name of the primeval sky god of Greek mythology. Also a male version of Urania.

Urban

Variants and diminutives: Orban,
Urbain, Urbaine, Urbane, Urbano,
Urbanus, Urvan.
Meaning: 'of the city' or 'citizen',
'polite', 'witty' or 'refined' (Latin).

Uri

Variants and diminutives: Uriah,
Urias, Urie, Uriel, Uriano, Yuri.
Meaning: 'light of God' (Hebrew) as
a diminutive of Uriah.

Uriah

Variants and diminutives: Uri,
Uriano, Urias, Urie, Uriel, Yuri.
Meaning: 'light of God' (Hebrew).

Urien

Variants and diminutives: Urian,
Uren, Uryan, Yurvan.
Meaning: 'town-born' or 'born into
privilege' (Old Welsh); derived from a
British family name.

Ursell

Variants and diminutives: Ursel,
Urshell.
Meaning: 'little bear' (Latin). Also a
male version of Ursula.

Uzi

Variants and diminutives: Uziel.
Meaning: 'my strength' (Hebrew).

Valentine

Variants and diminutives: Val, Vale,
Valentijn, Valentin, Valentinian,
Valentino, Valentinus, Valerius, Vallie.
Meaning: 'healthy' or 'vigorous'
(Latin). Also a girl's name.

Valerius

Variants and diminutives:
Valentine, Valerian, Valerio, Valery,
Vallie.
Meaning: 'to be healthy' or 'to be
vigorous' (Latin).

Van

Variants and diminutives: Vander,
Vann.
Meaning: 'God has favoured', 'God is
gracious' or 'God is merciful'
(Hebrew) as a diminutive of Ivan
(John); 'of' or 'from' (Dutch).

Vance

Variants and diminutives: Fance.
Meaning: 'of the fen' (Old English);
derived from an English family name.

Vane

Variants and diminutives: Fane,
Van, Vanne, Von.

Meaning: 'sanctuary temple' or
'cloth' (Latin); 'eager' or 'glad' (Old
English) when derived from an
English family name.

Varden

Variants and diminutives: Vardon,
Verdon, Verdin, Verduin, Verdon,
Verdun, Verdyn.
Meaning: 'green' and 'hill' or 'fort'
(Old French); derived from an English
family name, in turn derived from a
number of French place names.

Vassily

Variants and diminutives: Basil, Vas,
Vasil, Vasile, Vasilek, Vasili, Vasilis,
Vasily, Vassily, Vasya, Vasyl, Vazul,
William.
Meaning: 'kingly' or 'royal' (Greek) or
'war' (Irish Gaelic) as a Russian
variant of Basil; 'will' and 'helmet' or
'protection' (Germanic) as a Russian
variant of William.

Vaughan

Variants and diminutives: Vaughn,
Vaune, Vawn, Vawne, Von, Vonn,
Vonne.
Meaning: 'little' (Old Welsh).

Vere

Meaning: uncertain; possibly
'truthful' (Latin) or 'faith' (Russian) as

a male version of Vera; possibly 'a slave born in his [or her] master's house' or 'of spring' (Latin) as a male version of Verna; possibly 'alder tree' (Old French) as a variant of Vernon; derived from a French and English family name.

Vered

Meaning: 'rose' (Hebrew).

Vernon

Variants and diminutives: Lavern, Laverne, Laverno, Varney, Vern, Verne, Vernen, Vernice, Vernin, Vernn, Verrier. **Meaning:** 'alder tree' (Old French); derived from an English family name, in turn derived from a number of French place names.

Victor

Variants and diminutives: Vic, Vick, Victoir, Victorino, Victorio, Victuriano, Vika, Viktor, Vince, Vincent, Vitenka, Vitin, Vitka, Vito, Vitor, Vittore, Vittorio, Vitya, Wiktor, Witek. **Meaning:** 'victor' (Latin). Also male version of Victoria.

Vince

Variants and diminutives: Victor, Vin, Vincent. **Meaning:** 'conqueror' (Latin) as a diminutive of Vincent.

Vincent

Variants and diminutives: Bink,
Binkentios, Chenche, Enzo, Kesha,
Victor, Vika, Vikent, Vikenti, Vikesha,
Vin, Vince, Vincenc, Vincente,
Vincenz, Vicenso, Vinci, Vinco, Vine,
Vinicent, Vinn, Vinnie, Vinny, Vinsent,
Vinson, Vint, Wicek, Wicent, Wicus.
Meaning: 'conqueror' (Latin).

Virgil

Variants and diminutives: Verge,
Vergil, Vergit, Virge, Virgie, Virgilio.
Meaning: uncertain; derived from
the Roman family name Vergilius,
perhaps in turn derived from the
collective name of the Roman
goddesses of the Pleiades
constellation, the Vergiliae.

Vitas

Variants and diminutives: Vida,
Vidal, Viel, Vitalis, Vito, Vitus.
Meaning: 'life' (Latin). A male
version of Vita.

Vivian

Variants and diminutives: Bibiana,
Fithian, Phythian, Vivien, Vyvyan.
Meaning: 'living' (Latin); derived
from the Roman family name
Vivianus. Also a girl's name
(generally Vivien).

Vladimir

Variants and diminutives: Ladimir,
Ladislas, Ladislaw, Laidslaw,
Landislaus, Vladi, Vladko, Vladmir,
Vlady, Walter.
Meaning: 'prince of the world',
'mighty warrior' or 'army ruler' (Old
Slavonic).

Wade

Variants and diminutives: Wadell,
Wadsworth.
Meaning: uncertain; possibly
derived from the name of a hero of
English legend, Wada or Wade;
possibly 'at the ford' (Old English);
derived from an English family name,
in turn derived from an English place
name.

Waldemar

Variants and diminutives:
Valdemar, Wald, Waldo, Walter.
Meaning: 'power' or 'rule'
(Germanic).

Walden

Variants and diminutives: Wald,
Waldon.

Meaning: 'Welsh' or 'serfs' and 'valley'
(Old English); derived from an English
family name, in turn derived from a
number of English place names.

Waldo

Variants and diminutives: Wald,
Waldemar, Walter.
Meaning: 'power' or 'rule' (Germanic)
as a diminutive of Waldemar.

Walker

Variants and diminutives: Wal.
Meaning: 'fuller [of cloth]' (Old
English); derived from an English
family name.

Wallace

Variants and diminutives: Wal, Wall,
Wallache, Wallas, Wallie, Wallis, Wally,
Walsh, Welch, Welsh.
Meaning: 'Celt', 'Breton', 'Welshman'
or 'foreigner' (Old French) as a
Scottish variant of Wallis; derived
from an English family name.

Walter

Variants and diminutives: Dima,
Dimka, Gauther, Gauthier, Gautier,
Gualberto, Gualterio, Gualtiero,
Gutierre, Landislaus, Vacys, Valdemar,
Valter, Valters, Valtr, Vanda, Vandele,
Vladimir, Vladko, Volya, Vova, Vovka,

Wal, Wald, Waldemar, Walden, Waldo, Waldron, Walli, Wallie, Wally, Walt, Walther, Waltili, Waltr, Wat, Watkins, Watley, Watly, Watson, Wattie, Watty, Waud, Wilt, Wolli, Wollie, Wolly.
Meaning: 'power' or 'rule' and 'people' or 'army' (Germanic).

Wapi

Meaning: 'fortunate' (Native American).

Ward

Variants and diminutives: Warde, Warden, Winward, Wordon.
Meaning: 'watchman', 'protector' or 'guard' (Old English); derived from an English family name.

Warner

Variants and diminutives: Garnier, Warren, Warrener, Werner, Wernher.
Meaning: 'Warin's' or 'protector's' and 'army' or 'people' (Germanic); 'warrener' or 'keeper of the game preserve' (Old French) as a diminutive of Warrener; derived from an English family name.

Warren

Variants and diminutives: Varner, Vaney, Walena, Ware, Waring, Warner, Warrener.
Meaning: 'game preserve', 'wasteland' or 'sandy soil' (Gaulish) when derived from a French and English family name, in turn derived from name of the French town La Varenne; 'to protect' or 'to preserve' (Germanic).

Warwick

Variants and diminutives: Wick, Wickie, Wicky.
Meaning: 'dairy farm' and 'belonging to Wary's people', 'at the dam' or 'at the weir' (Old English); derived from an English family name, in turn derived from two English place names.

Washington

Variants and diminutives: Wash, Washburn.
Meaning: 'Wassa's kin's' and 'farm' or 'place' (Old English); derived from an English family name, in turn derived from two English place names.

Wat

Variants and diminutives: Walter, Watly, Wattie, Watty.
Meaning: 'power' or 'rule' and 'people' or 'army' (Germanic) as a diminutive of Walter.

Wayne

Variants and diminutives: Dwaine, Dwayne, Lewayne, Vaino, Wain, Waine, Wainwright, Wene.
Meaning: 'wain' or 'farm wagon', (Old English); denoting a maker or driver of wagons or carts derived from an English family name.

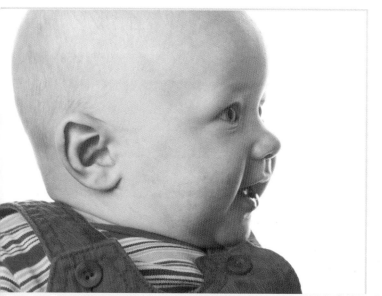

Webster

Variants and diminutives: Web, Webb, Weeb.
Meaning: 'weaver' (Old English); derived from an English family name.

Welby

Variants and diminutives: Welbon, Welburn, Weldon, Welford, Welham.
Meaning: 'spring' and 'farm' (Old Norse and Old English); derived from an English family name, in turn derived from two English place names.

Wendell

Variants and diminutives: Wendayne, Wendel, Wendelin, Wenford, Wentford, Wynn.
Meaning: 'wanderer' (Germanic); derived from an English family name.

Wesley

Variants and diminutives: Lee, Leigh, Wellesley, Wes, Wesleigh, Wesly, Wessley, West, Westbrook, Westcott, Westleigh, Westley, Weston, Wezley.
Meaning: 'western' and 'wood', 'meadow' or 'clearing' (Old English); derived from an English family name, in turn derived from a number of English place names.

Wilbert

Variants and diminutives: Bert, Bertie, Berty, Gilbert, Wilber, Wilbur, Wilburt.
Meaning: 'will' and 'bright' (Germanic and Old English); 'pledge' or 'hostage' and 'bright' (Germanic) or 'servant', 'servant of Saint Bridget' or 'servant of Saint Gilbert' (Scots Gaelic) as a variant of Gilbert.

Wilbur

Variants and diminutives: Gilbert, Wilbert, Wilburh, Wilburn, Wilburt, Wiley, Wilford, Wilgburh, Willard, Willmer, Wilmar, Wilmer, Wilt, Wilton, Wilver, Wylie.
Meaning: uncertain; possibly 'will' and 'defence' (Germanic and Old English); possibly derived from the English family name Wildbore, meaning 'wild' and 'boar' (Old English); possibly 'will and 'bright' (Germanic and Old English) as a variant of Wilbert; possibly 'pledge' or 'hostage' and 'bright' (Germanic) or 'servant', 'servant of Saint Bridget' or 'servant of Saint Gilbert' (Scots Gaelic) as a variant of Gilbert.

Wilfred

Variants and diminutives: Wilf, Wilfrid, Wilfried, Wilfredo.
Meaning: 'will' and 'peace' (Germanic).

Willard

Variants and diminutives: Will, Willie, Willy.
Meaning: 'will' and 'bold' or 'hard' (Old English).

William

Variants and diminutives: Bill, Billie, Billy, Giermo, Gigermo, Gijermo, Gillermo, Guglielmo, Guilermon, Guillamus, Guillaume, Guille, Guillelmo, Guillemot, Guillermino, Guillermo, Guillim, Guillo, Guillot, Guirmo, Gullermo, Gwilim, Gwilym, Gwylim, Gwyllim, Ilermo, Liam, Memo, Quillermo, Uilleam, Uilliam, Vas, Vasilak, Vasili, Vasilios, Vasiliy, Vaska, Vassili, Vassily, Vassos, Vasya, Vasyl, Vila, Vilek, Vilem, Vilhelm, Vili, Viliam, Viljo, Vilko, Ville, Vilmos, Vilous, Welfel, Wil, Wile, Wilem, Wilhelm, Will, Willard, Wille, Willem, Willi, Williamson, Willie, Willis, Willmer, Wills, Willy, Wilmar, Wilmer, Wilmot, Wilson, Wolf.
Meaning: 'will' and 'helmet' or 'protection' (Germanic).

Willis

Variants and diminutives: William, Wills, Willison.
Meaning: 'son of William'; derived from an English family name.

Willoughby

Variants and diminutives: Will.
Meaning: 'willow trees' and 'farm' (Old English and Old Norse); derived from an English family name, in turn derived from a number of English place names.

Wilmer

Variants and diminutives: Will, William.
Meaning: 'will' and 'fame' (Germanic).

Wilmot

Variants and diminutives: Will, William, Willmot, Willmott, Wilmut.
Meaning: 'will' and 'helmet' or 'protection' (Germanic) as a diminutive of William; derived from an English family name.

Windsor

Variants and diminutives: Win, Winsor.
Meaning: 'windlass' or 'winch' and 'riverbank' (Old English); derived from an English family name (including, since 1917, that of the British royal family), in turn derived from a number of English place names.

Winfred

Variants and diminutives: Fred, Freddie, Freddy, Win, Winfield, Winford, Winfrid.
Meaning: 'friend' and 'peace' (Old English).

Winston

Variants and diminutives: Win, Winfield, Wingate, Winn, Winnie, Winny, Winslow, Winsten, Winthrop, Winton, Wyn, Wystan, Wynston.
Meaning: 'Win's' or 'friend's' and 'place' or 'farm' (Old English); derived from an English family name, in turn derived from a number of English place names.

Winthrop

Variants and diminutives: Win, Winfield, Wingate, Winnie, Winny, Winslow, Winston, Winton, Wystan.
Meaning: 'Win's' or 'friend's' and 'farm' or 'village' (Old English and Old Norse); derived from an English family name, in turn derived from two English place names.

Wolf

Variants and diminutives: Wilf, Wolfe, Wolfgang, Wolfhart, Wolfie, Wolfy, Wulf.
Meaning: 'wolf' (Old English).

Wolfgang

Variants and diminutives: Wolf, Wolfhart, Wolfie, Wolfy, Wulf.
Meaning: 'wolf' and 'path' (Germanic).

Woodrow

Variants and diminutives: Wood, Woodie, Woodruff, Woodson, Woody.
Meaning: 'wood' and 'lane' or 'row [of cottages]' (Old English); derived from an English family name, in turn derived from a number of English place names.

Woody

Variants and diminutives: Wood, Woodie, Woodrow, Woodruff, Woodson.
Meaning: 'wood' and 'lane' or 'row [of cottages]' (Old English) as a diminutive of Woodrow; also an adjective relating to wood.

Wyatt

Variants and diminutives: Guy, Wayman, Wiatt, Wyat, Wyatte, Wyeth, Wyman.
Meaning: 'wood', 'wide', 'warrior' or 'guide' (Germanic) as a variant of Guy; derived from an English family name.

Wybert

Variants and diminutives: Bert, Bertie, Berty.
Meaning: 'battle' and 'bright' (Old English).

Wyndham

Variants and diminutives: Wyn.
Meaning: 'Wyman's' and 'homestead' or 'settlement' (Old English), Wyman meaning 'battle' and 'protector' (Old English); derived from an English family name, in turn derived from an English place name.

Wynford

Variants and diminutives: Ford, Winford, Wyn.
Meaning: 'white' or 'holy' and 'stream' (Old Welsh); derived from an English family name, in turn derived from an English place name.

Wynne

Variants and diminutives: Gwyn, Gwynfor, Win, Winn, Winne, Winnie, Winny, Wyn, Wynn.
Meaning: 'fair' (Welsh); 'friend' (Old English); derived from a British family name. Also a girl's name.

Wystan

Variants and diminutives: Wigstan.

Meaning: 'battle' and 'stone' (Old English).

Xanthus

Variants and diminutives: Zanth, Zanthos.
Meaning: 'yellow' or 'bright' (Greek). A male version of Xantha.

Xavier

Variants and diminutives: Javier, Saviero, Xaver, Zever.
Meaning: 'new house' (Basque) when derived from a Basque and Spanish family name; 'bright' or 'brilliant' (Arabic). Also a girl's name.

Xenophon

Variants and diminutives: Zeno, Zennie.
Meaning: 'strange' and 'voice' or 'sound' (Greek).

Xenos

Variants and diminutives: Zeno, Zenos.
Meaning: 'strange' (Greek).

Xerxes

Variants and diminutives: Circs.
Meaning: uncertain; possibly 'ruler' (Persian).

Xylon

Variants and diminutives: Xylo.
Meaning: 'wood' (Greek).

Yakir

Variants and diminutives: Yaki.

Meaning: 'precious' or 'beloved' (Hebrew). A male version of Yakira.

Yale

Meaning: 'fertile upland' (Welsh); derived from a Welsh family name.

Yannis

Variants and diminutives: Ioannis, Yanni, John.
Meaning: 'God has favoured', 'God is gracious' or 'God is merciful' (Hebrew) as a Greek variant of John.

Yardley

Variants and diminutives: Lee, Leigh, Yard.
Meaning: 'sticks' and 'wood' or 'clearing' (Old English); derived from an English family name, in turn derived from a number of English place names.

Yarkon

Meaning: 'green' (Hebrew). A male version of Yarkona.

Yasar

Variants and diminutives: Yaser, Yasir, Yasser.
Meaning: 'wealth' (Arabic).

Yehudi

Variants and diminutives: Judah, Jude, Yehuda, Yehudah.
Meaning: 'Jewish man' (Hebrew); 'praise' (Hebrew) as a variant of Judah or Jude.

Yigal

Variants and diminutives: Yagel, Yigael, Yigdal.
Meaning: 'God will redeem' (Hebrew).

Yora

Variants and diminutives: Jorah.
Meaning: 'to teach' (Hebrew).

Yorath

Variants and diminutives: Iolo, Iowerth.
Meaning: 'lord' and 'value' (Welsh) as an anglicised version of Iorwerth.

Yorick

Variants and diminutives: George, York, Yorke.
Meaning: 'farmer' (Greek) as a Danish variant of George.

Yoshi

Variants and diminutives: Yoshie, Yoshiko, Yoshio, Yoshiyo.
Meaning: 'respectful', 'well-behaved' or 'good' (Japanese). Also a girl's name.

Yukio

Variants and diminutives: Yuki, Yukiko.

Meaning: 'boy of the snow' (Japanese). A male version of Yuki.

Yule

Variants and diminutives: Yul, Youl.
Meaning: 'Christmas' or 'yuletide' (Old English), although the original yule referred to a Norse pagan feast rather than a Christian one.

Yuma

Meaning: 'son of the chief' (Native American).

Yuri

Variants and diminutives: George, Yura, Yurchik, Yuri, Yurik, Yurko, Yusha.
Meaning: 'farmer' (Greek) as a Russian variant of George.

Yusef

Variants and diminutives: Joseph, Yousef, Yusif, Yussuf, Yusuf.
Meaning: 'God will increase' (Hebrew) as an Arabic variant of Joseph.

Yves

Variants and diminutives: Evan, Ives, Ivo, John.
Meaning: 'yew' or 'small archer' (Germanic) as a French variant of Ivo; 'God has favoured', 'God is gracious' or 'God is merciful' (Hebrew) as a French variant of John.

Zacchaeus

Variants and diminutives: Zacc, Zach, Zachariah, Zacharias, Zacharie, Zachary, Zack, Zak, Zakarias, Zecharia, Zecharia, Zecharias, Zeke.
Meaning: uncertain; possibly 'pure' (Aramaic); possibly 'God has remembered' (Hebrew) as a variant of Zachariah.

Zachariah

Variants and diminutives: Benzecry, Sachar, Sacharja, Sakari, Sakarias, Sakarja, Zacaria, Zacarias, Zaccaria, Zacchaeus, Zach, Zacharia, Zacharias, Zacharie, Zachary, Zack, Zak, Zakarias, Zakhar, Zako, Zakris, Zecharia, Zechariah, Zecharias, Zeke.
Meaning: 'God has remembered' (Hebrew).

Zacharias

Variants and diminutives: Benzecry, Sachar, Sacharja, Sakari, Sakarias, Sakarja, Zacaria, Zacarias, Zaccaria, Zacchaeus, Zach, Zacharia, Zachariah, Zacharie, Zachary, Zack, Zak, Zakarias, Zakhar, Zako, Zakris, Zecharia, Zechariah, Zecharias, Zeke.
Meaning: 'God has remembered' (Hebrew) as a variant of Zachariah.

Zachary

Variants and diminutives: Benzecry, Sachar, Sacharja, Sakari, Sakarias, Sakarja, Zacaria, Zacarias, Zaccaria, Zacchaeus, Zach, Zacharia, Zachariah, Zacharias, Zacharie, Zack, Zak, Zakarias, Zakhar, Zako, Zakris, Zecharia, Zechariah, Zecharias, Zeke.
Meaning: 'God has remembered' (Hebrew) as a variant of Zachariah.

Zahid

Meaning: 'ascetic' (Arabic).

Zahur

Meaning: 'flower' (Swahili – Africa). A male version of Zahara.

Zak

Variants and diminutives: Sachar, Sacharja, Sakari, Sakarias, Sakarja, Zacaria, Zacarias, Zaccaria, Zacchaeus, Zach, Zacharia, Zachariah,

Zacharias, Zacharie, Zachary, Zack, Zakarias, Zakhar, Zako, Zakris, Zecharia, Zecharias, Zeke.
Meaning: 'God has remembered' (Hebrew) as a diminutive of Zachariah and its variants; 'laughter' (Hebrew) as a diminutive of Isaac.

Zamir

Variants and diminutives: Samir, Zemer.
Meaning: 'song' or 'bird' (Hebrew); 'entertainment' (Arabic) as a variant of Samir.

Zane

Variants and diminutives: John, Zan.
Meaning: uncertain; possibly 'God has favoured', 'God is gracious' or 'God is merciful' (Hebrew) as a Danish variant of John; possibly derived from a US family name of uncertain meaning.

Zared

Meaning: 'ambush' (Hebrew).

Zebedee

Variants and diminutives: Zeb.
Meaning: 'God has given' (Hebrew).

Zebulun

Variants and diminutives: Zeb,

Zebulon, Zev, Zevulum, Zubin.
Meaning: 'to praise' or 'to honour' (Hebrew).

Zechariah

Variants and diminutives: Zacchaeus, Zachariah, Zacharias, Zachary, Zack, Zak.
Meaning: 'God has remembered' (Hebrew) as a variant of Zachariah.

Zedekiah

Variants and diminutives: Zed.
Meaning: 'God is righteousness' or 'God is goodness' (Hebrew).

Zeke

Variants and diminutives: Ezekiel, Zacchaeus, Zachariah, Zacharias, Zachary, Zack, Zak.
Meaning: 'shooting star' or 'spark' (Aramaic); 'God give strength' (Hebrew) as a diminutive of Ezekiel; 'God has

remembered' (Hebrew) as a diminutive of Zachariah and its variants.

Zeno

Variants and diminutives: Cenon, Zenas, Zenon, Zenus, Zeus, Zewek, Zinon.
Meaning: 'given life by Zeus' (Greek), referring to the supreme god of Greek mythology, whose name means 'shining', 'bright' or 'bright sky', (Greek).

Zenos

Variants and diminutives: Zenas, Zeno, Zenon, Zenus, Zeus.
Meaning: 'gift of Zeus' (Greek), referring to the supreme god of Greek mythology, whose name means 'shining', 'bright' or 'bright sky', (Greek).

Zephaniah

Variants and diminutives: Zevadia.
Meaning: 'God has hidden' or 'God has protected' (Hebrew).

Zephyr

Variants and diminutives: Zephyr, Zephyrinus, Zephyrus.
Meaning: 'the west wind' (Greek); derived from the name of the god of the west wind in Greek mythology.

Zeus

Variants and diminutives: Zeno, Zenon, Zenos.
Meaning: 'shining', 'bright' or 'bright sky' (Greek); derived from the name of the supreme god of Greek mythology.

Zev

Variants and diminutives: Seef, Sef, Sif, Zeeb, Zeev.
Meaning: 'wolf' (Hebrew).

Zinan

Meaning: 'second son' (Japanese).

Ziv

Variants and diminutives: Zivi.
Meaning: 'to shine radiantly' (Hebrew). A male version of Ziva.

Ziven

Variants and diminutives: Ziv, Zivon.
Meaning: 'vigorous' (Slavic).

Zohar

Meaning: 'brilliant light' (Hebrew).
Notable namesakes: a mystical Hebrew commentary on sections of the Pentateuch and the Hagiographa.

Girls' Names

Abigail

Variants and diminutives: Abagael, Abagail, Abagil, Abaigeal, Abbe, Abbey, Abbie, Abby, Abigael, Gael, Gail, Gayle.
Meaning: 'my father rejoices' or 'source of joy' (Hebrew).

Abiola

Meaning: 'born into nobility' (Yoruban – West Africa).

Abira

Variants and diminutives: Adira, Amiza.
Meaning: 'strong' or 'heroic' (Hebrew).

Acacia

Variants and diminutives: Acaysha, Akaysha, Cacia, Casey, Casia, Kacie, Kasi, Kassie, Kassya.
Meaning: 'thorny' or 'without guile' (Greek).

Adah

Variants and diminutives: Ada, Adie, Adina, Dena, Dina.
Meaning: 'lovely ornament' (Hebrew); 'noble' (Latin); 'happy' (Old English).

Adamina

Variants and diminutives: Adama.
Meaning: 'red' or 'red earth' (Hebrew). A female version of Adam.

Adara

Meaning: 'loveliness' (Greek); 'exalted nobility' (Hebrew); 'virgin' (Arabic).

Adelaide

Variants and diminutives: Ada, Adalheid, Adalia, Addie, Addy, Adela, Adelaida, Adèle, Adelle, Adelheid, Adelia, Adelina, Adeline, Della, Heidi.
Meaning: 'noble' or 'nobility' (Germanic).

Adeline

Variants and diminutives: Ada, Addie, Addy, Adelin, Adelina, Adelind, Alina, Aline, Alyna, Della, Dellene, Edelin, Edalina, Edeline, Edolina, Lina.
Meaning: 'noble' or 'nobility' (Germanic). A variant of Adelaide.

Adesina

Meaning: 'my arrival opens the way for more' (Yoruba of West Africa).

Adina

Variants and diminutives: Adie, Ady.
Meaning: 'desire' or 'noble' (Hebrew).

Aditi

Meaning: 'free abundance' or 'unbounded creativity' (Sanskrit).

Adrienne

Variants and diminutives: Adriana, Adriane, Adrianna, Adrianne, Adrina, Drena, Drina.
Meaning: 'from Adria' (a city in northern Italy) or 'dark one' (Latin). A female version of Adrian.

Affrica

Variants and diminutives: Africa.
Meaning: 'beloved' and 'free' (Anglo-Saxon).

Agate

Meaning: 'precious stone' (Greek); derived from the gemstone of the same name.

Agatha

Variants and diminutives: Agacia, Agata, Agathe, Aggie, Aggy.
Meaning: 'good' or 'a good woman' (Greek).

Aglaia

Variants and diminutives: Aglae.
Meaning: 'brilliant' and 'splendour' (Greek).

Agnes

Variants and diminutives: Aggie, Agna, Agnella, Agnesa, Agneta, Agnette, Annais, Anis, Annice, Annis, Ina, Inez, Nessa, Nessie, Nessy, Nest, Nesta, Senga, Ynes, Ynez.
Meaning: 'pure' or 'chaste' (Greek); 'lamb' (Latin).

Ahimsa

Meaning: 'reverence of harmony' (Hindi).

Aida

Variants and diminutives: Iraida, Zaida.
Meaning: 'modesty' (Greek); 'reward' (Arabic); 'to assist' (French); 'happy' (Old English).

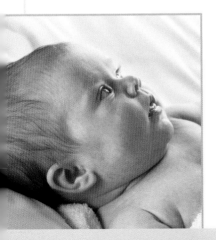

Aiko

Meaning: 'little beloved' (Japanese).

Ailsa

Variants and diminutives: Allile, Elsa.
Meaning: uncertain; derived from the Scottish island Ailsa Craig.

Aine

Variants and diminutives: Aithne, Ann, Anne, Annie, Ethne, Hannah.
Meaning: 'brightness', 'splendour', 'delight' or 'little fire' (Irish Gaelic).

Aisha

Variants and diminutives: Aesha, Asha, Ayasha, Ayesha, Aysha.
Meaning: 'woman' (Arabic); 'life' (Swahili).

Aisling

Variants and diminutives: Aislin, Aislinn, Ashlin, Ashling, Islinn.
Meaning: 'vision' or 'dream' (Irish Gaelic).

Aiyana

Meaning: 'eternal little flower' (Native American).

Akako

Meaning: 'red' (Japanese).

Aki

Meaning: 'autumn' (Japanese).

Alamea

Meaning: 'precious' or 'ripe' (Hawaiian).

Alana

Variants and diminutives: Alaina, Alaine, Alane, Alanis, Alanna, Alayne, Alina, Allanna, Alannah, Lana, Lane.
Meaning: 'rock' (Breton), 'harmony' (Celtic), 'good-looking' or 'cheerful' (Irish Gaelic) as a female version of Alan; 'child' or 'darling' (Irish Gaelic); 'an offering' or 'light' (Hawaiian).

Alaula

Meaning: 'light of the dawn' or 'the sunset's glow' (Hawaiian). Also a boy's name.

Alberta

Variants and diminutives: Alba, Albertha, Albertina, Albertine, Albertyna, Ali, Alli, Allie, Alverta, Auberta, Berta, Berti, Berty, Elba, Elberta, Elbertina, Elbertine, Elbi, Elbie, Elby, Elverta.
Meaning: 'noble' and 'notable' or 'brilliant' (Old English). A female version of Albert.

Albina

Variants and diminutives: Alba, Albigna, Albinia, Albinka, Alva, Alvina, Alvinia, Alwine, Aubine, Bina.
Meaning: 'white' (Latin). A female version of Albin.

Alcina

Variants and diminutives: Alcie, Alcine, Alcinia, Alzina, Elsie.
Meaning: 'strong-willed' (Greek). A female version of Alcander.

Alcyone

Variants and diminutives: Halcyone.
Meaning: 'sea' and 'I am pregnant' (Greek).

Alda

Variants and diminutives: Aldabella, Aldas, Aldina, Aldine, Aldis, Aldona, Aldya, Aldyne, Aldys, Aude, Auld.
Meaning: 'old and wise' (Germanic). A female version of Aldous.

Aldith

Variants and diminutives: Adelid, Aethelgith, Aild, Ailith, Alda, Aldis, Alditha.
Meaning: 'old' or 'experienced' and 'battle' (Old English).

Alethea

Variants and diminutives: Alatheia, Aletea, Aletha, Aletheia, Alethia, Aletta, Alithia, Allathea, Letitia, Letty.
Meaning: 'truth' (Greek).

Alexandra

Variants and diminutives: Al, Alejandra, Alejandrina, Alejo, Aleksandrina, Alessandra, Alex, Alexa, Alexandria, Alexandrina, Alexandrine, Alexia, Alexina, Alexis, Alescha, Ali, Alisaundre, Alix, Lexie, Lexine, Lexy, Lysandra, Sacha, Sandie, Sandra, Sandy, Sondra, Zandra.
Meaning: 'defender of men' or 'warrior' (Greek). A female version of Alexander.

Alfreda

Variants and diminutives: Aelfreda, Al, Albreda, Alfie, Alfy, Elfreda, Elfrieda, Elfrida, Freda, Freddie, Freddy, Frieda.
Meaning: 'elf' or 'good' and 'counsel' (Old English). A female version of Alfred.

Alice

Variants and diminutives: Al, Ali, Alicia, Allie, Allis, Alisa, Alise, Alison, Alissa, Alix, Allison, Ally, Alyce, Alys, Alyssa, Elsa, Lissie, Lissy.
Meaning: 'truthful' (Greek); 'noble' or 'nobility' (Germanic) as a variant of Adelaide.

Alida

Variants and diminutives: Aleda, Aleta, Aletta, Alette, Alidia, Alidita, Alita, Elida, Elita, Leda, Leeta, Lita, Oleda, Oleta.
Meaning: 'small winged one' (Latin); 'noble' (Spanish).

Alima

Meaning: 'expert in dancing and music-making' or 'sea maiden' (Arabic).

Alina

Variants and diminutives: Aleen, Aleena, Aleene, Alena, Alene, Aline, Alya, Lina.
Meaning: 'noble' (Arabic); 'small noble one' (Germanic); 'fair' (Celtic); 'bright' or 'lovely' (Slavic).

Alison

Variants and diminutives: Al, Ali, Alice, Alicia, Allie, Allis, Alisa, Alise, Alissa, Alix, Allison, Ally, Alyce, Alys, Alyssa, Elsa, Lissie, Lissy.
Meaning: 'truthful' (Greek) or 'noble' or 'nobility' (Germanic) as a variant of Alice.

Allegra

Meaning: 'cheerful', 'joyful' or 'lively' (Italian).

Alma

Meaning: 'maiden' (Hebrew); 'caring' or 'kind' (Latin); 'soul' (Italian); 'apple' (Turkish).

Almira

Meaning: 'princess' or 'unquestioning truth' (Arabic); 'basket for clothes' (Hindi).

Aloha

Meaning: a word used to convey warmth when greeting and parting (Hawaiian).

Alphonsine

Variants and diminutives: Alfonsina, Alphonsina.
Meaning: 'noble' and 'ready' (Germanic). A female version of Alphonse.

Altair

Meaning: 'bird' (Arabic). Also a boy's name.

Althea

Meaning: 'wholesome', 'good' or 'to heal' (Greek).

Alyssum

Variants and diminutives: Alison, Alissa, Ilyssa, Lyssa.
Meaning: 'sensible' (Greek).

Amabel

Variants and diminutives: Amabil, Amiable, Bel, Bell, Belle, Annabel, Annabella, Annabelle, Arabella, Mabel, Mabella, Mabelle, Mable.
Meaning: 'lovable' (Latin).

Amalia

Variants and diminutives: Amaliah, Amalthea, Amelia.
Meaning: 'God's labour' (Hebrew); 'hard-working' (Latin).

Amanda

Variants and diminutives: Amandine, Amata, Manda, Mandi, Mandie, Mandy.
Meaning: 'lovable' or 'fit to be loved' (Latin).

Amaryllis

Meaning: 'I sparkle' (Greek); often used to describe country girls in classical poetry.

Amber

Variants and diminutives: Amberlea, Amberlee, Amberly, Ambur, Amby.
Meaning: 'jewel' (Arabic); 'fierce' (Old French); derived from the decorative resin of the same name.

Amelia

Variants and diminutives: Amali, Amalia, Amalie, Amelina, Emilia, Emily, Millie, Milly.
Meaning: 'working hard' (Latin).

Aminta
Variants and diminutives: Amynta, Arminta, Minty.
Meaning: uncertain; possibly coined by Italian writer Torquato Tasso for the title of his eponymous play; possibly derived from Greek and Latin words for 'protector'.

Amira
Meaning: 'utterance' (Hebrew); 'princess' (Arabic).

Amy
Variants and diminutives: Aimée, Amata, Ami, Amice, Amie, Amicia, Esme, Esmee, Ismay.
Meaning: 'beloved' (French).

Ananda
Meaning: 'joy' (Sanskrit); 'bliss' (Hindi).

Anastasia
Variants and diminutives: Anastace, Anastice, Anastasie, Anastassia, Anastatia, Anstey, Anstice, Anya, Asia, Nastassia, Nastssja, Nastasya, Natia, Nestia, Stacey, Stacie, Stacy, Stasa, Stasya, Tansy, Tasia, Tasya.
Meaning: 'resurrection' or 'awakening' (Greek).

Andrea
Variants and diminutives: Aindrea, Anndee, Andie, Andra, Andreanna, Andrée, Andria, Andy.
Meaning: 'manly' (Greek) a the female version of Andreas (Andrew).

Andromache
Variants and diminutives: Andromaque
Meaning: 'she who fights men' (Greek).

Andromeda
Meaning: 'ruler of men' (Greek).

Anemone
Meaning: 'windflower' (Greek).

Angela
Variants and diminutives: Angel, Angelina, Angeline, Angie, Anjela, Anjelika.
Meaning: 'messenger' (Greek). A female version of Angel.

Angelica
Variants and diminutives: Angelique, Angie, Anjelica.
Meaning: 'angelic' (Latin).

Angharad
Variants and diminutives: Angahard.
Meaning: 'beloved' or 'without reproach' (Welsh).

Anika
Variants and diminutives: Anneka, Annika.
Meaning: 'sweet face' (Hausa). Also a variant of Anna.

Anita
Meaning: 'little Ann' (Spanish).

Anna
Variants and diminutives: Aine, Anika, Ann, Anne, Anneka, Annette, Annie, Annika, Anita, Anoushka, Anya, Hannah, Nan, Nancy, Nanette, Nannie, Nanny, Nina.
Meaning: 'I have been favoured (by God)' (Hebrew). A variant of Hannah.

Annabella
Variants and diminutives: Anabel, Annabel, Annabelle, Annaple, Barabel, Bel, Bell, Bella, Belle.
Meaning: Anna: 'I have been favoured (by God)' (Hebrew); -bella: 'beautiful' (Italian). Possibly also a variant of Amabel.

Annalisa

Variants and diminutives: Annaliese, Annelies, Anneliese, Annelisa.
Meaning: Anna: 'I have been favoured (by God)' (Hebrew); -lisa (Elizabeth): 'God is perfection', 'God is satisfaction', 'dedicated to God' or 'God's oath' (Hebrew).

Annwyl

Meaning: 'beloved' (Welsh).

Anona

Meaning: 'pineapple' or 'grain harvest' (Latin).

Anselma

Variants and diminutives: Selma, Zelma.
Meaning: 'divine' and 'helmet' (Germanic) or 'related to nobility' (Old French) as a female version of Anselm.

Anthea

Meaning: 'flowery' (Greek).

Antigone

Variants and diminutives: Tiggie, Tiggy.
Meaning: 'contrary-born' (Greek).

Antoinette

Variants and diminutives: Antonetta, Antonette, Antonietta, Netta, Nettie, Toinetta, Toinette, Toni.
Meaning: 'flourishing' (Greek); 'without price' (Latin); derived from the Roman family name Antonius. A female version of Anthony.

Antonia

Variants and diminutives: Toni, Tonia, Tonya.
Meaning: 'flourishing' (Greek); 'without price' (Latin); derived from the Roman family name Antonius. A female version of Anthony.

Anwen

Meaning: 'very beautiful' (Welsh).

Anzu

Meaning: 'apricot' (Japanese).

Aphra

Variants and diminutives: Affery, Afra.
Meaning: 'dust' (Hebrew).

Aphrodite

Meaning: 'sea foam' or 'foam-born' (Greek).

Apollonia

Variants and diminutives:
Appolina, Appoline.
Meaning: 'of Apollo' (Greek); 'to push back' or 'destroy' (Greek) as a female version of Apollo.

April

Variants and diminutives: Aprilette, Aprille, Averil, Averyl, Avril.
Meaning: 'to open' (Latin); derived from the name of the fourth month, April.

Arabella

Variants and diminutives: Amabel, Annabel, Ara, Arabel, Arabela, Arabelle, Arbela, Arbell, Bella, Belle.
Meaning: Ara: 'altar', 'obliging' or 'ceding to prayers' (Latin); 'eagle' (Germanic); -bella: 'beautiful' (Italian).

Araminta

Variants and diminutives: Minty.
Meaning: coined by English playwright Sir John Vanbrugh for a character in *The Confederacy* (possibly derived from Torquato Tasso's play *Aminta*).

Aranrhod

Variants and diminutives: Arianrhod.
Meaning: 'silver coin' or 'silver wheel' (Welsh).

Aretha

Variants and diminutives: Areta, Aretta, Arette.
Meaning: 'virtue' or 'best' (Greek).

Aria

Meaning: 'melody' (Latin).

Ariadne

Variants and diminutives: Ariane, Arianna, Arianne.
Meaning: 'very sacred', 'to delight' or 'very pure' (Greek).

Arianwen

Variants and diminutives: Argenta, Ariana.
Meaning: 'silver, beautiful and blessed' (Welsh).

Ariel

Variants and diminutives: Ariela, Ariella, Arielle.
Meaning: 'hearth of the altar' or 'lion of the earth or God' (Hebrew). Also a boy's name.

Arista

Meaning: 'best' (Greek); 'grain harvest' (Latin). A female version of Aristo.

Arline

Variants and diminutives: Aline, Arleen, Arlene, Lene, Lena, Lina.
Meaning: uncertain; possibly 'man' or 'free man' (Germanic) when derived from Karolina (Caroline), a Hungarian female version of Karl (Charles); coined by Irish composer Michael Balfe for a character in his opera *The Bohemian Girl*.

Armina

Variants and diminutives: Armine, Arminel.
Meaning: 'army' and 'man' (Germanic). A female version of Herman.

Artemis

Variants and diminutives: Arta, Arte, Artema, Artamas, Artemisa, Artemisia.
Meaning: 'strong-limbed', 'she who cuts up' or 'high law-giver' (Greek).

Asha
Meaning: 'woman' (Arabic); 'life' (Swahili).

Asoka
Variants and diminutives: Ashok, Ashoka.
Meaning: 'the flower that doesn't sorrow' (Hindi).

Aspasia
Variants and diminutives: Spase, Spasia.
Meaning: 'welcome' (Greek).

Astra
Variants and diminutives: Asta, Astera, Asteria, Astra, Astrea, Esther, Hester.
Meaning: 'of the stars' (Latin).

Astrid
Variants and diminutives: Asta, Astrud, Astyr.
Meaning: 'divine' and 'beauty' or 'strength' (Old Norse).

Atalanta
Meaning: 'full of joy' or 'of equal weight' (Greek).

Atara
Variants and diminutives: Ataret.
Meaning: 'crown' (Hebrew).

Athena
Variants and diminutives: Athene.
Meaning: 'unnursed' or 'immortal' (Greek).

Atida
Meaning: 'the future' (Hebrew).

Aude
Meaning: 'blessed' (Gaelic).

Audrey
Variants and diminutives: Aude, Audey, Audra, Audree, Audrie, Ethel, Etheldreda.
Meaning: 'noble' and 'strength' (Old English). A variant of Etheldreda.

Augusta
Variants and diminutives: Augustina, Austine, Gus, Gussie, Gusta.
Meaning: 'venerable' or 'great' (Latin). A female variant of Augustus; a title assumed by female members of the Roman imperial family.

Aurelia
Variants and diminutives: Arelia, Aura, Aurea, Aurelie, Aureola, Aureole, Auria, Auriel, Auriol, Auriole, Ora, Oralia, Oralie, Orelie, Oriel, Orielle.
Meaning: 'gold' (Latin); derived from the Roman family name Aurelius.

Aurora
Variants and diminutives: Aurore, Ora, Rora, Rory.
Meaning: 'dawn' (Latin).

Ava
Variants and diminutives: Eva, Eve.
Meaning: 'life' (Hebrew). A variant of Eva (Eve).

Avalon
Variants and diminutives: Avallon.
Meaning: 'apple' (Old Welsh).

Averil
Variants and diminutives: Averill, Averyl, Avril, Avrill, Eberhilda, Everild.

Meaning: 'boar' and 'protect' or 'battle' (Old English) when derived from Saint Everild's name. Also a variant of Avril, in turn the French variant of April.

Aviva

Variants and diminutives: Abibi, Abibiti, Avivah, Avivi, Avivice, Avivit, Avrit.
Meaning: 'springtime' (Hebrew).

Aziza

Variants and diminutives: Asisa.
Meaning: 'beloved' (Arabic); 'precious' (Swahili).

Bakula

Meaning: 'bakula flower' (Hindi).

Barbara

Variants and diminutives: Bab, Babara, Babb, Babbie, Babette, Babica, Babie, Babita, Babola, Babs, Bairbre, Bara, Barb, Barba, Barbarella, Barbarette, Barbary, Barbata, Barbe, Barbette, Barbi, Barbie, Barbo, Barbora, Barborka, Barbot, Barbota, Barbra, Barby, Barica, Barra, Barushka, Baubie,

Bob, Bobbie, Bobby, Bobs, Vara, Varenka, Varina, Varinka, Varka, Varvara, Varya, Voska.
Meaning: 'foreign' or 'strange' and 'woman' (Greek).

Basilia

Variants and diminutives: Basilie, Basilla, Basilly.
Meaning: 'kingly' or 'royal' (Greek); 'war' (Irish Gaelic). A female version of Basil.

Bathsheba

Variants and diminutives: Barsabe, Bathshua, Bathsua, Batsheva, Batsua, Sheba, Sheva.
Meaning: 'daughter of riches', 'daughter of a pledge', 'seventh daughter' or 'voluptuous' (Hebrew).

Batya

Variants and diminutives: Basia, Basya, Batia, Bethia, Bithia, Bitya.
Meaning: 'daughter of God' (Hebrew).

Beata

Variants and diminutives: Beate.
Meaning: 'blessed' or 'happy' (Latin).

Beatrice

Variants and diminutives: Bea, Beah,

Beat, Beata, Beate, Beaten, Beathy, Beatie, Beatisa, Beatrica, Beatrika, Beatriks, Beatrisa, Beatrise, Beatrix, Beatriz, Beattie, Beatty, Beautrice, Bebe, Bee, Beitris, Bertrice, Bettris, Bettrys, Betune, Bice, Blaza, Blazena, Ticha, Tris, Trisa, Trissie, Trissy, Trix, Trixie, Trixy.
Meaning: 'bringer of blessings' or 'traveller' (Latin).

Becky

Variants and diminutives: Becca, Beckie, Becks, Rebecca.
Meaning: 'binding' (Hebrew). A variant of Rebecca.

Behira

Meaning: 'brilliant' or 'clear' (Hebrew); 'dazzling' (Arabic).

Belinda

Variants and diminutives: Bel, Bell, Bella, Bellalinda, Belle, Bellinda, Bindy, Blenda, Linda, Lindi, Lindie, Lindy, Lynda, Lynde, Velinda.
Meaning: Bel: 'beautiful' (French); -linda: 'snake (Germanic), 'pretty' (Spanish) or 'neat' (Italian).

Bella

Variants and diminutives: Amabel, Annabel, Annabella, Arabella, Bel, Bela, Belicia, Belinda, Bell, Belle, Belvia, Isabel, Isabella, Isabelle, Isobel, Rosabella.
Meaning: 'beautiful' (Italian). Also a diminutive of any name ending in '-bella', such as Annabella.

Benedicta

Variants and diminutives: Bena, Bendetta, Bendite, Benedetta, Benedictine, Benedikta, Benet, Benetta, Benicia, Benita, Bennedett, Bennedette, Bennet, Bennie, Bennie,
Bennitt, Benoite, Betta, Bettina, Binnie, Binny, Dixie.
Meaning: 'blessed' (Latin). A female version of Benedict.

Berengaria

Meaning: 'bear' and 'spear' (Germanic). A female version of Berenger.

Berenice

Variants and diminutives: Berenice, Bernice, Bernie, Berniece, Bernine, Bernita, Berny, Neigy, Nicia, Nixie, Pherenice, Vernice.
Meaning: 'bringer of victory' (Greek).

Bernardette

Variants and diminutives: Bena, Berna, Bernadina, Bernadine, Bernadot, Bernadotte, Bernandina, Bernandine, Bernada, Bernadina, Bernela, Berneta, Bernetta, Bernette, Berni, Bernie, Bernine, Bernita, Berny, Dina, Ina, Nadette.
Meaning: 'bear' and 'strength' (Germanic). A female version of Bernard.

Bertha

Variants and diminutives: Berta, Berte, Berthe, Bertie, Bertina.
Meaning: 'bright' or 'famous' (Germanic).

Beryl

Variants and diminutives: Berura, Beruria, Berylla.
Meaning: 'precious gem' (Sanskrit); 'crystal clear' (Arabic); 'sea-green gem' (Greek); derived from the name of the family of precious minerals.

Beth

Variants and diminutives: Bess, Bessie, Bessy, Beta, Bethan, Bethany, Bethesda, Bethia, Bethseda, Elizabeth.
Meaning: 'God gave a pledge', 'house' or 'God's worshipper' (Hebrew); 'life's breath' (Scots Gaelic). Also a diminutive of Elizabeth.

Bethan

Variants and diminutives: Beth, Bethany, Elizabeth.
Meaning: 'life' (Scots Gaelic). Also a diminutive of Bethany and Elizabeth.

Bethany

Variants and diminutives: Beth, Bethan.
Meaning: 'house of figs' (Hebrew); 'poor house' (Arabic); derived from a place name in Israel.

Bette

Variants and diminutives: Betsie, Betsy, Bettie, Bettina, Betty, Elizabeth.
Meaning: 'God is perfection', 'God is

satisfaction', 'dedicated to God' or 'God's oath' (Hebrew). A diminutive of Elizabeth.

Bettula

Variants and diminutives: Betula.
Meaning: 'maiden' (Hebrew and Persian).

Beulah

Meaning: 'married' (Hebrew).

Beverley

Variants and diminutives: Bev, Beverie, Beverlee, Beverlie, Beverly, Buffy.
Meaning: 'beaver' and 'stream' or 'meadow' (Old English); derived from an English family name, itself derived from a town in Yorkshire. Also a boy's name.

Bianca

Variants and diminutives: Biancha, Blanche.
Meaning: 'white' (Italian).

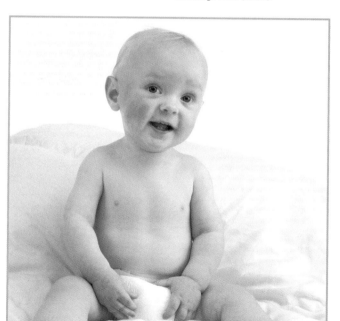

Bibi

Meaning: 'bauble' (French); 'lady' (Arabic).

Billie

Meaning: 'will' and 'helmet' or 'protection' (Germanic). A female version of Billy (William).

Bina

Variants and diminutives: Bena, Binah, Buna, Bunie.
Meaning: 'wisdom' (Hebrew); 'dance' (various African languages); 'fruits' (Arapaho).

Blanche

Variants and diminutives: Balaniki, Bela, Bellanca, Bianca, Blanca, Blanch, Blanchi, Blandina, Blanka, Blanquita, Blanshe, Blenda, Branca.
Meaning: 'white' (Old French).

Blodwedd

Variants and diminutives: Blod.
Meaning: 'flower' and 'face' (Welsh).

Blodwen

Variants and diminutives: Blod.
Meaning: 'flower' and 'white' (Welsh).

Blossom

Variants and diminutives: Blom, Bloom, Blum, Bluma.

Meaning: 'flower' (Old English).

Bo
Variants and diminutives: Bonita.
Meaning: 'precious' (Chinese);
'house-owner' (Old Norse).

Bonita
Variants and diminutives: Boni,
Bonie, Bonnie, Bonny, Nita.
Meaning: 'pretty' (Spanish).

Bonnie
Variants and diminutives: Bonita,
Bonnee, Bonni, Bonny, Bunni, Bunnie,
Bunny.
Meaning: 'good' or 'lovely' (Middle
English).

Brandy
Variants and diminutives: Brandee,
Brandi, Brandie.
Meaning: 'to burn wine' (Old
English); 'brandy wine' (Dutch).

Branwen
Meaning: 'blessed' or 'beautiful' and
'raven' (Welsh).

Brenda
Meaning: 'prince' or 'royal' (Irish
Gaelic) as a female version of
Brendan; 'fiery sword' or 'torch' (Old
Norse).

Brianna
Variants and diminutives: Brenna,
Briana.
Meaning: 'strong', 'hill' or 'elevated'
(Irish Gaelic) as a female version of
Brian.

Bridget
Variants and diminutives: Bedelia,
Berek, Beret, Berget, Bergette, Bergit,
Biddie, Biddu, Biddy, Bidu, Birget,
Birgit, Birgitta, Birte, Breeda, Brid, Bride,
Bridgid, Bridgit, Bridie, Bridita, Brietta,
Brigada, Briget, Brigette, Bridghde,
Brighid, Brigid, Brigida, Brigide,
Brigidita, Brigita, Brigit, Brigitta,
Brigitte, Brit, Brita, Britt, Bryde, Brydie,
Bryga, Brygida, Brygitka, Gidita, Gitta.
Meaning: 'strength' or 'high one'
(Irish Gaelic); 'protection'
(Scandinavian languages).

Britanny
Variants and diminutives: Brit, Brita,
Britany, Britney, Britt, Britta, Brittni.
Meaning: 'Breton' or 'Briton' (Latin);
'the ardent one's child' (Celtic). A
female version of Brett.

Bronwen
Variants and diminutives: Bron,
Bronnie, Bronny, Bronwyn.
Meaning: 'white' and 'breast' (Welsh);
'robust friend' (Middle English).

Brook
Variants and diminutives: Brooke,
Brooks.
Meaning: 'stream' (Old English). Also
a boy's name.

Brunella
Variants and diminutives: Brunetta,
Nella, Netta.
Meaning: 'brown' or 'like a bear'
(Germanic). A female version of Bruno.

Bryony
Variants and diminutives: Briony.
Meaning: uncertain; derived from
the name of a climbing plant,
Bryonia cretica.

Bunty
Variants and diminutives: Buntie.
Meaning: uncertain, probably
derived either from the English word
'bunny', denoting a rabbit, or from
the traditional English name for a
pet lamb.

Cadenza
Variants and diminutives: Cadence,
Cadina.
Meaning: 'to fall' (Latin).

Caitlin

Variants and diminutives: Cathleen, Kathleen.
Meaning: 'pure' (Greek). An Irish Gaelic variation of Catherine.

Calandra

Variants and diminutives: Cal, Calander, Calandré, Calandria, Cali, Calie, Calla, Calley, Calli, Callie, Cally, Kalandra, Kali, Kalie, Kalley, Kalli, Kallie, Kally, Kolandra, Landra.
Meaning: 'lark' or 'beauty' (Greek).

Calantha

Variants and diminutives: Cal, Calanthe, Calli, Callie, Cally.
Meaning: 'lovely flower' (Greek).

Calida

Meaning: 'warm' or 'loving' (Spanish).

Calista

Variants and diminutives: Calesta, Calisto, Calla, Calli, Callie, Callista, Cally, Calysta, Kallista.
Meaning: 'most beautiful' (Greek).

Calliope

Meaning: 'lovely voice' (Greek).

Callula

Meaning: 'lovely little girl' (Latin).

Calypso

Meaning: 'to cover' or 'to hide' (Greek).

Camellia

Variants and diminutives: Cam, Camel, Camille, Cammie, Cammy, Melia, Millie, Milly.
Meaning: derived from the name of the *Camellia* genus of flowering shrubs named for botanist Joseph Kamel.

Camilla

Variants and diminutives: Cam, Cama, Camala, Camel, Cami, Camila, Camille, Cammi, Cammie, Cammy, Kamila, Kamilka, Kamilla, Milla, Milli, Millie, Milly.
Meaning: 'messenger' or 'attendant at ritual' (Latin); derived from the Roman family name Camillus. A female version of Camillus.

Candice

Variants and diminutives: Candace, Candance, Candase, Candee, Candi, Candida, Candie, Candis, Candy, Candyce, Kandace, Kandee, Kandi, Kandice, Kandie, Kandy.
Meaning: 'to glow white hot' (Greek) or 'white' (Latin) as a variant of Candida.

Candida

Variants and diminutives: Candide, Candee, Candi, Candice, Candie, Candra, Candy, Kandee, Kandi, Kandie, Kandy.
Meaning: 'to glow white hot' (Greek); 'white' (Latin).

Caprice

Meaning: 'a hedgehog-like head' (Latin); 'fanciful' (Italian and French).

Cara

Variants and diminutives:
Carabelle, Carina, Carine, Carita, Carra, Carrie, Kara, Karina, Karine, Karra.
Meaning: 'dear' (Latin and Italian); 'friend' (Irish Gaelic); 'diamond' (Vietnamese).

Cari

Meaning: 'keel' (Latin); 'flowing' (Turkish). Also a diminutive of many girls' names beginning with 'Car-'.

Carla

Variants and diminutives: Arla, Carleen, Carlene, Carley, Carlia, Carli, Carlie, Carlita, Carlotta, Carly, Karla, Karli, Karlie, Karly.
Meaning: 'man' or 'free man' (Germanic) as a female version of Carl (Charles).

Carmel

Variants and diminutives: Carma, Carmania, Carmela, Carmelina, Carmelita, Carmelle, Carmen, Carmi, Carmie, Carmine, Carmit, Carmita, Carmiya, Carmy, Kaarmia, Karma, Karmel, Karmela, Karmelit, Karmit, Lita, Melina.

Meaning: 'fertile field' or 'garden' (Hebrew); 'fruit garden' or 'vineyard' (Arabic).

Carmen

Variants and diminutives: Carma, Carmel, Carmena, Carmencita, Carmia, Carmine, Carmino, Carmita, Chamain, Charmaine, Charmian, Charmion, Karma, Karmen, Karmia, Karmina, Karmine, Karmita, Mina.
Meaning: 'song' (Latin); 'crimson' (Spanish). Also a variant of Carmel.

Carol

Variants and diminutives: Carel, Carey, Caro, Carola, Carole, Carolee, Carrie, Carroll, Carry, Caryl, Kalola, Karel, Karol, Karole, Karyl, Sharyl, Sherrie, Sherry, Sherye, Sheryl.
Meaning: 'brave in battle' (Welsh); 'round dance' (Old French); 'man' or 'free man' (Germanic) as a female version of Charles. Also a diminutive of Caroline.

Caroline

Variants and diminutives: Arla, Cara, Carey, Cari, Carla, Carlana, Carleen, Carlen, Carlene, Carlera, Carley, Carli, Carlia, Carlie, Carlin, Carlina, Carline, Carlita, Carlite, Carley, Carlota, Carlotta, Carly, Carlyn, Carlynne, Caro, Carol, Carola, Carole, Caroleen, Carolina, Carolinda, Carolly, Caroly, Carolyn, Caron, Carona, Carri, Carrie, Carroll, Carry, Cary, Caryl, Cassie, Chariena, Charla, Charlayne, Charleen, Charlen, Charlena, Charlene, Charlet, Charline, Charlot, Charlotte, Charo, Cherlene, Ina, Inka, Kari, Karie, Karila, Karla, Karleen, Karlene, Karli, Karlie, Karlinka, Karlita, Karly, Karola, Karole, Karolina, Karoline, Karolinka, Karolyn, Lina, Linchen, Line, Linka, Lola, Lolita, Lolo, Lotchen, Lotta, Sharleen, Sharlene, Sharline, Tota.
Meaning: 'man' or 'free man' (Germanic) as a female version of Charles.

Caron

Variants and diminutives: Carren, Karen.

Meaning: 'pure' (Greek). A variant of Karen (Catherine).

Carys

Variants and diminutives: Caryl, Cerys, Cheryl.
Meaning: 'love' (Welsh).

Casey

Variants and diminutives: Cace, Case, Cassandra, Casi, Casie, Casy, Kace, Kacey, Kaci, Kacie, Kacy, Kase, Kasey, Kasy, KC.
Meaning: 'brave' (Irish Gaelic). Also a boy's name.

Cassandra

Variants and diminutives: Caasi, Casandra, Case, Casey, Cash, Caso, Cass, Cassander, Cassandre, Cassandry, Cassi, Cassie, Casson, Cassy, Kassandra, Sandi, Sandie, Sandra, Sandy.
Meaning: 'ensnarer of men' (Greek).

Catherine

Variants and diminutives: Caitlin, Caitlon, Caitria, Caitrin, Caren, Cari, Carin, Carina, Carita, Carolly, Caroly, Caronia, Caryn, Casey, Cass, Cassi, Cassie, Cassy, Casy, Cat, Catalina, Catant, Catarina, Cate, Caterina, Cath, Catha, Catharina, Catharine, Cathe, Cathee, Catheline, Cathi, Cathie, Cathleen, Cathlene, Cathlin, Cathrine, Cathryn, Cathy, Cati, Catie, Caton, Catlin, Catling, Catrin, Catrina, Catriona, Cattie, Caty, Caye, Cayla, Ekaterina, Kaety, Kaisa, Kaki, Kara, Karen, Karena, Karin, Karina, Kasia, Kasienka, Kasin, Kaska, Kassia, Kat, Kata, Katalin, Katarina, Katchen, Kate, Katee, Katelin, Katenka, Katerina, Katerine, Katerinka, Kateryn, Kath, Katha, Katharina, Katharine, Kathchen, Kathe, Katherin, Katherine, Kathi, Kathie, Kathleen, Kathlene, Kathline, Kathrene, Kathrina, Kathryn, Kathy, Kati, Katica, Katie, Katika, Katina, Katinka, Katja, Katka, Katla, Kato, Katoka, Katri, Katrin, Katrina, Katrine, Katrinka, Katryna, Katsa, Katty, Katus, Katuska, Katy, Katja, Katya, Kay, Kayce, Kaye, Kayla, Kaytlin, Kerry, Ketty, Ketya, Kinny, Kisa, Kiska, Kit, Kitti, Kittie, Kitty, Kofryna, Kolina, Kotinka, Kytte, Rina, Thrine, Treinel, Trina, Trinchen, Trine, Trinette, Trini.
Meaning: 'pure' (Greek).

Catriona

Variants and diminutives: Cat, Catrina, Katrina, Triona.
Meaning: 'pure' (Scots Gaelic). A variant of Catherine.

Cecilia

Variants and diminutives: Cacilia, Cacilie, Cecelia, Cecely, Cecil, Cecile, Cecilie, Cecilla, Cecille, Cecillia, Cecily, Cecilya, Cecyl, Cecyle, Cecylia, Ceil, Cele, Celia, Celie, Ces, Cesia, Chela, Chila, Cicely, Cicily, Ciel, Cile, Cili, Cilka, Cilly, Cis, Ciss, Cissi, Cissie, Cissy, Cycalye, Cycly, Kikelia, Kikilia, Sela, Sely, Sesilia, Sheila, Sile, Sileas, Sis, Sisile, Sisley, Sissela, Sissi, Sissie, Sissy.
Meaning: 'blind' (Latin) or 'sixth' (Welsh) as a female version of Cecil. Also a variant of Celia.

Ceinwen

Meaning: 'lovely jewels' (Welsh).

Celeste

Variants and diminutives: Cela, Cele, Celesta, Céleste, Celestia, Celestin, Celestina, Celestine, Celestyn, Celestyna, Celia, Celie, Celina, Celinka, Cesia, Inka, Selinka, Tyna, Tynka.
Meaning: 'celestial' or 'heavenly' (Latin).

Celia

Variants and diminutives: Caelia, Cecilia, Celie, Celina, Celinda, Selen, Selina, Sheelagh, Sheila, Shelagh, Sile.
Meaning: derived from the Roman family name Caelius, itself possibly meaning 'celestial' or 'heavenly' (Latin). Also a diminutive of Cecilia.

Celine

Variants and diminutives: Celina, Celinda, Céline, Celinka, Celka, Selen, Selena, Selene, Seline, Selina.
Meaning: 'celestial' or 'heavenly' (Latin).

Ceridwen

Meaning: 'beautiful poetry' (Welsh).

Chandelle

Variants and diminutives: Chan, Chandell, Shan, Shandell, Shandelle.
Meaning: 'candle' (Old French).

Chandra

Variants and diminutives: Chan, Chandra, Chandah, Shan, Shanda, Shandah, Shandra.
Meaning: 'illustrious' or 'like the moon' (Sanskrit).

Chantal

Variants and diminutives: Chantel, Chantele, Chantell, Chantelle, Shantal, Shantalle, Shantel, Shantell, Shantelle.
Meaning: 'to sing' or 'stone' (Old French) when derived from a French family name; 'to sing clearly' (Old French) as a female variant of Chanticleer.

Charity

Variants and diminutives: Carita, Carity, Charis, Charissa, Charita, Charito, Charry, Chattie, Cherry, Karita.
Meaning: 'grace' (Greek); 'kindness' (Latin); 'Christian love' (Old French).

Charlotte

Variants and diminutives: Cara, Carla, Carlene, Carli, Carlie, Carlota, Carlotta, Carly, Char, Charley, Charil, Charla, Charlayne, Charleen, Charlen, Charlena, Charlene, Charlet, Charlie, Charline, Charlot, Charlotta, Charlotty, Charly, Charyl, Chattie, Cheryl, Karla, Karlene, Karli, Karlicka, Karlie, Karline, Karlotta, Karlotte, Karly, Lola, Loleta, Loletta, Lolita, Lolotte, Lotta, Lottchen, Lotte, Lotti, Lottie, Lotty, Salote, Sari, Sarlote, Sarolta, Sharleen, Sharlene, Sharline, Sharyl, Sheree, Sheri, Sherisa, Sherissa, Sherri, Sherrie, Sherrill, Sherry, Sherrye, Sheryl, Totly, Totti, Tottie, Totty.
Meaning: 'man' or 'free man'

(Germanic) as a female version of Charles.

Charmaine

Variants and diminutives: Carman, Charmain, Charmayne, Charmian, Sharmain, Sharmaine, Sharmayne.
Meaning: 'joy' (Greek); 'song' (Latin).

Chastity

Meaning: 'pure' or 'chaste' (Latin).

Chaya

Variants and diminutives: Kaija.
Meaning: 'life' (Hebrew). A female version of Chaim.

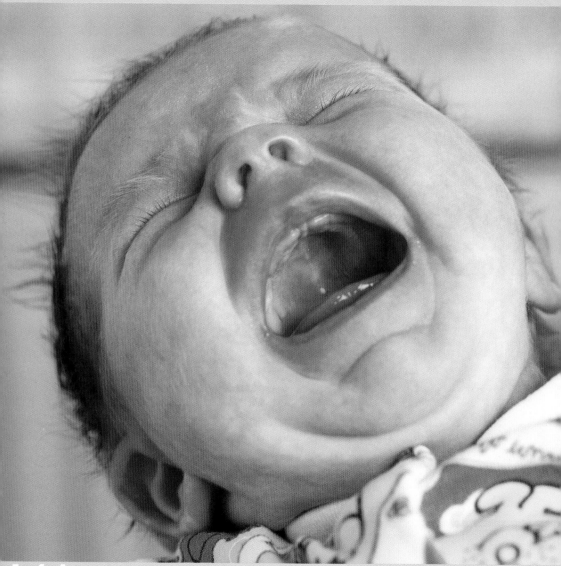

Chelsea

Variants and diminutives: Chelse, Chelsey, Chelsi.
Meaning: 'landing place of chalk' or 'port' (Old English); derived from the name of the London district and football club.

Chenoa

Meaning: 'white dove' (Native American).

Chérie

Variants and diminutives: Ceri, Cher, Cherami, Chere, Cheri, Cherie, Cherrie, Cherry, Chery, Cherye, Cheryl, Cheryle, Cherylie, Sharol, Sher, Sheral, Shere, Sheree, Sherell, Sheri, Sherelle, Sherri, Sherry, Sherye, Sheryl, Sheryle.
Meaning: 'darling' (French).

Cherry

Variants and diminutives: Cerise, Cherie, Chérie, Cheryl, Charity.
Meaning: derived from the Greek, Latin and Old English words for the fruit. Also a diminutive of Charity.

Cheryl

Variants and diminutives: Sheryl.
Meaning: uncertain; coined during the twentieth century, possibly by combining Cherry, 'cherry' (Greek, Latin and Old English) and Beryl, 'precious gem' (Sanskrit), 'crystal clear' (Arabic) or 'sea-green gem' (Greek).

Chloë

Variants and diminutives: Clela, Clo, Cloe.
Meaning: 'green' (Hebrew); 'tender green shoot' (Greek).

Christabel

Variants and diminutives: Christa, Christabell, Christabella, Christabelle, Christable, Christey, Christie, Christobelle, Christobella, Christy, Cristemberga, Cristemia, Cristie, Cristy, Bel, Bell, Bell.
Meaning: 'beautiful Christian' (Latin); possibly coined for his poem of the same name by English poet, Samuel Taylor Coleridge.

Christine

Variants and diminutives:
Cairistine, Cairistiona, Cauline, Chris, Chrissie, Chrissy, Christa, Christal, Christeen, Christeena, Christel, Christen, Christi, Christiana, Christiane, Christiania, Christie, Christina, Christy, Chrystal, Chryste, Chrystel, Ciorsdan, Crestienne, Crete, Crissie, Crista, Cristi, Cristiana, Cristin, Cristina, Cristine, Cristiona, Cristy, Crystal, Crystina, Kersti, Khristina, Khristyna, Kina, Kirsteen, Kirsten, Kirstin, Kirstie, Kirsto, Kirsty, Kris, Kriska, Kriss, Krissi, Krissie, Krissy, Krista, Kristel, Kristen, Kristi, Kristia, Kristian, Kristin, Kristina, Kristine, Kristinka, Kristin, Krysia, Krysta, Kryska, Krystyna, Krystynka, Stina, Stine, Teenie, Tina, Tinah, Tine, Tiny, Tyna, Xena, Xina.
Meaning: 'Christian' (Latin). A female version of Christian.

Ciara

Variants and diminutives: Ciar, Keera, Kiera, Kira, Kyara.
Meaning: 'dark' (Irish Gaelic).

Cilla

Variants and diminutives: Priscilla.
Meaning: 'of ancient times' (Latin). A diminutive of Priscilla.

Cindy

Variants and diminutives: Cindi, Cyndi, Sindy, Syndi.
Meaning: 'light' (Latin) as a diminutive of Lucinda (Lucia, in turn a female version of Lucius); possibly also a diminutive of Cinderella ('little cinder girl') and Cynthia (of Cynthus, Greek).

Clare

Variants and diminutives: Clara, Claramae, Clair, Claire, Clairene, Clairene, Clairette, Clareta, Claretha, Clarette, Clarey, Clari, Claribel, Claribele, Clarabella, Clarice, Claricia, Clarie, Clarimond, Clarina, Clarinda, Clarine, Claris, Clarisa, Clariscia, Clarissa, Clarisse, Clarita, Clarrie, Clarrie, Clarrisse, Clarus, Clary, Clerissa, Klara, Klarika, Klarissa, Larisa, Sorcha.
Meaning: 'clear', 'bright' or 'famous' (Latin).

Claudia

Variants and diminutives: Claude, Claudeen, Claudella, Claudeta, Claudette, Claudi, Claudie, Claudina, Claudine, Claudita, Clodia, Gladys,
Gwladys.
Meaning: 'lame' (Latin), derived from a Roman family name as a female version of Claude.

Cleantha

Variants and diminutives: Cleanthe, Cliantha.
Meaning: 'flower of glory' (Greek).

Clementine

Variants and diminutives: Clem, Clemence, Clemency, Clemense, Clementia, Clementina, Clemmie, Clemmy, Klementine, Klementina, Tina.
Meaning: 'merciful' or 'mild' (Latin). A female version of Clement.

Cleopatra

Variants and diminutives: Cleo, Cleta.
Meaning: 'fame of my father' (Greek).

Clio

Variants and diminutives: Cleo, Cleon, Cleona, Cleone, Cleora.
Meaning: 'fame-proclaimer' (Greek). Notable namesakes: one of the Muses – that of history and poetry in Greek mythology.

Clotilda

Variants and diminutives: Clothild, Clothilda, Clothilde, Clotilde, Klothilde, Klothilda.
Meaning: 'famous' and 'battle' (Germanic).

Clytie

Meaning: 'splendour' (Greek).

Colette

Variants and diminutives: Colecta, Colet, Coleta, Collect, Collett, Collette, Cosette, Cosetta, Kalotte.
Meaning: 'victory of the people' (Greek) as a diminutive of Nicolette, a female version of Nicholas.

Colleen
Variants and diminutives: Coleen, Colena, Colene, Coline, Collen, Collene, Collice, Colline.
Meaning: 'girl' (Irish Gaelic).

Columbine
Variants and diminutives: Columba, Columbia, Columbina.
Meaning: 'dove-like' (Latin); 'little dove' (Italian). A female version of Columba.

Concepta
Variants and diminutives: Conception, Concepcion, Concetta, Concha, Conchita.
Meaning: 'conceived' (Latin).

Constance
Variants and diminutives: Con, Concettina, Conetta, Conni, Connie, Conny, Constancia, Constancy, Constanta, Constantia, Constantina, Constanz, Constanza, Conte, Custance, Custancia, Custans, Custins, Kani, Konstantin, Konstanze, Kosta, Kostatina, Kostenka, Kostya, Kostyusha, Kotik, Tina.
Meaning: 'constancy' (Latin). A female version of Constantine.

Consuela
Variants and diminutives: Consolata, Consuelo.
Meaning: 'free of sadness', 'consoling' (Latin).

Cora
Variants and diminutives: Corabelle, Coralie, Corella, Corene, Coretta, Corette, Corey, Cori, Corie, Corin, Corina, Corine, Corinn, Corinna, Corinne, Corita, Correen, Correne, Corri, Corrina, Corrine, Corinna, Corrine, Corry, Cory, Kora, Korey, Kori, Korrie, Korry, Kory.
Meaning: uncertain; coined by US writer James Fennimore Cooper for his novel *The Last of the Mohicans*, probably drawing inspiration from the Greek word for 'maiden' (Greek).

Coral
Variants and diminutives: Coralie, Coraline.
Meaning: 'pebble' (Greek); derived from the name of the prized material produced by the aggregated skeletons of corals.

Cordelia
Variants and diminutives: Cordeilia, Cordeilla, Cordelie, Cordell, Cordelle, Cordie, Cordula, Cordy, Delia, Della, Kordel, Kordula.
Meaning: 'heart' or 'from her heart' (Latin); 'harmony' or 'daughter of the sea' (Celtic).

Corinna
Variants and diminutives: Cora, Corene, Corey, Cori, Corin, Corinn, Corinne, Correnen, Correne, Corri, Corrie, Corrina, Corrine, Corrinna, Corry, Cory, Kora, Korey, Kori, Korrie, Korry.
Meaning: 'maiden' (Greek).

Cornelia
Variants and diminutives: Cornela,

Cornelie, Cornella, Cornelle, Cornie, Corny, Kornelia, Kornelis, Melia, Neely, Neila, Nele, Nelia, Nell, Nelli, Nellie, Nelly.
Meaning: 'horn' or 'cornel tree' (Latin), derived from a Roman family name as a female version of Cornelius.

Cosima
Variants and diminutives: Cosi.
Meaning: 'order' (Greek). A female version of Cosmo.

Courtney
Variants and diminutives: Courtenay, Courtny.
Meaning: 'short nose', 'court-dweller' or 'the domain of Curtius' (Old French), derived from a French place name. Also a boy's name.

Cressida
Variants and diminutives: Briseida, Cressid, Criseida, Criseyde.
Meaning: 'golden' or 'stronger' (Greek).

Crystal
Variants and diminutives: Chris, Chrissie, Christal, Christel, Christelle, Christie, Christy, Chrys, Chrystal, Chrystie, Cristal, Cristel, Cristol, Cyrstle, Chrystol, Kristell, Krys, Krystal, Krystle, Kristol.
Meaning: 'ice' (Greek); derived from the name of the clear mineral.

Cynthia
Variants and diminutives: Cinda, Cindee, Cindi, Cindie, Cindy, Cinta, Cintia, Cyndi, Cyndie, Cyndy, Cynth, Cynthiana, Cynthie, Kynthia, Sindee, Sindy.
Meaning: 'of Cynthus' (Greek), Cynthus being Mount Cynthus, on the Greek island of Delos (Dhilos).

Cytherea
Meaning: 'of Cynthera', (Greek), Cynthera being equated with the island of Cyprus.

Daffodil
Variants and diminutives: Daff, Daffie, Daffy, Dilly, Margaret, Marguérite.
Meaning: 'asphodel' (Greek); derived from the name of the spring flower *Narcissus pseudonarcissus*.

Dagmar
Variants and diminutives: Daga, Dagi, Daggi, Dagmara, Dasa.
Meaning: 'maid of the famous day' or 'the Dane's joy' (Old Norse).

Dahlia
Variants and diminutives: Dalia, Daliah, Dahla.
Meaning: 'from the valley' (Old Norse).

Daisy
Variants and diminutives: Daisee, Daisey, Daisi, Daisia, Daisie, Dasey, Dasi, Dasie, Dasy, Daysee, Daysie, Daysy.
Meaning: 'day's eye' (Old English); derived from the name of the flower *Bellis perennis*.

Dakota
Meaning: 'friend' (Native American Sioux). Also a boy's name.

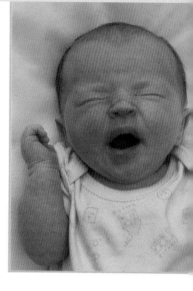

Dalila

Variants and diminutives: Dalilah, Lila, Lilah.
Meaning: 'gentle' (Swahili). Also a variant of Dahlia, Delia and Delilah.

Damaris

Variants and diminutives: Damara, Damaras, Damaress, Damiris, Demaras, Demaris, Mara, Mari, Maris.
Meaning: 'calf' or 'heifer' (Greek).

Dana

Variants and diminutives: Daina, Danae, Dane, Dania, Danice, Danit, Danita, Danna, Danni, Dannie, Dansy, Danu, Danuta, Danny, Dannye, Danya, Dayna.
Meaning: 'Dane' or 'from Denmark' (Celtic); 'mother of the gods', 'poet' or 'courageous' (Irish Gaelic); 'judgement of God' (Hebrew) as a diminutive of Danielle, in turn a female version of Daniel.

Danica

Variants and diminutives: Dan, Dani, Dany.
Meaning: 'morning star' (Old Slavic).

Danielle

Variants and diminutives: Dana, Danae, Danela, Danell, Danella, Danelle, Danette, Dani, Dania, Danica, Danice, Danika, Danikla, Danielka, Daniela, Daniele, Daniell, Daniella, Danila, Danilla, Danille, Danit, Danita, Danka, Danuta, Danya, Danyel, Danyell, Danyelle, Danni, Dannie, Danny, Dannye, Danya.
Meaning: 'judgement of God' (Hebrew). A female version of Daniel.

Daphne

Variants and diminutives: Daff, Daffi, Daffie, Daffy, Dafna, Dafne, Dafnee, Dafnit, Daph, Daphe, Daphna, Daphnee, Daphnit.
Meaning: 'laurel' (Greek).

Dara

Variants and diminutives: Darah, Daralice, Daralis, Darda, Dare, Darelle, Dareth, Daria, Darice, Darissa, Darra, Darryl, Darya, Daryl.
Meaning: 'fount of wisdom' (Hebrew); 'compassionate' or 'daring' (Middle English).

Darcy

Variants and diminutives: Dar, Darce, Darcey, Darci, Darcie, D'arcy, D'Arcy, Darsey, Darsi, Darsie, Darsey.
Meaning: 'dark' (Irish Gaelic); 'of the fortress' or 'of Arcy' (Old French); derived from an Irish family name, in turn derived from the French place name Arcy. Also a boy's name.

Daria
Variants and diminutives: Darice, Darya.
Meaning: 'rich' (Greek). A female version of Darius.

Darlene
Variants and diminutives: Dareen, Darelle, Dari, Darilyn, Darilynn, Darla, Darleen, Darlin, Darline, Darling,

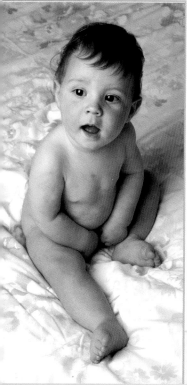

Darilynn, Darlyn, Darylyne, Darragh, Darrilyn, Daryl.
Meaning: 'darling' (Old English).

Davina
Variants and diminutives: Davene, Davi, Davida, Davinia, Davita, Devina, Veda, Veta, Vida, Vina, Vita, Vitia.
Meaning: 'beloved' or 'friend' (Hebrew). A female version of David.

Dawn
Variants and diminutives: Aurora, Dawna, Dawne, Dawnelle, Dawnette, Dawnta, Dawnyelle, Orrie, Rora.
Meaning: 'daybreak' (Old English).

Daya
Variants and diminutives: Dayah.
Meaning: 'bird' (Hebrew).

Deanna
Variants and diminutives: Dea, Deana, Deane, Deann, Deanne, Deena, Dena, Diana.
Meaning: uncertain; possibly 'one in charge of ten' or 'dean' (Latin) or 'valley' (Old English) as a female version of Dean; possibly a variant of Diana.

Deborah
Variants and diminutives: Deb, Debbe, Debbee, Debbi, Debbie, Debby, Debera,

Debi, Debire, Debo, Debor, Debora, Deboran, Debra, Debralee, Debs, Deva, Devera, Devora, Devorah, Devorit, Devra, Dobra, Dovra, Dvera, Dvorit, Dwora, Kepola.
Meaning: 'bee' (Hebrew).

Decima
Variants and diminutives: Deci, Deka.
Meaning: 'tenth' (Latin). A female version of Decimus.

Dee
Variants and diminutives: DD, Dede, Dee Dee, Didi.
Meaning: a diminutive of any name beginning with 'D-'; 'dark' (Welsh). Also a boy's name.

Deirdre
Variants and diminutives: Dede, Dedra, Dee, Deerdre, Deirdra, Deirdrie, Diedra, Dierdra, Dierdre, Dierdrie.
Meaning: 'broken-hearted', 'raging one', 'fearful' or 'wanderer' (Irish Gaelic).

Delia
Variants and diminutives: Adelia, Bedelia, Cordelia, Dahla, Dede, Dee, Dehlia, Delinda, Della, Didi.
Meaning: 'visible' or 'of Delos' (Greek), the former name of the Greek island of Dhilos.

Delicia

Variants and diminutives: Dee, Dela, Delesha, Delia, Delice, Delight, Delisa, Delise, Delisha, Delisiah, Delissa, Delizia, Delycia, Delys, Delyse, Delysha, Delysia, Delyssa.
Meaning: 'delight' (Latin).

Delilah

Variants and diminutives: Dalila, Delila, Lila, Lilah.
Meaning: 'delightful', 'amorous', 'hair', 'night' or 'poor' (Hebrew); 'leader' or 'flirt' (Arabic).

Della

Variants and diminutives: Adela, Dela, Dell, Delle.
Meaning: 'noble' or 'nobility' (Germanic) as a diminutive of Adela (Adelaide).

Delma

Variants and diminutives: Delmar, Delmi, Delmira.
Meaning: 'noble' and 'defender' (Germanic) as a diminutive of Adelma; 'of the sea' (Spanish).

Delphine

Variants and diminutives: Delfine, Delpha, Delphina, Delphinie, Delphinium.
Meaning: 'of Delphi' (Latin), Delphi ('dolphin' in Greek) being the site of the ancient Greek Delphic oracle on Mount Parnassus; also a variant of the botanical name of the larkspur flowering plant *Delphinium*.

Delyth

Meaning: 'lovely' or 'tidy' (Welsh).

Demelza

Meaning: uncertain; derived from a Cornish place name.

Demeter

Variants and diminutives: Demetra, Demetria, Demetris, Dimitra, Dimity.
Meaning: 'earth mother' (Greek).

Dena

Variants and diminutives: Dea, Deana, Deane, Deann, Deanna, Deanne, Deena, Dena, Dene, Denna, Dina.
Meaning: 'valley' (Old English and Native American). Also a female version of Dean.

Denise

Variants and diminutives: Danice, Danise, Deneice, Denese, Deney, Denice, Deniece, Deniese, Denis, Denisha, Denisse, Denize, Dennet, Dennie, Dennise, Denny, Denyce, Denyse, Deonysia, Dinnie, Dinny, Dion, Dione, Dionetta, Dionis, Dionise, Dionycia, Dionysia, Diot.
Meaning: 'deity of the Nysa' (Greek), Nysa being the birthplace of Dionysus, the Greek god of wine, fecundity, vegetation and revelry, as a variant of Dionysia and a female version of Dennis.

Derora

Variants and diminutives: Deroit, Derorice, Derorit.
Meaning: 'flowing stream', 'the swallow' (Hebrew).

Dervla

Meaning: 'poet's daughter' (Irish Gaelic).

Desdemona

Variants and diminutives: Desmona.
Meaning: 'unhappiness' or 'bad luck' (Greek).

Désirée

Variants and diminutives: Desarae, Desaree, Desi, Desideria, Desiraye, Desirita, Desiré, Dezarae, Dezaray, Dezirae, Deziree.
Meaning: 'desired' (French).

Deva

Variants and diminutives: Devaki, Devanee, Devi, Devika, Dewi.
Meaning: 'divine' (Sanskrit).

Dia

Meaning: 'divine' (Greek); 'middle child' (Mende, Africa). Also a variant of Diana.

Diamond

Variants and diminutives: Diamanta.
Meaning: 'hardest' or 'unconquerable' (Greek); derived from the name of the precious stone.

Diana

Variants and diminutives: Deana, Deane, Deanna, Deanne, Deannis, Dede, Dee, Denna, Di, Dia, Diahann, Dian, Diandra, Diane, Diani, Dianna, Dianne, Didi, Diona, Dione, Dionne, Dionetta, Dyan, Dyana, Dyane, Dyann, Dyanna, Dyanne, Kiana.
Meaning: 'divine' (Latin).

Dido

Meaning: 'bold' (Phoenician).

Dilys

Variants and diminutives: Dalice, Dalicia, Dalisha, Delicia, Delisha, Dilees, Dylice.
Meaning: 'sincere', 'genuine' or 'perfect' (Welsh).

Dinah

Variants and diminutives: Deanna, Deanne, Deena, Dena, Dina.
Meaning: 'proved right', 'revenged' or 'judged' (Hebrew).

Dion

Variants and diminutives: Diona, Dionaea, Diondra, Dione, Dionée, Dionis, Dionna, Dionne.
Meaning: 'divine' or 'deity of the Nysa' (Greek), Nysa being the birthplace of Dionysus, the Greek god of wine, fecundity, vegetation and revelry, as a variant of Dionysia and a female version of Dennis.

Dixie

Variants and diminutives: Dis, Disa, Dix.
Meaning: 'goddess' or 'sprite' (Old Norse). Also a boy's name.

Dolina

Variants and diminutives: Donalda, Donaldina.
Meaning: 'global might' (Scots Gaelic). A female version of Donald.

Dolores

Variants and diminutives: Dalores, Dela, Delora, Delores, Deloris, Delorita, Dola, Dolly, Dolo, Dolorcitas, Dolore, Dolorita, Doloritas, Dolours, Kololeke, Lo, Lola, Lolita, Lora, Loras.
Meaning: 'sorrows' (Spanish).

Dominique

Variants and diminutives: Chumina, Dom, Doma, Domek, Domenica, Domeninga, Domina, Dominee, Dominga, Domini, Dominic, Dominica, Dominick, Dominik, Dominika, Domka, Dumin, Mika, Nika, Niki.
Meaning: 'of the lord' (Latin). A female version of Dominic.

Donna

Variants and diminutives: Domella, Dona, Donalie, Donella, Donelle, Donetta, Donia, Donica, Doniella, Donita, Donnel, Donni, Donnie, Donnis, Donny, Kona, Ladonna.
Meaning: 'lady' (Italian).

Dora

Variants and diminutives: Dorah, Doralin, Doralyn, Doralynne, Doreen, Dorelia, Dorena, Dorette, Dori, Dorind, Dorinda, Dorita, Dorothy, Dorrie, Dorry, Theodora.

Meaning: 'God's gift' (Greek) as a diminutive of both Theodora (and other '-doras') and Dorothy.

Dorcas
Variants and diminutives: Dorcia.
Meaning: 'gazelle' or 'doe' (Greek).

Doris
Variants and diminutives: Dorea, Dori, Doria, Dorice, Dorie, Dorinda, Dorisa, Dorise, Dorit, Dorita, Dorith, Doritt, Dorri, Dorrie, Dorris, Dorrit, Dory, Kolika, Rinda.
Meaning: 'bountiful sea', 'sacrificial knife' or 'of Doris' (Greek), Doris being a Greek region north of the Gulf of Corinth. Also a female version of Dorian.

Dorit
Variants and diminutives: Dorice, Dorrit.
Meaning: 'generation' (Hebrew). Also a diminutive of Dorothy.

Dorothy
Variants and diminutives: Dahtee, Dasha, Dasya, Dede, Derede, Dode, Dodi, Dodie, Dodo, Dody, Doe, Doioreann, Dol, Doll, Dolley, Dolli, Dollie, Dolly, Dora, Doralane, Doraleen, Doralene, Doralia, Doralice, Doralyn, Dorann, Dorat, Dore, Doreen, Dorelia, Dorene, Doretta, Dorette, Dori, Dorinda, Dorisia, Dorit, Dorita, Dorka, Dorle, Dorlisa, Doro, Dorolice, Dorosia, Dorota, Dorotea, Doroteya, Doroteyo, Dorothea, Dorothee, Dorothiea, Dorotthea, Dorrie, Dorrie, Dorrit, Dorte, Dorthea, Dorthy, Dory, Dosi, Dosya, Dot, Dotti, Dottie, Dotty, Lolotea, Koleka, Kolokea, Thea, Theadora, Tiga, Tigo, Tio, Totie.
Meaning: 'God's gift' (Greek). A female variant of Theodore.

Drisa
Variants and diminutives: Dreesa, Dreesha, Drisana, Drisanna, Drisha, Risa, Risha.
Meaning: 'the sun's daughter' (Hindi).

Drusilla
Variants and diminutives: Dru, Druci, Drucilla, Drusa, Drusie, Drusus, Drusy.
Meaning: uncertain; possibly 'soft-eyed' (Greek); derived from the Roman family name Drusus.

Dulcie
Variants and diminutives: Delcina, Delcine, Dulce, Dulcea, Dulcee, Dulcia, Dulciana, Dulcibella, Dulcine, Dulcinea, Dulcy.
Meaning: 'sweet' (Latin).

Duscha
Variants and diminutives: Dusha.

Meaning: 'soul' (Russian).

Dymphna
Variants and diminutives: Damhnait, Daunat, Dympna.
Meaning: 'eligible' or 'little fawn' (Irish Gaelic).

Eartha
Variants and diminutives: Erda, Erde, Erna, Ertha, Herta, Hertha.
Meaning: 'earth' (Old English).

Easter
Variants and diminutives: Esther.
Meaning: 'radiant dawn' (Germanic). Also a variant of Esther.

Ebony
Variants and diminutives: Ebbony, Ebonee, Eboney, Eboni, Ebonie.
Meaning: 'the ebony tree' (Greek), derived from the name of the *Diospyros* genus of trees that produce dark hardwood.

Edda
Meaning: 'great-grandmother', 'poetry' or 'song-writer' (Old Norse); 'striver' (Germanic).

Eden

Meaning: 'delight' or 'paradise' (Hebrew). Also a boy's name.

Edith

Variants and diminutives: Ardith, Dita, Ditka, Duci, Eade, Eadita, Eady, Eda, Edda, Edde, Ede, Edetta, Edi, Edie, Edit, Edita, Edite, Editha, Edithe, Ediva, Edka, Edon, Edy, Edyta, Edyth, Edytha, Edythe, Eidita, Ekika, Eyde.
Meaning: 'happiness' or 'riches' and 'war' (Old English).

Edna

Variants and diminutives: Adena, Adina, Eda, Edana, Edena, Ednah, Eithne.
Meaning: 'delight' or 'rejuvenation' (Hebrew); 'pleasing gift' (Old English); 'kernel' or 'small fire' (Irish Gaelic) as a variant of Ethne.

Edwina

Variants and diminutives: Edina, Edna, Edweena, Edwene, Edwyna.
Meaning: 'happiness' or 'riches' and 'friend' (Old English). A female version of Edwin.

Eileen

Variants and diminutives: Aibhilin, Aileen, Eibhilin, Eila, Eilean, Eiley, Eilidh, Eilleen, Eily, Elie, Eveleen, Evelyn, Helen, Ilean, Ileen, Ileene, Ilene.
Meaning: 'bright' (Greek) as an Irish Gaelic variant of Helen; 'hazelnut' (Germanic) or 'bird' (Latin) as an Irish Gaelic variant of Evelyn.

Eira

Meaning: 'snow' (Welsh).

Eirian

Meaning: 'silver' (Welsh).

Elain

Meaning: 'fawn' (Welsh).

Elaine

Variants and diminutives: Elain, Elaina, Elane, Elayne, Ellaine, Helen.
Meaning: 'bright' (Greek) as an Old French variant of Helen.

Elana

Variants and diminutives: Ilana.
Meaning: 'tree' (Hebrew); 'spirited' (Latin); 'friendly' (Native American). A female version of Elan.

Eleanor

Variants and diminutives: Alianora, Alienor, Alienora, El, Ele, Elanora, Eleanora, Eleanore, Elen, Elena, Eleni, Elenor, Elenora, Elenorah, Eleonora, Eleonore, Eli, Elianor, Elianora, Elie, Elien, Elin, Elinor, Elinora, Elinore, Elinorr, Ella, Ellen, Ellenor, Ellenora, Ellenore, Ellette, Ellie, Ellin, Elly, Ellyn Elnore, Elnora, Elyenora, Elyn, Elynn, Heleanor, Leanor, Lennie, Lenora, Lenore, Leonora, Leonore, Leora, Nelda, Nora, Nell, Nella, Nellie, Nelly, Nora, Norah, Noreen, Norene, Norina, Norine, Nureen.
Meaning: 'bright' (Greek) as an Old French variant of Helen; 'foreign' (Germanic).

Electra

Variants and diminutives: Electre, Elektra.
Meaning: 'amber' or 'radiant' (Greek).

Elfrida

Variants and diminutives: Alfreda, Elfie, Eldreda, Frida, Freda.
Meaning: 'elf' and 'strength' (Old English).

Elissa

Variants and diminutives: Elisabeth, Lisa, Lissa.
Meaning: uncertain; possibly 'heroic' (Phoenician); possibly 'God is perfection', 'God is satisfaction', 'dedicated to God' or 'God's oath' (Hebrew) as a diminutive of Elizabeth.

Elita

Meaning: 'selected' (Latin).

Elizabeth

Variants and diminutives: Alzbeta, Bab, Babette, Bela, Belicia, Belita, Bella, Bess, Bessi, Bessie, Bessy, Bet, Beta, Beth, Bethan, Betka, Betsey, Betsi, Betsie, Betssy, Betsy, Bett, Betta, Bette, Betti, Bettina, Bettine, Betty, Betuska, Boski, Bozsi, Buffy, Chabica, Chavelle, Chela, Ealasaid, Eilie, Eilis, Ela, Elese, Elikapeka, Elis, Elisa, Elisabet, Elisabeta, Elisabeth, Elisabetta, Elisavet, Elise, Elisheba, Elisheva, Eliska, Elissa, Elisveta, Eliza, Elizabet, Elizabete, Elizbez, Elize, Elka, Ellie, Elsa, Elsavetta, Elsbet, Else, Elsebeth, Elschen, Elsebin, Elsey, Elsi, Elsie, Elspet, Elspeth, Elspie, Elsye, Elts, Elysa, Elyse, Elyssa, Elza, Elzbieta, Elsbietka, Elzunia, Erzebet, Erzsebet, Etti, Etty, Helsa, Ila, Ilisa, Ilise, Ilsa, Ilse, Ilyse, Isa, Isabel, Isabelita, Isabella, Isabelle, Isobel, Issa, Iza, Izabel, Izabela, Izabella, Letha, Lety, Libbi, Libbie, Libby, Lieschen, Liese, Liesel, Liesl, Liisa, Liisi, Lili, Lilian, Lilibet, Lila, Lilla, Lillah, Lisa, Lisbet, Lisbeth, Lise, Liselotta, Lieselotte, Lisbete, Lise, Lisenka, Liseta, Lisette, Lisettina, Lisl, Lista, Liszka, Liz, Liza, Lizabeth, Lizanka, Lizbeth, Lize, Lizette, Lizka, Lizzi, Lizzie, Lizzy, Lusa, Orse, Sabela, Tetsy, Tetty, Tibby, Yelisabeta, Yelizaveta, Ysabel, Yza, Yzabel, Yzabela, Zizi.

Ella

Meaning: 'God is perfection', 'God is satisfaction', 'dedicated to God' or 'God's oath' (Hebrew).

Variants and diminutives: Ala, Ela, Elizabeth, Ellen, Hela, Hele.

Meaning: 'all' (Germanic); 'fairy' and 'maiden' (Old English). Also a variant of Elizabeth and Ellen.

Ellama

Meaning: 'mother goddess' (Hindi).

Ellen

Variants and diminutives: Elea, Elen, Elin, Ella, Ellan, Elli, Ellie, Ellin, Ellon, Elly, Elyn, Nell, Nellie, Nelly.

Meaning: 'bright' (Greek) as a variant of Helen.

Elma

Variants and diminutives: Alma.

Meaning: 'apple' (Turkish).

Eloise

Variants and diminutives: Eloisa, Heloise, Lois, Louise.

Meaning: 'hale' and 'wide' (Germanic); 'famed' and 'warrior' (Germanic) as a variant of Louise.

Elsa

Variants and diminutives: Ailsa, Aliza, Else, Elsie, Elza.

Meaning: 'truthful' (Greek), 'noble' or 'nobility' (Germanic) as a variant of Alice (Adelaide); 'swan' (Anglo-Saxon); 'God is my joy' (Hebrew). Also a diminutive of Elizabeth.

Eluned

Variants and diminutives: Eiluned, Elined, Linet, Linette, Linnet, Lyn, Lynette, Lynne, Lynnette.

Meaning: 'idol' or 'adored one' (Welsh).

Elvira

Variants and diminutives: Ela, Elvire, Wirke, Wira.

Meaning: uncertain; possibly 'elf' or 'good' and 'counsel' (Germanic) as a variant of Alfreda; possibly 'white' (Latin).

Emily

Variants and diminutives: Aimil, Amalea, Amalie, Ameldy, Amelia, Amelie, Amella, Amilia, Amilie, Amma, Eimile, Em, Ema, Emalia, Emaline, Eme, Emele, Emelin, Emelina, Emeline, Emera, Emi, Emie, Emilia, Emilie, Emiley, Emilia, Emilie, Emiliia, Emilita, Emilka, Emlyn, Emlynn, Emlynne, Emm, Emma, Emmaline, Emmeleia, Emmeline, Emmi, Emmie, Emmy, Imma, Mema, Milka, Millie, Milly, Neneca, Nuela, Ymma.

Meaning: 'eager', 'flatter' or 'rival' (Latin); derived from the Roman family name Aemilius. A female version of Emile.

Emma

Variants and diminutives: Em, Emmeline, Emmi, Emmie, Emmy, Irma.
Meaning: 'whole' or 'universal' (Germanic).

Emmeline

Variants and diminutives: Amelia, Ameline, Em, Emaline, Emblem, Emblyn, Emelen, Emeline, Emelyn, Emiline, Emma, Emmie, Emmy, Emylynn.
Meaning: 'work' (Germanic). Also a variant of Emma and Emily.

Ena

Variants and diminutives: Aine, Aithne, Enya, Ethne, Eugénie, Helena, Ina.
Meaning: 'bright' (Greek) as a diminutive of Helena (Helen); 'kernel' or 'small fire' (Irish Gaelic) as a diminutive of Ethne; 'well-born' (Greek) as a diminutive of Eugénie.

Enid

Meaning: 'soul' or 'life force' (Welsh).

Enya

Variants and diminutives: Eithne, Ena, Etha, Ethenia, Ethna, Ethne, Etna, Etney.
Meaning: 'small fire' or 'kernel' (Irish Gaelic) as a diminutive of Ethne.

Erica

Variants and diminutives: Elika, Ericka, Erika, Errika, Rica, Rickee, Ricki, Rickie, Ricky, Rika, Rikki, Rikky.
Meaning: 'eternal', 'honourable' or 'island' and 'ruler' (Old Norse). A female version of Eric.

Erin

Variants and diminutives: Eri, Erina, Erinn, Erinna, Errin, Eryn.
Meaning: 'western island' or 'from Ireland' (Irish Gaelic); 'peace' (Old Norse).

Ermintrude

Variants and diminutives: Armigil, Ermegarde, Ermengarde, Ermyntrude, Trudi, Trudie, Trudy.
Meaning: 'universal' and 'strength' (Germanic).

Ernestina

Variants and diminutives: Erna, Ernesta, Ernestine.
Meaning: 'earnest' (Old English). A female version of Ernest.

Ersa

Variants and diminutives: Erse.
Meaning: 'dew' (Greek).

Esmé

Variants and diminutives: Amy, Amyas, Esmee.
Meaning: 'esteemed' (French). Also a boy's name.

Esmeralda

Variants and diminutives: Emerald, Emeralda, Emeraldine, Emerlin, Emerline, Esmeraldah, Esmaralda, Esmarelda, Esmerelda, Meraud.
Meaning: 'emerald' (Greek); derived from the name of the green precious stone, a variety of beryl.

Estelle

Variants and diminutives: Essie,

Estella, Estrelita, Estrella, Estrelletta, Estrellita, Stella, Stelle.
Meaning: 'star' (Latin).

Esther

Variants and diminutives: Easter, Eister, Eistir, Essa, Essi, Essie, Essy, Esta, Estee, Estella, Ester, Estercita, Estralita, Estrella, Etti, Ettie, Etty, Hadassah, Heddy, Hedy, Heidi, Heiki, Hester, Hesther, Hettie, Hetty, Trella.
Meaning: 'myrtle' or 'bride' (Hebrew); 'star' (Persian).

Ethel

Variants and diminutives: Adal, Adale, Adela, Adeline, Alice, Edel, Eth, Ethelda, Etheldreda, Ethelinda, Etheline, Ethelyn, Ethyl.
Meaning: 'noble' (Germanic).

Etheldreda

Variants and diminutives: Audrey, Dreda, Ethel.
Meaning: 'noble' and 'strength' (Old English).

Ethne

Variants and diminutives: Aine, Aithne, Eithne, Ena, Ethlinn, Ethnea, Ethnee.
Meaning: 'kernel' or 'small fire' (Irish Gaelic).

Eudora

Variants and diminutives: Dora.
Meaning: 'beneficial' and 'gifted' (Greek).

Eugénie

Variants and diminutives: Ena, Eugenia, Gene, Genie, Ina
Meaning: 'well-born' (Greek). A female version of Eugene.

Eulalia

Variants and diminutives: Eula, Eulalie.
Meaning: 'sweet talker' (Greek).

Eunice

Variants and diminutives: Niki, Nikki, Unice, Younice.
Meaning: 'victorious' (Greek).

Euphemia

Variants and diminutives: Eadaoine, Effie, Effim, Effum, Epham, Eppie, Eufemia, Eupham, Eupheme, Femie, Fanny, Oighrig, Phamie, Phemie.
Meaning: 'well thought of' or 'auspicious talk' (Greek).

Eustacia

Variants and diminutives: Stacey, Stacia, Stacie, Stacy.
Meaning: 'fruitful', 'good' or 'ear of corn' (Greek). A female version of Eustace.

Evangeline

Variants and diminutives: Angela, Eva, Evangela, Evangelia, Evangelina, Eve, Lia, Litsa.
Meaning: 'gospel' or 'good news' (Greek); 'messenger' (Greek) as a variant of Angela.

Eve

Variants and diminutives: Aoiffe, Ava, Chava, Eba, Ebba, Eeva, Eeve, Eubha, Ev,

Eva, Evadne, Evaine, Evalina, Evaline, Evathia, Evchen, Eveleen, Evelin, Evelina, Evelyn, Evetta, Evette, Evi, Evia,, Eviana, Evicka, Evie, Eviene, Evike, Evin, Evita, Evka, Evleen, Evlyn, Evonne, Evota, Evuska, Evy, Ewa, Ewalina, Ina, Lina, Vica, Yeva, Yevka, Zoe.
Meaning: 'life' (Hebrew).

Eveline
Variants and diminutives: Avelina, Aveline, Eileen, Eve, Eveleen, Evelina, Evelyn, Evie.
Meaning: 'hazelnut' (Germanic) or 'bird' (Latin) as a variant of Evelyn (also a boy's name).

Evita
Variants and diminutives: Eva, Eve.
Meaning: 'life' (Hebrew) as a diminutive of Eva (Eve).

Fabiola
Variants and diminutives: Fabia, Fabiana.
Meaning: uncertain; possibly 'bean' or 'skilful' (Latin); derived from the Roman family name Fabius. A female version of Fabian.

Faith
Variants and diminutives: Fae, Fay, Faye, Fayth, Faythe, Fe, Fidelia, Fidelity.
Meaning: 'trust' or 'faithful' (Latin). A female version of Fidel.

Farrah
Variants and diminutives: Fara, Farah, Farra.
Meaning: 'happiness' (Arabic); 'lovely' (Middle English).

Fatima
Variants and diminutives: Fatimah, Fatma.
Meaning: 'weaner' or 'abstainer' (Arabic).

Fawn
Variants and diminutives: Fauna, Fawna, Fawnah, Fawniah.
Meaning: 'offspring' (Latin).

Fay
Variants and diminutives: Fae, Faye, Fayette, Fayina.
Meaning: 'fairy' (Old French); 'trust' or 'faithful' (Latin) as a diminutive of Faith, in turn a female version of Fidel.

Felicity
Variants and diminutives: Falice, Falicia, Falasha, Fela, Felcia, Felecia,

Felice, Felicia, Feliciana, Felicidad, Felicie, Felicite, Felicitas, Felis, Felise, Felisha, Felisia, Felisse, Felita, Feliz, Feliza, Felka, Filicie, Filisia, Fillys, Flick, Lisha, Liss, Lissa, Lissie, Phelicia, Phil, Philicia.
Meaning: 'happy' or 'fortunate' (Latin). A female version of Felix.

Fenella
Variants and diminutives: Finella, Finnuala, Finola, Fionnghuala, Fionila, Fionnuala, Fionnula, Fionuala, Nuala.
Meaning: 'fair-shouldered' (Irish Gaelic) as an anglicised version of Fionnuala.

Fern
Variants and diminutives: Ferne.
Meaning: 'leaf' (Old English); derived from the Filicinophyta phylum of plants.

Fifi
Variants and diminutives: Fi.
Meaning: 'God will increase' (Hebrew) as a diminutive of Josephine, in turn a female version of Joseph.

Fiona
Variants and diminutives: Fee, Ffion, Fi, Fio, Fionna, Fione.
Meaning: 'fair' (Scots Gaelic); a name

coined for his pseudonym, Fiona Macleod, by Scottish poet William Sharp.

Flavia

Variants and diminutives: Flavus.
Meaning: 'yellow' (Latin) as the female version of Flavius.

Fleur

Variants and diminutives: Fflur, Fleurette, Flora, Flower.
Meaning: 'flower' or 'blossom' (French). A variant of Flora.

Flora

Variants and diminutives: Eloryn, Fflur, Fiora, Fiore, Fleur, Fleure, Fleurette, Flo, Flor, Flore, Florella, Flores, Floressa, Floretta, Florette, Flori, Floria, Floriana, Florianne, Florida, Floridita, Florie, Florinda, Floris, Florita, Florri, Florrie, Flory, Florry, Floss, Flossie, Flower, Kveta, Kvekta, Lora, Lorka.
Meaning: 'flower' or 'blossom' (Latin).

Florence

Variants and diminutives: Fiorella, Fiorenza, Flann, Flo, Flonda, Flor, Flora, Florance, Flore, Floreen, Floren, Florencia, Florentia, Florentina, Florenz, Florina, Florinda, Florine, Florri, Florrie, Floryn, Floss, Flossi, Flossie, Flossy.

Meaning: 'flowering' or 'blossoming' (Latin).

Fortuna

Variants and diminutives: Faustina, Faustine, Fortune, Fortunata.
Meaning: 'luck' (Latin).

Frances

Variants and diminutives: Cella, Chica, Fan, Fanchette, Fanchon, Fancy, Fanechka, Fani, Fania, Fanni, Fannie, Fanny, Fannye, Fanya, Fedora, Ferike, Fotina, Fraka, Fran, Franca, France, Francesca, Franci, Francie, Francina, Francine, Francisca, Franciska, Franciszka, Francise, Francka, Françoise, Franconia, Francyne, Frania, Franika, Frank, Frankey, Frankie, Franni, Frannie, Franny, Franja, Franny, Fanz, Franze, Franziska, Franziske, Fronia, Paca, Pancha, Panchita, Paquita, Ranny.
Meaning: 'French' (Latin). A female version of Francis.

Freda

Variants and diminutives: Elfrida, Fred, Fredda, Freddie, Freddy, Fredi, Fredie, Fredyne, Freida, Freide, Frieda, Friede, Frida, Fritzi, Fryda.
Meaning: 'peace' (Germanic); 'elf' and 'strength' (Old English) as a diminutive

of Elfrida; 'reconciliation' (Welsh) and 'peace' (Old English) as a diminutive of Winifred. Also a female version of Frederick.

Frederica

Variants and diminutives: Farica, Federica, Fedriska, Feriga, Fred, Freda, Fredda, Freddi, Freddie, Freddy, Fredericka, Frederika, Frederique, Fredrica, Fredrika, Frerika, Frici, Frida, Friederike, Fritze, Frizinn, Fryda, Fryderyka, Frydryka, Rica, Ricki, Ricky, Rika, Rike, Rikki.
Meaning: 'peace' and 'ruler' (Germanic). A female version of Frederick.

Freya

Variants and diminutives: Freja, Freyja, Froja.
Meaning: 'noble lady' (Old Norse).

Fulvia

Meaning: 'tawny' (Latin); derived from the Roman family name Fulvius.

Gabrielle

Variants and diminutives: Gabay, Gabbie, Gabby, Gabel, Gabell, Gabey, Gabi, Gabie, Gabriel, Gabriela, Gabriella, Gabryell, Gaby, Gavi, Gavra, Gavriela, Gavriella, Gavrielle, Gavrila, Gavrilla, Gay, Gaye, Gigi.
Meaning: 'man of God' or 'my strength is God' (Hebrew). A female version of Gabriel.

Gaia

Meaning: 'earth' (Greek).

Gail

Variants and diminutives: Gael, Gale, Gayel, Gayelle, Gayle, Gayleen, Gaylin, Gayline, Gaylyn, Gaylynn.
Meaning: 'my father rejoices' or

'source of joy' (Hebrew). A diminutive of Abigail.

Gardenia

Meaning: derived from the name of the Gardenia genus of flowering plants named for the botanist Dr Alexander Garden.

Garnet

Variants and diminutives: Garnett, Grania.
Meaning: 'grain' (Latin); 'pomegranate' (Old French); derived from the name of the silicate-mineral gemstone that ranges from pink to dark red in colour. Also a boy's name.

Gay

Variants and diminutives: Gae, Gaye.
Meaning: 'merry' (Old French). Also a diminutive of Gabrielle and Gaynor and a boy's name, although recently rendered unfashionable by its homosexual connotations.

Gaynor

Variants and diminutives: Gaenor, Gainer, Gaenor, Gay, Gayner.
Meaning: 'fair' and 'yielding' or 'ghost' (Welsh) as a diminutive of Guinevere.

Gemma

Variants and diminutives: Gem, Jem, Jemma.
Meaning: 'jewel' (Latin and Italian).

Geneva

Variants and diminutives: Gena, Genève, Genevia, Genna, Janeva, Janevra.
Meaning: 'juniper' or 'river mouth' (Latin).

Genevieve

Variants and diminutives: Gen, Gena, Genavieve, Gene, Geneva, Geneveeve, Genevra, Genie, Genivieve, Ginette, Genni, Gennie, Genny, Genovefa, Genovera, Genoveva, Gina, Guenevere, Guinevere, Janeva, Jen, Jenevieve, Jenni, Jennie, Jenny.
Meaning: uncertain; possibly 'race' and 'woman' (Germanic).

Georgia

Variants and diminutives: George, Georgea, Georgeanna, Georgeanne, Georgeen, Georgeene, Georgena, Georgene, Georgess, Georgett, Georgetta, Georgette, Georgi, Georgiana, Georgianna, Georgianne, Georgie, Georgienne, Georgina, Georgine, Georginita, Georgy, Gerda,

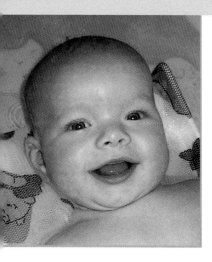

Gigi, Gina, Gyorci, Gyorgyi, Jirca, Jirina, Jirka, Jorgina.
Meaning: 'farmer' (Greek). A female version of George.

Georgina
Variants and diminutives: George, Georgea, Georgeanna, Georgeanne, Georgeen, Georgeene, Georgena, Georgene, Georgess, Georgett, Georgetta, Georgette, Georgi, Georgia, Georgiana, Georgianna, Georgianne, Georgie, Georgienne, Georgine, Georginita, Georgy, Gerda, Gigi, Gina, Gyorci, Gyorgyi, Jirca, Jirina, Jirka, Jorgina.
Meaning: 'farmer' (Greek). A female version of George.

Geraldine
Variants and diminutives: Deena, Dina, Geralda, Geraldene, Geraldina, Gerarda, Gerardine, Gerardine, Gererdina, Gererdine, Gerhardina, Gerhardine, Geri, Gerldine, Gerri, Gerrie, Gerry, Giralda, Jeralee, Jere, Jeri, Jerri, Jerrie, Jerry.
Meaning: 'spear' and 'rule' (Germanic). A female version of Gerald.

Gerda
Variants and diminutives: Gerde.
Meaning: 'protector' or 'enclosure' (Old Norse).

Germaine
Variants and diminutives: Germain, Germana, Germane, Germayne, Jermain, Jermaine, Jermane, Jermayn, Jermayne.
Meaning: 'brother' (Latin) or 'German' (Old French). A female version of Germain (Jermaine).

Gertrude
Variants and diminutives: Gatt, Gatty, Gerda, Gert, Gerte, Gertie, Gertruda, Gertrudis, Gerty, Jara, Jera, Jerica, Truda, Trude, Trudel, Trudi, Trudie, Trudy, Trula, Truta.
Meaning: 'spear' and 'strength' (Germanic).

Ghislaine
Variants and diminutives: Ghislain.

Meaning: 'pledge' (Germanic).

Gilberta
Variants and diminutives: Gil, Gilbertine.
Meaning: 'pledge' or 'hostage' and 'bright' (Germanic); 'servant', 'servant of Saint Bridget' or 'servant of Saint Gilbert' (Scots Gaelic). A female version of Gilbert.

Gilda
Variants and diminutives: Gilde, Gildi, Gildie, Gildita, Gildy, Gill, Gill, Jil, Jill.
Meaning: uncertain; possibly 'to gild' (Old English).

Gillian
Variants and diminutives: Gilian, Gill, Gillan, Gilli, Gilianne, Gillie, Gilly, Gillyanne, Jil, Jili, Jill, Jilli, Jillian, Jilliann, Jillianne, Jillie, Jilly, Jillyan, Juliana, Lian.
Meaning: uncertain; possibly 'fair-skinned' (Latin); derived from the Roman family name Julianus. A female version of Julian.

Gina
Variants and diminutives: Geena, Ginat.
Meaning: 'garden' (Hebrew); 'silvery' (Japanese); otherwise dependent on the name from which it is derived: for example, 'farmer' (Greek) as a diminutive of Georgina.

Gisela

Variants and diminutives: Ghislaine, Gigi, Gisele, Gisella, Giselle, Giza, Gizela, Gizi, Gizike, Gizus.
Meaning: 'pledge' or 'hostage' (Germanic).

Gladys

Variants and diminutives: Glad, Gladi, Gladis, Gleda, Gwladys.
Meaning: uncertain; possibly 'small sword' (Latin); possibly 'lame' (Latin), derived from a Roman family name, as the Welsh version of Claudia, in turn a female version of Claude; possibly 'territorial ruler' or 'delicate flower' (Welsh).

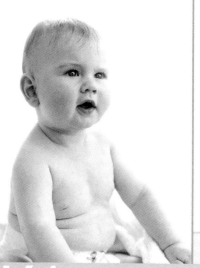

Glenda

Variants and diminutives: Glen, Glennie, Glenny.
Meaning: 'pure' or 'holy' and 'good' (Welsh).

Glenna

Variants and diminutives: Glen, Glena, Gleneen, Glenesha, Glenice, Glenine, Glenisha, Glenn, Glenne, Glenneen, Glennette, Glenni, Glennie, Glennine.
Meaning: 'valley' (Scots Gaelic); derived from a Scottish family name, in turn derived from a geographical feature. A female version of Glen.

Glenys

Variants and diminutives: Glen, Glenis, Glinys, Glyn, Glynis.
Meaning: 'pure' or 'holy' (Welsh).

Gloria

Variants and diminutives: Glora, Gloree, Glori, Gloriana, Gloriane, Glorianna, Glorianne, Glorie, Glorria, Glory.
Meaning: 'glory' (Latin).

Glynis

Variants and diminutives: Glenice, Glenis, Glenise, Glennice, Glennis, Glennys, Glenwys, Glenys, Glenyse, Glinnis, Glinys, Glyn, Glynn, Glynnis.
Meaning: 'little valley' (Welsh).

Golda

Variants and diminutives: Goldarina, Goldi, Goldia, Goldie, Goldina, Goldy.
Meaning: 'golden' (Germanic).

Grace

Variants and diminutives: Arete, Engracia, Giorsal, Graca, Gracia, Graciana, Gracie, Graciela, Gráinne, Grania, Grata, Gratia, Gratiana, Grayce, Grazia, Graziella, Grazielle, Grazina, Graziosa, Kaleki.
Meaning: 'grace' (Latin).

Gráinne

Variants and diminutives: Grace, Gráine, Grania, Granya.
Meaning: 'love', 'terrifier' or 'goddess of grain' (Irish Gaelic).

Greta

Variants and diminutives: Gretal, Gretchen, Grete, Gretel, Grethal, Grethel, Gretta, Grette, Gryta, Margareta, Margarete.
Meaning: 'pearl' (Greek) as a German and Scandinavian diminutive of Margareta (Margaret).

Griselda

Variants and diminutives: Chriselda, Criselda, Griseldis, Grishilda, Grishilde, Grissel, Grittie, Grizel, Grizelda, Grizzel, Grizzie, Selda, Zelda.
Meaning: 'grey' and 'battle' (Germanic).

Guadelupe

Variants and diminutives: Guada, Guadaloupa, Guadaloupe, Guadaloupa, Guadalupi, Guadelupe, Guadolupa, Guadolupe, Lupe, Lupeta, Lupina, Lupita.
Meaning: 'the world's valley' (Spanish); derived from the name of the West Indian island group in the Leeward Islands.

Guinevere

Variants and diminutives: Gaenor, Gaynor, Genevra, Ginevra, Guener, Guenever, Guenevere, Guenievre, Guinever, Gweniver, Jenifer, Jennifer, Jenniver.
Meaning: 'fair' and 'yielding' or 'ghost' (Welsh).

Gwen

Variants and diminutives: Gwena, Gwenna, Gwinn, Gwynn, Gwynne, Wynne.
Meaning: 'fair' (Welsh). Also a diminutive of Gwendolyn and other names beginning with 'Gwen-'. A female version of Gwyn.

Gwendolyn

Variants and diminutives: Guendolen, Gwen, Gwena, Gwenda, Gwendaline, Gwendeth, Gwendi, Gwendolen, Gwendolin, Gwendolina, Gwendoline, Gwendolyne, Gwendolynn, Gwenna, Gwennie, Gwenny, Wenda, Wendi, Wendie, Wendoline, Wendy, Wyn, Wynelle, Wynette, Wynne.
Meaning: 'fair' and 'ring' (Welsh).

Gwyneth

Variants and diminutives: Gwen, Gwenda, Gwenith, Gwenn, Gwenne, Gwennie, Gwenny, Gwenth, Gwyn, Gwynne, Gwynedd, Gwynneth, Wendi, Wendie, Wendy, Winni, Winnie, Winny, Wynne.
Meaning: 'happiness' or 'luck' (Welsh).

Habiba

Variants and diminutives: Haviva.
Meaning: 'lover' or 'beloved' (Arabic). A female version of Habib.

Hadara

Meaning: 'bedeck with loveliness' (Hebrew).

Hadassah

Variants and diminutives: Dasi, Dassi, Hadassa.
Meaning: 'myrtle' or 'bride' (Hebrew).

Hagar

Meaning: 'abandoned' (Hebrew).

Hana

Variants and diminutives: Hanae, Hanako.
Meaning: 'blossom' (Japanese); 'sky' or 'dark cloud' (Arapaho).

Hannah

Variants and diminutives: Anci, Aniko, Ann, Anna, Anne, Annuska, Chana, Chanah, Chani, Hana, Hania, Hanicka, Hanita, Hanka, Hanna, Hanne, Hannele, Hanni, Hannie, Hanny, Johannah, Nan, Nana, Nina, Ninascka, Nusi, Ona.
Meaning: 'I have been favoured (by God)' (Hebrew).

Harmony

Variants and diminutives: Harmonee, Harmoni, Harmonia, Harmonie.
Meaning: 'harmony' (Greek).

Harriet

Variants and diminutives: Arriet, Enrica, Enrichetta, Enrieta, Enriqueta, Enriquita, Etta, Etti, Ettie, Haliaka, Harri, Harrie, Harrietta, Harriette, Harriot, Harriott, Hatti, Hattie, Hatty, Hendrike, Henia, Henka, Henrie, Henrieta, Henriete, Henrietta, Henriette, Henrinka, Henriqueta, Hetta, Hetti, Hettie, Hetty, Jarri, Jindraska, Kika, Kiki, Minette, Queta, Yetta, Yettie, Yetty.
Meaning: 'home' and 'ruler' (Germanic) as a female version of Harry (Henry).

Hasika

Meaning: 'laughter' (Sanskrit).

Hayat

Meaning: 'life' (Arabic).

Hayley

Variants and diminutives: Haile, Hailey, Haley, Hali, Halie, Halli, Hallie, Hally, Haylie.
Meaning: 'hay' and 'meadow' (Old English); derived from an English family name, in turn derived from a place name; 'hero' (Norse); 'ingenious' (Irish Gaelic).

Hazel

Meaning: 'hazelnut' (Old English); derived from the common name of the *Corylus* genus of nut-bearing trees.

Heather

Meaning: 'flowering heath' or 'heather' (Middle English); derived from the common name of ericaceous shrubs, such as *Calluna vulgaris* and *Erica*.

Hebe

Meaning: 'young' (Greek).

Hedwig

Variants and diminutives: Eda, Heda, Hedda, Heddi, Heddie, Heddy, Hede, Hedi, Hedvick, Hedvika, Hedy.
Meaning: 'struggle' or 'refuge' and 'during war' (Germanic).

Heidi

Variants and diminutives: Heide, Heidie.
Meaning: 'noble' or 'nobility' (Germanic) as a diminutive of Adelheid (Adelaide).

Helen

Variants and diminutives: Ailie, Ale, Alena, Alenka, Aliute, Eileen, Eilidh, Elaina, Elaine, Elana, Elane, Elayne, Eleanor, Eleanora, Eleanore, Elen, Elena, Elene, Eleni, Elenita, Elenitsa, Elenka, Elenoa, Elenola, Elenor, Elenora, Elenore, Elenuta, Eleonor, Eleonora, Elia, Elianora, Elin, Elinor, Elle, Ellen, Elli, Ellie, Ellin, Elly, Ellyn, Elnora, Elyn, Ena, Halina, Hela, Helaine, Helayne, Hele, Helena, Hélène, Helenka, Helina, Hella, Helli, Heluska, Jelena, Jelika, Ila, Ileana, Ileanna, Ilena, Iliana, Ilka, Ilona, Ilonka, Iluska, Laina, Lana, Léan, Leena, Lena, Lenci, Lene, Leni, Lenka, Lenni, Lenore, Leona, Leonora, Leonor, Leonore, Leontina, Leora, Liana, Lili, Lina, Lino, Liolya, Liora, Nel, Nell, Nella, Nellene, Nelli, Nellie, Nelly, Nelya, Nitsa, Nora, Norah, Olena, Olenka, Yelena.
Meaning: 'bright' (Greek).

Helga

Variants and diminutives: Olga.
Meaning: 'prosperous' or 'pious' (Old Norse).

Henrietta

Variants and diminutives: Enrica, Enrichetta, Enrieta, Enriqueta, Enriquitta, Etta, Etti, Ettie, Etty, Haliaka, Harri, Harrie, Harriet, Harrietta, Harriette, Harriot, Harriott, Hatti, Hattie, Hatty, Hen, Hendrike, Henia, Henka, Henni, Hennie, Henny, Henrie, Henrieta, Henriete, Henriette, Henrinka, Henriqueta, Hetta, Hetti, Hettie, Hetty, Jarri, Jindraska, Kika, Kiki, Minette, Netta, Nettie, Netty, Oighrig, Queta, Yetta, Yettie, Yetty.
Meaning: 'home' and 'ruler' (Germanic) as a female variant of Henry.

Hephzibah

Variants and diminutives: Eppie, Eppy, Hephziba, Hepsey, Hepsie, Hepsy, Hepzi, Hepziba, Hepzibah, Hesba.
Meaning: 'she is my delight' or 'she is my desire' (Hebrew).

Hera

Meaning: 'lady' (Greek).

Hermione

Variants and diminutives: Erma, Herma, Hermia, Hermina, Hermine, Herminia, Mina.
Meaning: 'support' or 'stone' (Greek). A female variant of Hermes.

Hero

Meaning: 'hero' (Greek).

Hesper

Variants and diminutives: Hespera, Hesperia.
Meaning: 'evening' or 'evening star' (Greek).

Hester

Variants and diminutives: Esther, Hettie, Hetty.
Meaning: 'myrtle' or 'bride' (Hebrew) or 'star' (Persian) as a variant of Esther.

Hestia

Meaning: 'hearth' (Greek).

Hilary

Variants and diminutives: Hilaire, Hilaria, Hilarie, Hillarie, Hillary, Ilaria.
Meaning: 'cheerfulness' (Latin). Also a boy's name.

Hilda

Variants and diminutives: Hild, Hilde, Hildegard, Hildi, Hildie, Hildy, Hylda.
Meaning: 'battle' (Germanic).

Hippolyta

Variants and diminutives: Pollie, Polly.
Meaning: 'horse' and 'release' (Greek) as a female version of Hippolytus.

Holly

Variants and diminutives: Holley, Holli, Hollie, Hollye.
Meaning: 'holy' or 'holly tree' (Old English); derived from the common name of the *Ilex* genus of plants.

Honey

Meaning: 'honey' (Old English); derived from the name of the bee-produced food-stuff.

Honor

Variants and diminutives: Annora, Honora, Honoria, Honorine, Honour, Nora, Norah, Noreen, Norine, Norrie, Nureen, Onóra.
Meaning: 'honour' (Latin).

Hope

Variants and diminutives: Esperance, Esperanza, Hopi, Hopie.
Meaning: 'hope' (Old English); 'little valley' (Old English) when derived from an English family name and place name.

Horatia

Meaning: uncertain; possibly 'time' or 'hour' (Latin); derived from the Roman family name Horatius. A female version of Horatio (Horace).

Hortensia
Variants and diminutives: Hortense, Ortense, Ortensia.
Meaning: 'garden' (Latin); derived from the Roman family name Hortensius.

Hoshi
Variants and diminutives: Hoshie, Hoshiko, Hoshiyo.
Meaning: 'star' (Japanese).

Hulda
Variants and diminutives: Hildie, Huldah, Huldi, Huldy.
Meaning: 'weasel' (Hebrew); 'covered' or 'muffled' (Old Norse); 'beloved' or 'gracious' (Germanic).

Hyacinth
Variants and diminutives: Cinthie, Cynthia, Cynthie, Giacinta, Hy, Hyacintha, Hyacinthe, Hyacinthia, Jacenta, Jacinda, Jacinta, Jacinth, Jacintha, Jacinthe, Jackie, Jacky.
Meaning: 'precious blue stone' (Greek); derived from the name of the *Hyacinthus* genus of flowering plants. Once also a boy's name.

Hypatia
Meaning: 'highest' (Greek).

Ianthe
Variants and diminutives: Iantha, Iola, Iolanthe, Iole, Ione.
Meaning: 'violet' or 'dawn cloud' (Greek).

Ida
Variants and diminutives: Aida, Edonia, Edony, Idalee, Idaleene, Idalene, Idalia, Idalina, Idaline, Idalou, Idana, Idande, Idane, Iddes, Ide, Idel, Idella, Idelle, Idena, Ideny, Idette, Idhuna, Idina, Idona, Idonea, Idonia, Idony, Idun, Iduna, Idunn, Iduska, Ita, Itka, Ydonea.

Meaning: 'work' (Germanic); 'protection' or 'prosperity' (Old English).

Ilia
Meaning: 'from Ilium' (Latin), Ilium being Troy, the ancient city in Asia Minor.

Ilka
Variants and diminutives: Ilke.
Meaning: 'striving' or 'flattering' (Slavic).

Ilona
Variants and diminutives: Helen, Ili, Ilonka, Lonci.
Meaning: 'bright' (Greek) as a Hungarian variant of Helen; 'beautiful' (Hungarian).

Ilse
Variants and diminutives: Ilsa.
Meaning: 'God is perfection', 'God is satisfaction', 'dedicated to God' or 'God's oath' (Hebrew). A German variant of Elizabeth.

Imogen
Variants and diminutives: Emogene, Imagina, Immie, Immy, Imogene, Imogine, Imojean, Innogen, Inogen.
Meaning: uncertain; possibly 'innocent' or 'image' (Latin); possibly 'daughter'

(Irish Gaelic) as a misprint of Innogen that first appeared as the name of the daughter of Cymbeline in William Shakespeare's play *Cymbeline*.

India

Variants and diminutives: Indie, Indy.
Meaning: 'river' (Sanskrit); derived from the name of the country, itself derived from the river Indus.

Indigo

Variants and diminutives: Indie, Indy.
Meaning: 'from India' (Greek).

Indira

Variants and diminutives: Indie, Indy.
Meaning: 'splendid' (Hindi).

Inez

Variants and diminutives: Ines, Inesita, Inessa, Ynes, Ynesita, Ynez.
Meaning: 'pure' or 'chaste' (Greek) or 'lamb' (Latin) as a Spanish version of Agnes.

Ingeborg

Variants and diminutives: Inga, Ingaberg, Inge, Ingeberg, Inger, Ingmar, Ingunna, Inky.

Meaning: 'Ing's protection' (Old Norse), Ing being a Norse fertility god.

Ingrid

Variants and diminutives: Inga, Inge, Inger, Ingerith, Ingmar, Ingrede, Ingunna, Inky.
Meaning: 'Ing's beautiful one', 'Ing's daughter' or 'Ing's ride (referring to a golden boar]' (Old Norse), Ing being a Norse fertility god.

Iolanthe

Variants and diminutives: Ianthe, Iola, Iole, Yolanda, Yolande.
Meaning: 'violet' or 'dawn cloud' (Greek) as a variant of Iole.

Iole

Variants and diminutives: Ianthe, Iola, Iolanthe, Iona, Ione.
Meaning: 'violet' or 'dawn cloud' (Greek).

Iona

Variants and diminutives: Ione, Ionia.
Meaning: uncertain; possibly 'violet' or 'dawn cloud' (Greek); possibly 'island' (Old Norse); derived from the name of the Scottish Hebridean island.

Iphigenia

Variants and diminutives: Iffie, Iphie, Iphy.
Meaning: 'sacrifice' (Greek).

Irene

Variants and diminutives: Ailine, Arina, Arinka, Eireen, Eirena, Eirene, Eireni, Erena, Erene, Ereni, Ira, Ireen, Iren, Irena, Irenea, Irenee, Irenka, Irenke, Iriana, Irin, Irina, Irine, Irini, Irisha, Irka, Irusya, Irynam Jereni, Nitsa, Orina, Orya, Oryna, Rena, Rene, Renette, Reney, Renie, Renny, Rina, Yarina, Yaryna.
Meaning: 'peace' (Greek).

Iris

Variants and diminutives: Irisa, Irisha, Irissa, Irita, Iryl, Irys, Risa, Risha, Rissa.
Meaning: 'messenger of light' or 'rainbow' (Greek).

Irma

Variants and diminutives: Emma, Erma, Irmina, Irmintrude.
Meaning: 'universal' or 'whole' (Germanic).

Isabel

Variants and diminutives: Bel, Bela, Belia, Belica, Belicia, Belita, Bell, Bella,

Belle, Chabela, Chabi, Chava, Elisa, Ella, Ezabel, Ib, Ibbie, Ibbot, Ibby, Isa, Isabeau, Isabele, Isabelita, Isabella, Isabelle, Isbel, Iseabal, Iseabail, Ishbel, Isla, Isobel, Isopel, Issabell, Issi, Issie, Issy, Iza, Izabel, Izabela, Izabele, Izabella, Izzie, Izzy, Liseta, Nib, Tibbi, Tibbie, Tibbs, Tibby, Ysabel.
Meaning: 'God is perfection', 'God is satisfaction', 'dedicated to God' or 'God's oath' (Hebrew) as a variant of Elizabeth, the '-bel' (and also '-bella' and '-belle') additionally signifying 'beautiful' in Romance languages.

Ishana

Variants and diminutives: Ishani.
Meaning: 'desirable' (Sanskrit).

Isidora

Variants and diminutives: Dora, Isadora, Isadore, Isidore, Izzy.
Meaning: 'gift of Isis' (Greek), Isis being the supreme goddess of Egyptian mythology whose cult was subsequently adopted by the Greeks and Romans. A female version of Isidore.

Isla

Meaning: uncertain; possibly 'God is perfection', 'God is satisfaction', 'dedicated to God' or 'God's oath' (Hebrew) as a Scots Gaelic version of Isabel (Elizabeth); possibly derived from the name of the Scottish Hebridean island of Islay or a Scottish river.

Isolde

Variants and diminutives: Isaut, Iseult, Iseut, Isola, Isolda, Isolt, Yseult.
Meaning: 'ice' and 'rule' (Germanic); 'lovely' (Welsh).

Ita

Variants and diminutives: Ide.
Meaning: 'thirst' (Irish Gaelic).

Ivana

Variants and diminutives: Ivania, Ivanka, Ivanna, Ivannia, Ivanya, Vana.
Meaning: 'God has favoured', 'God is gracious' or 'God is merciful' (Hebrew) as a female version of Ivan, in turn a Slavic version of John.

Ivy

Variants and diminutives: Iva, Ivie, Ivi.
Meaning: 'plant' (Greek); derived from the common name of the *Hedera* genus of climbing plants.

Jacinta

Variants and diminutives: Cinthie, Cynthia, Cynthie, Giacinta, Hy, Hyacinth, Hyacintha, Hyacinthe, Hyacinthia, Jacenta, Jacinda, Jacinna, Jacinta,

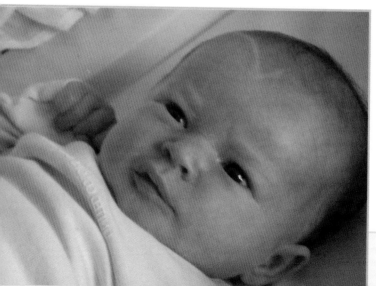

Jacinth, Jacintha, Jacinthe, Jackie, Jacky, Jacyth.
Meaning: 'precious blue stone' (Greek); derived from the name of the *Hyacinthus* genus of flowering plants. A Spanish version of Hyacinth.

Jacqueline

Variants and diminutives: Jacaline, Jacalyn, Jackalin, Jackalyn, Jackelyn, Jacket, Jackey, Jacki, Jackie, Jacklyn, Jacky, Jaclyn, Jacoba, Jacobina, Jacolyn, Jacquelyn, Jacquelynne, Jacquenetta, Jacquenette, Jaqueta, Jacquetta, Jacquette, Jacqui, Jacquie, Jaculyn, Jakelyn, Jakolina, Jaqualine, Jaqueline, Jaquelina, Jaquetta, Jaquith.
Meaning: 'supplanter' (Hebrew) as a female French version of Jacques, in turn derived from Jacob via James.

Jade

Variants and diminutives: Jayde.
Meaning: 'flank' or 'groin' (Latin); derived from the name of the jadeite or nephrite semi-precious stone that was once believed to cure renal colic.

Jael

Meaning: 'wild goat' or 'mountain goat' (Hebrew).

Jaime

Variants and diminutives: Jaimee, Jaimi, Jaimie, Jaimy, Jamee, Jamey, Jami, Jamie, Jamielee, Jaymee, Jaymi, Jaymie, Jymie.
Meaning: 'supplanter' (Hebrew) as a Spanish and Portuguese variant of James (Jacob) and thus also a boy's name.

Jamesina

Variants and diminutives: Jaime, Jamie, Jamesena, Jamie, Ina.
Meaning: 'supplanter' (Hebrew) as a female version of James (Jacob).

Jamila

Variants and diminutives: Jameela, Jameelah, Jamilah, Jamillah, Jamillia.
Meaning: 'beautiful' (Arabic). A female version of Jamal.

Jan

Variants and diminutives: Jane, Janet.
Meaning: 'God has favoured', 'God is gracious' or 'God is merciful' (Hebrew), both as a female version of John and a diminutive of Janet and of other names beginning with 'Jan-'. Also a boy's name.

Jane

Variants and diminutives: Gian, Giann, Gianna, Giannetta, Giannina, Giovanna, Hanne, Ioanna, Iva, Ivana, Ivanka, Ivanna, Jama, Jan, Jana, Janae, Janean, Janee, Janeen, Janel, Janela, Janella, Janelle, Janerette, Janess, Janessa, Janet, Janeta, Janetta, Janette, Janey, Jani, Jania, Janica, Janice, Janie, Janina, Janine, Janis, Janita, Janith, Janka, Janna, Janne, Janessa, Janissa, Jantina, Jany, Jasia, Jasisa, Jatney, Jayne, Jaynell, Jayney, Jayni, Jaynie, Jean, Jeanette, Jeani, Jeanie, Jeanine, Jeanne, Jehane, Jehanne, Jene, Jenica, Jenine, Jenka, Jenni, Jennie, Jenny, Jensine, Jess, Jessi, Jessie, Jessy, Jinni, Jinnie, Jinny, Joan, Joana, Joanka, Joanna, Joanne, Joasta, Joeann, Johanka, Johanna, Johanne, Jone, Joni, Jonie, Jony, Jovanna, Juana, Juanita, Jutta, Nita, Ohanna, Seini, Seonaid, Sheena, Shena, Sian, Sine, Sinéad, Siobhan, Vania, Yoana, Zaneta, Zanna, Zannz, Zsanett.
Meaning: 'God has favoured', 'God is gracious' or 'God is merciful' (Hebrew) as a female version of John.

Janet

Variants and diminutives: Jan, Jane, Janella, Janelle, Janeta, Janete, Janetta, Janette, Janice, Janis, Janot, Jeanette, Jenetta, Jennie, Jennit, Jenny, Jessie, Netta, Nettie, Netty, Seonaid, Shona, Sinéid.

Meaning: 'God has favoured', 'God is gracious' or 'God is merciful' (Hebrew) as a female version of John.

Janice

Variants and diminutives: Jan, Jane, Janess, Janessa, Janis, Janissa, Janith, Janissa, Jansisa.

Meaning: 'God has favoured', 'God is gracious' or 'God is merciful' (Hebrew) as a female version of John.

Janine

Variants and diminutives: Jan, Jane, Janeen, Janina, Janita, Jeanine, Jeannine, Jenine.

Meaning: 'God has favoured', 'God is gracious' or 'God is merciful' (Hebrew) as a female version of John.

Jardena

Variants and diminutives: Jordan, Jordana, Jordane, Jordann, Jordanne, Jordyn.

Meaning: 'to flow down' (Hebrew), a female variant of the boy's (and increasingly girl's) name Jordan.

Jasmine

Variants and diminutives: Jasmin, Jasmina, Jazmin, Jazmina, Jesmond, Jess, Jessamine, Jessamy, Jessamyn, Jessi, Jessie, Jessy, Yasiman, Yasmin, Yasmina, Yasmine.

Meaning: 'jasmine flower' (Persian and Arabic) as an anglicised form of Yasmin; derived from the common name of the *Jasminum* genus of fragrant flowering plants.

Jean

Variants and diminutives: Gene, Genie, Genna, Gianina, Giovanna, Giovanni, Ivana, Jana, Jane, Janeska, Janina, Janka, Janne, Jasia, Jeane, Jeanette, Jeani, Jeanice, Jeanie, Jeanine, Jeanne, Jeannette, Jeannie, Jeannine, Jehane, Jehanne, Jen, Jena, Jenalyn, Jenat, Jenda, Jenica, Jenni, Jennica, Jennie, Jennine, Jinny, Joan, Joanna, Joanne, Johanna, Johanne, Kini, Netta, Nettie, Netty, Nina.

Meaning: 'God has favoured', 'God is gracious' or 'God is merciful' (Hebrew) as a female Scottish version of John.

Jeanette

Variants and diminutives: Janet, Jean, Jeannette.

Meaning: 'God has favoured', 'God is gracious' or 'God is merciful' (Hebrew) as a female version of John, as well as a variant of Janet and Jean.

Jemima

Variants and diminutives: Jem, Jemimah, Jemma, Jona, Jonati, Jonina, Jonit, Mima, Yonina, Yemima.

Meaning: 'dove' (Hebrew and Arabic).

Jenna

Variants and diminutives: Genna, Janet, Jen, Jennabel, Jennalee, Jennalyn, Jennanne, Jennarae, Jenni, Jennie, Jennifer, Jenniver, Jenny.

Meaning: 'God has favoured', 'God is gracious' or 'God is merciful' (Hebrew) as a variant of Janet, in turn a female version of John; 'fair' and 'yielding' or 'ghost' (Welsh) as a Cornish variant of Jenny, a diminutive of Jennifer, in turn derived from Guinevere.

Jennifer

Variants and diminutives: Gaenor, Ganor, Gaynor, Genevra, Genn, Gennfer, Genny, Ginevra, Ginnifer, Ginny, Guener, Guenever, Guenevere, Guenievre, Guinever, Guinivere, Gweniver, Gwinny, Gwyneth, Jen, Jenefer, Jenifer, Jeniffer, Jenn, Jennelle, Jenni, Jennie, Jennilee, Jenniver, Jenny, Jeny, Jinny, Vanora.

Meaning: 'fair' and 'yielding' or 'ghost' (Welsh) as a Cornish variant of Guinevere.

Jenny

Variants and diminutives: Genn, Genny, Ginny, Jen, Jenn, Jenna, Jenni,

Jennie, Jenifer, Jennifer, Jenniver, Jenny, Jeny, Jinny.
Meaning: 'God has favoured', 'God is gracious' or 'God is merciful' (Hebrew) as a variant of Janet, in turn a female version of John; 'fair' and 'yielding' or 'ghost' (Welsh) as a diminutive of Jennifer, in turn derived from Guinevere.

Jessica
Variants and diminutives: Gessica, Iscah, Janka, Jesca, Jess, Jessalyn, Jesse, Jessi, Jessie, Jesslyn, Jessy.
Meaning: uncertain; possibly 'God sees' or 'wealthy' (Hebrew) as a variant of Iscah.

Jessie
Variants and diminutives: Jess, Jesse, Jessey, Jessi, Jessica, Jessy.
Meaning: 'God has favoured', 'God is gracious' or 'God is merciful' (Hebrew) as a Scottish version of Janet, in turn a female version of John; possibly 'God sees' or 'wealthy' (Hebrew) as a diminutive of Jessica, in turn a possible variant of Iscah; 'gift' or 'God exists' (Hebrew) as a female version of Jesse.

Jetta
Variants and diminutives: Jet, Jette, Jetti, Jettie, Jetty.

Meaning: 'stone of Gagai' (Greek), Gagai being a town in Lycia, Asia Minor, where jet, a decorative black variety of lignite, was once mined.

Jewel
Variants and diminutives: Jewell.
Meaning: 'plaything' (Old French); 'jewel' (Old English).

Jezebel
Meaning: 'domination' or 'impure' (Hebrew).

Jill
Variants and diminutives: Gill, Gilli, Gillian, Gillie, Gilly, Jilli, Jillian, Jilliana, Jillie, Jilly.
Meaning: uncertain; possibly 'fair-skinned' (Latin) as a diminutive of Jillian (Gillian, in turn a female variant of Julian).

Joan
Variants and diminutives:
Giovanna, Giovannina, Hanne, Ione, Ivanna, Jane, Janis, Janna, Jean, Jehane, Jenise, Jhone, Jo, Joanie, Joann, Joanna, Joanne, Joeann, Joeanna, Joeanne, Johan, Johanna, Johannah, Johanne, Johna, Johnna, Johnnie, Jonet, Joni, Jonie, Jonnie, Jovana, Jovanna, Juan, Juana, Juanita, Nita, Seonag, Siobhan, Zaneta.

Meaning: 'God has favoured', 'God is gracious' or 'God is merciful' (Hebrew) as a female variant of John.

Joanna
Variants and diminutives:
Giovanna, Giovannina, Hanne, Ivanna, Janna, Jo, Joan, Joanie, Joann, Joanne, Joeann, Joeanna, Joeanne, Johan, Johanna, Johannah, Johanne, Johna, Johnna, Johnnie, Joni, Jonnie, Jonnie, Jovana, Jovanna.
Meaning: 'God has favoured', 'God is gracious' or 'God is merciful' (Hebrew) as a female variant of John.

Jobina
Variants and diminutives: Jobey, Jobi, Jobie, Joby.
Meaning: 'persecuted' (Hebrew). A female version of Job.

Jocasta
Meaning: 'shining moon' or 'woe adorned' (Greek).

Jocelyn
Variants and diminutives: Jocelin, Joceline, Jocelynd, Jocelyne, Jos, Joscelin, Joscelind, Josceline, Joscelyn, Josceline, Joslyn, Joss.

Meaning: uncertain; possibly 'a Goth' or 'a Gaut' (Germanic), referring to a Germanic tribe; possibly 'champion' (Celtic). Also a boy's name.

Jodie
Variants and diminutives: Jodi, Jody.
Meaning: 'Jewish woman' (Hebrew) as a diminutive of Judith; 'praise' (Hebrew) as a female version of Jude, a diminutive of Judah.

Joella
Variants and diminutives: Joel, Joela, Joelle, Joellen, Joellyn.
Meaning: 'Jehovah is God' or 'God is willing' (Hebrew) as a female version of Joel.

Jolie
Variants and diminutives: Joleen, Jolene, Joletta, Joliet, Jolly.
Meaning: 'pretty' (Old French); 'jolly' (Middle English).

Joline
Variants and diminutives: Josepha, Josephine, Joleen, Jolene.
Meaning: 'God will increase' (Hebrew). A female version of Joseph.

Jonquil
Variants and diminutives: Jonquilla, Jonquille.
Meaning: 'reed' (Spanish); derived from the common name of the *Narcissus jonquilla* flowering plant.

Josephine
Variants and diminutives: Fife, Fifi, Fifine, Jo, Joe, Josepha, Josèphe, Josephina, Josette, Josie, Pepita, Peppie, Peppy, Pheenie, Pheeny, Posie, Posy, Yosepha, Yosifa.
Meaning: 'God will increase' (Hebrew). A female version of Joseph.

Joy
Variants and diminutives: Joia, Joya, Joye, Joyita.
Meaning: 'happiness' (Old French).

Joyce
Variants and diminutives: Jocea, Jocey, Jocosa, Joice, Jolia, Jooss, Josse, Jossi, Jossie, Jossy.
Meaning: uncertain; possibly 'Lord' (Breton); derived from a British family

name, in turn derived from the Latin name Jodocus via the French Breton name Joisse. Also a boy's name.

Juanita
Variants and diminutives: Juana, Nita, Wanika, Wanita.
Meaning: 'God has favoured', 'God is gracious' or 'God is merciful' (Hebrew) as a female Spanish variant of Juan (John).

Judith
Variants and diminutives: Eudice, Giulia, Ioudith, Jodette, Jodi, Jodie, Jody, Juci, Jicika, Jude, Judi, Judie, Judit, Judita, Judite, Judithe, Jitka, Judy, Jutka, Yehudit, Yudif, Yudit, Yudita, Yuta.
Meaning: 'Jewish woman' (Hebrew); 'praise' (Hebrew) as a female version of Jude, a diminutive of Judah.

Julia
Variants and diminutives: Gillie, Giula, Giulia, Giuletta, Iulia, Jula, Julca, Julcia, Jule, Jules, Juli, Juliaca, Juliana, Juliane, Julianna, Julianne, Julie, Julienne, Juliet, Julieta, Julietta, Juliette, Julina, Julinda, Juline, Julinka, Juliska, Julissa, Julita, Julitta, Julka, Julyann, Sheila, Sile, Sileas, Utili, Yula, Yulinka, Yuliya, Yulka, Yulya.
Meaning: uncertain; possibly 'fair-skinned' (Latin). A female version of Julian.

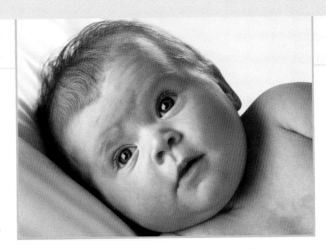

Juliana

Variants and diminutives: Julia, Jule, Jules, Juliane, Julianna, Julianne, Julie, Julienne, Juliet, Julitta, Liana, Lianne, Julyan.
Meaning: uncertain; possibly 'fair-skinned' (Latin). A female version of Julian.

Julie

Variants and diminutives: Juli, Julia, Juliana, Julianne, Jule, Jules, Julienne, Juliet, Julitta.
Meaning: uncertain; possibly 'fair-skinned' (Latin). A French version of Julia, in turn derived from Julian.

Juliet

Variants and diminutives: Giuletta, Giulietta, Juet, Juetta, Jule, Jules, Julia, Juliana, Julie, Julieta, Julietta, Juliette, Julitta, Jules.
Meaning: uncertain; possibly 'fair-skinned' (Latin). A French version of Julia, in turn derived from Julian.

June

Variants and diminutives: Juno, Junella, Unella.
Meaning: 'younger' or 'the month of June' (Latin); probably derived from the Roman family name Junius, but also linked with Juno, the Roman supreme goddess for whom the month of June may have been named.

Justine

Variants and diminutives: Jestine, Jestina, Jussie, Jussy, Justeen, Justina, Justyne.
Meaning: 'just' (Latin). A female version of Justin.

Kagami

Meaning: 'mirror' (Japanese).

Kalinda

Variants and diminutives: Kaleenda.

Meaning: 'the sun' (Hindi).

Kalindi

Variants and diminutives: Kali, Lindi.
Meaning: 'the Jumna' (Hindi), Jumna being a sacred Hindu river.

Kalyca

Variants and diminutives: Kali, Kalica, Kalie, Kalika, Kaly.
Meaning: 'rosebud' (Greek).

Kamea

Variants and diminutives: Kameo.
Meaning: 'the one' (Hawaiian).

Kammile

Variants and diminutives: Kameel, Kamil, Kamila, Kamilla, Kamillah.
Meaning: 'perfection' (Arabic) as a female version of Kamil.

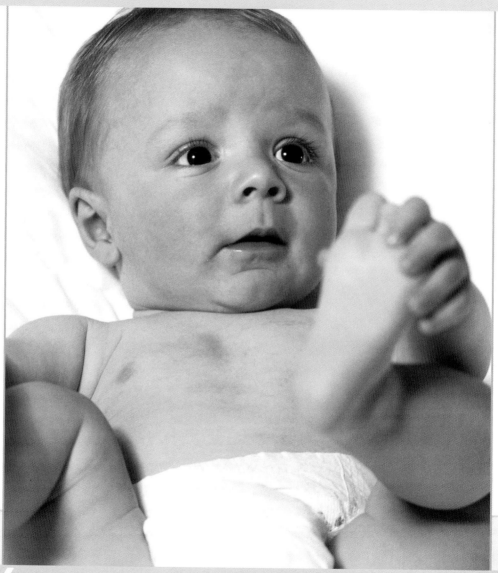

Kanani

Variants and diminutives: Ani, Nani.
Meaning: 'beautiful' (Hawaiian).

Karen

Variants and diminutives: Caren, Carin, Caron, Carren, Caryn, Kaarina, Kalena, Kalina, Kar, Kari, Karin, Karina, Karine, Karon, Karyn, Karyna, Kaz.
Meaning: 'pure' (Greek) as a Danish diminutive of Katherine (Catherine).

Karima

Variants and diminutives: Kareema, Karimah.
Meaning: 'noble' or 'generous' (Arabic). A female version of Karim.

Karita

Variants and diminutives: Cara, Cari, Carita, Carity, Charis, Charissa, Charita, Charito, Charry, Chattie, Cherry, Kara, Kari, Karina.
Meaning: 'grace' (Greek); 'kindness' (Latin); 'Christian love' (Old French). A variant of Charity.

Karma

Meaning: 'action' (Sanskrit).

Kasimira

Variants and diminutives: Kasi, Mira.
Meaning: 'peace is proclamed' (Old Slavic). A female version of Kasimir (Casimir).

Kasota

Meaning: 'cloudless sky' (Native American).

Kassia

Variants and diminutives: Kasia, Kasienka, Kasin, Kaska.
Meaning: 'pure' (Greek) as a Polish version of Katherine (Catherine).

Kate

Variants and diminutives: Cate, Catey, Catharine, Catherine, Cathy, Catie, Kadee, Kadi, Kadia, Kadiane, Kadianne, Kadie, Kadienne, Kady, Kaety, Kaiti, Kaity, Kassia, Kat, Katelyn, Katey, Katharine, Käthe, Katherine, Katee, Kati, Katie, Katy, Kay, Keti, Kit, Kittie, Kitty.
Meaning: 'pure' (Greek) as a diminutive of Katherine (Catherine).

Katherine

Variants and diminutives: Caitlin, Caitlon, Caitria, Caitrin, Cari, Cass, Cassi, Cassie, Cassy, Casy, Catalina, Catant, Cate, Catey, Catarina, Caterina, Cath, Catharin, Catharina, Catharine, Cathe, Catheline, Catherine, Cathi, Cathie, Cathleen, Cathy, Catie, Catrin, Catriona, Cayla, Ekaterina, Kaety, Kaisa, Kara, Karen, Karena, Karin, Karina, Kasia, Kasienka, Kasin, Kaska, Kassia, Kat, Kata, Katalin, Katarina, Katchen, Kate, Katee, Katelyn, Katenka, Katerina, Katerinka, Katey, Kath, Katharina, Katharine, Kathe, Katherin, Kathi, Kathie, Kathleen, Kathryn, Kathy, Kati, Katica, Katie, Katika, Katinka, Katka, Katla, Kato, Katoka, Katri, Katrin, Katrina, Katrine, Katryna, Katsa, Katus, Katuska, Katy, Katya, Kay, Kayce, Kayla, Ketya, Kisa, Kiska, Kit, Kitti, Kittie, Kitty, Kofryna, Kolina, Kotinka, Rina, Trina, Trinchen, Trine, Trinette.
Meaning: 'pure' (Greek) as a variant of Catherine.

Kathleen

Variants and diminutives: Caitlin, Cath, Catharin, Catharine, Catherin, Catherine, Cathleen, Cathy, Kaitlan, Kaitleen, Kaitlen, Kaitlin, Kaitlinn, Kaitlyn, Kaitlynn, Kate, Katelyn, Kath, Kathie, Kathlee, Kathy, Katie, Katlin, Katy, Kay, Kit, Kittie, Kitty.
Meaning: 'pure' (Greek) as an Irish variant of Katherine (Catherine).

Kathy

Variants and diminutives: Cath, Catharine, Catherine, Cathy, Kat, Kath, Katharine, Katerine, Kath, Katherine, Kathie, Kay.
Meaning: 'pure' (Greek) as a diminutive of Katherine (Catherine).

Katrina

Variants and diminutives: Cat,

Catrina, Catrine, Catriona, Kat, Katrine, Trina.
Meaning: 'pure' (Greek) as a variant of Katherine (Catherine).

Katya

Variants and diminutives: Ekaterina, Katenka, Kaaterinka, Katinka, Katka, Katryna, Katya, Ketya, Kisa, Kiska, Kitti, Kotinka.
Meaning: 'pure' (Greek) as a diminutive of Ekaterina, a Russian variant of Katherine (Catherine).

Kay

Variants and diminutives: Kai, Kailee, Kailey, Kailin, Kaye, Kayla, Kaylee, Kayley, Kaylin, Kayly, Kaylyn, Kaylynn.
Meaning: 'pure' (Greek) as a diminutive of Katherine (Catherine); 'rejoice' (Greek); 'fence' (Old Breton); 'quay' (Old French); 'spear' (Middle Low German); 'key' (Old English). Also a boy's name (see Kai).

Kayley

Variants and diminutives: Kailee, Kailey, Kay, Kayla, Kaylee, Kayleigh, Kayley, Kayly.
Meaning: 'slim' (Irish Gaelic); derived from an Irish family name.

Keely

Variants and diminutives: Keelin, Keelyn.
Meaning: 'beautiful' (Irish Gaelic).

Kelda

Variants and diminutives: Keli, Kelie, Kelli, Kellie, Kelley, Kelly.
Meaning: uncertain; possibly 'fountain', 'well' or 'spring' (Old Norse).

Kelila

Variants and diminutives: Kaila, Kaile, Kayle, Kelilah, Kelula, Kyla, Kyle, Kylene, Lylia.
Meaning: 'crowned with laurel' (Hebrew). Also a female version of Kyle.

Kelly

Variants and diminutives: Kaley, Keeley, Keely, Keli, Kelia, Kellee, Kellen, Kelley, Kelli, Kellia, Kellie, Kellina, Kelisa, Kelton, Kylie.
Meaning: uncertain; possibly 'Celtic warrior' (Greek); possibly 'warrior' or 'attender of church' (Irish Gaelic) when derived from an Irish family name; possibly 'wood' (Scots Gaelic) when derived from a Scottish family name, in turn derived from a British place name. Also a boy's name.

Kendra

Variants and diminutives: Ken, Kendis, Kenna.
Meaning: uncertain; possibly 'knowledge' (Old English).

Kenina

Variants and diminutives: Kenna, Nina.
Meaning: 'born of fire' or 'handsome' (Scottish and Irish Gaelic); 'royal oath' (Old English). A female version of Kenneth.

Keren

Variants and diminutives: Kaaren, Kareen, Karen, Karin, Karon, Karyn, Kerenhappuch, Kyran.
Meaning: 'animal horn' or 'horn of antimony' (Hebrew), antimony being a metal that was once used to beautify the eyes. A dimutive of Kerenhappuch.

Meaning: 'cassia tree', 'fragrant bark' or 'bark like cinnamon' (Hebrew).

Kim

Variants and diminutives: Kimberlee, Kimberley, Kimberli, Kimberlie, Kimberly, Kimmi, Kimmie, Kym.
Meaning: 'ruler' (Old English); 'Cyneburga's clearing' (Old English), Cyneburga being a 7th century English abbess and saint, as a diminutive of Kimberley. Also a boy's name.

Kimberley

Variants and diminutives: Kim, Kimberlee, Kimberli, Kimberlie, Kimberly, Kimmi, Kimmie, Kym.
Meaning: 'Cyneburga's clearing' (Old English), Cyneburga being a 7th century English abbess and saint; derived from an English family name, in turn derived from a number of English place names. Also a boy's name.

Kimi

Variants and diminutives: Kimie, Kimoko, Kimiyo.
Meaning: 'without equal' (Japanese).

Kira

Variants and diminutives: Kiran,

Kerry

Variants and diminutives: Ceri, Cerrie, Cerry, Keree, Keri, Kerie, Kerrey, Kerri, Kerrie.
Meaning: 'descendants of Ciar' or 'dark children' (Irish Gaelic); derived from the name of the Irish county. Also a boy's name.

Keshisha

Meaning: 'an elder' (Aramaic).

Keturah

Meaning: 'fragrance' or 'incense' (Hebrew).

Kezia

Variants and diminutives: Kerzia, Kesia, Kesiah, Ketzi, Ketzia, Kez, Kezi, Keziah, Kezzie, Kezzy, Kissie, Kiz, Kizzie, Kizzy.

Kiri, Kiriana, Kirina, Kirini, Klla, Kirra, Kyra.
Meaning: 'sun', 'throne' or 'shepherd' (Persian) as a female variant of Cyrus.

Kirby

Variants and diminutives: Kirbie.
Meaning: 'church village' (Old Norse); derived from an English family name, in turn derived from a number of English place names. Also a boy's name.

Kirsten

Variants and diminutives: Christine, Keirstan, Kersten, Kerstine, Kireen, Kirsteen, Kirstene, Kirstie, Kirstien, Kirstin, Kirstine, Kirston, Kirsty, Kirstyn.
Meaning: 'Christian' (Latin) as a Scandinavian variant of Christine (Christian).

Kirsty

Variants and diminutives: Christine, Kersty, Kirsteen, Kirsten, Kirsti, Kirstie, Kirstene, Kyrsty.
Meaning: 'Christian' (Latin) as a Scottish diminutive of Kirstene (Christine, in turn derived from Christian).

Kismet

Meaning: 'destiny' (Arabic).

Kitty
Variants and diminutives: Catherine, Kit, Kittie.
Meaning: 'pure' (Greek) as a diminutive of Katherine (Catherine).

Koko
Meaning: 'stork' (Japanese).

Kristen
Variants and diminutives: Christin, Christine, Krista, Kristan, Kristene, Kristin, Kristina, Kristine, Krysta, Krystena.
Meaning: 'Christian' (Latin) as a Danish version of Christine (Christian).

Kylie
Variants and diminutives: Keeley, Kellie, Kelly, Kilie.

Meaning: 'boomerang' (Western Australian Aboriginal); as a variant of Kelly, possibly 'Celtic warrior' (Greek); 'warrior' or 'attender of church' (Irish Gaelic) when derived from an Irish family name; 'wood' (Scots Gaelic) when derived from a Scottish family name, in turn derived from a British place name.

Lacey
Variants and diminutives: Lacee, Lacie, Lacy, Larissa.
Meaning: uncertain; possibly 'merry' (Latin) or 'citadel' (Greek) as a diminutive of Larissa; possibly 'frisky' or 'noose' (Latin) when derived from a British family name. Also a boy's name.

Laelia
Variants and diminutives: Lelia.
Meaning: 'jolly' or 'garrulous' (Latin).

Lalage
Variants and diminutives: Lala.
Meaning: 'babbling' or 'chattering' (Greek).

Lalita
Variants and diminutives: Lal, Lalie, Lita.
Meaning: 'honest' or 'charming' (Sanskrit).

Lana
Variants and diminutives: Alana, Lanna, Lanne, Lannie, Lanny.
Meaning: uncertain; possibly 'woolly' (Latin); possibly 'buoyant' (Hawaiian); possibly 'rock' (Breton), 'harmony' (Celtic), 'good-looking', 'cheerful', 'child' or 'darling' (Irish Gaelic), 'an offering' or 'light' (Hawaiian) as a diminutive of Alana (Alan).

Lara
Variants and diminutives: Larissa.
Meaning: uncertain; possibly 'merry' (Latin) or 'citadel' (Greek) as a Russian diminutive of Larissa.

Larissa

Variants and diminutives: Lacey, Lara, Laris, Larisa, Larochka, Lissa.
Meaning: uncertain; possibly 'merry' (Latin); possibly 'citadel' (Greek).

Lark

Meaning: 'lark' (Germanic); derived from the common name of the Alaudidae family of songbirds.

Laura

Variants and diminutives: Lara, Laraine, Lari, Larilia, Larinda, Lauraine, Lauran, Laurane, Laure, Laureana, Laureen, Laurel, Laurella, Lauren, Laurena, Laurene, Laurestine, Lauretta, Laurette, Lauri, Laurice, Laurie, Lauriette, Laurina, Laurinda, Laurine, Laurka, Lawrie, Lavra, Lola,
Lollie, Lolly, Lora, Lorain, Loraine, Loral, Lorann, Lorayne, Loree, Loreen, Lorell, Loren, Lorena, Lorene, Lorenza, Loretah, Loretta, Lorette, Lori, Lorie, Lorinda, Lorine, Lorita, Lorna, Lorraine, Lorri, Lorrie, Lorry, Loura, Lourana.
Meaning: 'laurel' (Latin); 'from Laurentum' (Latin), Laurentum being the Roman name of an Italian town, as a female version of Laurence.

Laurel

Variants and diminutives: Laura, Laure, Laurella, Loral, Lorell.
Meaning: 'laurel' (Latin) as a variant of Laura; 'from Laurentum' (Latin), Laurentum being the Roman name of an Italian town, as a female version of Laurence.
Notable namesakes: a character in Arthurian legend.

Lauren

Variants and diminutives: Laura, Lauran, Laurena, Laurene, Laurencia, Laurentia, Laurenza, Laurie, Laurin, Laurine, Lauryn, Loreen, Loren, Lorena, Lorene, Lorenza, Lorin, Lorine, Lorrin, Loryn, Lorynn, Lorynne.
Meaning: 'laurel' (Latin) as a variant of Laura; 'from Laurentum' (Latin), Laurentum being the Roman name
of an Italian town, as a female version of Laurence.

Lavender

Meaning: 'to wash' (Latin); derived from the common name of the *Lavandula* genus of fragrant plants.

Laverne

Variants and diminutives: Lavern, Laverna, LaVerne, La Verne, Luvern.
Meaning: 'the springtime' (Latin); 'the green one' (Old French).

Lavinia

Variants and diminutives: Lavena, Lavina, Lavinie, Vin, Vina, Vinia, Vinnie, Vinny.
Meaning: uncertain; possibly 'woman of Rome' (Latin).

Leah

Variants and diminutives: Lea, Lee, Leigh, Lia, Liah.
Meaning: 'weary', 'gazelle' or 'cow' (Hebrew).

Leanne

Variants and diminutives: Ann, Anne, Lee, Leeanne, Lee-Ann, Leigh-Anne, Liane, Lianne.
Meaning: uncertain; probably a compound name comprising Lee,

'meadow', 'clearing' or 'wood' (Old English), and Anne (Hannah), 'I have been favoured (by God)' (Hebrew).

Leda

Variants and diminutives: Ledah, Lida, Lidah, Lidia.
Meaning: 'woman' (Lycian).

Leeba

Variants and diminutives: Liba, Luba.
Meaning: 'heart' (Hebrew); 'dear one' (Yiddish).

Leila

Variants and diminutives: Laila, Laili, Lailie, Laleh, Layla, Leila, Leilah, Leilia, Lela, Lelah, Lelia, Lila, Leyla.
Meaning: 'dark' or 'night' (Arabic).

Leilani

Variants and diminutives: Lei, Lelani.
Meaning: 'heavenly' and 'child' or 'flower' (Hawaiian).

Lelia

Variants and diminutives: Lela, Lélia.
Meaning: uncertain; derived from the Roman family name Laelius.

Lena

Variants and diminutives: Galina, Helena, Leena, Lenah, Lene, Lenea, Lenette, Liene, Lina, Linah, Magdalene.

Meaning: 'lodging place' (Hebrew); 'seductress' (Latin); 'bright' (Greek) as a diminutive of Helena (Helen).

Leona

Variants and diminutives: Leola, Leoma, Leonarda, Leone, Leonel, Leonia, Leonice, Léonie, Leonina, Leonine, Leonora, Leontine, Leontyne, Leora, Leota, Liona, Lona, Loni.
Meaning: 'lion' (Latin) as a female variant of Leo.

Léonie

Variants and diminutives: Leona, Leone, Leonia, Leonice, Leonina, Leonine, Liona, Lona.
Meaning: 'lion' (Latin) as a female French variant of Leo.

Leonora

Variants and diminutives: Eleanora, Leonarda, Lenora, Lenore, Nora, Norah, Nornie.
Meaning: 'bright' (Greek) as a diminutive of Eleanora (Helen via Eleanor), and, as such, also 'foreign' (Germanic); 'lion' (Latin) as a variation of Leona (Leo).

Leora

Meaning: 'light' (Hebrew) as a female version of Leor; 'lion' (Latin) as a variant of Leona (Leo).

Leta

Variants and diminutives: Letitia.
Meaning: 'joyful' (Latin) as a diminutive of Letitia; 'bringer' (Swahili).

Letifa

Variants and diminutives: Letipha.
Meaning: 'gentle' (Arabic).

Letitia

Variants and diminutives: Laetitia, Latisha, Laytisha, Lece, Lecelina, Lecia, Leda, Leetice, Leta, Lethia, Letice, Leticia, Letisha, Letizia, Letti, Lettice, Lettie, Letty, Letycia, Loutitia, Tish, Tisha, Titia.
Meaning: 'joyful' (Latin).

Levana

Variants and diminutives: Levanna, Levona, Livana, Livona.
Meaning: 'rising sun' or 'lifter' (Latin).

Levia

Variants and diminutives: Livia, Liviya.
Meaning: 'attached' or 'pledged' (Hebrew) as a female version of Levi.

Lexa

Variants and diminutives: Lecksi, Leksi, Leksie, Lexi, Lexie, Lexia.

Meaning: 'word' (Greek) as a female version of Lex; 'defender of men' or 'warrior' (Greek) as a diminutive of Alexandra (Alexander).

Liana

Variants and diminutives: Juliana, Lean, Leana, Leane, Leanna, Leanne, Lia, Liane, Lianna, Lianne, Oliana.
Meaning: uncertain; possibly 'fair-skinned' (Latin) as a diminutive of Juliana (Julian); 'to bind' (French).

Libby

Variants and diminutives: Elizabeth, Lib, Libbie.
Meaning: 'God is perfection', 'God is satisfaction', 'dedicated to God' or 'God's oath' (Hebrew) as a diminutive of Elizabeth.

Liberty

Variants and diminutives: Lib, Libbie, Libby.
Meaning: 'freedom' (Latin).

Liesel

Variants and diminutives: Elizabeth, Liese, Lieselotte, Liesl, Lise, Lisette.
Meaning: 'God is perfection', 'God is satisfaction', 'dedicated to God' or 'God's oath' (Hebrew) as a German diminutive of Elizabeth.

Lilac
Variants and diminutives: Lila, Lilah.
Meaning: 'bluish' (Persian); derived from the common name of the *Syringa* genus of flowering shrubs.

Lilith
Variants and diminutives: Lilis, Lilita, Lillith, Lillus.
Meaning: uncertain; possibly 'storm goddess' or 'of the night' (East Semitic).

Lillian
Variants and diminutives: Boske, Bozsi, Elizabeth, Leka, Lelya, Lena, Lenka, Liana, Lieschen, Liesel, Lil, Lila, Lilana, Lileana, Lili, Lilia, Lilian, Liliana, Liliane, Lilias, Lilie, Lilike, Lilion, Liliosa, Liljana, Lill, Lilla, Lilli, Lillias, Lillie, Lillis, Lilly, Lily, Lilyan, Olena, Olenka.

Meaning: 'lily' (Greek) as a variant of Lily; 'God is perfection', 'God is satisfaction', 'dedicated to God' or 'God's oath' (Hebrew) as a variant of Elizabeth.

Lily
Variants and diminutives: Boske, Bozsi, Elizabeth, Leka, Lelya, Lena, Lenka, Liana, Lieschen, Liesel, Lil, Lila, Lilana, Lileana, Lili, Lilia, Lilian, Liliana, Liliane, Lilias, Lilie, Lilike, Lilion, Liliosa, Liljana, Lilla, Lillah, Lilli, Lillian, Lillie, Lillis, Lilly, Lilya, Lilyan, Olena, Olenka.
Meaning: 'lily' (Greek) when derived from the common name of the Lilium genus of flowering plants; 'God is perfection', 'God is satisfaction', 'dedicated to God' or 'God's oath' (Hebrew) as a variant of Elizabeth.

Linda
Variants and diminutives: Belinda, Lin, Lindi, Lindia, Lindie, Lindita, Lindy, Lyn, Lynda, Lynn, Lynne.
Meaning: 'snake' (Germanic); 'pretty' (Spanish); 'neat' (Italian); also a diminutive of any name ending in '-linda', such as Belinda.

Lindsay
Variants and diminutives: Linda, Lindsey, Lindsie, Linsey, Linsi, Linsie, Linsy, Lyndsay, Lyndsey, Lyndsy, Lynsey.

Meaning: 'island' or 'wetland' and 'of lime trees' or 'of Lincoln' (Old English); derived from a Scottish family name, in turn derived from the English place name Lindsey. Also a boy's name.

Linnea
Variants and diminutives: Linea, Linna, Linnae, Linnaea, Lynea, Lynnea.
Meaning: derived from the Linnaea (twin flower) genus of flowering plants named for the Swedish botanist Carolus Linnaeus (Carl von Linné).

Lirit
Variants and diminutives: Lyra, Lyre, Lyris.
Meaning: 'lyrical' (Hebrew).

Liron
Variants and diminutives: Lirone.
Meaning: 'my song' (Hebrew) or 'the circle' (Old French) as a female version of Leron.

Lisa
Variants and diminutives: Elizabeth, Liese, Lis, Lisbeth, Lise, Liseta, Lisette, Liza, Lizette.
Meaning: 'God is perfection', 'God is satisfaction', 'dedicated to God' or 'God's oath' (Hebrew) as a diminutive of Elizabeth.

Livia

Variants and diminutives: Olivia, Levia, Liv, Livie, Liviya, Livy, Livvie, Livvy

Meaning: 'black and blue' (Latin) when derived from the Roman family name Livius; 'olive' (Latin) as a diminutive of Olivia; 'crown' (Hebrew).

Liz

Variants and diminutives: Elizabeth, Lisa, Lisabet, Lisabeth, Lisabette, Lisbet, Lisbeth, Liz, Liza, Lizana, Lizanne, Lizabeth, Lizabette, Lizbeth, Lizbett, Lizet, Lizette, Lizina, Lizzie, Lizzy, Lyza, Lyzbeth, Lyzet, Lyzett, Lyzette.

Meaning: 'God is perfection', 'God is satisfaction', 'dedicated to God' or 'God's oath' (Hebrew) as a diminutive of Elizabeth.

Llewella

Variants and diminutives: Lewella, Louella, Luella.

Meaning: 'leader' or 'lion' and 'resemblance' (Welsh) as a female version of Llewellyn.

Lois

Variants and diminutives: Eloise, Louise.

Meaning: uncertain; possibly 'desirable' or 'good' (Greek); possibly 'famed' and 'warrior' (Germanic) as a variant of Louise, in turn a female version of Louis (Ludwig).

Lola

Variants and diminutives: Dolores, Lo, Lolita, Lita, Loleta, Luchel, Lurleen, Lurline.

Meaning: 'sorrows' (Spanish) as a diminutive of Dolores.

Lorelei

Variants and diminutives: Lorelie, Lorilee, Lura, Lurette, Lurleen, Lurlene, Lurline.

Meaning: uncertain; derived from Lurlei, the name of a rock on the German river Rhine, south of Koblenz.

Lorna

Variants and diminutives: Lona, Lornna.

Meaning: uncertain; possibly 'forlorn' (Old English); possibly 'from Laurentum' (Latin), Laurentum being the Roman name of an Italian town, as a variant of Laura (Laurence); possibly derived from a Scottish place name; coined by the English writer R D Blackmore for the eponymous heroine of his novel *Lorna Doone, A Romance of Exmoor*.

Lorraine

Variants and diminutives: Laraine, Larraine, Lauraine, Laurraine, Lorain, Loraine, Lorayna, Lorayne, Lorrane, Lorrayne, Raina, Rayna.

Meaning: 'Lothar's kingdom' (Latin); derived from the name of the Lorraine region of eastern France that was once ruled by the Holy Roman emperor Lothar (Lothair) I.

Lottie

Variants and diminutives: Charlotte, Elizabeth, Lieselotte, Lotta, Lotte, Lotty.

Meaning: 'man' or 'free man' (Germanic) as diminutive of Charlotte, in turn a female version of Charles; 'God is perfection', 'God is satisfaction', 'dedicated to God' or 'God's oath' (Hebrew) as a diminutive of Lieselotte (Elizabeth).

Louella

Variants and diminutives: Llewella, Lewella, Luella.

Meaning: a compound name comprising Lou, 'famed' and 'warrior' (Germanic) as a diminutive of Louise, in turn a female version of Louis (Ludwig), and Ella, 'all' (Germanic) or 'fairy' and 'maiden' (Old English), also a variant of Elizabeth and Ellen.

Louise

Variants and diminutives: Aloisa, Aloise, Aloisia, Alouise, Aloys, Aloyse, Aloysia, Aluisa, Eloisa, Eloise, Eloisia, Heloise, Isa, Iza, Lewes, Lisette, Lodoiska, Lois, Loise, Lou, Louie, Louisa, Louisetta, Louisette, Lovisa, Loyce, Lu, Ludka, Ludwika, Luisa, Luisana, Luisanna, Luise, Luisetta, Luisina, Luiza, Lujza, Lula, Lulita, Lulu, Lutza, Luyiza, Ouida.
Meaning: 'famed' and 'warrior' (Germanic) as a female version of Louis (Ludwig).

Lourdes

Meaning: uncertain; derived from the name of the French place of pilgrimage.

Loveday

Variants and diminutives: Lovdie, Lowdy, Luveday.
Meaning: 'day of love' (Old English).

Lucia

Variants and diminutives: Cindie, Cindy, Lu, Luce, Lucetta, Lucette, Luci, Luciana, Lucie, Lucienne, Lucija, Lucile, Lucilla, Lucille, Lucina, Lucinda, Lucine, Lucita, Lucky, Lucy, Lusita, Luz, Luzia, Luzija, Luzine.
Meaning: 'light' (Latin) as a female version of Lucius.

Lucilla

Variants and diminutives: Cilla, Lu, Luce, Lucia, Lucile, Lucille, Lucy.
Meaning: 'light' (Latin) as a variant of Lucia, in turn a female version of Lucius.

Lucinda

Variants and diminutives: Cindie, Cindy, Lu, Lucia, Lucinde, Lucy.
Meaning: 'light' (Latin) as a diminutive of Lucia, in turn a female version of Lucius.

Lucretia

Variants and diminutives: Lucrece, Lucrecia, Lucretzia, Lucrezia.
Meaning: uncertain; possibly 'gain' (Latin); derived from the Roman family name Lucretius.

Lucy

Variants and diminutives: Cindy, Laoise, Lu, Luca, Luce, Lucetta, Lucette, Luci, Lucia, Luciana, Luciane, Lucida, Lucie, Lucienne, Lucija, Lucika, Lucila, Lucile, Lucilla, Lucille, Lucina, Lucinda, Lucine, Lucita, Lucka, Lucky, Lucya, Lulu, Lusita, Luz, Luzi, Luzie, Luzia, Luzija, Luzine.
Meaning: 'light' (Latin) as an English variant of Lucia, in turn a female version of Lucius.

Ludmilla

Variants and diminutives: Ludie, Ludmila, Ludovika.
Meaning: 'people' and 'grace' or 'beloved' (Slavonic).

Lulu

Variants and diminutives: Lleulu, Louise, Lu, Lucy.
Meaning: 'rabbit' (Native American); 'famed' and 'warrior' (Germanic) as a diminutive of Louise, in turn a female version of Louis (Ludwig); 'light' (Latin) as a diminutive of Lucy (Lucia), in turn a female version of Lucius.

Luna

Variants and diminutives: Lunette.
Meaning: 'moon', 'month' or 'crescent' (Latin).

Lydia

Variants and diminutives: Liddie, Liddy, Lida, Lidi, Lidia, Lidie, Lidiya, Lidka, Lidochka, Lyda, Lydda, Lydie.
Meaning: 'from Lydia' (Greek), Lydia being an ancient region of Asia Minor.

Lynette

Variants and diminutives: Eiluned, Eluned, Lanette, Linet, Linetta, Linette, Linnet, Linnett, Linette, Luned, Lyn, Lynette, Lynn, Lynne, Lynnet, Lynnette.
Meaning: uncertain; possibly 'flax' (Latin) as a variant of Linnet, linnet being the common name of the flax-eating finch Acanthis cannabina; possibly 'idol' or 'adored one' (Welsh) as a variant of Eluned.

Lynn

Variants and diminutives: Carolyn, Eluned, Lin, Lina, Linda, Linell, Linelle, Linn, Linne, Linnet, Linnette, Lyn, Lynda, Lyndel, Lyndell, Lyndelle, Lynell, Lynelle, Lynette, Lynna, Lynne, Lynelle.

Meaning: 'lake' (Celtic); 'snake' (Germanic), 'pretty' (Spanish) or 'neat' (Italian) as a diminutive of Lynda (Linda); 'flax' (Latin), 'idol' or 'adored one' (Welsh) as a diminutive of Lynette; also a diminutive of a number of names containing the '-lyn-' element, such as Carolyn. Also a boy's name (generally Lyn).

Lyra

Variants and diminutives: Lirit, Lyre, Lyris.
Meaning: 'lyre' (Greek).

Lysandra

Variants and diminutives: Sandie, Sandra, Sandy.
Meaning: 'freer of men' (Greek) as a female version of Lysander.

Mabel

Variants and diminutives: Amabel, Amabella, Maeve, Mab, Mabb, Mabbit, Mabbot, Mabbs, Mabell, Mabella, Mabelle, Mabilia, Mabilla, Mable, Mably, Mapp, Mappin, Mapps, Mave, Mavis.
Meaning: 'lovable' (Latin) as a

diminutive of Amabel; 'intoxicating' (Irish Gaelic) as a variant of Maeve.

Madeleine

Variants and diminutives: Lena, Lenna, Lina, Linn, Lynn, Lynne, Mada, Madia, Madaleine, Madalina, Madaliene, Madaline, Madalyn, Madalyne, Madalynn, Madalynne, Maddi, Maddie, Maddy, Madelaine, Madelena, Madelina, Madeline, Madena, Madge, Madina, Madlen, Madlin, Madlyn, Mady, Magaly, Magda, Magdalen, Magdalena, Magdalene, Magdalina, Magola, Mahda, Mala, Malena, Marla, Marleen, Marlena, Marlene, Marlina, Marline.
Meaning: 'woman from Magdala' (Hebrew), Magdala being a place on the Sea of Galilee, as a French variant of Magdalene.

Madonna

Variants and diminutives: Donna, Maria, Mary.
Meaning: 'my lady' (Italian), usually referring to the Virgin Mary.

Maeve

Variants and diminutives: Mab, Mabel, Madhbh, Mauve, Mave, Mavis, Meadhbh, Meave, Medb.
Meaning: 'intoxicating' (Irish Gaelic).

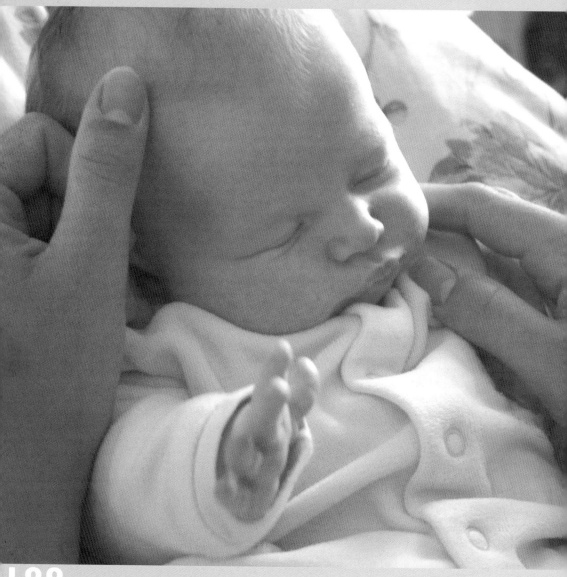

Magdalene

Variants and diminutives: Delenna, Leli, Lena, Lene, Lenna, Lina, Linn, Lynn, Lynne, Mada, Madaleine, Madalena, Madaliene, Madaline, Madalyn, Madalyne, Madeline, Madalynne, Maddalena, Maddi, Maddie, Maddy, Madeena, Madel, Madelaine, Madeleine, Madelena, Madelia, Madelina, Madeline, Madella, Madelle, Madelon, Madelyn, Madge, Madia, Madina, Madlen, Madli, Madlin, Madlyn, Madlynn, Madlynne, Mady, Mag, Magaly, Magda, Magdale, Magdalen, Magdalena, Magdalina, Magdaline, Magdelina, Magia, Magli, Magola, Mahda, Mai, Mala, Malena, Mali, Malin, Manda, Marla, Marleen, Marlena, Marlene, Marlie, Marlina, Marline, Marlo, Marlowe, Marlys, Maudlin, Migdana.
Meaning: 'woman from Magdala' (Hebrew), Magdala being a place on the Sea of Galilee.

Maggie

Variants and diminutives: Mag, Maggi, Maggy, Margaret.
Meaning: 'pearl' (Greek) as a diminutive of Margaret.

Magnolia

Variants and diminutives: Lia.
Meaning: uncertain; derived from the *Magnolia* genus of flowering shrubs named for the French botanist Pierre Magnol.

Mahala

Variants and diminutives: Mahalah, Mahalia, Mahela, Mahelia, Mahila, Mahilia, Mehala, Mehalah, Mehalia.
Meaning: 'tenderness' or 'infertile' (Hebrew); 'woman' (Native American).

Mahina

Variants and diminutives: Hina.
Meaning: 'moon' (Hawaiian).

Mahira

Variants and diminutives: Mehira.
Meaning: 'energetic' or 'quick' (Hebrew).

Maia

Variants and diminutives: Mae, Mai, May, Maya.
Meaning: 'mother' or 'nurse' (Greek).

Maidie

Variants and diminutives: Maddie, Maddy, Maid, Maida, Maidel, Maidie, Maidey, Margaret, Mary.
Meaning: uncertain; possibly 'little maid' (Old English); possibly 'pearl' (Greek) as a diminutive of Margaret; possibly 'longed-for child' or 'rebellion' (Hebrew) as a diminutive of Mary (Miriam).

Maire

Variants and diminutives: Mair, Mary.
Meaning: 'dark' (Celtic); 'longed-for child' or 'rebellion' (Hebrew) as an Irish Gaelic variant of Mary (Miriam).

Maisie

Variants and diminutives: Mairead, Maise, Margaret, Mysie.
Meaning: 'pearl' (Greek) as a diminutive of Margaret; 'maize' (French).

Maja

Variants and diminutives: Majidah.
Meaning: 'splendid' (Arabic).

Malka

Variants and diminutives: Malkah.
Meaning: 'queen' (Hebrew and Arabic).

Malu

Variants and diminutives: Malulani.
Meaning: 'peace' (Hawaiian).

Malvina

Variants and diminutives: Melvina, Vina.

Meaning: uncertain; possibly 'smooth' and 'brow' (Scots Gaelic); coined by the Scottish writer James Macpherson.

Mamie
Variants and diminutives: Mary, Miriam.
Meaning: 'my darling' (French); 'longed-for child' or 'rebellion' (Hebrew) as a diminutive of Mary (Miriam).

Mandy
Variants and diminutives: Amanda, Armanda, Mand, Manda, Mandi, Mandie.
Meaning: 'lovable' or 'fit to be loved' (Latin) as a diminutive of Amanda.

Mangena
Variants and diminutives: Mangena.
Meaning: 'song' or 'melody' (Hebrew).

Manuela
Variants and diminutives: Emanuella, Emmanuela.
Meaning: 'God is with us' (Hebrew) as a female version of Manuel (Emmanuel).

Mara
Variants and diminutives: Marah.
Meaning: 'bitter' (Hebrew).

Marcella
Variants and diminutives: Malinda, Marcela, Marcelia, Marcelinda, Marcelle, Marcellina, Marcelline, Marcelyn, Marcha, Marci, Marcia, Marcie, Marcile, Marcilen, Marcille, Marcy, Marisella, Marquita, Marsha, Marshe, Melinda.
Meaning: uncertain; possibly 'martial' (Latin) through association with Mars, the god of war in Roman mythology, as a female version of Marcellus.

Marcia
Variants and diminutives: Marcelia, Marcella, Marcelle, Marcha, Marci, Marcie, Marcile, Marcille, Marcy, Marquita, Marsha, Marshe, Marsi, Marsie, Marsy.
Meaning: uncertain; possibly 'martial' (Latin) through association with Mars, the god of war in Roman mythology, as a female version of Marcus.

Margaret
Variants and diminutives: Daisy, Ghita, Gita, Gitka, Gitta, Gituska, Gogo, Greta, Gretal, Gretchen, Grete, Gretel, Gretie, Gretta, Grieta, Gritty, Madge, Madie, Mady, Mae, Maergrethe, Mag, Magge, Maggi, Maggie, Maggy, Mago, Maidie, Maiga, Mairead, Maisie, Maisy, Makelesi, Mamie, Manci, Mared, Marga, Margalit, Margalith, Margara, Margareta, Margarete, Margaretha, Margarethe, Margaretta, Margarette, Margarid, Margarida, Margarinda, Margarita, Margaritis, Margaro, Margat, Margaux, Marge, Margebelle, Marged, Margene,

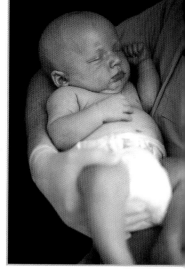

Margerie, Margery, Marget, Marghanita, Margherita, Margiad, Margie, Margisia, Margit, Margita, Margo, Margot, Margret, Margreta, Margrete, Margrethe, Margrieta, Marguarita, Marguerita, Marguerite, Marguita, Margy, Mari, Marjarie, Marjary, Marjatta, Marje, Marjie, Marjorie, Marjory, Marka, Marketa, Marleah, Marles, May, Meaghan, Meeri, Meg, Megan, Meggi, Meggie, Meggy, Meghan, Mergret, Meta, Midge, Mittie, Mog, Moggie, Moggy, Molly, Mysie, Peg, Peggi, Peggie, Peggy, Penina, Perla, Polly, Reatha, Reet, Reta, Rita, Tita.
Meaning: 'pearl' (Greek).

Maria

Variants and diminutives: Carmen, Dolores, Jesusa, Lucita, Luz, Mareea, Mariabella, Mari, Mariah, Mariamne, Mary, Marya, Mia, Mitzi.
Meaning: 'longed-for child' or 'rebellion' (Hebrew) as the Latin form of Mary (Miriam).

Marian

Variants and diminutives: Ann, Anna, Anne, Mari, Mariamne, Mariane, Mariann, Marianne, Marien, Marion, Meirion, Mor, Morag.
Meaning: 'longed-for child' or 'rebellion' (Hebrew) as a variant of Marianne and Mary (Miriam).

Marianne

Variants and diminutives: Ann, Anna, Anne, Mari, Mariamne, Marian, Mariana, Mariane, Mariann, Marianna, Marien, Mary, Maryam, Maryann, Maryanna, Maryanne.
Meaning: a compound name comprising Marie (Miriam via Mary), 'longed-for child' or 'rebellion' (Hebrew), and Anne (Hannah via Anna), 'I have been favoured (by God)' (Hebrew).

Marie

Variants and diminutives: Maree, Mari, Marietta, Mariette.

Meaning: 'longed-for child' or 'rebellion' (Hebrew) as a French variant of Mary (Miriam).

Marigold

Variants and diminutives: Goldie, Goldy, Mari, Marie, Mary, Marygold.
Meaning: 'Mary's gold' (Old English); derived from the common name of the *Tagetes* genus of flowering plants.

Marilyn

Variants and diminutives: Maralin, Maralyn, Mara-Lyn, MaraLyn, Maralyne, Maralynn, Mari, Marilee, Marilene, Marilil, Marillin, Marillyn, Marilynn, Marilynne, Marlyn, Marolyn, Marrilyn, Marylin, Maryline, Marylyn, Marylynn, Merili, Merilyn, Merilynn, Merrilyn.
Meaning: a composite name comprising Mary (Miriam), 'longed-for child' or 'rebellion' (Hebrew), and Lyn (Lynn), 'lake' (Celtic), 'snake' (Germanic), 'pretty' (Spanish), 'neat' (Italian), 'flax' (Latin), 'idol' or 'adored one' (Welsh).

Marina

Variants and diminutives: Mare, Maren, Marena, Marie, Maris, Marisa, Marisella, Marissa, Marna, Marne, Marni, Marnie, Marnina, Marys,

Meris, Rina.
Meaning: 'of the sea' (Latin).

Marisa

Variants and diminutives: Mareesa, Mari, Maris, Marissa, Marisella, Marita, Maritza, Marrisa, Mary, Marysa, Maryse, Maryssa, Meris, Merisa, Merissa, Morissa, Risa, Rissa.
Meaning: 'longed-for child' or 'rebellion' (Hebrew) as a variant of Mary (Miriam).

Marjorie

Variants and diminutives: Margaret, Marge, Margerie, Margery, Margie, Marjarie, Marjary, Marje, Marjie, Marjory, Marsali.
Meaning: 'pearl' (Greek) as a variant of Margaret.

Marlene

Variants and diminutives: Layna, Lene, Lena, Leyna, Lina, Linn, Lynn, Lynne, Magdalena, Magdalene, Mala, Malena, Marla, Marlaina, Marlaine, Marlane, Marle, Marlea, Marleah, Marlee, Marleen, Marlena, Marley, Marlie, Marlies, Marlin, Marlina, Marline, Marlyn, Mary.
Meaning: a compound name comprising Maria (Miriam via Mary), 'longed-for child' or 'rebellion'

(Hebrew), and Magdalena (Magdalene), 'woman from Magdala' (Hebrew).

Marnie
Variants and diminutives: Marina, Marna, Marni.
Meaning: 'of the sea' (Latin) as a variant of Marina.

Marnina
Variants and diminutives: Marni, Marnie, Marny, Nina.
Meaning: 'rejoicer' or 'singer' (Hebrew). A female version of Marnin.

Martha
Variants and diminutives: Maita, Marcia, Mardeth, Mardie, Mart, Marta, Martelle, Marthe, Marthena, Marti, Marticka, Martie, Martina, Martita, Martus, Martuska, Marty, Masia, Matti, Mattie, Matty, Merta, Moireach, Pat, Pattie, Patty.
Meaning: 'lady' (Aramaic).

Martina
Variants and diminutives: Marta, Martella, Marti, Martie, Martine, Marty, Martyna, Martyne, Tina.
Meaning: uncertain; possibly 'martial' (Latin) through association with Mars, the god of war in Roman mythology, as a female version of Martin.

Mary
Variants and diminutives: Macia, Mae, Mai, Maidie, Maie, Maija, Maijii, Maikki, Mair, Maire, Mairi, Mairin, Maisie, Malia, Maralou, Mame, Mamie, Manette, Manka, Manon, Manya, Mara, Marabel, Marca, Marcsa, Mare, Maree, Mareea, Marella, Maren, Marenka, Mari, Maria, Mariah, Mariam, Mariamne, Marian, Mariana, Mariane, Marianna, Marianne, Maribel, Maribella, Maribeth, Maricara, Marice, Maridel, Marie, Mariel, Mariele, Mariene, Marienka, Mariesa, Mariessa, Marietta, Mariette, Marija, Marijon, Marijune, Marika, Marilee, Marilin, Marilu, Marilyn, Marinka, Marion, Mariquilla, Mariquita, Marisa, Marisha, Mariska, Marissa, Marita, Mariwin, Mariya, Marja, Marla, Marlo, Maroula, Maruca, Maruja, Maruska, Marya, Maryalice, Maryam, Maryann, Maryanna, Maryanne, Marybeth, Marye, Maryla, Marylin, Marylinn, Marylois, Marylou, Marylyn, Maryna, Maryse, Masha, Mashenka, Mashka, Maura, Maure, Maureen, Maurene, Maurine, May, Meirion, Mele, Meli, Meri, Meriel, Merrill, Meryl, Mhairi, Miliama, Millie, Mim, Mimi, Min, Minette, Minni, Minnie, Mira, Miri, Miriam, Mirit, Mirjam, Mirjana, Mirra, Miryam, Mitzi, Mo, Moira, Moire, Moll, Molli, Mollie, Molly, Mollye, Morine, Moya, Moyra, Muire, Mura, Muriel, Muriell, Poll, Polli, Pollie, Polly, Roula.

Meaning: 'longed-for child' or 'rebellion' (Hebrew) as a variant of Miriam.

Matana
Meaning: 'gift' (Hebrew).

Matilda
Variants and diminutives: Hilda, Hilde, Macia, Maddy, Mahaut, Mala, Malkin, Mat, Matelda, Mathilda, Mathilde, Mati, Matilde, Matilldis, Matti, Mattie, Matty, Mattye, Matya, Matylda, Maud, Maude, Maudene, Maudie, Mawde, Mechthild, Metilda, Mold, Pattie, Patty, Tila, Tilda, Tilde, Tildie, Tildy, Tillie, Tilly, Tylda.
Meaning: 'mighty' and 'battle' (Germanic).

Maud
Variants and diminutives: Matilda, Maude, Maudie.
Meaning: 'mighty' and 'battle' (Germanic) as a variant of Matilda.

Maura
Variants and diminutives: Maire, Mary, Maureen, Maurene, Maurine, Moira, Mora.
Meaning: 'dark' (Celtic); 'longed-for child' or 'rebellion' (Hebrew) as an anglicised form of Maire, an Irish Gaelic variant of Mary (Miriam).

Maureen
Variants and diminutives: Maire, Mairin, Mary, Maura, Maurene, Maurine, Mo, Moira, Mora, Moreen, Morena.
Meaning: 'dark' (Celtic); 'longed-for child' or 'rebellion' (Hebrew) as an anglicised form of Maire, an Irish Gaelic variant of Mary (Miriam).

Mavis
Variants and diminutives: Maeve, Mave.
Meaning: 'song thrush' (Old French); derived from the common name of the song thrush, Turdus philomelos.

Maxine
Variants and diminutives: Max, Maxencia, Maxi, Maxie, Maxima, Maxime, Maxy.
Meaning: 'great' (Latin).

May
Variants and diminutives: Mae, Maia, Margaret, Mary, Maya, Maybelle, Mei.
Meaning: 'the month of Maia' (Latin); 'longed-for child' or 'rebellion' (Hebrew) as a diminutive of Mary (Miriam); 'pearl' (Greek) as a diminutive of Margaret.

Maya
Variants and diminutives: Maia, May.
Meaning: 'illusion' (Sanskrit).

Meena
Variants and diminutives: Mina.
Meaning: 'precious stone' or 'fish' (Sanskrit).

Megan
Variants and diminutives: Meagan, Meaghan, Meaghen, Meg, Megen, Meggie, Meggy, Meghan, Meghann.
Meaning: 'pearl' (Greek) as a Welsh variant of Margaret.

Meira
Variants and diminutives: Meera, Mira.
Meaning: 'radiant' or 'light' (Hebrew).

Meirion
Variants and diminutives: Merrion.
Meaning: 'longed-for child' or 'rebellion' (Hebrew) as a Welsh variant of Marian (Miriam via Mary).

Melanie
Variants and diminutives: Ela, Mel, Mela, Melana, Melani, Melania, Melaniya, Melanka, Melantha, Melany, Melanya, Melashka, Melasya, Melena, Melenia, Melka, Melli, Mellie, Melloney, Mellony, Melly, Meloni, Melonie, Meloney, Melony, Milena, Milya.
Meaning: 'black' or 'dark' (Greek).

Melinda
Variants and diminutives: Linda, Lynda, Malinda, Malinde, Mallie, Mally, Mel, Meli, Melissa, Melli, Mellie, Melly, Melynda.
Meaning: a composite name comprising 'Mel', 'honey' (Greek), and '-linda', 'snake' (Germanic), 'pretty' (Spanish), or 'neat' (Italian).

Meliora
Meaning: 'better' (Latin).

Melissa
Variants and diminutives: Lissa, Lisse, Malina, Malinda, Malinde, Malissa, Mallie, Mally, Mel, Melesa, Melessa, Meli, Melina, Melinda, Melisa, Melisande, Melise, Melisenda, Mell, Melli, Mellie, Melly, Melynda, Misha, Missie, Missy.
Meaning: 'bee' (Greek).

Melody
Variants and diminutives: Medosa, Mel, Melina, Melodi, Melodie, Melodye, Meldoy.

Meaning: 'harmonious tune' or 'singer of songs' (Greek).

Melora
Variants and diminutives: Mel, Lora.
Meaning: uncertain; possibly 'honey' and 'gold' (Greek).

Melosa
Variants and diminutives: Mel.
Meaning: 'honey-sweet' or 'gentle' (Spanish).

Melvina
Variants and diminutives: Malva, Malvina, Malvinda, Melevine, Melva, Melveen, Melvene, Melvine.
Meaning: uncertain; possibly 'smooth' and 'brow' (Scots Gaelic) as a variant of Malvina; possibly 'Amalo's settlement' (Germanic) or 'bad' and 'town' (Old French) as a female version of Melvin.

Menora
Variants and diminutives: Menorah.
Meaning: 'candelabrum' (Hebrew).

Mercedes
Variants and diminutives: Mercy, Sadie.
Meaning: 'mercy' (Spanish).

Mercia
Variants and diminutives: Mercy.

Meaning: 'people of the borderland' (Old English); derived from the name of an Anglo-Saxon kingdom.

Mercy
Variants and diminutives: Mercedes, Mercia, Mercille, Merri, Merry.
Meaning: 'recompense' (Latin); 'clemency' (English).

Meredith
Variants and diminutives: Bedo, Maredudd, Meri, Merideth, Meridith, Merri, Merridie, Merrie, Merry.
Meaning: 'great' and 'chief' or 'lord' (Old Welsh). Also a boy's name.

Merle
Variants and diminutives: Meriel, Muriel, Merla, Merlina, Merline, Merola, Merril, Merrill, Merryl, Meryl, Meryle, Morell, Murle.
Meaning: 'blackbird' (Latin); 'sea' and 'bright' (Irish Gaelic) as a variant of Muriel. Also a boy's name.

Merry
Variants and diminutives: Marrilee, Mercy, Meredith, Meri, Merie, Meridee, Merri, Merrie, Merrielle, Merrili, Merris, Merrita.
Meaning: 'agreeable' or 'jolly' (Old English); 'recompense' (Latin) or

'clemency' (English) as a diminutive of Mercy; 'great' and 'chief' or 'lord' (Old Welsh) as a diminutive of Meredith.

Meryl
Variants and diminutives: Maryl, Meriel, Merilyn, Merril, Merrill, Merrilyn, Merryl, Merle, Meryle, Muriel.
Meaning: 'sea' and 'bright' (Irish Gaelic) as a variant of Muriel; 'longed-for child' or 'rebellion' (Hebrew) as a variant of Mary (Miriam).

Mia
Variants and diminutives: Maria.
Meaning: 'my' (Italian and Spanish); 'longed-for child' or 'rebellion' (Hebrew) as a diminutive of Maria, the Latin form of Mary (Miriam).

Michaela

Variants and diminutives: Miia, Mica, Michael, Michaelle, Michal, Michel, Michele, Michelina, Micheline, Michelle, Micki, Mickie, Micky, Miguella, Mikaela, Mikelina.
Meaning: 'who is like God?' (Hebrew) as a female version of Michael.

Michelle

Variants and diminutives: Michael, Michaela, Michaelle, Michal, Michel, Michèle, Michelina, Micheline, Micki, Mickie, Micky.
Meaning: 'who is like God?' (Hebrew) as a female French version of Michael.

Mignon

Variants and diminutives: Mignonette.
Meaning: 'darling' (French).

Mildred

Variants and diminutives: Melicent, Mélisande, Melisent, Mil, Milda, Millie, Milly, Mindy.
Meaning: 'mild' and 'strength' (Old English).

Millicent

Variants and diminutives: Mel, Meli, Melicent, Mélisande, Melisent, Melita, Melleta, Melli, Mellicent, Mellie, Mellisent, Melly, Melusine, Mil, Mili, Milli, Millie, Millisent, Milly.
Meaning: 'work' and 'strength' (Germanic).

Mima

Variants and diminutives: Jemima.
Meaning: 'dove' (Hebrew and Arabic) as a diminutive of Jemima.

Mimi

Variants and diminutives: Helmine, Maria, Mary, Miriam.
Meaning: 'longed-for child' or 'rebellion' (Hebrew) as an Italian diminutive of Maria, the Latin form of Mary (Miriam).

Mina

Variants and diminutives: Helmine, Hermina, Meena, Mena, Minna, Wilhelmina.
Meaning: 'will' and 'helmet' or 'protection' (Germanic) as a diminutive of Wilhelmina (William). Also a diminutive of any other name ending in '-mina'.

Minerva

Variants and diminutives: Min, Minette, Minni, Minnie, Minny.
Meaning: uncertain; possibly 'mind' or 'remember' (Latin); derived from the name of the goddess of wisdom, martial skills and household arts and crafts in Roman mythology.

Minna

Variants and diminutives: Helmine, Mina, Minda, Mindi, Mindie, Mindy, Minee, Minetta, Minette, Minne, Minnie, Minny, Wilhelmina.
Meaning: 'love' (Germanic); 'will' and 'helmet' or 'protection' (Germanic) as a diminutive of Wilhelmina (William).

Minnie

Variants and diminutives: Mina, Minee, Minna, Minni, Minny, Wilhelmina.
Meaning: 'will' and 'helmet' or 'protection' (Germanic) as a diminutive of Wilhelmina (William). Also a diminutive of Mary (Miriam).

Mirabelle

Variants and diminutives: Bella, Belle, Mira, Mirabel, Mirabell, Mirabella, Mirabelle, Mirella.
Meaning: 'wonderful' or 'extraordinary' (Latin); 'beautiful' (Spanish).

Miranda

Variants and diminutives: Maranda, Marenda, Meranda, Mina, Mira, Mirabel, Mirinda, Mironda, Mirranda,

Myranda, Randa, Randee, Randi, Randie, Randy.
Meaning: 'wonderful' or 'admirable' (Latin); possibly coined by William Shakespeare for the heroine of his play *The Tempest*.

Miriam

Variants and diminutives: Mary, Maria, Marian, Marianne, Meliame, Meryem,

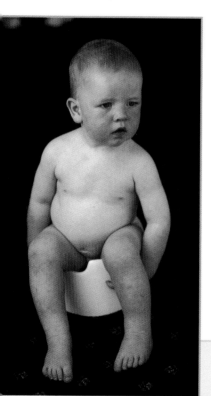

Mimi, Minni, Minnie, Miri, Mirjam, Mitzi, Myriam.
Meaning: 'longed-for child' or 'rebellion' (Hebrew).

Misty

Variants and diminutives: Misti, Mistie, Mystee, Mysti, Mystie, Mystique.
Meaning: 'obscure' or 'foggy' (Old English).

Mitzi

Variants and diminutives: Mitz, Mitzie, Mitzy.
Meaning: 'longed-for child' or 'rebellion' (Hebrew) as a German diminutive of Maria, the Latin form of Mary (Miriam).

Modesty

Variants and diminutives: Modesta, Modeste, Modestee, Modestene, Modestia, Modestina, Modestine.
Meaning: 'humble' or 'temperate' (Latin).

Moira

Variants and diminutives: Maire, Mary, Maura, Moyra, Myra.
Meaning: 'dark' (Celtic); 'longed-for child' or 'rebellion' (Hebrew) as an anglicised form of Maire, an Irish Gaelic version of Mary (Miriam).

Molly

Variants and diminutives: Mary, Moll, Molli, Mollie.
Meaning: 'longed-for child' or 'rebellion' (Hebrew) as a diminutive of Mary (Miriam).

Mona

Variants and diminutives: Madonna, Monica, Monique, Monna, Moyna, Muadhnait, Muna.
Meaning: uncertain; possibly 'alone' or 'just' (Greek); possibly 'admonish' or 'warn' (Latin); possibly 'my lady' (Italian); possibly 'noble', 'nun' or 'angel' (Irish Gaelic); possibly 'wish' (Arabic); possibly 'month' (Old English).

Monica

Variants and diminutives: Mona, Monca, Monique, Monika, Monna, Muna.
Meaning: uncertain; as a variant of Mona, possibly 'alone' or 'just' (Greek), 'admonish' or 'warn' (Latin), 'my lady' (Italian) 'noble', 'nun' or 'angel' (Irish Gaelic), 'wish' (Arabic) or 'month' (Old English).

Morag

Variants and diminutives: Marion, Moirin, Moreen, Sarah.
Meaning: 'great' and 'sun' or 'young

one' (Scottish and Irish Gaelic); 'princess' (Hebrew) as a Scots Gaelic variant of Sarah.

Morgan

Variants and diminutives: Morcant, Morgain, Morgana, Morganne, Morgen, Morgenne, Morien.

Meaning: uncertain; possibly 'morning' (Germanic); possibly 'sea' or 'great' and 'bright' (Celtic); derived from a British family name. Also a boy's name.

Moriah

Variants and diminutives: Mariah, Morel, Moria, Morice, Moriel, Morit.

Meaning: 'my teacher is God' (Hebrew).

Morna

Variants and diminutives: Morrow, Muirne, Myrna.

Meaning: 'spirited' or 'beloved' (Irish Gaelic).

Morven

Variants and diminutives: Morve, Ven, Venna, Venni, Vennie, Venny.

Meaning: uncertain; possibly 'big mountain' or 'sea gap' (Scots Gaelic); derived from a number of Scottish place names. Also a boy's name.

Morwenna

Variants and diminutives: Wenna, Wennie, Wenny.

Meaning: 'maiden' or 'sea' and 'wave' (Welsh).

Muriel

Variants and diminutives: Marial, Meriel, Merril, Merrill, Merryle, Meryl, Meryle, Miriel, Muireall, Muirgheal, Murial, Muriell, Murielle.

Meaning: 'sea' and 'bright' (Irish Gaelic).

Myfanwy

Variants and diminutives: Fanni, Fannie, Fanny, Myf, Myvanwy.

Meaning: 'my fine', 'my rare' or 'my dear' and 'one' (Welsh).

Myra

Variants and diminutives: Mira.

Meaning: uncertain; as a variant of Myrna, possibly 'myrrh' (Aramaic and Arabic); 'spirited' or 'beloved' (Irish Gaelic); coined for various poems by the English poet Fulke Greville, Baron Brooke. Also a female version of Myron.

Myrna

Variants and diminutives: Merna, Mirna, Moina, Morna, Muirna, Muirne, Murnia, Moyna.

Meaning: 'myrrh' (Aramaic and Arabic); 'spirited' or 'beloved' (Irish Gaelic) as a variant of Morna.

Myrtle

Variants and diminutives: Myrta, Myrtia, Myrtice, Myrtilla.

Meaning: 'myrtle' (Greek); derived from the common name of the *Myrtus* genus of evergreen shrubs.

Nabila

Variants and diminutives: Nabeela, Nabiha, Nabilah.

Meaning: 'noble' (Arabic). A female version of Nabil.

Nadia

Variants and diminutives: Dusya, Nada, Nadeen, Nadenka, Nadezhda, Nadie, Nadina, Nadine, Nadiya, Nadja, Nadka, Nado, Nady, Nadya, Nata, Natka.

Meaning: 'hope' (Slavonic) as as diminutive of Nadezhda.

Nagida

Meaning: 'noble', 'wealthy' or 'ruler' (Hebrew). A female version of Nagid.

Nancy
Variants and diminutives: Ann, Anna, Anne, Hannah, Nan, Nana, Nance, Nancey, Nanci, Nancie, Nanette, Nani, Nanice, Nannie, Nanny.
Meaning: 'I have been favoured (by God)' (Hebrew) as a diminutive of Ann, Anna, Anne and other variants of Hannah.

Nanette
Variants and diminutives: Ann, Anna, Anne, Annette, Hannah, Nan, Nana, Nancy, Nannette, Nannie, Nanny.
Meaning: 'I have been favoured (by God)' (Hebrew) as a diminutive of Ann, Anna, Anne and other variants of Hannah.

Naomi
Variants and diminutives: Naoma, Naome, Noami, Noemi, Nomi.
Meaning: 'pleasant' or 'my delight' (Hebrew).

Narcissa
Variants and diminutives: Narcisse.
Meaning: 'numbness' (Greek) as a female version of Narcissus.

Nasia
Variants and diminutives: Nasya.
Meaning: 'miracle of God' (Hebrew).

Natalia
Variants and diminutives: Nacia, Nat, Nata, Natacha, Natala, Natalie, Natalina, Nataline, Natalka, Natalle, Natalya, Natasa, Natasha, Nathalia, Nathalie, Nati, Natie, Natka, Nattie, Nattie, Natty, Neda, Netti, Nettie, Netty, Noel, Noelle, Novella, Talia, Talya, Tasha, Tashka, Taska, Tasya, Tata, Tuska, Tusya.
Meaning: 'birthday' (Latin); 'Christ's birthday' or 'Christmas' (Slavonic).

Natania
Variants and diminutives: Nataniella, Natanielle, Nathania, Nathaniella, Nathanielle, Netania, Netanya, Nethania.
Meaning: 'gift' (Hebrew) as a female version of Nathan.

Natasha
Variants and diminutives: Nat, Nata, Natacha, Natala, Natalia, Natalya, Nathalie, Natasa, Nati, Natie, Natti, Nattie, Natty, Talia, Talya, Tasha, Tashka, Tashua, Taska, Tasya, Tata, Tuska, Tusya.
Meaning: 'birthday' (Latin); 'Christ's birthday' or 'Christmas' (Slavonic) as a Russian diminutive of Natalya (Natalia).

Neala
Variants and diminutives: Nea, Neala, Neali, Nealie, Nealy, Nelda, Neela, Neeli, Neelie, Neely, Neili, Neily, Nia, Nigella.

Meaning: 'champion', 'cloud' or 'vehement' (Irish Gaelic) as a female version of Neal (Neil).

Nell
Variants and diminutives: Eleanor, Ellen, Helen, Nel, Nelli, Nellie, Nellwyn, Nelly.
Meaning: 'bright' (Greek) as a diminutive of Eleanor, Ellen and other variants of Helen; also 'foreign' (Germanic) as a diminutive of Eleanor.

Neola
Variants and diminutives: Neolie, Neoly.
Meaning: 'new' (Greek).

Neoma
Meaning: 'new moon' (Greek).

Nerissa
Variants and diminutives: Nerice, Nerina, Nerine, Nerisse, Nerita, Nissa, Rissa.
Meaning: uncertain; possibly 'sea nymph' (Greek); derived from the name of the Nereides, sea nymphs of Greek mythology.

Nerys
Meaning: 'lord' (Welsh).
Notable namesakes: Nerys Hughes (British actress).

Nesta
Variants and diminutives: Agnes, Nesha, Nessa, Nessie, Nessy, Nest.
Meaning: 'pure' or 'chaste' (Greek) or 'lamb' (Latin) as a variant of Agnes.

Netta
Variants and diminutives: Antoinetta, Antoinette, Jeanetta, Jeanette, Neata, Neta, Nettie, Netty.
Meaning: 'door' (Mende – Africa); also a diminutive of any name ending in '-netta' or '-nette', such as Jeanette, meaning 'God has favoured', 'God is gracious' or 'God is merciful' (Hebrew) as a female version of John.

Neva
Variants and diminutives: Nevada.
Meaning: 'to snow' or 'snow white' (Spanish).

Ngaio
Meaning: 'clever' (Maori).

Niamh
Meaning: 'bright' (Irish Gaelic).

Nicola
Variants and diminutives: Colette, Collete, Cosette, Nic, Nicci, Nichele, Nichelle, Nichol, Nichola, Nichole, Nicholle, Nicki, Nickie, Nicky, Nico, Nicol, Nicole, Nicoleen, Nicolete, Nicoletta, Nicolette, Nicoli, Nicolina, Nicoline, Nicolle, Nijole, Nika, Nike, Niki, Nikki, Nikolette, Nikolia.
Meaning: 'victory of the people' (Greek) as a female Italian version of Nicholas.

Nigella
Variants and diminutives: Gella, Jella, Neala, Nigie.
Meaning: 'black' (Latin) when derived from the Nigella genus of flowering plants, commonly known as love-in-the-mist, which have black seeds; 'champion', 'cloud' or 'vehement' (Irish Gaelic) as a female version of Nigel, Neil.

Nike
Variants and diminutives: Niki.
Meaning: 'victory' (Greek); derived from the name of the winged goddess of victory in war in Greek mythology.

Nina
Variants and diminutives: Nena, Nenah, Neneh, Ninetta, Ninette, Ninita, Ninnetta, Ninnette, Ninon.
Meaning: 'girl' (Spanish); 'mighty' (Native American); 'I have been favoured (by God)' (Hebrew) as a Russian form of Anna (Hannah); also a diminutive of any name ending in '-nina'.

Nisha
Variants and diminutives: Neesh, Neesha, Neisha, Nesha, Neshia, Nishi.
Meaning: 'night' (Sanskrit).

Nissa
Variants and diminutives: Nisa, Nisse, Nissie, Nissy.
Meaning: 'sign' or 'to test' (Hebrew); 'a never-forgotten loved one' (Hausa – Africa)

Nita
Variants and diminutives: Anita, Juanita.

Meaning: 'bear' (Chocktaw – Native American); also a diminutive of any name ending in '-nita', such as Anita (Hannah via Anna), meaning 'I have been favoured (by God)' (Hebrew).

Nitza
Variants and diminutives: Nitzana, Nizana, Zana, Zanah.
Meaning: 'bud' (Hebrew).

Nixie
Variants and diminutives: Nix, Nixe, Nixy.
Meaning: 'water spirit' or 'nymph' (German); derived from the name of the Nixen, river spirits of Germanic mythology.

Noëlle
Variants and diminutives: Natalia, Natasha, Noel, Noele, Noeleen, Noelene, Noeline, Noell, Noella, Noelle, Nolene, Novelia, Nowlle.
Meaning: 'birthday' (Latin), 'Christ's birthday' or 'Christmas' (French) as a female version of Noël.

Nofia
Variants and diminutives: Nophia.
Meaning: 'panorama' (Hebrew).

Nola
Variants and diminutives: Finnuala, Finola, Nolana, Noleen, Nolena, Nuala.
Meaning: 'son of the noble one' (Irish Gaelic) as a female version of Nolan; 'fair-shouldered' (Irish Gaelic) as a variant of Fionnuala (Fenella).

Nolene
Variants and diminutives: Noalene, Noelle, Nola, Nolana, Noleen, Nolena.
Meaning: 'son of the noble one' (Irish Gaelic) as a female version of Nolan; 'birthday' (Latin), 'Christ's birthday' or 'Christmas' (French) as a female version of Noël.

Nona
Variants and diminutives: Noni, Nonie.
Meaning: 'ninth' (Latin).

Nora
Variants and diminutives: Annora, Honor, Honora, Leonora, Norah, Noreen, Norene, Norine.
Meaning: 'honour' (Latin) as a diminutive of Honora (Honor); 'bright' (Greek) as a diminutive of most names ending in '-nora', such as Eleanora (Helen via Eleanor), which also means 'foreign' (Germanic).

Norma
Variants and diminutives: Normie, Normy.
Meaning: 'rule' or 'pattern' (Latin); 'north'

and 'man' [Norseman or Viking] (Germanic) as a female version of Norman.

Norna
Variants and diminutives: Nornie, Norny.
Meaning: 'fate' (Old Norse); derived from the name of the Norns (or Nornir), the three Fates of Norse mythology.

Nova
Variants and diminutives: Novia.
Meaning: 'new' (Latin).

Noya

Meaning: 'bejewelled by nature' (Hebrew).

Nuala

Variants and diminutives: Fenella, Fionnghuala, Fionnuala, Nola.
Meaning: 'fair-shouldered' (Irish Gaelic) as a variant of Fionnuala (Fenella).

Nydia

Variants and diminutives: Neda, Nedda, Nydie, Nydy.
Meaning: 'nest' or 'home' (Latin).

Nyree

Variants and diminutives: Ngaire.
Meaning: uncertain; an anglicised version of the Maori name Ngaire.

Nysa

Variants and diminutives: Nissa, Nisse, Nissie, Isy, Nyssa.
Meaning: 'beginning' (Greek); 'striving' or 'soaring' (Latin).

Nyx

Meaning: 'night' (Greek); derived from the name of the underworld goddess of the night in Greek mythology.

Obelia

Variants and diminutives: Belia, Belya.
Meaning: 'pillar', 'pointer' or 'marker' (Greek); 'off the beaten track' (Bini – Africa).

Octavia

Variants and diminutives: Octaviana, Octavie, Ottavia, Tavi, Tavia, Tavie.
Meaning: 'eighth' (Latin); derived from the Roman family name Octavius. A female version of Octavius.

Odelia

Variants and diminutives: Delia, Detta, Oda, Odelet, Odelinda, Odell, Odella, Odelyn, Odetta, Odette, Odila, Odile, Odilia, Otha, Othelia, Othilia, Othilie, Ottilia, Ottilie, Ottoline, Uta.
Meaning: 'song' or 'ode' (Greek); 'praise be to God' (Hebrew); 'where woad grows' (Old English) or 'otter' (Danish) as a female version of Odell; 'riches' (Germanic) as a female version of Odo.

Odette

Variants and diminutives: Oda, Oddetta, Odelia, Odetta, Odile, Odilia, Otilie, Ottilia, Ottoline.
Meaning: 'riches' (Germanic) as a female version of Odo.

Ola

Meaning: 'protector' or 'nourisher' (Old Norse); 'forebear' and 'relics' (Old Norse) as a female version of Olaf.

Oleander

Variants and diminutives: Oliana, Olinda, Olynda.
Meaning: 'rose tree' (Greek); derived from the common name of the flowering shrub *Nerium oleander*.

Olena

Variants and diminutives: Helen, Lena.
Meaning: 'bright' (Greek) as a Russian variant of Helen.

Olga

Variants and diminutives: Elga, Helga, Lelya, Lesya, Ola, Olenka, Olesya, Olia, Olina, Olka, Olli, Ollie, Olly, Olunka, Oluska, Olva, Olya, Olyusha.
Meaning: 'prosperous' or 'pious' (Old Norse) as a Russian variant of Helga.

Olive

Variants and diminutives: Liv, Liva, Livie, Livrie, Livvy, Livy, Nola, Nolana, Nollie, Oli, Olia, Oliff, Oliva, Olivet, Olivette, Olivia, Oliwia, Ollett, Oli, Ollie, Olliffe, Olly, Ollye, Olva.
Meaning: 'olive' (Latin); derived from the common name of the olive-bearing *Olea europaea* genus of trees. Also a female variant of Oliver.

Olivia

Variants and diminutives: Liv, Liva, Livia, Livie, Livrie, Livvy, LIvy, Nola, Nolana, Nollie, Oli, Olia, Oliff, Oliva, Olive, Olivet, Olivette, Oliwia, Ollett, Olli, Ollie, Olliffe, Olly, Ollye, Olva.
Meaning: 'olive' (Latin) as an Italian variant of Olive.

Olwen

Variants and diminutives: Olwin, Olwyn.
Meaning: 'white tracks' (Old Welsh).

Olympia

Variants and diminutives: Olimpe, Olimpia, Olimpie, Olympe, Olympias, Olympie.
Meaning: 'from Olympus' (Greek), Olympus being Mount Olympus, home of the gods in Greek mythology, or 'from Olympia' (Greek), the original site of the Olympic Games.

Omega

Variants and diminutives: Mega.
Meaning: 'great "O"' (Greek); derived from the name of the last letter of the Greek alphabet.

Oona

Variants and diminutives: Oonagh, Oonie, Ona, Una.
Meaning: 'one' or 'together' (Latin) or 'lamb' (Irish Gaelic) as an Irish Gaelic form of Una.

Opal

Variants and diminutives: Opalina, Opaline.
Meaning: 'precious stone' (Sanskrit); derived from the name of the decorative iridescent mineral.

Ophelia

Variants and diminutives: Ofelia, Oilia, Ophelie.
Meaning: 'help' (Greek).

Ophira

Variants and diminutives: Ofira.
Meaning: 'gold' (Hebrew).

Oprah

Variants and diminutives: Ofra, Ophra, Ophrah, Opra, Orfa, Orpah.
Meaning: uncertain; possibly 'fawn' or 'runaway' (Hebrew) as a variant of Orpah.

Ora

Variants and diminutives: Aurora, Cora, Dora, Orah.
Meaning: 'edge' or 'boundary' (Latin); also a diminutive of any name ending in '-ora', such as Aurora, meaning 'dawn' (Latin).

Orah

Variants and diminutives: Ora, Oralee, Orit, Orlice, Orly.
Meaning: 'light' (Hebrew).

Oriana

Variants and diminutives: Oralia, Orelda, Orella, Orelle, Oria, Oriande, Oriane, Oriente, Orlann, Orlene.
Meaning: 'to rise' or 'sunrise' (Latin).

Oriel

Variants and diminutives: Auriel, Aurelia, Aurildis, Nehora, Ora, Orah, Orabel, Oralia, Orieldis, Orielle, Oriole, Orit.
Meaning: 'fire' and 'strife' (Germanic); 'niche' (Latin); 'gallery' (Old French); 'gold' (Latin) as a variant of Aurelia.

Oriole

Variants and diminutives: Oriel.
Meaning: 'golden one' (Latin); derived from the common name of the *Oriolus* genus of songbirds.

Orla

Variants and diminutives: Oria, Orlagh, Orlaidh.
Meaning: 'golden princess' (Irish Gaelic).

Orpah

Variants and diminutives: Ofra, Ophra, Ophrah, Opra, Oprah, Orfa, Orpha, Orpra, Orphy.
Meaning: uncertain; possibly 'fawn' or 'runaway' (Hebrew).

Osanna

Variants and diminutives: Hosana, Hosanna, Osana.
Meaning: 'save now, we pray' (Hebrew); 'praise be to God' (Latin); a diminutive of Hosanna, a Judaeo-Christian exclamation of praise.

Ottilie

Variants and diminutives: Odala, Odette, Odila, Odile, Odilia, Odille, Otilie, Ottalie, Ottilia, Ottoline, Uta.
Meaning: 'of the fatherland' (Germanic); 'riches' (Germanic) as a female version of Otto (Odo).

Ottoline

Variants and diminutives: Odette, Odile, Otilie, Ottilie.
Meaning: 'riches' (Germanic) as a female version of Otto (Odo).

Ouida

Variants and diminutives: Louise.
Meaning: 'famed' and 'warrior' (Germanic) as a diminutive of Louise, in turn a female version of Louis (Ludwig).

Ova

Meaning: 'egg' or 'to celebrate a small triumph' (Latin); 'sunshine' (Bini – Africa); 'January-born' (Hausa – Africa).

Padma

Meaning: 'lotus' (Hindi).

Paige

Variants and diminutives: Page, Paget, Pagett.
Meaning: 'child' (Greek); 'page boy' or 'boy attendant' (Old French); derived from an English family name. Also a boy's name (generally Page).

Paloma

Variants and diminutives: Palometa, Palomita.
Meaning: 'dove' (Spanish).

Pamela

Variants and diminutives: Pam, Pamala, Pamelia, Pamelina, Pamella, Pammi, Pammie, Pammy.
Meaning: uncertain; possibly 'all' and 'honey' (Greek); coined by the English poet Philip Sidney for a heroine of his romance *Arcadia*.

Pandora

Variants and diminutives: Dora, Pandore, Polydora.
Meaning: 'all' and 'gift' (Greek).

Pansy

Variants and diminutives: Pansie.
Meaning: 'thought' (Old French); derived from the common name of the *Viola tricolor* genus of flowering plants.

Parthenia

Variants and diminutives: Partha, Parthenope, Parthenos.
Meaning: 'virgin' (Greek).

Pascale

Variants and diminutives: Pascha.
Meaning: 'to pass over' (Hebrew) or 'of Easter' (Old French) as a female version of Pascal.

Pat

Variants and diminutives: Patricia, Patsy, Patti, Pattie, Patty.
Meaning: 'noble' or 'patrician' (Latin) as a diminutive of Patricia (and of Patrick).

Patience

Variants and diminutives: Pat, Patia, Pattie, Patty.
Meaning: 'endurance' (Latin).

Patricia

Variants and diminutives: Paddie, Paddy, Pat, Patia, Patrice, Patrizia, Patsy, Patti, Pattie, Patty, Tricia, Trish, Trisha.
Meaning: 'noble' or 'patrician' (Latin). A female version of Patrick.

Patsy

Variants and diminutives: Pat, Patricia, Patsi, Patsie, Patty.
Meaning: 'noble' or 'patrician' (Latin) as a diminutive of Patricia (and of Patrick).

Patty

Variants and diminutives: Martha, Matilda, Pat, Patti, Patricia, Patsy, Patty.
Meaning: 'noble' or 'patrician' (Latin) as

a diminutive of Patricia; 'lady' (Aramaic) as a diminutive of Martha; 'mighty' and 'battle' (Germanic) as a diminutive of Matilda.

Paula

Variants and diminutives: Paola, Paolina, Paule, Pauleen, Paulene, Pauletta, Paulette, Pauli, Paulie, Paulina, Pauline, Paulita, Pauly, Pavia, Pavla, Pavlina, Pavlinka, Pawlina, Pola, Polcia, Polli, Pollie, Polly.
Meaning: 'small' (Latin) as a female version of Paul.

Paulette

Variants and diminutives: Paula, Pauletta, Pauline, Paulita.
Meaning: 'small' (Latin) as a female version of Paul.

Pauline

Variants and diminutives: Paula, Pauleen, Paulene, Paulette, Pauli, Paulie, Paulina, Paulita, Pavlina, Pavlinka, Pawlina.
Meaning: 'small' (Latin) as a female version of Paul.

Pazia

Variants and diminutives: Paz, Paza, Pazice, Pazit.
Meaning: 'gold' (Hebrew). Also a boy's name.

Peace
Variants and diminutives: Pax, Paz.
Meaning: 'peace' (English).

Pearl
Variants and diminutives:
Margaret, Pearla, Pearle, Pearlie,
Pearline, Perla, Perle, Perly, Perry.
Meaning: 'sea mussel' (Latin);
derived from the lustrous gem
produced by oysters.

Peggy
Variants and diminutives:
Margaret, Meg, Peg, Peggi, Peggie.
Meaning: 'pearl' (Greek) as a
diminutive of Margaret.

Pelagia
Variants and diminutives: Palasha,
Pasha, Pashka, Pelageya.
Meaning: 'sea' (Greek).

Penelope
Variants and diminutives: Fenella,
Fionnghuala, Lopa, Pela, Pelcha,
Pelcia, Pen, Peneli, Penelopa,
Penélope, Penina, Penine, Penni,
Pennie, Penny, Pinelopi, Pipitsa, Popi.
Meaning: uncertain; possibly
'bobbin', 'thread' or 'weaver' (Greek).

Penina
Variants and diminutives: Peninah,
Peninit.
Meaning: 'pearl' or 'coral' (Hebrew).

Penny
Variants and diminutives: Pen,
Penelope, Penney, Penni, Pennie.
Meaning: uncertain; possibly
'bobbin', 'thread' or 'weaver' (Greek)
as a diminutive of Penelope.

Peony
Variants and diminutives: Paeony,
Peonie.
Meaning: 'healing' (Greek); derived
from the common name of the
Paeonia genus of flowering plants.

Pepita
Variants and diminutives: Josefina,
Josephine.
Meaning: 'God will increase'
(Hebrew) as a Spanish diminutive of
Josefina (Josephine).

Perdita
Variants and diminutives: Purdey,
Purdie.
Meaning: 'lost' (Latin); coined by
William Shakespeare for the heroine
of his play *A Winter's Tale*.

Perpetua
Variants and diminutives: Pet,
Petua.
Meaning: 'perpetual' (Latin).

Persephone

Variants and diminutives: Persephassa, Perseponeia, Proserpina.
Meaning: 'bearer of death', 'destroyer of light' or 'dazzling radiance' (Greek); derived from the name of the daughter of Demeter and Zeus, and, as the wife of Pluto or Hades, queen of the underworld for six months of the year in Greek mythology.

Peta

Variants and diminutives: Pet, Petena, Peterina, Peternella, Petie, Petra, Petrina, Petrona, Petty.
Meaning: 'rock' (Greek) as a female version of Peter.

Petal

Variants and diminutives: Pet.
Meaning: 'leaf' (Greek); derived from the name of the flower component.

Petra

Variants and diminutives: Pet, Peta, Petie, Petrina, Petrona, Petty.
Meaning: 'rock' (Greek) as a female version of Peter.

Petronella

Variants and diminutives: Parnall, Parnel, Parnell, Patch, Pernel, Peronel, Peronnelle, Perri, Perrin, Perrine, Perry, Perryne, Pet, Peta, Peternella, Petrina, Petrona, Petronel, Petronia, Petronilla, Petronille, Petty.
Meaning: uncertain; possibly 'rock' (Greek); derived from the Roman family name Petronius.

Petula

Variants and diminutives: Pet.
Meaning: uncertain; possibly 'pert' or 'to assail' (Latin).

Petunia

Variants and diminutives: Pet.
Meaning: 'tobacco' (Old French); derived from the name of the *Petunia* genus of flowering plants.

Phaedra

Variants and diminutives: Phaidra, Phèdre.
Meaning: 'shining brightly' (Greek).

Phila

Variants and diminutives: Philadelphia, Philana, Philantha, Philberta.
Meaning: 'love' or 'beloved' (Greek).

Philadelphia

Variants and diminutives: Delphia, Delphie, Delphy, Phil, Phila, Phillie, Philly.
Meaning: 'brotherly love' (Greek).

Philana

Variants and diminutives: Lana, Phil, Phila, Philene, Philina, Phillie, Phillina, Philly.
Meaning: 'lover of humanity' (Greek).

Philantha

Variants and diminutives: Lantha, Phil, Phila, Phillie, Philly.
Meaning: 'flower-lover' (Greek).

Philippa

Variants and diminutives: Felipa, Fiipote, Filipa, Filippa, Filippina, Filpina, Flippa, Ina, Inka, Pelipa, Phelypp, Phil, Philipa, Philippe, Philippine, Philli, Phillie,

Phillipa, Phillippa, Philly, Pine, Pip,
Pippa, Pippi, Pippie, Pippy.
Meaning: 'horse-lover' (Greek) as a
female version of Philip.

Philomela

Variants and diminutives: Filomela,
Phil, Phillie, Philly, Mela, Mellie, Melly.
Meaning: 'loving' or 'sweet' and
'song' (Greek).

Philomena

Variants and diminutives:
Filomena, Phil, Phillie, Philly, Philomina.
Meaning: 'love' and 'harmony' or
'strength' (Greek); 'peace' and
'beloved' (Latin).

Phoebe

Variants and diminutives: Phebe,
Pheobe, Pheoby.
Meaning: 'shining' or 'radiant'
(Greek).

Phoenix

Variants and diminutives: Phenice,
Phenix.
Meaning: 'purple' (Phoenician). Also
a boy's name.

Phyllida

Variants and diminutives: Filide,
Phil, Phillida, Phillie, Philly, Phyllada,
Phyllis.

Meaning: 'foliage' or 'leafy' (Greek) as
a variant of Phyllis.

Phyllis

Variants and diminutives: Filide,
Filis, Phil, Philis, Phillida, Phillie, Phillis,
Philliss, Philly, Phyllys, Phyl, Phylis,
Phyliss, Phyllada, Phyllida, Phyllie,
Phyllys, Phylys, Pilisi.
Meaning: 'foliage' or 'leafy' (Greek).

Pia

Meaning: 'pious' or 'dutiful' (Latin). A
female version of Pius.

Pilar

Meaning: 'pillar' or 'fountain base'
(Spanish). Also a boy's name.

Pippa

Variants and diminutives: Philippa,
Pip.
Meaning: 'horse-lover' (Greek) as a
diminutive of Philippa (Philip).

Placida

Variants and diminutives: Placidia.
Meaning: 'peaceful' (Latin) as a
female version of Placido.

Pleasance

Variants and diminutives:
Plaisance, Pleasant.
Meaning: 'pleasure' (Old French).

Polly

Variants and diminutives: Pol, Poli,
Poll, Polley, Polli, Pollie, Pollyanna.
Meaning: 'longed-for child' or
'rebellion' (Hebrew) as a variant of
Molly (Miriam via Mary); 'small'
(Latin) as a diminutive of Paula
(Paul).

Polydora

Variants and diminutives: Dora,
Pandora, Pol, Poli, Poly.
Meaning: 'many' and 'gift' (Greek).

Pomona

Variants and diminutives: Mona,
Pom, Pommie, Pommy.
Meaning: 'fruit' (Latin).

Poppy

Variants and diminutives: Poppi,
Poppie.
Meaning: 'poppy' (Latin); derived
from the common name of the
Papaver genus of flowering plants.

Pora

Meaning: 'fruitful' (Hebrew).

Portia

Variants and diminutives: Porsha.
Meaning: 'entrance', 'gate' or 'pig'
(Latin); derived from the Roman
family name Porcius.

Posy

Variants and diminutives: Poesie, Poesy, Posie.
Meaning: 'poetic creativity' (Greek); 'a small bunch of flowers' (English); 'God will increase' (Hebrew) as a diminutive of Josephine.

Primrose

Variants and diminutives: Primula, Rose.
Meaning: 'first rose' (Latin); derived from the common name of the *Primula* genus of flowering plants.

Primula

Variants and diminutives: Primrose.
Meaning: 'little first one' (Latin); derived from the *Primula* genus of flowering plants.

Priscilla

Variants and diminutives: Cilla, Precilla, Prescilla, Pricilla, Pris, Prisca, Priscella, Priscila, Prisilla, Priss, Prissie, Prissila, Prissy, Scilla, Sila.
Meaning: 'of ancient times' (Latin).

Priya

Variants and diminutives: Priyal, Priyam, Priyanka, Priyata, Pryasha, Pryati.
Meaning: 'endearing' or 'sweet-natured' (Hindi).

Prudence

Variants and diminutives: Pru, Prude, Prudencia, Prudentia, Prudi, Prudie, Prudy, Prue, Pruedi.
Meaning: 'discretion' (Latin).

Prunella

Variants and diminutives: Ella, Nella, Pru, Prue.
Meaning: 'little plum' (Latin).

Pyralis

Variants and diminutives: Pyrene.
Meaning: 'fire' (Greek).

Queenie

Variants and diminutives: Quanda, Queena, Queenby, Queeny, Quenie, Quinn, Regina, Victoria.
Meaning: 'wife' (Old Norse) or 'queen' (Old English) as a diminutive of the highest female rank of nobility.

Quella

Variants and diminutives: Ella.
Meaning: 'to kill' or 'to quell' (Old English).

Querida

Variants and diminutives: Rida.
Meaning: 'to query' or 'beloved' (Spanish).

Questa

Variants and diminutives: Esta.
Meaning: 'searcher' (Old French).

Quinta

Variants and diminutives: Quin, Quinci, Quincie, Quincy, Quinetta, Quinette, Quintessa, Quintilla, Quintina.
Meaning: 'fifth' (Latin) as a female variant of Quintin (Quentin).

Quintessa

Variants and diminutives: Quentessa, Quentice, Quinta, Quintice, Tess, Tessa, Tessi, Tessie, Tessy.
Meaning: 'the fifth essence' or 'quintessence' (Latin).

Quirina
Variants and diminutives: Rina.
Meaning: 'of Romulus' (Latin) as a female version of Quirinal.

Rabia
Variants and diminutives: Rabi, Rabiah.
Meaning: 'breeze' (Arabic).

Rachel
Variants and diminutives: Lahela, Lesieli, Rachael, Rachele, Racheli, Rachelle, Rachie, Rae, Ragnhildr, Rahel, Rahela, Rahil, Rakel, Rakhil, Rakhhila, Raoghnald, Raquel, Raquela, Rashel, Ray, Raye, Rochell, Ruchel, Shell, Shelley, Shellie, Shelly.
Meaning: 'ewe' (Hebrew).

Rae
Variants and diminutives: Rachel, Raelene, Ray, Raye.
Meaning: 'ewe' (Hebrew) as a diminutive of Rachel.

Raina
Variants and diminutives: Raine, Raini, Rainie, Rana, Rane, Rayna, Rayne, Raynell, Raynette, Regina, Reina, Reine, Reyna, Reyne.
Meaning: 'queen' (Latin) as a Russian variant of Regina; 'advice' or 'might' and 'army' (Germanic) as a female version of Rayner; 'pure' (Yiddish).

Raisa
Variants and diminutives: Raissa, Raiza, Raizel, Rayzel, Rayzil, Razil.
Meaning: 'rose' (Yiddish).

Ramona
Variants and diminutives: Mona, Raymonda, Raymonde, Romona.
Meaning: 'advice' or 'might' and 'protector' (Germanic) as a female version of Ramon (Raymond).

Rana
Variants and diminutives: Raniyah, Ranya.
Meaning: 'pleasing to the eye' (Arabic).

Ranana
Meaning: 'fresh' (Hebrew).

Randa
Variants and diminutives: Randi, Randie, Randy.
Meaning: 'the randa tree' (Arabic); 'shield' or 'raven' and 'wolf' (Old

English) as a female version of Randall.

Rani
Variants and diminutives: Raina, Rana, Rancie, Ranee, Rania, Regina.
Meaning: 'queen' (Sanskrit). A female version of Raja.

Raphaela
Variants and diminutives: Rafaela, Rafaele.
Meaning: 'healed by God' (Hebrew) as a female version of Raphael.

Rashida
Variants and diminutives: Rasheeda, Rashi.
Meaning: 'follower of the correct path' (Sanskrit and Arabic); 'righteous' (Swahili). A female version of Rashid.

Rawnie
Variants and diminutives: Rawni, Ronni, Ronnie, Ronny.
Meaning: 'lady' (English Gypsy).

Raya
Meaning: 'friend' (Hebrew).

Raz
Variants and diminutives: Razi, Razia, Raziah, Raziel, Raziela, Razilee, Razille, Razili, Raziye.
Meaning: 'secret' (Hebrew and Aramaic). Also a boy's name.

Rea
Variants and diminutives: Poppy, Rhea, Ria.
Meaning: 'poppy' (Greek).

Rebecca
Variants and diminutives: Becca, Beck, Becka, Becki, Beckie, Becks, Becky, Bekka, Bekki, Bekkie, Bekky, Reba, Rebe, Rebeca, Rebeka, Rebekah, Rena, Reva, Reveca, Reveka, Revekka, Rifka, Rivca, Rivka.
Meaning: 'binding', 'knotted cord' or 'to fatten' (Hebrew); 'gentle' (Akkadian).

Regan
Variants and diminutives: Reagan, Reaganne, Reagen, Regen, Regin, Regina.
Meaning: uncertain; possibly 'wise' (Germanic); possibly 'queen' (Latin) as a variant of Regina; possibly 'descendant of the little king' or 'queen' (Irish Gaelic) when derived from an Irish family name; coined by William Shakespeare for a character in his play *King Lear*. Also a boy's name.

Regina
Variants and diminutives: Gina, Ina, Queenie, Raina, Raine, Raini, Rainie, Rane, Rani, Rayna, Raynell, Raynette, Reena, Reene, Regan, Regi, Regie, Reggi, Reggie, Reggy, Regine, Reina, Reine, Reinette, Rena, Rene, Renia, Reyna, Reyne, Rina.
Meaning: 'queen' (Latin). A female version of Rex.

Renata
Variants and diminutives: Rene, Renée, Renette, Renita.
Meaning: 'reborn' (Latin); 'joyful song' (Hebrew); 'lovely melody' (Arabic).

Rene
Variants and diminutives: Irene, Reenie, Rena, Renah, Renie, Renna.
Meaning: 'peace' (Greek) as as diminutive of Irene.

Renée
Variants and diminutives: Reenie, Rena, Renata, Rene, Renette, Renita.
Meaning: 'reborn' (French). A female version of René.

Rhea
Variants and diminutives: Rea, Reanna, Ria.
Meaning: uncertain; possibly 'flowing' or 'protector' (Greek); derived from the name of the Titan wife of Kronos and the mother of many gods, including Zeus, in Greek mythology.

Rheta
Variants and diminutives: Reeta, Rita.
Meaning: 'well-spoken' (Greek).

Rhian
Variants and diminutives: Reanna, Rhiana, Rhianna, Rhianne, Rhianu, Rian, Riana, Riane, Rianne.
Meaning: 'maiden' (Welsh); 'great queen', 'goddess', 'moon goddess' or 'nymph' (Welsh) as a diminutive of Rhiannon.

Rhiannon
Variants and diminutives: Reanna, Rhiana, Rhianna, Rhianne, Rhona, Rian, Riana, Riane, Rianne.

Meaning: 'great queen', 'goddess', 'moon goddess' or 'nymph' (Welsh); derived from the name of a moon goddess, the daughter of Hefeydd Hen, wife of Pwyll and Manawydan fab Llyr and mother of Pryderi in Welsh mythology.

Rhoda

Variants and diminutives: Rhode, Rhodeia, Rhodope, Rhodie, Rhody, Rhona, Rhosanna, Roda, Rodina, Rona, Rosa, Rose.
Meaning: 'rose' or 'woman from Rhodes [a Greek island]' (Greek).

Rhona

Variants and diminutives: Rhon, Rhonette, Rhonni, Rhonnie, Rhonny, Ron, Rona, Ronni, Ronnie, Ronny.
Meaning: uncertain; possibly 'little seal' (Irish Gaelic) as a female version of Ronan; possibly derived from the Hebridean island of Rona.

Rhonda

Variants and diminutives: Rhon, Rhondda, Rhonnie, Rhonny, Rhonwen, Ronda.
Meaning: uncertain; possibly 'powerful river' (Celtic); possibly 'noisy' or 'gift' (Welsh); possibly derived from the Rhondda Valley in Wales.

Rhonwen

Variants and diminutives: Rhona, Rowena.
Meaning: 'lance' or 'slim' and 'fair' (Welsh).

Ria

Variants and diminutives: Maria, Rhea, Victoria.
Meaning: 'little river' or 'river mouth' (Spanish). Also a diminutive of any name ending in '-ria', such as Victoria, 'victory' (Latin).

Rica

Variants and diminutives: Erica, Erika, Ricki, Ricky, Rika, Rikki, Rikkie, Rikky, Roderica.
Meaning: 'eternal', 'honourable' or 'island' and 'ruler' (Old Norse) as a diminutive of Erica. Also a diminutive of any name ending in '-rica', such as Roderica (Roderick), 'renowned' and 'ruler' (Germanic).

Ricarda

Variants and diminutives: Rica, Richanda, Richarda, Richardyne, Richela, Richella, Richelle, Richenda, Richenza, Richia, Richmal, Ricka, Ricki, Rickie, Ricky, Riki, Rikki, Rikkie, Rikky.
Meaning: 'ruler' and 'hard' (Germanic) as a female version of Richard.

Richmal

Variants and diminutives: Ricarda, Richarda, Richenda.
Meaning: uncertain; possibly a composite name comprising 'Rich-', 'ruler' and 'hard' (Germanic), as a diminutive of Richard, and '-mal', 'who is like God?' (Hebrew) as a diminutive of Michael.

Rilla

Meaning: 'little stream' (Low German).

Rimona

Variants and diminutives: Mona.
Meaning: 'pomegranate' (Arabic).

Rina

Variants and diminutives: Katrina, Marina, Reena, Rena, Sabrina.
Meaning: a diminutive of any name ending in '-rina', such as Marina, 'of the sea' (Latin).

Rishona

Meaning: 'first' (Hebrew).

Rita

Variants and diminutives: Margarita, Margherita, Marguerita, Reda, Reeta, Reida, Rheta.
Meaning: 'pearl' (Greek) as a diminutive of Margarita (Margaret); 'proper' (Hindi).

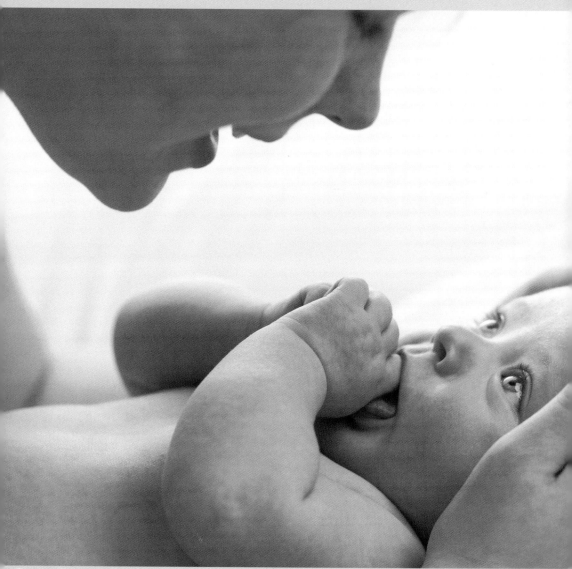

Riva
Variants and diminutives: Ree, Reeva, Reva, Rivana, River, Rivi, Rivy.
Meaning: 'river bank' (Latin).

Roberta
Variants and diminutives: Berta, Bertha, Bertunga, Bobbet, Bobbette, Bobbi, Bobbie, Bobby, Bobbye, Bobina, Bobine, Bobinetta, Bobinette, Erta, Rebinah, Roba, Robbi, Robbie, Robbin, Robby, Robena, Robenia, Robin, Robina, Robine, Robinette, Robinia, Robonia, Robyn, Robynn, Robynne, Rori, Rory, Rubinah, Ruby, Ruperta.
Meaning: 'fame' and 'bright' (Germanic) as a female version of Robert.

Robina
Variants and diminutives: Bina, Bobina, Bobine, Bobinetta, Bobinette, Robbie, Robbin, Robby, Robena, Robenia, Roberta, Robin, Robina, Robine, Robinette, Robinia, Robonia, Robyn, Robynn, Robynne.
Meaning: 'fame' and 'bright' (Germanic) as a variant of Robin (Robert).

Rochelle
Variants and diminutives: Roch, Rochele, Rochella, Rochette, Roshele, Roshelle, Shell, Shelley, Shelli, Shellie, Shelly.
Meaning: 'little rock' (French); possibly derived from the western French port La Rochelle.

Roderica
Variants and diminutives: Rod, Roddi, Roddie, Roddy, Rori, Rory.
Meaning: 'renowned' and 'ruler' (Germanic) as a female version of Roderick.

Róisín
Variants and diminutives: Rosaleen, Rose, Rosheen.
Meaning: 'little rose' (Irish Gaelic).

Rolanda
Variants and diminutives: Orlanda, Ralna, Rolaine, Rolande, Rolene, Roll, Rolleen, Rolli, Rollie, Rolly.
Meaning: 'fame' and 'land' (Germanic) as a female version of Roland.

Roma
Variants and diminutives: Romaine, Romelda, Romia, Romilda, Romola.
Meaning: 'Rome' (Latin and Italian); derived from the Latin and Italian name for the city of Rome, in turn named for Romulus, its legendary co-founder. A female version of Roman.

Romaine
Variants and diminutives: Roma, Romain, Romana, Romayne, Romola, Romy.
Meaning: 'of Rome' (French). A female version of Romain.

Romelda
Variants and diminutives: Roma, Romaine, Romilda.
Meaning: 'Roman warrior' (Germanic).

Romia
Variants and diminutives: Roma, Romaine, Romelda.
Meaning: 'exalted' (Hebrew).

Ronalda
Variants and diminutives: Rona, Roni, Ronl, Ronna, Ronne, Ronnette, Ronnie, Ronny, Ronsie, Ronsy.
Meaning: 'advice' or 'might' and 'power' (Germanic) as a female version of Ronald (Reynold).

Roni
Variants and diminutives: Rani, Ranit, Ranita, Renana, Renanit, Ronia, Ronit, Ronli, Ronnit.
Meaning: 'joy' (Hebrew).

Rosa
Variants and diminutives: Rosabella, Rosaleen, Rosalie, Rosalind,

Rosaline, Rosamund, Rose.
Meaning: 'rose' (Latin).

Rosabella

Variants and diminutives: Bell, Bella, Belle, Ros, Rosa, Rosabel, Rosabelle, Roz.
Meaning: a composite name comprising 'Rosa-', 'rose' (Latin), and '-bella', 'beautiful' (Italian).

Rosaleen

Variants and diminutives: Rosa, Rosalie, Rosalind, Rosaline, Rose, Roseleen.
Meaning: 'little rose' (Latin) as an Irish variant of Rosa.

Rosalie

Variants and diminutives: Ros, Rosa, Rosaleen, Rosalia, Rosaline, Rose, Rosele, Roz, Rozalia, Rozalie.
Meaning: 'little rose' (Latin).

Rosalind

Variants and diminutives: Lindi, Lindie, Lindy, Rhodalind, Ros, Rosa, Rosaleen, Rosalin, Rosalinda, Rosalinde, Rosaline, Rosalyn, Rosalynd, Rosalynde, Rose, Roseleen, Roselyn, Rosilyn, Rosina, Roslyn, Roslyne, Roslynn, Roz, Rozalin, Rozlyn.
Meaning: 'horse' or 'fame' and 'snake' or 'tender' (Germanic); 'rose' and 'lovely' (Spanish).

Rosaline

Variants and diminutives: Ros, Rosa, Rosaleen, Rosalin, Rosalina, Rosalind, Rosalinda, Rosalyn, Rosalynd, Roseleen, Roseline, Roselyn, Rosilyn, Roslyn, Roslyne, Roslynn, Rosslyn, Roz, Rozalin, Rozalina, Rozaline, Rozlyn.
Meaning: 'horse' or 'fame' and 'snake' or 'tender' (Germanic) or 'rose' and 'lovely' (Spanish) as a variant of Rosalind.

Rosamund

Variants and diminutives: Ros, Rosamond, Rosamunda, Rosamunde, Roseaman, Roseman, Rosemunda, Rosomon, Roz, Rozamond.
Meaning: 'horse' or 'fame' and 'protection' (Germanic); 'rose' and 'of the world' or 'pure' (Latin).

Rosanne

Variants and diminutives: Ann, Anna, Anne, Roanne, Ros, Rosa, Rosana, Rose, Roseann, Rosanna, Roseanna, Roseanne, Roz, Rozanne.
Meaning: a composite name comprising 'Rosa-', 'rose' (Latin), and '-anne' (Hannah), 'I have been favoured (by God)' (Hebrew).

Rose

Variants and diminutives: Chalina, Chara, Charo, Losa, Lose, Rhoda, Ricki, Roanne, Roese, Roesia, Rohana, Rohese, Rois, Róisín, Rosa, Rosabel, Rosabella, Rosabelle, Rosabeth, Rosalba, Rosaleen, Rosalia, Rosalie, Rosalin, Rosalina, Rosalind, Rosalinda, Rosamund, Rosana, Rosanna, Rosanne, Rosaura, Roesia, Rosebud, Rosedale, Rosel, Roselani, Rosella, Rosele, Rosella, Roselle, Rosellen, Roselotte, Roselynde, Rosemary, Rosena, Rosetta, Rosette, Rosi, Rosie, Rosina, Rosine, Rosita, Roslyn, Rosy, Royse, Roza, Rozalia, Rozalie, Roze, Rozele, Rozene, Rozina, Rozsa, Rozsi, Rozy, Rozyte, Ruusu, Ruza, Ruzena, Ruzenka, Ruzha, Ruzsa, Shaba, Zita.
Meaning: 'horse' or 'fame' (Germanic); 'rose' (Latin) when derived from the common name of the *Rosa* genus of flowering plants.

Rosemary

Variants and diminutives: Marie, Mary, Romy, Ros, Rose, Rosemaree, Rosemaria, Rosemarie, Rosie, Rosmarie, Roz, Rozmary.
Meaning: 'sea dew' (Latin) or 'rose of the sea' (Latin) when derived from the common name of the *Rosmarinus* genus of herbs; as a composite name, 'Rose-', 'horse' or 'fame' (Germanic) or 'rose' (Latin), and '-mary' (Miriam), 'longed-for child' or 'rebellion' (Hebrew).

Rosetta

Variants and diminutives: Ros, Rose,

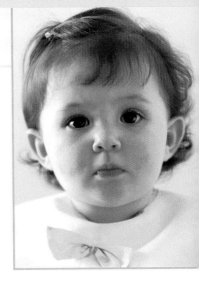

Rosette, Rosita, Roz.
Meaning: 'rose' (Latin) as an Italian variant of Rose.

Rosina
Variants and diminutives: Ros, Rose, Rosetta, Rosita, Roz.
Meaning: 'rose' (Latin) as an Italian variant of Rose.

Rosita
Variants and diminutives: Ros, Rose, Rosetta, Roz.
Meaning: 'rose' (Latin) as a Spanish variant of Rose.

Rosslyn
Variants and diminutives: Ros, Ross, Rosslinda, Rosslynda, Roz, Lyn, Lynn, Lynne.
Meaning: 'horse' or 'fame' and 'snake' or 'tender' (Germanic) or 'rose' and 'lovely' (Spanish) as a variant of Roslyn (Rosalind via Roseline); 'cape' or 'promontory' (Scots Gaelic), 'wood' (Scottish and Irish Gaelic) or 'moor' (Cornish and Welsh) as a female version of Ross.

Rowena
Variants and diminutives: Rhona, Rhonwen, Roanna, Roanne, Rowan, Weena, Wena.

Meaning: 'lance' or 'slim' and 'fair' (Welsh) as a variant of Rhonwen; 'fame' and 'joy' (Germanic); 'mountain ash' (Old Norse) or 'red' (Irish Gaelic) as a female version of Rowan.

Roxanne
Variants and diminutives: Rosana, Roxana, Roxane, Roxann, Roxanna, Roxi, Roxianne, Roxie, Roxine, Roxy.
Meaning: 'dawn' (Persian).

Ruby
Variants and diminutives: Rubetta, Rubette, Rubey, Rubi, Rubia, Rubie, Rubina, Rubye.
Meaning: 'red' (Latin); derived from the name of the precious stone, a variety of corundum.

Rula
Meaning: 'rule' or 'pattern' (Latin).

Rumer
Meaning: 'Gypsy' (English Gypsy).

Ruth
Variants and diminutives: Ruthann, Ruthanne, Ruthi, Ruthie, Ruthina, Ruthine, Ruthven.
Meaning: 'friend', 'companion' or 'lovely sight' (Hebrew); 'compassion', 'remorse' or 'grief' (Old English).

Saada
Meaning: 'help' or 'support' (Hebrew).

Sabina
Variants and diminutives: Bina, Sabcia, Sabia, Sabin, Sabine, Sabinka, Sabka, Savina, Savya.
Meaning: 'a Sabine woman' (Latin), Sabine referring to an ancient central Italian tribe whose women were abducted by the Romans.

Sabira
Meaning: 'patient' (Arabic).

Sabra
Variants and diminutives: Sabrina, Zabra, Zabrina.
Meaning: 'prickly pear' or 'thorny cactus' (Hebrew and Arabic).

Sabrina
Variants and diminutives: Brina, Sabra, Sabreen, Sabreena, Sabrinna, Sabryna.
Meaning: 'the river Severn [in England]' (Latin).

Sadie
Variants and diminutives: Mercedes, Sada, Sadella, Sadi, Sady, Sadye, Saida, Saidee, Sara, Sarah, Zaidee.
Meaning: 'princess' (Hebrew) as a diminutive of Sarah; 'mercy' (Spanish) as a diminutive of Mercedes.

Sadira
Meaning: 'lotus' (Persian).

Saffron
Variants and diminutives: Saffie, Safflower, Saffrey, Saffy.
Meaning: 'saffron' or 'crocus' (Arabic); derived from the common name of the *Crocus sativus* genus of flowers, whose dried stigmas impart a yellow colour and spicy taste to food.

Sagara
Meaning: 'ocean' (Hindi).

Sahara
Variants and diminutives: Zahara.
Meaning: 'desert' (Arabic), referring to the Sahara desert in North Africa, the largest in the world.

Sakura
Meaning: 'cherry blossom' (Japanese).

Sally
Variants and diminutives: Sal, Salena, Salina, Sall, Salley, Salli, Sallie, Sara, Sarah.
Meaning: 'princess' (Hebrew) as a diminutive of Sarah.

Salome
Variants and diminutives: Sal, Salama, Saloma, Salomi, Shulamit, Shulamith, Shuly, Zulema.
Meaning: 'peace' or 'peace of Zion' (Hebrew).

Samantha
Variants and diminutives: Sam, Sami, Sammi, Sammie, Sammy.
Meaning: uncertain; possibly 'to listen' (Hebrew).

Samara
Variants and diminutives: Mara, Sam, Sami, Sammie, Sammy.
Meaning: 'guarded by God' or 'guardian' (Hebrew).

Samira
Variants and diminutives: Mira, Sam, Sami, Sammie, Sammy.
Meaning: 'entertainment' (Arabic) as a female version of Samir.

Sanchia
Variants and diminutives: Saint, Sancha, Santa, Sayntes, Sence, Senses.
Meaning: 'holy' (Latin).

Sandra
Variants and diminutives: Alessandra, Alexandra, Cassandra, Sanda, Sandi, Sandie, Sandy, Saundra, Sondra, Zandra.
Meaning: 'defender of men' or 'warrior' (Greek) as a diminutive of Alexandra, in turn a female version of Alexander; 'ensnarer of men' (Greek) as a diminutive of Cassandra.

Sanne
Variants and diminutives: Susannah.
Meaning: 'lily' (Hebrew) as a diminutive of Susannah.

Santa
Variants and diminutives: Saint, Sancha, Sanchia, Santina.
Meaning: 'holy' (Latin); 'saint' (Portuguese and Spanish). A female version of Santo.

Sapphire
Variants and diminutives: Sapir, Sapira, Sapphira.
Meaning: 'beloved by the planet Saturn' (Sanskrit); 'sapphire' (Hebrew); derived from the common name of the blue corundum gemstone.

Sarah
Variants and diminutives: Chara, Charita, Kala, Morag, Sada, Sadella, Sadie, Sady, Sadye, Saida, Saidee, Sal, Sala, Salaidh, Salcia, Saliee, Sallie, Sally, Sara, Sarai, Saran, Sarann, Saranna, Saranne, Sareen, Sarena, Sarene, Saretta, Sarette, Sari, Sarice, Sarika, Sarina, Sarine, Sarinia, Sarita, Sarka, Sarolta, Sarotte, Sarra, Sasa, Satette, Sayre, Sela, Shara, Sharai, Shari, Sher, Sherrie, Socha, Sorale, Soralie, Sorcha, Sorolie, Zaidee, Zara, Zarah, Zaria, Zora, Zorana, Zoreen, Zorene, Zorna.
Meaning: 'princess' (Hebrew).

Sasha
Variants and diminutives: Alexandra, Sacha.
Meaning: 'defender of men' or 'warrior' (Greek) as a Russian diminutive of Alexandra (Alexander). Also a boy's name (generally Sacha).

Saskia
Variants and diminutives: Alexandra.
Meaning: uncertain; possibly 'Saxon' (Old Dutch); possibly 'defender of men' or 'warrior' (Greek) as a Dutch diminutive of Alexandra (Alexander).

Savannah
Variants and diminutives: Sav, Savana, Savanna, Savanah, Savi, Savie, Savy.
Meaning: 'open grasslands' (Spanish); derived from the topographical feature.

Scarlett
Variants and diminutives: Scarlet.
Meaning: 'fine cloth' (Old French); derived from a British family name.

Scilla
Variants and diminutives: Cilla, Priscilla, Scylla, Sila.
Meaning: 'of ancient times' (Latin) as a diminutive of Priscilla.

Sela
Variants and diminutives: Selena.
Meaning: 'rock' (Hebrew).

Selena
Variants and diminutives: Cela, Celena, Celene, Celie, Celina, Celinda, Celine, Cellina, Salena, Salina, Sela, Selene, Selia, Selie, Selina, Selinda, Seline, Selinka, Sena, Sillina.
Meaning: 'bright light' or 'moon' (Greek) when derived from Selene, a moon goddess of Greek mythology; 'celestial' or 'heavenly' (Latin) as a variant of Celine.

Selima
Variants and diminutives: Selimah.
Meaning: 'healthy' or 'well-made' (Arabic).

Selma

Variants and diminutives: Anselma, Aselma, Zelma.
Meaning: 'divine' and 'helmet' (Germanic) or 'related to nobility' (Old French); as a diminutive of Anselma, in turn a female version of Anselm; 'fair' (Celtic); 'secure' (Arabic).

Senga

Variants and diminutives: Agnes.
Meaning: 'pure' or 'chaste' (Greek) or 'lamb' (Latin), or maybe the reverse because this name results from spelling Agnes backwards.

Septima

Meaning: 'seventh' (Latin). A female version of Septimus.

Seraphina

Variants and diminutives: Serafina, Serafine, Seraphine.
Meaning: 'winged' or 'fiery' (Hebrew); derived from the name of the highest order of angels, the seraphs, or seraphim, in Judaeo-Christian belief.

Serena

Variants and diminutives: Reena, Rena, Rina, Saryna, Sereena, Serene, Serepta, Serina, Seryna, Sirena.
Meaning: 'calm' (Latin).

Shani

Variants and diminutives: Shan, Shannon, Shauna.
Meaning: 'wonderful' (Swahili); 'God has favoured', 'God is gracious' or 'God is merciful' (Hebrew) as a female version of Shane (John via Sean); 'old' (Irish Gaelic) as a diminutive of Shannon.

Shanna

Variants and diminutives: Shan, Shana, Shannah, Shannan, Shannon.
Meaning: 'old' (Irish Gaelic) as a diminutive of Shannon.

Shannon

Variants and diminutives: Shan, Shani, Shanna, Shannagh, Shannah, Shannan, Shannen, Shanon, Shauna, Shawna, Shawni.
Meaning: 'old' (Irish Gaelic); derived from an Irish family name, in turn derived from the name of the longest river in Ireland. Also a boy's name.

Sharifa

Variants and diminutives: Shareefa, Shari, Sharifah.
Meaning: 'honest' or 'noble' (Arabic) as a female version of Sharif.

Sharman

Variants and diminutives: Charmian, Sherman.
Meaning: 'joy' (Greek) or 'song' (Latin) as a variant of Charmian (Charmaine); 'shears' and 'man' (Old English) when derived from an English family name, when it can also be used as a boy's name.

Sharon

Variants and diminutives: Shaaron, Shara, Sharai, Sharan, Shareen, Shari, Sharma, Sharona, Sharron, Sharry, Sharyn, Sheri, Sherisa, Sherissa, Sherry, Sherryn, Shery.
Meaning: 'a plain' (Hebrew), referring to the Plain of Sharon in Israel. Also a boy's name.

Shauna

Variants and diminutives: Seana, Seanna, Shana, Shanna, Shannah, Shawna, Shawnee, Shawni, Shawnie, Siana.
Meaning: 'God has favoured', 'God is gracious' or 'God is merciful' (Hebrew) as a female version of Shaun (John via Sean); 'old' (Irish Gaelic) as a diminutive of Shannon.

Sheba

Variants and diminutives: Bathsheba, Sheva.
Meaning: 'daughter of riches', 'daughter

of a pledge', 'seventh daughter' or 'voluptuous' (Hebrew) as a diminutive of Bathsheba.

Sheena

Variants and diminutives: Jane, Jean, Shayna, Sheenah, Sheina, Shena, Shina, Shiona, Sine.
Meaning: 'God has favoured', 'God is gracious' or 'God is merciful' (Hebrew) as an anglicised version of Sine, in turn a Scots Gaelic variant of Jane or Jean (John).

Sheila

Variants and diminutives: Cecilia, Celia, Seila, Selia, Shayla, Shaylah, Sheela, Sheelagh, Sheelah, Sheilah, Sheilla, Shela, Shelagh, Shelia, Shelley, Shelli, Shelly, Shiela, Shielah, Sighile, Sile.
Meaning: 'celestial' or 'heavenly' (Latin) as an Irish Gaelic variant of Celia; 'blind' (Latin) or 'sixth' (Welsh) as an Irish Gaelic variant of Cecilia.

Shelley

Variants and diminutives: Shell, Shelli, Shellie, Shelly.
Meaning: 'bank', 'plateau' or 'ledge' and 'wood' or 'clearing' (Old English); derived from an English family name, in turn derived from a number of English place names. Also a boy's name.

Sherry

Variants and diminutives: Chérie, Sharee, Shari, Sharie, Sher, Sheree, Sherey, Sheri, Sherie, Sherill, Sherilyn, Sherina, Sherisa, Sherissa, Sherita, Sherree, Sherrey, Sherri, Sherrie, Sherrita, Sherryn, Shery, Sherye, Sheryl.
Meaning: 'darling' (French) as an anglicised version of Chérie; 'from Jerez' (Spanish) when referring to the fortified wine, which was originally made in the Jerez region of Spain.

Sheryl

Variants and diminutives: Cheryl, Sharell, Sheralin, Sheralyn, Sherileen, Sherill, Sherilyn, Sherlynn, Sherrill, Sherryl, Sheryll.
Meaning: uncertain; possibly a variant of Cheryl, a composite name comprising Cherry, 'cherry' (Greek, Latin and Old English) and Beryl, 'precious gem' (Sanskrit), 'crystal clear' (Arabic) or 'sea-green gem' (Greek).

Shira

Variants and diminutives: Shirah, Shiri, Shirlee.
Meaning: 'song' (Hebrew).

Shirley

Variants and diminutives: Sher, Sheree, Sheri, Sherill, Sherline, Sherri, Sherrie, Sherry, Sherye, Sheryl, Shir, Shirl, Shirlee, Shirleen, Shirleigh, Shirlene, Shirli, Shirlie, Shirline, Shirly, Shirlyn, Shirlynn.
Meaning: 'bright' or 'shire' and 'wood' or 'clearing' (Old English); derived from an English family name, in turn derived from a number of English place names.

Shizu

Variants and diminutives: Shizue, Shizuka, Shizuko, Shizuyo, Suizuka.
Meaning: 'clear' or 'quiet' (Japanese).

Shona

Variants and diminutives: Janet, Seonaid, Shaina, Shaine, Shana, Shanie, Shannon, Shayna, Shayne, Shonagh, Shoni, Shonie.
Meaning: 'God has favoured', 'God is gracious' or 'God is merciful' (Hebrew) as an anglicised variant of Seonaid, in turn a Scots Gaelic version of Jane or Janet (John).

Shula

Variants and diminutives: Shulamit.
Meaning: 'peace' (Hebrew).

Siân
Variants and diminutives: Jane.
Meaning: 'God has favoured', 'God is gracious' or 'God is merciful' (Hebrew) as a Welsh variant of Jane (John).

Sidony
Variants and diminutives: Sidney, Sidonia, Sidonie, Sydney.
Meaning: 'from Sidon' (Latin), Sidon being a city of ancient Phoenicia, today the Lebanese city of Saïda; 'linen' (Greek).

Signy
Variants and diminutives: Signe, Signi.
Meaning: 'victory' and 'new' (Old Norse).

Sigrid
Variants and diminutives: Siggi, Siggie, Siggy, Siri.
Meaning: 'victory' and 'beautiful' or 'advice' (Old Norse); 'victory' and 'peace' (Germanic) as a female version of Siegfried.

Silvana
Variants and diminutives: Silva, Silvano, Silvia, Sylva, Sylvana, Sylverta, Sylvi, Sylvia, Sylvie, Vana, Xylia, Xylina, Zilvana.
Meaning: 'sylvan' or 'of the woods' (Latin) as a female version of Silvanus.

Silver
Variants and diminutives: Silva, Silveria, Silvie.
Meaning: 'silver' (Old English); derived from the name of the metal. Also a boy's name.

Silvestra
Variants and diminutives: Silvia, Sylvia, Sylvestra.
Meaning: 'sylvan' or 'of the woods' (Latin) as a female version of Silvester.

Simone
Variants and diminutives: Simeona, Simona, Simonetta, Simonette, Simonia, Simonne.
Meaning: 'God has heard', 'listening' or 'little hyena' (Hebrew) or 'snub-nosed' (Greek) as a female French version of Simon.

Síne
Meaning: 'God has favoured', 'God is gracious' or 'God is merciful' (Hebrew) as a Scots Gaelic version of Jane or Janet (John).

Sinéad
Variants and diminutives: Janet, Seonaid.
Meaning: 'God has favoured', 'God is gracious' or 'God is merciful' (Hebrew) as an Irish Gaelic version of Jane or Janet (John).

Siobhán
Variants and diminutives: Charvon, Chavon, Chavonn, Chavonne, Chevon, Chevonne, Chivon, Shavon, Shavone, Shavonne, Shervan, Shevaun, Shevon, Shevonne, Siobhan, Shivohn, Siobahn, Siobhian.
Meaning: 'God has favoured', 'God is gracious' or 'God is merciful' (Hebrew) as an Irish Gaelic variant of Jane or Joan (John).

Sissy
Variants and diminutives: Cis, Cissie,

Cissy, Sis, Sisi, Sissi, Sissie.
Meaning: 'blind' (Latin) or 'sixth' (Welsh) as a diminutive of Cecilia; 'little sister' (English).

Sita

Variants and diminutives: Zita.
Meaning: 'furrow' (Sanskrit); derived from the name of a goddess of agriculture, who arose from a furrow, beloved by Vishnu in his incarnation as Rama in Hindu mythology.

Sky

Variants and diminutives: Skye.
Meaning: 'transparent skin' (Old Norse); 'cloud' Old English.

Solange

Meaning: 'alone' (Latin).

Soma

Meaning: 'intoxicating juice' (Sanskrit), referring to an extract of the *Asclepias acida* plant used in Vedic ritual; 'moon' (Hindi); 'body' (Greek).

Sonia

Variants and diminutives: Sondya, Sonja, Sonya, Sophia, Zonya.
Meaning: 'wisdom' (Greek) as a Russian variant of Sophia.

Sophia

Variants and diminutives: Chofa, Chofie, Fifi, Sofi, Sofia, Soficita, Sofka, Sofya, Sonia, Sondya, Sonja, Sonni, Sonny, Sonya, Sophie, Sophoon, Sophronia, Sophy, Sunny, Sunya, Zocha, Zofia, Zofie, Zofka, Zonya, Zophia, Zosha, Zosia.
Meaning: 'wisdom' (Greek).

Sophronia

Meaning: 'prudent' (Greek).

Sorcha

Variants and diminutives: Sarah, Sorcka, Sorka.
Meaning: 'radiant' or 'bright' (Irish Gaelic).

Sorrel

Variants and diminutives: Sorel, Sorell, Sorelle, Sorrell.
Meaning: 'sour' (Germanic) when derived from the name of both the sorrel tree (or sourwood), *Oxydendrum arboreum*, and the Rumex genus of plants, which have edible, bitter-tasting leaves; 'chestnut-coloured' or 'reddish-brown' (Old French).

Stacey

Variants and diminutives: Anastasia,

Staci, Stacia, Stacie, Stacy, Stasa, Staska, Stasya, Tasenka, Tasia, Taska, Tasya.
Meaning: 'resurrection' or 'awakening' (Greek) as a diminutive of Anastasia. Also a boy's name as a diminutive of Eustace, 'fruitful', 'good' or 'ear of corn' (Greek).

Star

Variants and diminutives: Estella, Estelle, Starla, Starlit, Starr, Starry, Stella.
Meaning: 'star' (Old English); derived from the generic name for a celestial object.

Stella

Variants and diminutives: Estella, Estelle, Esther, Hester, Star.
Meaning: 'star' (Latin); derived from the generic name for a celestial object.

Stephanie

Variants and diminutives:
Estephania, Etienette, Stamatios, Stef, Stefa, Stefani, Stefania, Stefanida, Stefanie, Stefcia, Stefenie, Steffi, Steffie, Stefka, Stepa, Stepania, Stepanida, Stepanie, Stepanyda, Stepha, Stephana, Stephanine, Stephenie, Stesha, Steshka, Stevana,

Stevena, Stevi, Stevie, Stevy, Panya,
Teena, Trinette.
Meaning: 'crown' (Greek) as a female
version of Stephen.

Stina

Variants and diminutives: Christina,
Stine.
Meaning: 'Christian' (Latin) as a German
diminutive of Christina (Christine).

Storm

Variants and diminutives: Stormie,
Stormy.
Meaning: 'storm' (Old English); derived
from the name for a tempestuous
weather condition. Also a boy's name.

Sukie

Variants and diminutives: Kukana, Su,
Sue, Suka, Suke, Sukee, Sukey, Suki, Suky,
Susan, Susannah.
Meaning: 'lily' (Hebrew) as a diminutive
of Susan or Susannah.

Summer

Meaning: 'season' (Sanskrit); 'the season
of summer' (Old English).

Susan

Variants and diminutives: Chana,
Shoshan, Shoushan, Shushan, Siusan,
Sonel, Su, Suanne, Sudi, Sue, Suella, Suka,
Sukee, Sukey, Suki, Suki, Sukie, Suky,
Susana, Susanka, Susanna, Susanne,
Susannah, Suse, Susetta, Susette, Susi,
Susie, Susy, Suzan, Suzana, Suze, Suzetta,
Suzette, Suzi, Suzie, Suzy, Zuska, Zuza,
Zuzana, Zuzanka, Zuzca, Zuzia, Zuzka.
Meaning: 'lily' (Hebrew) as a diminutive
of Susannah.

Susannah

Variants and diminutives: Chana,
Kukana, Sanne, Shoushan, Siusaidh,
Siusan, Sanna, Sanne, Shoshan,
Shoshana, Shoshanah, Shushan,
Shushana, Shushanah, Shushanna,
Siusan, Sonel, Sosanna, Su, Suanne, Sudi,
Sue, Suella, Suka, Suke, Sukee, Sukey,
Suki, Sukie, Sukey, Suky, Susan, Susana,
Susanka, Susanna, Susanne, Suse,
Susetta, Susette, Susi, Susie, Susy, Suzan,
Suzana, Suzanna, Suzannah, Suzanne,
Suze, Suzetta, Suzette, Suzi, Suzie, Suzy,
Xuxu, Zana, Zsa Zsa, Zuska, Zuza, Zuzana,
Zuzanna, Zuzia, Zuzka, Zuzanka.
Meaning: 'lily' (Hebrew).

Sybil

Variants and diminutives: Cybele,
Cybil, Sevilla, Sib, Sibbie, Sibby, Sibel,
Sibell, Sibella, Sibelle, Sibett, Sibeal, Sibil,
Sibilla, Sibille, Sibley, Sibyl, Sibylla, Sibylle,
Sibyllina, Sybella, Sybilla, Sybille, Sybyl,
Sybylla.

Meaning: uncertain; possibly
'prophetess' (Greek); possibly 'whistle' or
'hiss' (Latin).

Sylvia

Variants and diminutives: Silivia, Silva,
Silvana, Silvano, Silveria, Silvestra, Silvia,
Silvie, Silvina, Sylva, Sylvana, Sylverta,
Sylvestra, Sylvi, Sylvie, Xylia, Xylina,
Zilvia.
Meaning: 'wood' (Latin).

Tabitha

Variants and diminutives: Tab,
Tabatha, Tabbi, Tabbie, Tabbitha, Tabby.
Meaning: 'gazelle' (Aramaic).

Tacey

Variants and diminutives: Tace, Tacie,
Tacita, Tacy, Tacye.
Meaning: 'to be silent' (Latin).

Tacita

Variants and diminutives: Tacey, Tacye.
Meaning: 'the silent' (Latin).

Taja

Variants and diminutives: Tajah,
Talajara, Tejab, Tejal.

Meaning: 'crown' (Urdu and Arabic). A female version of Taj.

Takara
Variants and diminutives: Kara.
Meaning: 'treasure' or 'precious' (Japanese).

Talia
Variants and diminutives: Tal, Tali, Tallie, Tally, Talor, Talora, Talya, Teli, Thalia.
Meaning: 'lamb' (Aramaic); 'dew of heaven' (Hebrew); 'birthday' (Latin), 'Christ's birthday' or 'Christmas' (Slavonic) as a diminutive of Natalia.

Talitha
Variants and diminutives: Tali, Talith.
Meaning: 'little girl' (Aramaic).

Tallulah
Variants and diminutives: Lula, Lulah, Talli, Talie, Tallis, Talllou, Tally, Tallula, Talula, Talulla.
Meaning: 'spring' or 'running' or 'leaping' and 'water' (Choctaw – Native American); derived from a North American place name.

Talulla
Variants and diminutives: Lula, Lulla, Tali, Talie, Talullah.

Meaning: 'abundance' and 'princess' or 'lady' (Irish Gaelic).

Tamar
Variants and diminutives: Tam, Tama, Tamah, Tamara, Tamarah, Tamarra, Tamer, Tami, Tamie, Tamimah, Tammi, Tammie, Tammy, Tamor, Tamour, Tamra, Tamyra, Temima, Temira, Timora, Timi.
Meaning: 'date palm' or 'palm tree' (Hebrew).

Tamara
Variants and diminutives: Mara, Tam, Tama, Tamah, Tamar, Tamarah, Tamarka, Tamarra, Tamer, Tami, Tamie, Tammara, Tammera, Tammi, Tammie, Tammy, Tamor, Tamour, Tamra, Tamyra, Temira, Timora, Tomochka.
Meaning: 'date palm' or 'palm tree' (Hebrew) as a Russian variant of Tamar.

Tamsin
Variants and diminutives: Tamasin, Tamasine, Tami, Tammie, Tammy, Tansin, Tamzin, Tamzine, Tamzon, Thomasina, Thomasine.
Meaning: 'twin' (Aramaic) as a variant of Thomasina (Thomas).

Tanith
Variants and diminutives: Tanit.

Meaning: 'great mother' (Phoenician) when derived from the name of the supreme goddess of Carthage; 'estate' (Irish Gaelic).

Tansy
Variants and diminutives: Tansie.
Meaning: 'immortality' (Greek); derived from the common name of the *Tanacetum vulgare* flowering plant, which has edible leaves.

Tanya
Variants and diminutives: Tanhya, Tania, Tatiana, Tiana.
Meaning: uncertain; possibly 'fairy queen' (Old Slavonic), 'I arrange' (Greek) or derived from the Sabine and Roman family name Tatius as a diminutive of Tatiana.

Tara

Variants and diminutives: Tarah, Tarra, Taryn, Tatiana, Teamhair, Tera, Terra.
Meaning: uncertain; possibly 'hill' (Irish Gaelic); possibly 'star' (Sanskrit) when derived from the name of the Hindu, Jain and Buddhist Tantric mother goddess; possibly 'to carry' or 'to throw' (Aramaic).

Tasha

Variants and diminutives: Talia, Natasha.
Meaning: 'birthday' (Latin), 'Christ's birthday' or 'Christmas' (Slavonic) as a diminutive of Natasha, in turn a diminutive of Natalya (Natalia).

Tasya

Variants and diminutives: Anastasia, Tasia.
Meaning: 'resurrection' or 'awakening' (Greek) as a diminutive of Anastasia.

Tatiana

Variants and diminutives: Tanhya, Tania, Tanya, Tara, Tiana, Tita, Titania.
Meaning: uncertain; possibly 'fairy queen' (Old Slavonic); possibly 'I arrange' (Greek); possibly derived from the Sabine and Roman family name Tatius.

Tatum

Variants and diminutives: Tait, Taite, Tata, Tate, Tayte.
Meaning: uncertain; possibly 'windy' or 'garrulous' (Native American), 'cheerful' (Old Norse), 'dear', 'happy', 'dice', 'hilltop', 'tress of hair', 'father' or 'teat' (Old English) as a female version of Tate.

Tauba

Variants and diminutives: Dove, Taube, Toby.
Meaning: 'dove' (Germanic).

Tawny

Variants and diminutives: Tawni, Tawnie.
Meaning: 'tan' (Old French) when derived from the name of the light-orange-brown colour; 'little one' (English Gypsy).

Teal

Variants and diminutives: Teale.

Meaning: 'teal' (Middle English); derived from an English family name, in turn derived from the common name of a number of small ducks.

Tegan

Variants and diminutives: Taegen, Taygan, Teagan, Teegan, Tegan, Tegin, Tegwen, Tiegan, Tigan.
Meaning: 'lovely' (Welsh); 'poet' or 'philosopher' (Irish Gaelic) as a female version of Teague.

Tegwen

Variants and diminutives: Tegan.
Meaning: 'lovely' and 'fair' or 'blessed' (Welsh).

Temima

Variants and diminutives: Tamar, Tamimah.
Meaning: 'honest' or 'entire' (Hebrew and Arabic).

Temperance

Variants and diminutives: Temp, Tempi, Tempie, Tempy.
Meaning: 'to regulate' (Latin).

Tempest

Variants and diminutives: Tempestt.
Meaning: 'storm' (Old French).

Tertia
Variants and diminutives: Terti,
Tertie, Terty, Tia.
Meaning: 'third' (Latin). A female
version of Tertius.

Tesia
Variants and diminutives: Taisha,
Taysha, Tesha, Teysha, Theophila.
Meaning: 'God-loving' (Greek) as a
Polish diminutive of Theophila
(Theophilus).

Tessa
Variants and diminutives: Teresa,
Tersa, Tesa, Tess, Tessi, Tessia, Tessie,
Tessy, Theresa, Tresa.
Meaning: uncertain; possibly
'harvest', 'reap' or 'from Thera [or
Therasia]' (Greek) as a diminutive of
Theresa.

Thalassa
Variants and diminutives: Thalli,
Thallie, Thally, Lassa.
Meaning: 'sea' (Greek), with particular
reference to the Mediterranean Sea.

Thalia
Variants and diminutives: Talia,
Talya, Thaleia.
Meaning: 'to prosper', 'to flourish' or
'to bloom' (Greek).

Thea
Variants and diminutives:
Dorothea, Dorothy, Theia, Theodora.
Meaning: 'goddess' (Greek) as a
female version of Theo; 'God's gift'
(Greek) as a diminutive of Dorothea
(Dorothy), in turn a female version of
Theodore.

Thekla
Variants and diminutives: Tecla,
Tecle, Thecla, Thea, Theodora,
Theodosia, Theophania, Theophila.
Meaning: 'God' and 'renowned'
(Greek).

Thelma
Variants and diminutives: Kama,
Teli, Telma.
Meaning: uncertain; possibly 'will',
'wish' or 'nursling' (Greek); coined by
British writer Marie Corelli for the
heroine of her novel of the same
name.

Theodora
Variants and diminutives: Dora,
Dorothea, Dorothy, Fedora, Feodora,
Ted, Tedda, Teddi, Teddy, Tedra,
Teodora, Thaddea, Thadine, Thea,
Theda, Thekla, Theo, Theodosia,
Theophania, Theophila.
Meaning: 'God's gift' (Greek) as a
female version of Theodore.

Theodosia
Variants and diminutives: Thea,
Thekla, Theodora, Theophania,
Theophila.
Meaning: 'given by God' (Greek).

Theophania
Variants and diminutives: Thea,
Theodora, Theodosia, Theophila,
Tiffany.
Meaning: 'God's manifestation' or
'epiphany' (Greek).

Theophila
Variants and diminutives: Offie,
Offy, Phila, Tesia, Thea, Theodora,
Theodosia, Theophania.
Meaning: 'God-loving' (Greek) as a
female version of Theophilus.

Theresa
Variants and diminutives: Renia,
Resel, Resi, Rezi, Riza, Rizua, Tassos,
Teca, Techa, Tera, Tercsa, Tere, Terenia,
Teresa, Terese, Teresina, Teresita,
Tereska, Teressa, Terez, Tereza, Terezia,
Terezie, Terezilya, Terezka, Teri, Terie,
Terike, Terri, Terrie, Terry, Tery, Tersa,
Teruska, Tesa, Tesia, Tess, Tessa, Tessi,
Tessie, Tessy, Tete, Therese, Thérèse,
Theresia, Trace, Tracey, Traci, Tracie,
Tracy, Tresa, Trescha, Treszka, Zilya,
Zita.
Meaning: uncertain; possibly

'harvest', 'reap' or 'from Thera [or Therasia]' (Greek), Thera (Thíra) being a Greek island in the Aegean Sea, also known as Santorini.

Thirza

Variants and diminutives: Thirsa, Thirzah, Thyrza, Tirza, Tirzah.
Meaning: uncertain; possibly 'pleasantness' or 'acceptance' (Hebrew).

Thomasina

Variants and diminutives: Tamanique, Tamasin, Tamasine, Tami, Tammie, Tammy, Tamsin, Tamzin, Tamzine, Tamzon, Thomasa, Thomasin, Thomasine, Thomasing, Thomassine, Thomson, Toma, Tomasa, Tomasina, Tomasine, Tommi, Tommianne, Tommy.
Meaning: 'twin' (Aramaic) as a female version of Thomas.

Thora

Variants and diminutives: Thodia, Thordis, Thyra, Tora, Tyra.
Meaning: uncertain; possibly 'of Thor' or 'the thunderer' (Old Norse), Thor being the thunder god of Norse mythology. A female version of Thor.

Tiana

Variants and diminutives: Christiana, Tania, Tanya, Tatiana, Tia, Tiane, Tianna, Tianne.

Meaning: 'Christian' (Latin) as a diminutive of Christiana (Christine); possibly 'fairy queen' (Old Slavonic), 'I arrange' (Greek) or derived from the Sabine and Roman family name Tatius as a diminutive of Tatiana.

Tibby

Variants and diminutives: Isabel, Tibbi, Tibbie, Tibbs.
Meaning: 'God is perfection', 'God is satisfaction', 'dedicated to God' or 'God's oath' (Hebrew) and 'beautiful' (French, Italian and Spanish) as a diminutive of Isabel.

Tiffany

Variants and diminutives: Teffan, Teffany, Thefania, Theophania, Tifaine, Tiff, Tiffan, Tiffani, Tiffanie, Tiffy, Tiphaine, Thiphania, Tyfanny.
Meaning: 'God's manifestation' or 'epiphany' (Greek) as a diminutive of Theophania.

Tilda

Variants and diminutives: Matilda, Tila, Tilda, Tilde, Tildie, Tildy, Tillie, Tilly, Tylda
Meaning: 'mighty' and 'battle' as a diminutive of Matilda.

Timothea

Variants and diminutives: Timi, Timie, Timmie, Timmy.

Meaning: 'in honour of God' (Greek) as a female version of Timothy.

Tina

Variants and diminutives: Christina, Constantina, Tiana, Tyna, Valentina.
Meaning: a diminutive of any name ending in '-tina', such as Christina (Christine), 'Christian' (Latin).

Tisha

Variants and diminutives: Letitia, Tish, Titia.
Meaning: 'joyful' (Latin) as a diminutive of Letitia.

Tivona

Variants and diminutives: Tibona, Tiboni, Tivony.
Meaning: 'nature-lover' (Hebrew). A female version of Tivon.

Tonia

Variants and diminutives: Antonia, Toni, Tonie, Tonya, Tosia.
Meaning: 'flourishing' (Greek) or 'without price' (Latin) as a diminutive of Antonia (Anthony).

Topaz

Variants and diminutives: Topaza.
Meaning: 'topaz' (Greek); derived from the name of the usually golden-coloured gemstone.

Tora

Variants and diminutives: Tori, Tory.
Meaning: 'tiger' (Japanese).

Tori

Variants and diminutives: Tora, Tory.
Meaning: 'bird' (Japanese).

Toyah

Variants and diminutives: Toya.
Meaning: 'toying' or 'trifling' (Middle English).

Tracy

Variants and diminutives: Teresa, Theresa, Trace, Tracey, Traci, Tracie, Trasey.
Meaning: 'Thracian' or 'of Thrace' (Latin), Thrace being an ancient kingdom in the south-eastern Balkans, when derived from an English family name, in turn derived from two French place names; possibly 'harvest', 'reap' or 'from Thera [or Therasia]' (Greek) as a diminutive of Theresa. Also a boy's name.

Trina

Variants and diminutives: Catriona, Katrina, Trinete.
Meaning: 'pure' (Greek) as a diminutive of Catriona and Katrina, both variants of Catherine; 'piercing' (Hindi).

Trisha

Variants and diminutives: Patricia, Tricia, Trish.
Meaning: 'noble' or 'patrician' (Latin) as a diminutive of Patricia (Patrick); 'thirst' (Hindi).

Trixie

Variants and diminutives: Beatrice, Beatrix, Tris, Trissie, Trix, Trixy.
Meaning: 'bringer of blessings' or 'traveller' (Latin) as a diminutive of Beatrix (Beatrice).

Trudy

Variants and diminutives: Ermintrude, Gertrude, Truda, Trude, Trudey, Trudi, Trudie.
Meaning: 'spear' and 'strength' (Germanic) as a diminutive of Gertrude; 'universal' and 'strength' (Germanic) as a diminutive of Ermintrude.

Tryphena

Variants and diminutives: Phena, Truffeni, Tryphosa.
Meaning: 'delicacy' or 'daintiness' (Greek).

Twyla

Variants and diminutives: Twila, Twilla.
Meaning: 'woven with a double thread' (Old English).

Tyra

Variants and diminutives: Thora, Thyra.
Meaning: uncertain; possibly 'of Tyr' or 'warrior' (Old Norse), Tyr being a god of war in Norse mythology.

Udelle

Variants and diminutives: Ella, Elle, Udella, Ula.
Meaning: 'yew' and 'valley' (Old English) as a female version of Udell; 'wealth' (Old Norse), 'owner' (Germanic) or 'sea jewel' (Irish Gaelic) as a variant of Ula.

Ula
Variants and diminutives: Udelle, Ulani, Ulla.
Meaning: 'wealth' (Old Norse); 'owner' (Germanic); 'sea jewel' (Irish Gaelic).

Ulani
Variants and diminutives: Lani, Ula.
Meaning: 'light-hearted', 'cheerful' or 'bright' (Hawaiian).

Ulima
Variants and diminutives: Ulema.
Meaning: 'wise' or 'learned' (Arabic). A female version of Ulim.

Ulrica
Variants and diminutives: Rica, Ula, Ulla, Ulli, Ullie, Ully, Ulrika, Ulrike.
Meaning: 'wolf' and 'ruler' (Germanic) as a female version of Ulric.

Ultima
Variants and diminutives: Ulti, Ultie, Ulty.
Meaning: 'furthest' or 'last' (Latin). A female version of Ultimus.

Ulva
Variants and diminutives: Ulvi, Ulvie, Ulvy.
Meaning: 'she-wolf' (Old English).

Uma
Variants and diminutives: Ama, Amma.
Meaning: 'mother', 'light', 'peace of night' or 'desist' (Sanskrit); derived from the name of an ancient Indian creator goddess, also the shakti (female power) of Shiva, the Hindu god of destruction and personal destiny.

Umay
Variants and diminutives: Umai.
Meaning: 'hopeful' (Turkish).

Umeko
Variants and diminutives: Ume, Umeyo.
Meaning: 'plum blossom' (Japanese).

Una
Variants and diminutives: Juno, Ona, Oona, Oonagh, Oonie, Unique, Unity.
Meaning: 'one' or 'together' (Latin); 'lamb' (Irish Gaelic).

Undina
Variants and diminutives: Ondine, Undine.
Meaning: 'wave' or 'water', 'surge' or 'stream' (Latin).

Unice
Variants and diminutives: Eunice.
Meaning: 'victorious' (Greek) as a variant of Eunice.

Unique
Variants and diminutives: Una, Unity.
Meaning: 'unparalleled' (Latin).

Unity
Variants and diminutives: Una, Unique.
Meaning: 'one' or 'together' (Latin).

Urania
Variants and diminutives: Ourania.
Meaning: 'heavenly' (Greek). Also a female version of Uranus.

Urith
Variants and diminutives: Urice, Urit.
Meaning: 'light' or 'bright' (Hebrew). Also a female version of Uriah.

Ursula
Variants and diminutives: Orsa, Orsel, Orsola, Sula, Ulla, Ulli, Urmi, Ursa, Ursala, Urse, Ursel, Ursie, Ursina, Ursine, Ursley, Ursola, Ursule, Ursulina, Ursuline, Ursi, Ursie, Ursy, Uschi, Urzula, Vorsila, Wuschi, Wuschie, Wuschy.
Meaning: 'little she-bear' (Latin). Also a female version of Ursell.

Usha
Variants and diminutives: Ushi.
Meaning: 'dawn' or 'sunrise' (Hindi).

Utako
Variants and diminutives: Tako.
Meaning: 'poem' (Japanese).

Valda
Variants and diminutives: Velda.
Meaning: 'power' or 'rule' (Germanic) as a female version of Waldo.

Valentina
Variants and diminutives: Teena, Tina, Val, Vale, Valencia, Valentia, Valera, Valerie, Valida, Vallie.
Meaning: 'healthy' or 'vigorous' (Latin) as a female version of Valentine.

Valerie
Variants and diminutives: Lera, Lerka, Val, Valaree, Valaria, Valarie, Valarie, Valary, Vale, Valentina, Valentine, Valerey, Valeria, Valeriana, Valery, Valerye, Valka, Valli, Vallie, Vally, Valora, Valry, Valya, Wala, Waleria, .
Meaning: 'to be healthy' or 'to be vigorous' (Latin) as a female French version of Valerius.

Valeska
Variants and diminutives: Val.
Meaning: 'glorious' (Russian).

Valma
Variants and diminutives: Alma, Val, Velma, Vilma.
Meaning: uncertain; possibly 'may flower' (Celtic).

Valonia
Variants and diminutives: Val, Vallonia.
Meaning: 'acorn' (Greek); derived from a name for the unripe acorns and acorn cups of the *Quercus aegilops* species of oak tree, which are used for tanning, dyeing and ink-making.

Vanda
Variants and diminutives: Wanda.
Meaning: uncertain; possibly 'family' or 'wanderer' (Germanic) or derived from the name of a Germanic people, the Vandals, or 'wand' or 'shoot' (Old Norse) as a variant of Wanda; 'plait' (Congo and Mende – Africa).

Vanessa
Variants and diminutives: Essa, Ness, Nessa, Nessi, Nessie, Nessy, Van, Vana, Vania, Vanna, Vanni, Vannie, Vanny, Vanya, Venesa, Venessa.
Meaning: uncertain; possibly 'butterflies' (Greek); a name coined by the Irish writer Jonathan Swift by combining and reversing components of the name of one of his friends, Esther Vanhomrigh, for the eponymous heroine of his poem *Cadenus and Vanessa*.

Vania
Variants and diminutives: Ivana, Ivanna, Vanessa, Vanna, Vanya.
Meaning: 'God has favoured', 'God is gracious' or 'God is merciful' (Hebrew) as a diminutive of Ivanna (Ivana); possibly 'butterflies' (Greek) as a variant of Vanessa.

Vanna
Variants and diminutives: Ivana, Ivanna, Vanessa, Vania.
Meaning: 'God has favoured', 'God is gracious' or 'God is merciful' (Hebrew) as a diminutive of Ivanna (Ivana); possibly 'butterflies' (Greek) as a variant of Vanessa.

Vanora
Variants and diminutives: Vevay.
Meaning: 'white wave' (Celtic).

Varda

Variants and diminutives: Vardia, Vardice, Vardina, Vardis, Vardit, Vered.
Meaning: 'rose' (Hebrew and Arabic).

Vashti

Meaning: 'best' or 'lovely' (Persian).

Veda

Meaning: 'knowledge' or 'I know' (Sanskrit).

Vela

Variants and diminutives: Vella.
Meaning: 'sail' (Latin); derived from the name of a constellation of the Southern Hemisphere.

Velda

Variants and diminutives: Valda.
Meaning: uncertain; possibly 'power' or 'rule' (Germanic) as a variant of Valda; possibly 'field' (Germanic).

Velika

Variants and diminutives: Lika, Veli.
Meaning: 'great' (Slavonic).

Velma

Variants and diminutives: Valma, Vilma, Wilhelmina, Willa, Wilma.
Meaning: uncertain; possibly 'will' and 'helmet' or 'protection' (Germanic) as a diminutive of Wilhelmina (William).

Velvet

Variants and diminutives: Velve, Velvi, Velvie, Velvy.
Meaning: 'hairy' (Old French).

Venetia

Variants and diminutives: Venda, Veneta, Venezia, Venita, Venus, Vinetia, Vinita.
Meaning: 'district of the Veneti' (Latin), the Veneti referring to the ancient people who established Venetia, today the Veneto (Venezia-Euganea) region of Italy, whose capital is Venice (Venezia).

Ventura

Meaning: 'good fortune' (Spanish).

Venus

Variants and diminutives: Venita, Vespera, Vin, Vinita, Vinnie, Vinny.
Meaning: 'beauty', 'charm' or 'love' (Latin); derived from the name of the goddess of love and beauty in Roman mythology.

Vera

Variants and diminutives: Verasha, Vere, Verena, Verene, Verina, Verine, Verinka, Verity, Verka, Verla, Veronica, Verusya, Viera, Wera, Wiera, Wiercia, Wierka.
Meaning: 'truthful' (Latin); 'faith' (Russian).

Verena

Variants and diminutives: Vera, Veradis, Vere, Verene, Verina, Verine, Verinka, Verita, Verity, Verla, Verna, Verochka, Veronica, Virna.
Meaning: uncertain; possibly 'truthful' (Latin) or 'faith' (Russian) as a variant of Vera; possibly 'a slave born in [his or] her master's house' or 'of spring' (Latin) or 'alder tree' (Old French) as a variant of Verna.

Verity

Variants and diminutives: Vera, Verena.
Meaning: 'truth' (Latin).

Verna

Variants and diminutives: Verena, Verona.
Meaning: 'a slave born in [his or] her master's house' or 'of spring' (Latin); 'alder tree' (Old French) as a female version of Vernon.

Verona

Variants and diminutives: Rona, Verna, Verone, Veronica.
Meaning: uncertain; possibly 'certainly' or 'indeed' (Latin) when derived from the name of the city in the Veneto region of Italy; possibly 'true image' (Latin) as a variant of Veronica.

Veronica

Variants and diminutives: Berenice, Berenike, Bernice, Nika, Ron, Roni, Ronie, Ronni, Ronnie, Ronny, Vera, Verenice, Verona, Verone, Veronika, Veronike, Véronique, Veronka, Vonni, Vonnie, Vonny, Vron, Vronni, Vronnie, Vronny.
Meaning: 'true image' (Latin), referring to the cloth that, according to traditional Christian belief, was miraculously imprinted with the image of Christ's face after Saint Veronica offered it to him to wipe away his sweat on the road to Calgary.

Vespera

Variants and diminutives: Vespi, Vespie, Vespy.
Meaning: 'evening' or 'evening star' (Latin); derived from Vesper, the alternative name of the planet Venus when visible in the evening.

Vesta

Variants and diminutives: Vessi, Vessie, Vessy, Star.
Meaning: uncertain; possibly 'goddess of the hearth' or 'keeper of the sacred flame' (Latin); derived from the name of the goddess of the hearth in Roman mythology, in whose temple in Rome the Vestal virgins tended a perpetual flame. Notable namesakes: an asteroid; an alternative name for a match.

Vevila

Variants and diminutives: Vevi, Vila.
Meaning: 'harmonious' or 'together' (Celtic).

Victoria

Variants and diminutives: Nike, Tora, Tory, Vic, Vici, Vick, Vicki, Vickie, Vicky, Victoire, Victoriana, Victorina, Victorine, Vika, Viki, Vikie, Vikki, Vikkie, Vikky, Viktoria, Viktorie, Viktorija, Viktorka, Viky, Vita, Vitoria, Vittoria, Viqui.
Meaning: 'victory' (Latin).

Victorine

Variants and diminutives: Tori, Vic, Vicki, Vickie, Vicky, Victoria, Victoriana, Victorina, Vikki, Vikkie, Vikky.
Meaning: 'victor' (Latin) as a female version of Victor.

Vida

Variants and diminutives: Davida.
Meaning: 'beloved' or 'friend' (Hebrew) as a diminutive of Davida (David).

Vina

Variants and diminutives: Davina, Lavina, Vinia.
Meaning: 'wine' (Latin); also a diminutive of any name ending in '-vina', such as Davina, meaning 'beloved' or friend' (Hebrew) as a female version of David.

Vincentia

Variants and diminutives: Centia, Vin, Vince, Vinnie, Vinny.
Meaning: 'conqueror' (Latin) as a female version of Vincent.

Viola

Variants and diminutives: Vi, Violet, Violetta, Violette.
Meaning: 'violet' (Latin); derived from the name of the genus of flowering plants that includes violets and pansies.

Violet

Variants and diminutives: Vi, Viola, Violante, Violeta, Violetta, Violette, Voleta, Voletta, Yolanda, Yolande, Yolane.

Meaning: 'little violet' (Old French) as a variant of Viola; derived from the common name of various species of the Viola genus of flowering plants.

Violetta

Variants and diminutives: Vi, Viola, Violet, Violeta, Violette, Voleta, Voletta.
Meaning: 'little violet' (Italian) as a variant of Viola.

Virginia

Variants and diminutives: Gina, Ginata, Ginger, Ginia, Ginney, Ginni, Ginnie, Ginny, Jinni, Jinnie, Jinny, Vegenia, Vergie, Vinnie, Vinny, Virgie, Virginie, Virgy, Wilikinia.
Meaning: 'virgin' or 'maiden' (Latin); derived from the Roman family name Verginius or Virginius.

Vita

Variants and diminutives: Victoria, Vida, Viva, Viviana, Vivien.
Meaning: 'life' (Latin); 'victory' (Latin) as a diminutive of Victoria.

Viva

Variants and diminutives: Vita, Viv, Vivia, Viviana, Vivien.
Meaning: 'to live' (Latin).

Vivia

Variants and diminutives: Vita, Viv, Viva, Viviana, Vivien.
Meaning: 'to live' (Latin) as a variant of Viva; 'living' (Latin) as a variant of Vivien.

Vivien

Variants and diminutives: Bibiana, Fithian, Vevay, Vita, Viv, Viva, Viveca, Vivevca, Vivi, Vivia, Vivian, Viviana, Viviane, Vivianne, Vivie, Vivien, Vivienne, Vivyan, Vyvyan.
Meaning: 'living' (Latin); derived fom the Roman family name Vivianus. Also a boy's name (generally Vivian or Vyvyan).

Waikiki

Variants and diminutives: Kiki.
Meaning: 'spring' or 'flowing water' (Hawaiian).

Walburga

Variants and diminutives: Walpurga.
Meaning: 'power' and 'protection' or 'fortress' (Germanic and Old English).

Walda

Variants and diminutives: Waldi, Waldie, Waldy.
Meaning: 'power' or 'rule' and 'people' or 'army' (Germanic) as a female version of Walter.

Wallis

Variants and diminutives: Wallace, Wallie, Wally.
Meaning: 'Celt', 'Breton', 'Welshman' or 'foreigner' (Old French); derived from an English family name. Also a boy's name.

Wanda

Variants and diminutives: Vanda, Vandis, Vona, Vonda, Wanaka, Wandi, Wandie, Wandis, Wandy, Wandzia, Wanja, Wenda, Wendeline, Wendi, Wendy, Wendye.
Meaning: uncertain; possibly 'family' or 'wanderer' (Germanic) or derived from the name of a Germanic people, the Vandals; possibly 'wand' or 'shoot' (Old Norse).

Warrene

Variants and diminutives: Warnette, Waurene.
Meaning: 'game preserve', 'wasteland' or 'sandy soil' (Gaulish) or 'to protect' or 'to preserve' (Germanic) as a female version of Warren.

Welcome

Meaning: 'welcome' (Old English). Also a boy's name.

Wenda

Variants and diminutives: Vendelin, Wanda, Wendeline, Wendey, Wendi, Wendoline, Wendy.

Meaning: uncertain; possibly 'to change course' (Old Norse); possibly 'family' or 'wanderer' (Germanic) or derived from the name of a Germanic people, the Vandals, or 'wand' or 'shoot' (Old Norse) as a variant of Wanda; possibly 'fair' and 'ring' (Welsh) as a diminutive of Wendoline (Gwendolyn); possibly a variant of Wendy. Also a female version of Wendell.

Wendoline

Variants and diminutives: Gwendoline, Gwendolyn, Vendelin, Wenda, Wendelin, Wendeline, Wendey, Wendi, Wendie, Wendolin, Wendy.
Meaning: 'fair' and 'ring' (Welsh) as a variant of Gwendolyn.

Wendy

Variants and diminutives: Wenda, Wendey, Wendi, Wendie.
Meaning: uncertain; coined by the Scottish writer J M Barrie for the leading female character of his play *Peter Pan*, having been inspired by Margaret Henley, a young girl who called him her 'friendy-wendy' or 'fwendy-wendy'.

Whitney

Variants and diminutives: Whitley, Whitnee, Whitni, Whitnie, Whitny, Witney.
Meaning: 'white' or 'White's' and 'island' (Old English); derived from an English family name, in turn derived from an English place name. Also a boy's name.

Wilfreda

Variants and diminutives: Freda, Frida, Wilfrida.
Meaning: 'will' and 'peace' (Germanic) as a female version of Wilfred.

Wilhelmina

Variants and diminutives: Bill, Billi, Billie, Billy, Guglielma, Guilette, Guilla, Guillelmine, Guillema, Guillemette, Guillerma, Guillermina, Helma, Helmine, Ilma, Mimi, Min, Mina, Minchen, Minka, Minna, Minette, Mini, Minni, Minnie, Minny, Valma, Velma, Vilhelmina, Vilma, Vilna, Wileen, Wiletta, Wilette, Wilhelma, Wilhelmine, Willa, Willabelle, Willamae, Willamina, Willandra, Willene, Willeta, Willetta, Willette, Willi, Williamina, Willie, Willy, Wilma, Wilmena, Wilmet, Wilmette, Wylma.
Meaning: 'will' and 'helmet' or 'protection' (Germanic) as a female version of William.

Willa

Variants and diminutives: Wilhelmina, Willabelle, Willamae, Willamina, Willandra, Willlene, Willeta, Willetta, Willette, Willi, Williamina, Willow, Willy, Wilma.

Meaning: 'continuation' (Arabic); 'will' and 'helmet' or 'protection' (Germanic) as a female version of William.

Willow

Variants and diminutives: Willa, Wilda.
Meaning: 'twisted' (Greek); 'willow tree' (Old English); derived from the common name of the Salix genus of trees and shrubs.

Wilma

Variants and diminutives: Vilma, Vilna, Wilhelmina, Willa, Williamina, Wilmena, Wilmet, Wilmette, Wylma.
Meaning: 'will' and 'helmet' or 'protection' (Germanic) as a diminutive of Wilhelmina; 'will' and 'fame' (Germanic) as a female version of Wilmer.

Winema

Variants and diminutives: Nema, Win, Winnie, Winny.
Meaning: 'female chief' (Miwok – Native American).

Winifred

Variants and diminutives: Freda, Freddi, Freddie, Freddy, Fredi, Guinever, Gwenevere, Gwenfrewi, Gwinevere, Oona, Una, Usa, Vinette, Wenefreda, Win, Winefred, Winefride, Winie, Winifrin,

Winn, Winnie, Winnifred, Winnifride, Winny, Wyn, Wynelle, Wynifred, Wynn, Wynne.
Meaning: 'reconciliation' (Welsh) and 'peace' (Old English); 'friend' and 'peace' (Old English) as a female version of Winfred.

Winna

Variants and diminutives: Winn, Winni, Winnie, Winny.
Meaning: 'relaxed' (Arabic).

Winona

Variants and diminutives: Wenona, Wenonah, Wenonoah, Winnie, Winonah, Wynona.
Meaning: 'bliss' or 'joy' (Germanic); 'first-born daughter' (Sioux – Native American).

Xanthe

Variants and diminutives: Xantha, Xantho, Zanth, Zantha, Zanthe.
Meaning: 'yellow' or 'bright' (Greek). A female version of Xanthus.

Xanthippe

Variants and diminutives: Xantippe.
Meaning: 'yellow' and 'horse' (Greek).

Xaviera

Variants and diminutives: Javier, Xavier.
Meaning: 'new house' (Basque) or 'bright' or 'brilliant' (Arabic) as a female version of Xavier.

Xenia

Variants and diminutives: Cena, Chimene, Xena, Xene, Ximena, Xiomara, Zena, Zenia.
Meaning: 'hospitable' (Greek).

Xylophila

Variants and diminutives: Phil, Phila, Philli, Phillie, Philly, Xylo, Xylona, Zilo.
Meaning: 'wood' and 'lover' (Greek).

Yakira

Variants and diminutives: Kira, Yaki.
Meaning: 'precious' or 'beloved' (Hebrew). A female version of Yakir.

Yarkona

Variants and diminutives: Kona.
Meaning: 'green' (Hebrew).

Yarmilla

Variants and diminutives: Milla.
Meaning: 'market trader' (Slavonic).

Yasmin

Variants and diminutives: Jasmeen, Jasmin, Jasmine, Yasiman, Yasmeen, Yasmin, Yasmina, Yasmine.
Meaning: 'jasmine flower' (Persian and Arabic).

Yasu

Variants and diminutives: Yasuko, Yasuyo.
Meaning: 'calm' or 'peaceful' (Japanese).

Yedida

Variants and diminutives: Yedidah.
Meaning: 'beloved friend' (Hebrew).

Yehuda

Variants and diminutives: Judith, Yehudit, Yudif, Yudit, Yudita, Yuta.
Meaning: 'Jewish woman' (Hebrew) as a variant of Judith; 'praise' (Hebrew) as a female variant of Judah or Jude. Also a boy's name.

Yelena

Variants and diminutives: Helen, Helena.
Meaning: 'bright' (Greek) as a Russian version of Helena (Helen).

Yemina

Variants and diminutives: Mina.
Meaning: 'child of my right hand' or

'favourite child' (Hebrew) as a female
version of Benjamin.

Yeshisha
Variants and diminutives: Shisha,
Yeshi.
Meaning: 'old' (Hebrew)

Yigala
Variants and diminutives: Yigaala.
Meaning: 'God will redeem' (Hebrew) as
a female version of Yigal.

Yoko
Meaning: 'across', 'ocean', 'female' or
'positive' (Japanese).

Yolande
Variants and diminutives: Eolanda,
Eolande, Iolanda, Iolande, Iolanthe,
Iolende, Jola, Jolan, Jolande, Jolanka,
Jolanta, Joleicia, Jolenta, Joli, Olinda,
Viola, Violet, Violante, Yola, Yolanda,
Yolane, Yolanta, Yolanthe, Yoli.
Meaning: 'little violet' (Old French) as a
variant of Violet, in turn a French variant
of Viola; 'violet' or 'dawn cloud' (Greek)
as a variant of Iolanthe.

Yovela
Variants and diminutives: Vela, Yovi.
Meaning: 'ram's horn', 'rejoicing' or
'celebration' (Hebrew).

Yseult
Variants and diminutives: Isaut, Iseult,
Iseut, Isola, Isolda, Isolde, Isolt.
Meaning: 'ice' and 'rule' (Germanic) or
'lovely' (Welsh) as a French variant of
Iseult (Isolde).

Yuki
Variants and diminutives: Yukie,
Yukiko, Yukiyo.
Meaning: 'fortunate' or 'snow'
(Japanese).

Yulan
Meaning: 'gem' and 'plant' (Chinese);
derived from the name of a Chinese
magnolia, *Magnolia denudata*.

Yvette
Variants and diminutives: Ivetta,
Yevette, Yve, Yvonne.
Meaning: 'yew' or 'small archer'
(Germanic) or 'God has favoured', 'God is
gracious' or 'God is merciful' (Hebrew) as
a female version of Yves (Ivo and John).

Yvonne
Variants and diminutives: Evon, Evona,
Evonne, Ivona, Ivone, Iwona, Iwonka,
Yvone, Yvette.
Meaning: 'yew' or 'small archer'
(Germanic) or 'God has favoured', 'God is
gracious' or 'God is merciful' (Hebrew) as
a female version of Yves (Ivo and John).

Zada
Variants and diminutives: Zada, Zaida,
Zayda.
Meaning: 'fortunate' (Arabic).

Zahara
Variants and diminutives: Sahara,
Zahra.
Meaning: 'flower' (Swahili – Africa) as a
female version of Zahur; 'desert' (Arabic)
as a variant of Sahara.

Zahira
Variants and diminutives: Sarah,
Zaharita, Zaira, Zara.
Meaning: uncertain; possibly 'flower',
'splendour', 'eastern splendour' or 'dawn
brightness' (Arabic) as a variant of Zara;
possibly 'princess' (Hebrew) as a variant
of Zara and Sarah.

Zaida
Variants and diminutives: Zadam,
Zaidah, Zayda.
Meaning: 'growth', 'prosperity' or 'good
luck' (Arabic).

Zalika
Variants and diminutives: Zuleika.
Meaning: 'well-born' (Swahili – African).

Zana

Variants and diminutives:
Susannah, Zsa Zsa, Zuska, Zuza,
Zuzana, Zuzanna, Zuzia, Zuzka,
Zuzanka
Meaning: uncertain; possibly
'woman' (Persian); possibly 'alert' or
'vivacious' (Arabic); possibly 'lily'
(Hebrew) as a diminutive of
Susannah.

Zandra

Variants and diminutives:
Alexandra, Sandra.
Meaning: 'defender of men' or
'warrior' (Greek) as a diminutive of
Alexandra, in turn a female version of
Alexander.

Zara

Variants and diminutives: Sara,
Sarah, Zahira, Zahirita, Zaira, Zarah.
Meaning: uncertain; possibly 'flower',
'splendour', 'eastern splendour' or
'dawn brightness' (Arabic); possibly
'princess' (Hebrew) as a variant of
Sarah.

Zarifa

Meaning: 'graceful' (Arabic).

Zarina

Meaning: 'golden' or 'golden vessel'
(Persian).

Zariza

Variants and diminutives: Zeriza.
Meaning: 'hard-working' (Hebrew).

Zayit

Variants and diminutives: Zeta,
Zetana.
Meaning: 'olive' (Hebrew). Also a
boy's name.

Zaza

Variants and diminutives: Zazu.
Meaning: 'movement' (Hebrew).

Zea

Variants and diminutives: Zia.
Meaning: 'grain' (Latin).

Zehava

Variants and diminutives: Zehara,
Zehari, Zehavi, Zehavit, Zehuva,
Zohar, Zoheret.
Meaning: 'gold' or 'brilliant' (Hebrew).

Zehira

Meaning: 'protected' (Hebrew).

Zelda

Variants and diminutives: Griselda,
Selda, Zelde.
Meaning: uncertain; possibly
'happiness' (Yiddish); possibly 'grey'
and 'battle' (Germanic) as a
diminutive of Griselda.

Zelia

Variants and diminutives: Zele,
Zelie, Zelina.
Meaning: 'zealous' (Hebrew).

Zelma

Variants and diminutives: Anselma,
Selma.
Meaning: 'divine' and 'helmet' (Old
German) or 'related to nobility' (Old
French) as a diminutive of Anselma,
in turn a female version of Anselm.

Zena

Variants and diminutives: Xena,
Xenia, Zenia.
Meaning: uncertain; possibly
'woman' (Persian); possibly
'hospitable' (Greek) as a variant of
Xenia.

Zenda

Meaning: 'sacred' (Persian).

Zenobia

Variants and diminutives: Zena,
Zenaida, Zenda, Zenia, Zenna,
Zenobie, Zinaida.
Meaning: 'power of Zeus' (Greek),
referring to the supreme god of
Greek mythology, whose name
means 'shining', 'bright' or 'bright sky'
(Greek).

Zephira

Variants and diminutives: Zephyr.
Meaning: 'morning' (Hebrew); also 'the west wind' (Greek) as a female version of Zephyr.

Zeta

Variants and diminutives: Zayit, Zetana, Zetta, Zita.
Meaning: 'sixth' (Greek), referring to the name of the sixth letter of the Greek alphabet; possibly 'to seek' (Greek), 'girl' (Italian), 'little rose' (Spanish) or 'harvest', 'reap' or 'from Thera [or Therasia]' (Greek) as a variant of Zita.

Zevida

Variants and diminutives: Zevuda.
Meaning: 'gift' (Hebrew).

Zhen

Meaning: 'treasure' (Chinese).

Zia

Variants and diminutives: Zea.
Meaning: 'to shiver' or 'to tremble' (Hebrew). Also a boy's name.

Zigana

Meaning: 'Gypsy' (Hungarian).

Zilla

Variants and diminutives: Zila, Zillah, Zilli.

Meaning: 'shadow' or 'shade' (Hebrew).

Zilpah

Meaning: 'sprinkling' or 'dripping' (Hebrew).

Zina

Variants and diminutives: Zeena, Zinaida, Zinnia.
Meaning: 'mystical name' (Nsenga – Africa).

Zinnia

Variants and diminutives: Zeena, Zina.
Meaning: uncertain; derived from the name of the genus of flowering plants named for the German botanist Johann Gottfried Zinn.

Zipporah

Variants and diminutives: Cipora, Zippora.
Meaning: 'bird' (Hebrew).

Zita

Variants and diminutives: Citha, Rosita, Sitha, Zeta.
Meaning: uncertain; possibly 'to seek' (Greek); possibly 'girl' (Italian); possibly 'little rose' (Spanish) as a diminutive of Rosita (Rosa); possibly 'harvest', 'reap' or 'from Thera [or Therasia]' (Greek) as a diminutive of Theresa.

Ziva

Variants and diminutives: Siva, Zivit.
Meaning: 'to shine radiantly' (Hebrew). A female version of Ziv.

Zizi

Variants and diminutives: Elizabeth.
Meaning: 'God is perfection', 'God is satisfaction', 'dedicated to God' or 'God's oath' (Hebrew) as a Hungarian diminutive of Elizabeth.

Zoë

Variants and diminutives: Eve, Vita, Zoe, Zoé, Zoey.
Meaning: 'life' (Greek).

Zohra

Variants and diminutives: Zarya, Zora, Zorah, Zorana, Zoreen, Zoreene, Zorene, Zorina, Zorine, Zorna.
Meaning: 'blooming' or 'dawning' (Arabic).

Zola

Meaning: uncertain; possibly derived from a French family name, a famous bearer of which was the French writer Emile Zola, in turn possibly derived from the German word for 'toll'. Also a boy's name.

Zorya

Variants and diminutives: Zarya, Zohra, Zora, Zorah, Zorana, Zoreen,

Zoreene, Zorene, Zori, Zorie, Zorina,
Zorine, Zorna, Zory.
Meaning: 'golden dawn' (Slavonic).

Zsa Zsa
Variants and diminutives:
Susannah, Zana, Zuza.

Meaning: 'lily' (Hebrew) as a Hungarian
diminutive of Susannah.

Zuleika
Variants and diminutives: Zalika.
Meaning: 'radiant beauty' (Persian);
'lovely girl' (Arabic).

Zulema
Variants and diminutives: Salome,
Suleima, Zuelia, Zuleika, Zuleima.
Meaning: 'peace' (Arabic); 'peace' or
'peace of Zion' (Hebrew) as a variant of
Salome.

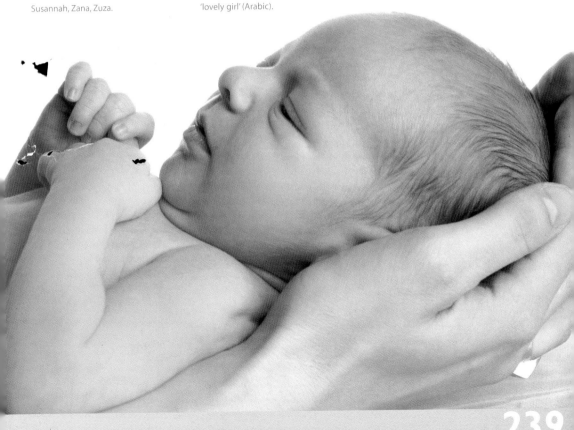

Credits and acknowledgements

The author would like to thank Emily Wood, Judith Millidge, Mark Akiwumi and Mike Haworth-Maden for their help in contributing to, and clarifying, some of the source material used in the writing of this book. Thanks, too, to John and Marianne Gibson for sharing their impressive knowledge of matters etymological and philological.

All images © stockbyte, except pages 23, 39, 45, 48, 53, 61, 86, 89, 100, 123, 135, 148, 160, 162, 165, 170, 188, 202 and 217.

Bibliography

Ann, Martha and Myers Imel, Dorothy, *Goddesses in World Mythology*, Oxford University Press, Oxford, 1993.

Benét, William Rose, *The Reader's Encyclopedia*, Guild Publishing, London, 1988.

Browder, Sue, *The New Age Baby Name Book*, Workman Publishing, New York, 1998.

Byars, Mel, *The Design Encyclopedia*, Laurence King Publishing, London, 1994.

Celtic Mythology, Gedded & Grosset, New Lanark, 1999.

Cottle, Basil, *The Penguin Dictionary of Surnames*, Penguin Books, London, 1978.

Crystal, David, *The Cambridge Encyclopedia of Language*, Cambridge University Press, Cambridge, 1987.

Fergusson, Rosalind, *Choose Your Baby's Name*, Penguin Books, London, 1987.

The Hutchinson Softback Encyclopedia, The Softback Preview, London, 1987.

Macleod, Iseabail, and Freedman, Terry, *The Wordsworth Dictionary of First Names*, Wordsworth Editions Ltd, Ware, 1995.

Nicholson, Louise, *The Best Baby Name Book*, Thorsons, London, 1990.

Read, Herbert (Consulting Editor), *The Thames and Hudson Dictionary of Art and Artists*, Thames and Hudson Ltd, London, 1994.